S0-BYY-474

ENGLISH LITERATURE

THE BEGINNINGS TO 1500
JAMES DOW McCALLUM
Dartmouth College

THE RENAISSANCE
ROBERT WHITNEY BOLWELL
George Washington University

THE SEVENTEENTH CENTURY
EVERT MORDECAI CLARK
University of Texas

THE EIGHTEENTH CENTURY
JOSEPH P. BLICKENSDERFER
University of Oklahoma

THE ROMANTIC PERIOD
ALBERT GRANBERRY REED
Louisiana State University

THE VICTORIAN PERIOD
GEORGE MOREY MILLER
University of Idaho

This series of anthologies of English literature
is under the general editorship of

JAMES DOW McCALLUM
Professor of English, Dartmouth College

ENGLISH LITERATURE

THE RENAISSANCE

EDITED BY

ROBERT WHITNEY BOLWELL

Associate Professor of English Literature
George Washington University

CHARLES SCRIBNER'S SONS

NEW YORK   CHICAGO   BOSTON   ATLANTA
SAN FRANCISCO   DALLAS

Copyright, 1929, by
CHARLES SCRIBNER'S SONS

———

Printed in the United States of America

*All rights reserved. No part of this book
may be reproduced in any form without
the permission of Charles Scribner's Sons*

E

CONTENTS

Lyrics:

INTRODUCTION

The Renaissance

THE sixteenth century, culminating in the Elizabethan period, marks a most important step in the modernizing of English thought. Behind this century lay the medieval world, with its art and literature bounded by two powerful institutions, the feudal system and the Church. During this century English culture passed over a vague line and entered a new world. By the end of the period Englishmen were generally thinking, living, and expressing themselves in a manner greatly different from that of their grandfathers. Perhaps no other century in the history of English literature shows changes so radical and significant as this, from the work of Malory and Hawes to that of Bacon and Shakespeare.

During the Middle Ages man had his interests fixed primarily on his immortal soul; life was essentially a preparation for eternity. A religious seriousness dominated humanity, so that the infrequent humor and pleasantness of some works of Middle English literature stand out as grateful exceptions. Largely because of the rigid organization of society into the ranks of the feudal system, and the universal supervision and influence of the Church, there was little opportunity for the assertion or development of individual personality. It is significant that most medieval literature is anonymous, and in comparison with the coming age, its thought seems ordered and systematized. This condition, however much it helps toward spiritual serenity, brings monotony and often dulness to the arts.

The Renaissance, as the period which effects the change into modernism has been called, was the rebirth of an attitude toward life which medieval thought had stifled. Its tendency was worldly in a wide sense, as contrasted with the medieval emphasis upon immortality. The renaissance man was awakened to the possibility of beauty and gratification in this mortal life. He did not abandon religion, but he enlarged his life to include many new interests. These enthusiasms stimulated him in personal and individual ways, so that in the art and literature which he produced we can see more clearly than before a variety, a freshness, a desire to create, which give vitality and distinction to the Elizabethans.

The Reformation

The great change which the Renaissance brings is not a single abrupt revolution. Its causes are many and diverse, and some of its phases develop slowly. But only by combining the separate factors into one general attitude of mind can the Elizabethan temper be understood. At the beginning of the sixteenth century, all Englishmen were Catholics varying somewhat in their religious ardor; at the close of the same century, most of them were Protestants divided into many degrees of anti-Catholic fervor. The forces which made this change are not found entirely in the political events of the period. During the early Middle Ages the Church was fired by a militant zeal for converts, and its kingdom spread in triumph over the peoples of Europe. In the later Middle Ages the problem was not to convert, but to serve and control the religious needs and habits of many nations of orthodox Christians. This new emphasis evoked an administrative system which, as it grew more effective, became increasingly involved in political and material interests. Disputes with na-

tional parties and rulers became frequent. Also, the
Church as a religious institution had grown so large
that a natural division in matters of faith and doctrine
was imminent. In the days of Chaucer there were pro-
tests against the teachings and policies of the Church,
illustrated in the writings of Wiclif and his Lollards,
and in sections of the *Piers Plowman* poetry. This
discord becomes open rebellion in the Protestant Reformation of the sixteenth century. Of course, the details
of the revolt in terms of political history vary with the
nations involved; German Protestantism, led by Martin
Luther, moves by steps which are different from those
of English Protestantism under Henry VIII. But in
both cases the absolute power of a great institution,
which with its temporal and spiritual strength might
be likened to a sort of world state, was challenged.
The greatest fixed influence over human thought and
conduct, unbroken in western Europe for nearly a thousand years, was defied. In England a state church was
established, with the monarch at its head. But it did
not wield a power so complete as the Roman Catholic
rule had been, and throughout the sixteenth century differences grew in the Anglican church which eventually
brought about a civil war in the next century, and later
the establishment of numerous sects and sub-divisions of
Protestantism. One essential interpretation of this
great shift from a centralized, international religious
institution with its control over even the material forces
of life, to a national church quarrelling with a fringe
of dissenting, antagonistic sects, is that England had
seized and amplified the opportunities for a more personal, individual understanding and use of religion.
The power of disciplined authority over human aspirations was broken. This is the chief contribution of the
Reformation to the English Renaissance.

Humanism

During the late fifteenth century the English baronage engaged in the civil strife for control of the kingdom known as the Wars of the Roses. Because of this preoccupation, England was slow to react to a new force which had begun to move the intellectual life of Italy. This influence, inclusively termed Humanism, resulted from the discovery of forgotten Greek and Roman writings, and a subsequent enthusiasm for classical art and learning. Greek scholars living at Constantinople had preserved since the break-up of the Roman Empire, the works of their ancient poets, historians, and philosophers. This pagan culture had been neglected throughout the Middle Ages because it was unimportant in the study and expression of Christian theology, which was the primary concern of students in the universities of western Europe. Encouraged by the interest of Italian scholars from Petrarch on, Greek teachers brought their manuscripts from the east. Aided by the disorders of the Turkish invasions of eastern Europe, which drove westward to a place of refuge the treasures of this ancient culture, a vogue for Greek learning rapidly developed. Roman civilization also was studied and readily included in this revival of the classics. A new attitude toward life had been maturing during the late Middle Ages. The discovery of the beauty and wisdom in the poetry of Homer and the Greek dramatists, of Virgil and Ovid, and in the prose of Plato and Cicero, at once stimulated and gratified both the scholar and the artist of the Renaissance. They found in the classical culture a new combination, stressing equally a mental poise and physical beauty, a material well-being which enjoyed the experiences of life without anxiety concerning eternity. The pagan attitude well suited the intellectual tendency of the times.

sixteenth century had use for their humanism in the religious discussions and spiritual issues of the day. It was not until after these were resolved into a fixed Protestant policy in the reign of Elizabeth that the pagan element of the classical revival blossomed into an artistic literature. In Italy, where there was no open warfare against the Catholic church, the poet was the scholar and his art immediately reflected his new learning; in England, because of the Reformation, the poets followed after the scholars.

Discovery and Invention

Under one large theme may be grouped a number of events which emphasized the break between the medieval world and the period of Renaissance. Science during the Middle Ages did not contribute much in a practical way to the advancement of civilization, in spite of the fact that many valuable discoveries, such as gunpowder, the mariner's compass, and the lens, were then made. The Renaissance developed and utilized what medieval science passed on. By the beginning of the sixteenth century, gunpowder had practically displaced the military equipment and devices of feudalism. Cannon destroyed medieval castles and walled towns, and the social system which they protected. Voyages of discovery and exploration expanded the limits of a world which Marco Polo had already stretched. Columbus, Vasco da Gama, the Cabots, rounded the seas to discover new continents, and finally with the enterprise of such successors as Magellan and Drake, made the old hazardous guess that the world was a sphere a common fact. These men in a direct and physical sense enlarged the world of the Renaissance, and necessarily increased man's interest therein and aroused his imagination. Even the universe at

New forms and manners, therefore, were introd
into poetry, painting, sculpture, and architecture;
flourished under this stimulation, and renaissance
added its glories to the achievements of mankind.

It was not until the sixteenth century, after Englan
had settled into the reign of the Tudor dynasty at the
close of the Wars of the Roses, that the influences of
humanism crossed the Channel. Humanism was not
introduced under the same auspices as in Italy, where
the artists and poets, men of creative imagination, kept
pace with scholars and antiquarians. In England the
first humanists were scholars of a critical and intellectual cast, not primarily creative or artistic. Greek instruction was received by men who were swept into the
disputes and controversies of the national religious tur-
moil. Their chief use of a knowledge of Greek was in
a new study of the New Testament. The Latin version
which the Church had used for centuries was discarded
in their zeal for precision. There was little time in the
stirring days of Henry VIII, in the midst of a religious
revolution, for the imitation of pagan art and its delights. Sir Thomas More, famous for his ideal of
government in the *Utopia*, which derived much from his
study of Plato, used his energies on the side of religious conservatism in his numerous tracts attacking
the Protestant position. Erasmus, the great Dutch
humanist, allied himself with More on his long visits
to England, although he refrained from much controversy and devoted himself to academic pursuits. On the
Protestant side humanism was well represented by such
men as John Colet, dean of St. Paul's, and Roger
Ascham, both accomplished teachers and leaders of the
educational reform which was made necessary by th
changed conditions of life. The founders of classi
scholarship in England during the first half of

large took on a different aspect under the new scientific curiosity. Medieval astrologers had read in the relation of the planets a trivial interpretation of human events, but now the new science of astronomy emerged. The Renaissance produced Galileo and Copernicus, who outlined our solar system and enlarged the conception of the material universe, and from a scientific point of view reduced tremendously the size of man standing in his conceit at its center. Nature and its laws were now perceived as independent of man's desires and self-importance. Such material and scientific discoveries as these, although not directly concerned with the arts, made deep impressions upon the thought of the age, and their influences slowly but definitely modernized the life and interests upon which the arts rest.

But by far the most influential material contribution of the Renaissance to literature and learning was the printing press. Accustomed as we are today to think of literature immediately in terms of printed matter, we may fail to realize the revolution caused in the literary world by the first production of books by printing with movable type. Before the fifteenth century Europe depended upon the inaccurate, slow-writing scribe or copyist for its reading. Costly parchment manuscripts, one copy alone requiring months of labor, were the treasures of large monasteries and wealthy men of culture. Now, at the close of the Middle Ages, all human thought was made available, inexpensive and abundant for those who would read. William Caxton established the first press in England in 1476; after him followed presses at Oxford, St. Albans, and London. The Renaissance is remarkable for its combination of coincidences; many diverse things occurred within a comparatively short period of time, and all worked toward the same general result: religious reform, revolt against established authority, change in political and social structure, revival of ancient culture and philosophy, discovery of a new hemisphere, a redefining of the universe, and scientific inventions. Nothing, however, was more opportune than that printing presses should have been started over Europe in order to express adequately the ferment and activity of a newly stimulated humanity. The printing presses of the Renaissance claim their due in giving the widest expression possible to the revived thought of the age.

The English Background

The best effects of the Renaissance appear in England at the close of the sixteenth century. Queen Elizabeth, coming to the throne in 1558, had for a score of years to set her realm in order, to subdue political and religious factions, to reform her government and its laws. By about 1580 a national unity and harmony are perceptible, and in the quarter-century of her reign which followed, the great Elizabethan literature was produced. Conditions then favored the arts as never before. Indeed, under the stimulation of the Renaissance, the writers of this age show a literary activity and spontaneity unique in the history of our literature. In the first half of the century, literature was largely an affair of the upper classes and the court. The Tudors were all patrons of the arts. Elizabeth herself had received an excellent classical education from Roger Ascham, the great humanist teacher. Her court, the people who surrounded her public and private life, were all thoroughly imbued with renaissance culture. It became fashionable then to be a patron of poets and artists. In the later part of her reign, however, a new factor aided literary production,—the rising power and prosperity of the middle classes. The tradesmen of

London founded schools for the education of their children, who received the new learning which earlier had come only to the sons of the nobility. The universities, meanwhile, had been revolutionized by the Protestant Reformation and the Renaissance. Medieval studies, the *trivium* and *quadrivium,* and the theological emphasis, were abandoned for the new Greek learning, classical history and philosophy. The young noblemen of the day attended Oxford and Cambridge for a secular, cultural education, not theological training for a religious ministry. With these students came the sons of London's citizens from their new schools. These commoners, because of their general affluence and the establishment of many scholarships at the colleges, increased steadily in number throughout the latter part of the century. Thus renaissance culture spread at once to the court and to the city from the universities, and both the courtier and the commoner felt equally the urge to write of the new ideas and beauty which their studies had revealed.

Particularly significant is the coming into formal literature of these well-educated sons of tradesfolk. They mark the beginning of professional writing, for they generally sustained themselves by the use of their pens. Stimulated by the poetry and art of the day, and not wishing to take up the trades of their fathers, they wrote for a growing reading public, and made a living thereby. They wrote all kinds of literature,—songs and lyrics, long narrative poems, short stories, novels, historical and theological discussions, tracts and pamphlets on politics, on social conditions, sensational articles exposing the shady side of London life, literary criticism, etc. But the most valuable contribution of these "university wits," as they were called, was to the theater. The Elizabethan drama, capped by the plays of

Shakespeare, is not only the highest product of the age; it is one of the chief glories of English literature.

Narrative Poetry

Long narrative poems were a heritage from the Middle English period and continued throughout the sixteenth century, modified of course by renaissance influences. Writers in the days of Henry VIII were feeling their way in a new world, but in general they trusted to the old medieval traditions passed down from Chaucer and Lydgate. The use of allegory, the rime-royal or seven-line Chaucerian stanza, and certain mannerisms sanctified by custom, are all observed in such works as Stephen Hawes' *Pastime of Pleasure* (1506), telling in the form of a chivalric romance the efforts of a young knight to gain learning, or John Skelton's *Bowge of Court* (about 1505), which satirizes the evils of court life in the story of a voyage in a ship full of rascals. The same device is used by Alexander Barclay in his *Ship of Fools* (1509) to describe the various kinds of folly in human society. In John Heywood's *The Spider and the Fly* (begun about 1536, not printed until 1556) a social and religious conflict between wealthy barons and dependent commons is depicted. But even in such medieval survivals as these there is a growing realism and concreteness in the story and its interpretation. Where medieval allegorists were general and abstract, the early Tudor poets related their work more definitely to the life and problems of the day.

The reader notices in these writers and others of the first half of the century a ruggedness and irregularity of meter and accent which mar the smoothness of the verse. This is due to the change in the language which marks the close of the Middle English period, when pronunciation was altered by the loss of inflectional endings common in Chaucer's day. Early Tudor poets, unable to read the verse of their medieval predecessors with the regularity of rhythm which only a knowledge of the speech could supply, either neglected or experimented with their meter and achieved no fixed, common standard. It is not until after the work of Henry Howard, Earl of Surrey, that modern English scansion is possible.

On the eve of Elizabeth's accession was projected *The Mirror for Magistrates,* a huge narrative collection which appeared in many editions with new material by different poets throughout the latter half of the century. These tragic stories, full of moral warning, were taken from the storehouse of English history, tradition, and legend. The background of this popular work is distinctly medieval; Chaucer's *Monk's Tale* and Lydgate's *Falls of Princes* are its two most distinguished forerunners. But it also shows the increasing interest of the Elizabethans in their national past, and it was used largely by the dramatists of the day who were writing patriotic plays on the theme of English history. This patriotic or national narrative poetry continues into the next century, the most popular works being Daniel's *Civil Wars* (1595-1609) and Drayton's *Polyolbion* (1613-1622).

The best of the Elizabethan narrative verse, however, shows the romantic use of classical myth and legend. In such poems as Shakespeare's *Venus and Adonis* (1593) and Marlowe's *Hero and Leander* (completed by Chapman in 1598) there is a pagan abandon to sensuous beauty and a lyrical passion which well illustrate the contrast between the medieval and the renaissance material and technique. In Spenser's *Faerie Queene* (1590-1596), however, is a remarkable combination of old and new elements. This magnificent fragment, little more than half finished, was to have been twelve books of twelve cantos each. A knight as the chief character of each book portrays one of the twelve moral virtues, which are all embodied in the main hero, Prince Arthur. The poem, like its medieval precursors, is a vast allegory representing Spenser's Puritan view of moral philosophy, of the conflict between Protestantism and Catholicism, of the political situation in England, and even of the poet's personal relationships. The story of the poem is an Arthurian romance; knights undertake quests, rescue ladies, fight giants and dragons, and win tourneys and jousts. But inserted into this medieval fabric are a wealth of allusion to classical myth and story, the poetic devices of Virgil, the idealism of Platonic philosophy, the ethics of Aristotle, and other humanistic enthusiasms to which Italian poets had pointed the way. Added to all this is the renaissance love of beauty, of color and life, which lifts his matter into the realm of poetry. Spenser is a poet of smooth-flowing music, stately and resonant, with vivid descriptions which show the artist at his best, profiting alike by his medieval and classical background.

Lyric and Pastoral Poetry

The lyric in English literature dates properly from the Renaissance. The lyric poem, originally the words of a song, preserves its essential musical quality by the combination of a simple stanza form, a tuneful rime scheme, and a marked rhythm. In addition to these matters of form, the lyric expresses a personal mood or emotion which springs from the inner feelings of the poet. This type of poem, therefore, unites a highly individualized fervor with an artistic appeal which carries it from the interpretation of the poet's own emotions to the acceptance and sympathy of the reader. In spite of some exceptions, the earlier literature did not produce lyric poetry because the conception of medieval writing was objective, and was not an expression of personal moods and feelings. The state of mind necessary to the composition of this kind of poetry did not exist as a rule before the Renaissance. The first important collection of English lyric poetry was *Tottel's Miscellany* (1557), which included the best of the courtier poets of Henry VIII's reign. These men represent the first fruits of renaissance influences brought from Italy and France into England. The lyric soon became the most popular literary form of the age. It appeared in a host of song-books and collections with such alluring titles as *A Paradise of Dainty Devices* (1576), *A Gorgeous Gallery of Gallant Inventions* (1578), *A Handful of Pleasant Delights* (1584), *England's Helicon* (1600), and many others. These anthologies reached all classes; some were made up of street ballads, and others of elaborate courtly fancies. The stories and novels, even the pamphlets, of the Elizabethans contained many lyrics, and the plays willingly halted their action for a song. Practically all literary men wrote at least a few lyrics, and all gentlemen of culture attempted to. It was an age of song.

The sonnet, the most frequent Elizabethan lyric form, like many other new fashions of the century, came from Italy. Petrarch (1304-1374) had written a Platonic idealization of love for his lady in a series of short lyrics (*sonetti*). These were widely imitated, and the vogue of sonnet writing which developed in Italy spread to France and was introduced by Sir Thomas Wyatt into England early in the sixteenth century. By the time English poets took up the sonnet it had developed many conventions; it was limited to fourteen lines with a somewhat fixed rime scheme, and it observed certain customary attitudes toward its subject. Metaphorical treatment of the lady's beauty, her coldness, and the sufferings of the repulsed lover became staples of the sonneteer. Slight changes in form and rime were made by English writers, but in general the sonnet was a piece of international literary currency during the Renaissance. The poets, restricted by these conventions, vied with each other to obtain distinction in new-turned figures of speech, in forceful images and high-flung phrases, which give to the Elizabethan sonnet a peculiar graciousness and exaggeration of sentiment. As the sonnet itself was not long enough to cover a theme so enticing as the love and beauty of the poet's lady, the custom of writing a series of sonnets after the manner of Petrarch was adopted. These cycles were produced in abundance during the 1590's, the best examples of such collections being Sidney's *Astrophel and Stella* (1591), Daniel's *Delia* (1592), and Spenser's *Amoretti* (1595). By the beginning of the seventeenth century, however, they were disfavored because their tone had become so extravagant as to render any further statement of the poetic idea impossible or absurd. In fact, an anti-Petrarchan tendency, with almost the force of a reform, is observed in the cooler attitude and more restrained phrasing of Ben Jonson and the later lyric writers.

Another poetic type which entered Elizabethan literature through the Renaissance was the pastoral. In classical poetry Theocritus and Virgil had sung the praise of the simple life of peaceful shepherds and their lasses. These children of nature, in poetry at least, spend most of their time in weaving garlands, playing at games and dances, in making love and song. Coming from a sophisticated civilization, the pastoral is highly artificial; its attitude is exquisite and dainty, not realistic. Italian and French poets had revived this classical mode, and it was imported into England by Alexander Barclay in his *Eclogues* (about 1514), in which he writes of the miseries of the courtier in contrast with the joys of the rural shepherd. The English pastoral is seen at its best in the *Shepherd's Calendar* of Spenser (1579). In an eclogue devoted to each month of the year, Spenser includes all the traditional uses of the form; Colin (Spenser himself) tells of his love for the shepherdess Rosalind, and shepherds hold singing matches and long discussions about the duties of their calling, in which political and religious issues are allegorized. A rustic dialect and old-fashioned speech savoring of Chaucer's English are used by Spenser to give the rural flavor. The lyric poetry was quick to absorb this pastoral attitude. It gave to the poet the romantic displacement for which he was striving; it heightened with a pagan charm the beauty and emotions which moved him to sing. This pastoral element also enters the prose fiction of the Elizabethans, and even the drama reflects the arcadianism which symbolized the combination of elegance and simplicity of ancient art to the Renaissance. The pastoral lyric continued into the seventeenth century, somewhat cooled by the rational temper which was growing, but always representing a pleasant retreat for those poets who sought the romantic and exquisite. Nature poetry was strengthened by it, in spite of the many artifices into which it was forced, for it not only presented the courtly attitude toward the simple life, but frequently sang of the natural beauties of the English countryside.

The Drama

The service of the Renaissance to English drama was to divorce it from a treatment of Biblical story and religious doctrine. The first step toward a drama dealing with the common life of actual men and women came in the reign of Henry VIII, when short *interludes* were devised for entertainments at court, along the lines of farces then popular in France. These racy stories put into dialogue, such as the plays written by John Heywood between 1530 and 1540, are the feeble beginnings of modern comedy. It was not until after the middle of the century that the direct influences of humanism reached the drama. English university students then learned from Italian writers the knack of modeling plays after the manner of Greek and Roman dramatists. Thus the first full-grown English comedy, *Ralph Roister Doister* (about 1553), was in careful imitation of Plautus, and *Gammer Gurton's Needle* (about 1560) combined elements of the earlier farce with methods of Roman comedy in an effective play of English village life. Classical tragedy also was imitated; the first English play of this sort was *Gorboduc* (1561), dealing with an early British legend and patterned after the plays of Seneca. Numerous other dramas in the early years of Elizabeth's reign show the influences of classical technique. In the years between 1560 and 1580 there was a rapid assimilation of classical and continental methods in English drama, as though in preparation for the greater writers who were to come.

After 1580 Elizabethan drama burst into full flower. The age was one of excitement and action, and the vitality of the drama is the reflection of the life with which it deals. The drama, like the lyric, had no restricted patronage; it was performed in the schools, at the universities, at the court of the queen, at the Inns of Court by the students of law. Also, by 1580 troupes of professional actors had given their plays before the citizens of London and other large towns, on improvised stages in the inn-yards. The first regular theaters of London had been built (1576) and were enjoying an ever-increasing business. Drama had become the outstanding literary commodity of the day, and had attracted the most brilliant and versatile writers to its service. The Elizabethan drama is not limited in its theme or manner of treatment. Romantic plays, both comedy and tragedy, of the most imaginative and poetic sort, vied with realistic and satiric pictures of London life. The stately panorama of English history was unrolled in a series of chronicle plays which held their audiences for two decades. Melodrama, violent and sensational, competed with pastoral plays, fanciful and delicate. Cheerful comedies on the life and aspirations of London's apprentices were produced along with studies of human depravity, of exaggerated lust and horror. Perhaps no other form of Elizabethan literature is so inclusive in its interests and materials as the drama.

The modern reader is impressed by the literary excellence and power of these plays. Indeed, the moving words of the dramatist performed for his audiences what our present-day scenery, properties, and lighting effects do for us. The Elizabethan stage was practically bare, hence the necessity of this verbal appeal. The atmosphere of reality or the illusion of romance had to reach the Elizabethans through the words of the actors. In these plays, therefore, are long descriptive passages on which the finest poetry at the command of the dramatist is lavished. Long speeches of a highly oratorical nature are frequent, and the stirring lines of verse stimulated and worked upon the audiences with telling effect. Blank verse was the most generally used form,—flexible, stately in its rhythm, and not impeding the thought so much as the more artificial couplets which were also employed. Prose was sometimes used, particularly in comic scenes or by persons not involved in the main action.

The dramatists and the great plays of this age are too numerous for individual treatment. Some writers will serve to illustrate certain outstanding types of drama. John Lyly, for instance, should be mentioned as the leader of a witty and colorful comedy which was presented at court,—plays built about classical myths and which could be interpreted politically by the courtiers who knew the trend of public affairs. Lyly used the pastoral scene, with nymphs and satyrs, and introduced dances and many songs. His plays, written in his Euphuistic prose, were given by boys whom he trained as actors. In contrast with the prettiness of his work which was obviously designed to please the feminine tastes of the queen's court, stands Christopher Marlowe and his powerful tragedies, which under a highly poetic treatment deal with the human spirit in its desire for unattainable things, beating against the limitations of the flesh. In no other plays of the age do we find such bombast and rant or at times such moving poetry as in his blank verse. Marlowe more than any other single writer led the drama to poetry as the medium of expressing the passions and yearnings of humanity.

William Shakespeare is, of course, the most brilliant of the poets who gave eminence to the drama. In his earlier plays we see him quick to observe and follow the fashions which his immediate predecessors, the "university wits," had established. With skill he adapted earlier plays and stories to meet the demands of the day. Lyly, Greene, and Marlowe showed him the way, but not for long. By the end of the century he led the large group who were then writing, especially in the field of romantic comedy. Toward the latter part of his career, however, he leaves the path of popular taste and goes his own way, writing tragedies which are increasingly analytical of the human motives portrayed, and richer in an understanding of life and its forces than had been written by any dramatist since the Greeks.

There were may literary partnerships among the dramatists, which hastened the production of plays and permitted the peculiar gifts of certain writers a readier expression. Shakespeare sometimes combined his work with that of other writers in such collaboration. The most notable partnership of the period was that of Francis Beaumont and John Fletcher. This pair wrote many plays of general popularity, chiefly in the field of comedy, polished, witty, frequently indecent, but always deft in the handling of plot and dramatic situation. In their tragedies and romantic plays they readily dropped the sophisticated, courtly manner, and wrote some of the most stirring and powerful melodramas of the age.

In the crowd of playwrights who wrote through the opening years of the seventeenth century were many of real ability and merit. But the sensation-loving audiences encouraged some writers, such as John Webster, to a violence of action, an exaggeration of sentiment, of vice and of virtue, which produced sheer melodrama. Soon there developed a movement to check this unrestraint. The popular drama had gone far from the practice of the classical writers who had originally given the Elizabethan playwrights much of their technique.

Ben Jonson, cool and clever in the handling of his materials, led this movement against romantic excesses and sensationalism. He observed a more careful adherence to the classical manner, a truer conception of dramatic character, and a more highly unified plot construction. He did not completely reform the practice of his contemporaries, but before the close of the seventeenth century the drama had rid itself of most of the absurdities which he attacked and satirized.

Puritan opposition to the theater was constant during Elizabeth's reign, and it grew in power under the early Stuart kings. The first chapter of modern English drama closes when the government passed into the hands of the Puritan party, and a law was enacted by Parliament in 1642, closing the playhouses and forbidding the performance of any kind of drama. After the Commonwealth, when Charles II came to the throne, the reestablished drama utilized the work of the earlier playwrights as a basis for a development which forms another important chapter—the Restoration drama. But the Elizabethan period had given the drama life and widespread popularity. To the royal court and the crowded city alike, it had pictured the welter of human passions and desires, the baseness and nobility of man's nature, the comedy and romance of his relations with his fellows, all expressed in a spirited poetry which has won permanent literary fame for its distinguished writers.

The Rise of Prose

Prose writing was established as a reputable literary form during the sixteenth century. Before this time, the best and most important works were all written in poetry; literature, in fact, meant poetry throughout the Middle Ages. There was some prose written in the earlier periods, but it was not regarded as involving literary art, and most of it was translated from Latin or French sources. During the Renaissance, however, a change developed in the attitude toward prose as a vehicle of literary art. Students of the classics had discovered a perfection of style in the works of the ancient prose writers as well as in the poets. Cicero and Aurelius, Plato and Demosthenes were studied and eventually imitated. Schoolboys were required to emulate the classical style in their language exercises. By the middle of the century some conscious efforts were made in the new schools to build up an English style comparable to that of Greece and Rome. Rhetorics were written, stylistic devices were borrowed from the classics, new words and phrases were coined or imported, and the art of English prose writing was begun.

Quite naturally, mistakes were made. In their efforts to make an art of prose, the early Elizabethans used excessive ornamentation. They thought that complexity and elaboration, not simplicity, would render this new literary form most artistic. The result of this tendency is seen in the amusing abnormalities of Lyly's *Euphues*. In this style the devices common to poetry were combined with those of classical rhetoric and the aureate diction of the medieval diplomatic correspondence,—alliteration, metaphorical expressions, balance of phrase and sentence, antithesis, rhetorical question and exclamation, etc. Lyly represents the high point of this florid and artificial prose; other writers strove for the same effects, but they were surpassed by him. By the end of the century, however, prose style had settled into saner channels. A reaction toward the other extreme had begun; men came to realize the artistic virtues of clearness, directness, and simplicity. The finest example of the simple, direct prose style is in the King James version of the Bible (1611). With this tendency there came a new emphasis on the difference between prose and poetry. Prose was perceived to be a more effective vehicle for expressing thought and idea than poetry, which appealed to the feelings and emotions in the expression of beauty. Thus the Elizabethans, from Ascham to Bacon, by a varied use of prose established it as a flexible and worthy form, no longer subordinate to poetry, or a catch-all for material which poetry refused to touch. By the close of this period, the prose writer was considered as much a man of letters as the poet.

Prose Literature

Most of the modern types of English prose literature grew out of the sixteenth century. Fiction, as it exists today in the short story and the novel, began with the translation of short tales, *novelle,* written in Italy by Boccaccio, Bandello, and others. True, Malory's *Le Morte d'Arthur,* a long prose romance, had appeared at the close of the Middle Ages, but the *novella* with its emphasis on sex, its romantic sophistication, and the pointed nature of its climax, superseded the medieval type of story. Many collections of *novelle* were printed; Painter's *Palace of Pleasure* (1566-7) and Fenton's *Tragical Discourses* (1567) mark the beginning of the popularity of prose fiction. The Elizabethan dramatists soon discovered in these stories abundant plot material for their plays, and some of the most outstanding dramas of the age, such as *Romeo and Juliet* and *Othello,* were derived from these collections. The modern novel was slowly forming in the hands of fiction writers, although it did not get far beyond a plot made up of separate episodes strung together like beads on the thread of a hero's life and adventures. In the two volumes of Lyly's *Euphues* (1578-80) there are several *novelle* pieced together as the adventures of two young gentlemen, and added to these are many letters, debates, and discussions which gave valuable hints about conduct to the renaissance courtier. The stories, the instruction, and the highly mannered style all combine to make this one of the most successful prose works of the century. Sir Philip Sidney's *Arcadia* (written between 1580-85, printed 1590), in a long story with a bewildering number of episodes, united the chivalric element of the medieval romances and the pastoral. Knights and ladies play at shepherd games and pastimes, endure war's hardships in besieged castles, and love in the ineffable style of royalty. The same combination of chivalric and pastoral elements is seen in Thomas Lodge's *Rosalind* (1590), the best of the romantic novels and famous as the source of Shakespeare's *As You Like It*. Robert Greene, facile and quick to imitate, wrote several novels in this pastoral vein while the fashion was at its height.

In sharp contrast with these courtly, romantic novels are the realistic stories which were written at the close of the century, dealing with London's apprentices, rascals, and under-world characters. Thomas Nashe's *The Unfortunate Traveller, or the Life of Jack Wilton* (1594) is also composed of many short episodes; pranks, amours, and murders are linked together as the confession of a vagabond who serves as the hero. This type of story, similar to the *picaresco* tales of the same period in Spanish literature, offers little of moral elevation to the reader; its tone is cynical, its object amusement and excitement. Vivid details of scene and action are given to shock or disgust; everything makes for a sense of actuality. Thomas Deloney also helped to bring the novel into a closer relation to actual life in a series of three stories, *Thomas of Reading, Jack of Newbury,* and *The Gentle Craft* (about 1597), concerning craftsmen and the dignity of their calling. The heroes are clothiers, weavers, and shoemakers, and although the tales have much of sentiment and romance in them, the medium through which they pass is the life of the common people and their interests.

Very close to the realistic novels are the numerous pamphlets which were written to expose the squalor, disorder, and crime of London life. Much of this material is pure fiction, purporting to be the career of a noted cutthroat or sharper. With journalistic shrewdness in the handling of this sensational matter, writers like Greene, Nashe, and Dekker gave the good citizens a picture of their own city which thrilled and warned them. The prose pamphlet also became a convenient form for almost any purpose. Religious controversy, early in the century between Catholic and Protestant, later between the conservative and Puritan elements in the Church of England, had established it as most useful in debating public issues. It was used in personal attacks and satires, as well as in all kinds of inviting things which were written to catch the eyes of the bourgeois reading public that had grown up during the Renaissance.

The excitement and restlessness of the Renaissance which sent many Englishmen to sea, adventure-bound in fighting the Spaniard or exploring the new hemisphere, is recorded in the accounts which Richard Hakluyt collected in a huge work entitled *The Principal Navigations, Voyages, and Discoveries of the English Nation* (1589, 1598, 1600), in which Sir John Hawkins, Sir Francis Drake, and Sir Humphrey Gilbert are commanding figures. Perhaps the most vivid single story of the English exploits on the seas during the century is Sir Walter Raleigh's *The Last Fight of the Revenge* (1591). Such narratives as these, in direct and unaffected prose, rise to epic strength as they reflect the individual heroism and national spirit which the times called forth.

Under the same impulse of an awakened national consciousness, history in its modern sense was first written. The earlier Elizabethan historians pieced together the materials in the fashion of medieval chroniclers. The greatest of these compilations was the *Chronicles of England, Scotland, and Ireland* (1578), supervised by Ralph Holinshed. This book appeared on the eve of the popularity of the chronicle history plays, and was used extensively by the dramatists. Partisan feeling naturally prevailed on the writers of religious history. In John Foxe's *Book of Martyrs* (1563) was united Protestant zeal and patriotism, and in spite of its distortion it was carried over into the next century as one of the most widely read books of the age. Late in Elizabeth's reign there grew up a spirit of research and impartial scholarship which supplanted the older manner of recording unrelated events in chronological sequence. William Camden, though writing most of his work in Latin, is outstanding among the historians; Sir John Hayward and Sir Walter Raleigh were also creditable writers in this field. The greatest achievement in the new manner, however, was Bacon's *History of Henry VII* (1622), which is the first work to show a philosophy of history and a careful, impartial interpretation of its materials.

The men of learning gave a dignity and richness to the new English prose. In a scholarly work combining religious philosophy and history, *Of the Laws of Ecclesiastical Polity* (1594-97), Richard Hooker gave a defense of the position of the Church of England in its attitude toward Calvinism and the Puritans. There is a breadth of view and a restraint of manner in Hooker which is unique in the religious prose of the century. By far the brightest name among the late Elizabethan prose writers is Lord Bacon. His native good sense, his well-trained mind with its speculative curiosity, produced works of great significance in the history of human thought. In his famous *Essays* (1597, 1612, 1625) he expresses the practical, worldly philosophy which the Renaissance had evolved. These general statements on conduct and human affairs, however, illustrate a typical view of life, and do not show the individual force of Bacon's thinking. More important, then, is *The Advancement of Learning* (1605), which surveys all existing knowledge in order to suggest possibilities for its enlargement. Here we have an early suggestion of a new way of thinking, the beginning of inductive reasoning and the scientific method. In his greatest work, the *Novum Organum* (1620), written in Latin, he carried further this new approach to knowledge, and encouraged a scientific rationalism which was to establish a new philosophy in the next literary period.

Literary Criticism

Although the prose writings of the Elizabethans ran into many types and forms too numerous even for general discussion, the ideas which they expressed relating to literary criticism deserve some attention. Literature during the earlier periods was objective and did not arouse much thought about it as an art. Medieval writers worked with their interests focused on their themes and were not self-conscious or bothered with theories of expression. The Renaissance, however, gave Englishmen the opportunity to compare classical literature with their own. From Ascham on, comments on the differences between the ancients and the moderns grew more frequent and emphatic. These writers found

that English literature was decidedly inferior, and that
its background was, by comparison, barbaric. It is
from such thinking that English literary criticism takes
its beginning. It may also be said that the writing of
criticism was called forth by the attacks of Puritan
reformers against poetry and the drama for being im-
moral and dangerous to religion. It was fictional,
therefore not "true"; it dealt with love, sometimes sin
and crime; it was, in short, worldly. These charges
were answered in several defenses of poetry, Sidney and
Lodge first coming to its rescue. In their essays, after
establishing the antiquity, dignity, and moral elevation
of poetry, they added a consideration of its nature and
its technique. The function of literary art was discussed, and tentative proposals for its improvement were
suggested. Thus criticism was put on a constructive
basis, as the statement of a theory and method which
underlies artistic creation. Criticism not only attempted
to analyze and judge a writer's achievement in itself, it
also implied or stated a conception of what is the best
in literature, by which individual work may be judged.
With the development of criticism, the study of literature becomes incomplete unless the principles which
mold it are understood.

Since renaissance thought conceived the classical culture as perfect, it was natural for Elizabethan critics to
adopt classical literature as a model, and by it to note
the shortcomings of their own. They observed, for example, that Greek and Latin poetry did not use rime,
and that rhythm was obtained by a quantitative scansion
of long and short syllables, instead of by stressed and
unstressed, as in English versification. They suggested,
therefore, that rime was uncouth, that it should be
abandoned for the unrimed verse of classical usage. A
group of writers, among whom were Sidney and Spenser,

experimented with quantitative meter, attempting to imitate the smooth-flowing hexameters of Virgil. This effort to abolish stressed rhythm failed in time, although some promising results were in sight. Later poets, such as Swinburne, Meredith, and Bridges, have occasionally written beautiful verse in the quantitative meter. The drama also was found to differ from the classical, and to the critics seemed absurd and childish. Sidney, for example, condemned the lack of unity, and the mixing of different types of drama in one play. After him Ben Jonson applied his own critical theories in his plays which were built along classical lines. The new criticism also appraised contemporary writers, and several essays were written which discussed outstanding poets of the age. In general, however, it may be said that the critics went one way, and the poets another. Criticism was in its infancy, it had not yet acquired an authority which could direct the literary output of the period. But already it had established a method of judging merit by a comparison with classical excellence. This return to the ancients, so natural to a renaissance critic, continued into later periods, building up a critical apparatus which affected all men of letters in the age of Dryden and Pope.

Conclusion

The literary period which has been so roughly surveyed possessed many forms of writing which have not been discussed. The activity of the age, running into many channels of expression, produced literature in confusing abundance. The strong individuality of the writers so affected their work that even within the same type of writing a richness and perplexing variability are found. Influences from the continent, through the works of important Italian and French writers who were readily translated, moved English thought and set up literary fashions. Classical literature was translated into English idiom for popular reading. National issues and policies were reflected in all the forms of poetry and prose. The thought and life of the age flowed freely into the literary expression of its writers.

No literary epoch, however, is distinct and isolated in its qualities. It has been convenient to treat the sixteenth century as the first of a new world; yet the persistence of medieval ideas and forms can easily be shown. Conversely, there are some writers and tendencies in the Middle English period that are not basically different from those of the Renaissance. So it is also, in looking forward into the seventeenth century, with its Puritan and Restoration literature; although it is helpful to stress differences between these two periods, the careful student will perceive the beginnings of one literary age in the achievements of its predecessor. But the Elizabethan period, extending its characteristic flourish into the reigns of the early Stuart kings, has its distinction and made its large contributions to literary history. The forces which vitalized it evoked new thoughts and ideas of life; the rising middle classes found expression and gratification through their popular writers. The age recorded high ideals and sound thinking; it dramatized life in a vivid and poetic way. Moreover, it gave to all readers of literature Marlowe and Spenser, Bacon and Shakespeare. Thus it has won its honorable place in the story of English literature.

Robert Whitney Bolwell

EARLY TUDOR LYRICS

SIR THOMAS WYATT (1503?-1542)

THE LOVER BESEECHETH HIS MISTRESS NOT TO FORGET HIS STEADFAST FAITH AND TRUE INTENT

FORGET not yet the tried intent
Of such a truth as I have meant;
My great travail so gladly spent,
Forget not yet!

Forget not yet when first began
The weary life ye know, since whan
The suit, the service none tell can;
Forget not yet!

Forget not yet the great assays,
The cruel wrong, the scornful ways,   10
The painful patience in delays,
Forget not yet!

Forget not! O, forget not this,
How long ago hath been, and is,
The mind that never meant amiss—
Forget not yet!

Forget not then thine own approved,
The which so long hath thee so loved.
Whose steadfast faith yet never moved:
Forget not this!   20

AN EARNEST SUIT TO HIS UNKIND MISTRESS
NOT TO FORSAKE HIM

AND wilt thou leave me thus?
Say nay, say nay, for shame!
To save thee from the blame
Of all my grief and grame.[1]
And wilt thou leave me thus?
Say nay! say nay!

And wilt thou leave me thus,
That hath loved thee so long
In wealth and woe among:
And is thy heart so strong   10
As for to leave me thus?
Say nay! say nay!

And wilt thou leave me thus,
That hath given thee my heart
Never for to depart
Neither for pain nor smart:
And wilt thou leave me thus?
Say nay! say nay!

And wilt thou leave me thus,
And have no more pity   20
Of him that loveth thee?
Alas, thy cruelty!
And wilt thou leave me thus?
Say nay! say nay!

[1] sorrow

THE LOVER FOR SHAME-FASTNESS HIDETH HIS DESIRE WITHIN HIS FAITHFUL HEART

Petrarchan

THE long love that in my thought I harbor,
And in my heart doth keep his residence,
Into my face presseth with bold pretence,
And there campeth displaying his banner.
She that me learns to love and to suffer,
And wills that my trust, and lust's negligence
Be reined by reason, shame, and reverence,
With his hardiness takes displeasure.
Wherewith love to the heart's forest he fleeth,
Leaving his enterprise with pain and cry,   10
And there him hideth, and not appeareth.
What may I do, when my master feareth?
But in the field with him to live and die?
For good is the life, ending faithfully.

THE LOVER COMPARETH HIS STATE TO A SHIP IN PERILOUS STORM TOSSED ON THE SEA

MY GALLEY chargèd with forgetfulness
Thorough sharp seas, in winter nights doth pass,
'Tween rock and rock; and eke my foe, alas,
That is my lord, steereth with cruelness,
And every hour, a thought in readiness,
As though that death were light in such a case.
An endless wind doth tear the sail apace
Of forcèd sighs, and trusty fearfulness.
A rain of tears, a cloud of dark disdain
Hath done the wearied cords great hinderance,   10
Wreathèd with error, and with ignorance.
The stars be hid that led me to this pain;

Drowned is reason that should be my comfort,
And I remain, despairing of the port.

A RENOUNCING OF LOVE

FAREWELL, Love, and all thy laws for ever!
Thy baited hooks shall tangle me no more:
Senec and Plato call me from thy lore
To perfect wealth my wit for to endeavor.
In blind error when I did persèver,
Thy sharp repulse, that pricketh aye so sore,
Hath taught me to set in trifles no store;
And 'scape forth, since liberty is lever.[1]
Therefore, farewell; go trouble younger hearts,
And in me claim no more authority.   1C
With idle youth go use thy property,
And thereon spend thy many brittle darts;
For hitherto though I have lost my time,
Me list no longer rotten boughs to climb.

THE LOVER SENDETH SIGHS TO MOVE HIS SUIT

Go, BURNING sighs, unto the frozen heart
Go, break the ice which pity's painful dart
Might never pierce: and if mortal prayer
In heaven may be heard, at least I desire
That death or mercy be end of smart.
Take with thee pain, whereof I have my part,
And eke the flame from which I cannot start,
And leave me then in rest, I you require.
Go, burning sighs, fulfill that I desire,
I must go work, I see, by craft and art,   10
For truth and faith in her is laid apart:

[1] dearer

Alas, I cannot therefore assail her,
With pitiful complaint and scalding fire,
That from my breast deceivably doth start.

TO A LADY TO ANSWER DIRECTLY WITH YEA OR NAY

MADAM, withouten many words,
   Once, I am sure, ye will or no;
And if ye will, then leave your bords [1]
   And use your wit and show it so:
And with a beck ye shall me call;
   And if of one, that burneth alway,
Ye have any pity at all,
   Answer him fair with yea, or nay.
If it be yea, I shall be fain; [2]
   If it be nay, friends as before;   10
Ye shall another man obtain,
   And I mine own and yours no more.

OF THE MEAN AND SURE ESTATE

Country mouse and city mouse

Written to John Poins

MY MOTHER's maids, when they did sew and spin,
They sung sometime a song of the field mouse
That, for because her livelihood was but thin,
Would needs go seek her townish sister's house.
She thought herself endurèd too much pain;
The stormy blasts her cave so sore did souse
That when the furrows swimmèd with the rain,
She must lie cold and wet in sorry plight;
And worse than that, bare meat there did remain

[1] teasings   [2] happy

To comfort her when she her house had dight;[1]   10
Sometime a barley corn; sometime a bean,
For which she labored hard both day and night
In harvest time whilst she might go and glean;
And when her store was stroyèd with the flood,
Then welaway! for she undone was clean.
Then was she fain to take, instead of food,
Sleep, if she might, her hunger to beguile.
    'My sister,' quoth she, 'hath a living good,
And hence from me she dwelleth not a mile.
In cold and storm she lieth warm and dry   20
In bed of down, the dirt doth not defile
Her tender foot, she laboreth not as I.
Richly she feedeth, and at the rich man's cost,
And for her meat she needs not crave nor cry.
By sea, by land, of the delicates, the most
Her cater[2] seeks and spareth for no peril,
She feedeth on boiled bacon, meat, and roast,
And hath thereof neither charge nor travail;
And, when she list, the liquor of the grape
Doth glad her heart till that her belly swell.'   30
    And at this journey she maketh but a jape;[3]
So forth she goeth, trusting of all this wealth
With her sister her part so for to shape,
That if she might keep herself in health,
To live a lady while her life doth last.
    And to the door now is she come by stealth,
And with her foot anon she scrapeth full fast.
Th' other, for fear, durst not well scarce appear,
Of every noise so was the wretch aghast.
At last she askèd softly who was there,   40
And in her language as well as she could.
'Peep!' quoth the other sister, 'I am here.'

---

[1] made orderly   [2] caterer   [3] joke

'Peace,' quoth the town mouse, 'why speakest thou
    so loud?'
And by the hand she took her fair and well.
'Welcome,' quoth she, 'my sister, by the Rood!' *Cross of Christ*
    She feasted her, that joy it was to tell
The fare they had; they drank the wine so clear,
And, as to purpose now and then it fell,
She cheerèd her with 'How, sister, what cheer!'
    Amid this joy befell a sorry chance,   50
That, welaway! the stranger bought full dear
The fare she had, for, as she looked askance,
Under a stool she spied two steaming[1] eyes
In a round head with sharp ears. In France
Was never mouse so feared, for, though unwise
Had not y-seen such a beast before,
Yet had nature taught her after her guise
To know her foe and dread him evermore.
The towny mouse fled, she knew whither to go;
Th' other had no shift, but wonders sore   60
Feared of her life. At home she wished her tho,
And to the door, alas! as she did skip.
The heaven it would, lo! and eke her chance was so,
At the threshold her silly foot did trip;
And ere she might recover it again,
The traitor cat had caught her by the hip,
And made her there against her will remain,
That had forgot her poor surety and rest
For seeming wealth wherein she thought to reign.
    Alas, my Poins, how men do seek the best   70
And find the worst by error as they stray!
And no marvel; when sight is so opprest,
And blinds the guide, anon out of the way
Goeth guide and all in seeking quiet life.
O wretched minds, there is no gold that may

[1] flashing

Grant that you seek; no war, no peace, no strife.
No, no, although thy head were hooped with gold,
Sergeant with mace, halberd, sword, nor knife,
Cannot repulse the care that follow should.
Each kind of life hath with him his disease.   80
Live in delight even as thy lust would,
And thou shalt find, when lust doth most thee please,
It irketh straight, and by itself doth fade.
A small thing is it that may thy mind appease.
None of ye all there is that is so mad
To seek for grapes on brambles or on briars;
Nor none, I trow, that hath his wit so bad
To set his hay [1] for conies [2] over rivers,
Nor ye set not a drag-net for an hare;
And yet the thing that most is your desire   90
Ye do mis-seek with more travail and care.
Make plain thine heart, that it be not knotted
With hope or dread, and see thy will be bare
From all effects whom vice hath ever spotted.
Thyself content with that is thee assigned,
And use it well that is to thee allotted.
Then seek no more out of thyself to find
The thing that thou hast sought so long before,
For thou shalt feel it sticking in thy mind.
Mad, if ye list to continue your sore,   100
Let present pass and gape on time to come,
And deep yourself in travail more and more.

Henceforth, my Poins, this shall be all and some,
These wretched fools shall have naught else of me;
But to the great God and to his high dome,[3]
None other pain pray I for them to be,
But, when the rage doth lead them from the right,
That, looking backward, virtue they may see,
Even as she is so goodly fair and bright,

[1] traps   [2] rabbits   [3] judgment

And whilst they clasp their lusts in arms across, 110
Grant them, good Lord, as thou mayst of thy might,
To fret inward for losing such a loss.

HENRY HOWARD, EARL OF SURREY

(1517?-1547)

DESCRIPTION OF SPRING, WHEREIN EACH THING RENEWS, SAVE ONLY THE LOVER

THE soote [1] season that bud and bloom forth brings,
With green hath clad the hill and eke the vale;
The nightingale with feathers new she sings;
The turtle [2] to her mate hath told her tale:
Summer is come, for every spray now springs;
The hart hath hung his old head on the pale;
The buck in brake his winter coat he flings;
The fishes float with new repairèd scale;
The adder all her slough away she slings;
The swift swallow pursueth the flies smale;   10
The busy bee her honey now she mings. [3]
Winter is worn, that was the flowers' bale:
And thus I see among these pleasant things
Each care decays, and yet my sorrow springs!

COMPLAINT OF A LOVER REBUKED

LOVE, that liveth and reigneth in my thought,
That built his seat within my captive breast,
Clad in the arms wherein with me he fought,
Oft in my face he doth his banner rest.
She that me taught to love, and suffer pain,
My doubtful hope and eke my hot desire

[1] sweet   [2] dove   [3] mingles, mixes.

With shamefast cloak to shadow and refrain,
Her smiling grace converteth straight to ire.
The coward Love then to the heart apace
Taketh his flight, whereas he lurks and plains,   10
His purpose lost, and dare not show his face.
For my lord's guilt thus faultless bide I pains.
Yet from my lord shall not my foot remove;
Sweet is his death that takes his end by love.

COMPLAINT OF THE LOVER DISDAINED

In Cyprus springs, whereas dame Venus dwelt,
A well so hot, that whoso tastes the same,
Were he of stone, as thawèd ice should melt,
And kindled find his breast with firèd flame;
Whose moist poison dissolvèd hath my heart.
With creeping fire my cold limbs are supprest,
Feeleth the heart that harbored freedom, smart:
Endless despair long thraldom hath imprest.
Another well of frozen ice is found,
Whose chilling venom of repugnant kind,   10
The fervent heat doth quench of Cupid's wound,
And with the spot of change infects the mind;
Whereof my dear hath tasted, to my pain:
Whereby my service grows into disdain.

VOW TO LOVE FAITHFULLY HOWSOEVER HE
BE REWARDED

Set me whereas the sun doth parch the green,
Or where his beams do not dissolve the ice;
In temperate heat, where he is felt and seen;
In presence prest of people, mad or wise;
Set me in high, or yet in low degree;
In longest night, or in the longest day;

In clearest sky, or where clouds thickest be;
In lusty youth, or when my hairs are gray:
Set me in heaven, in earth, or else in hell;
In hill, or dale, or in the foaming flood;   10
Thrall, or at large, alive whereso I dwell;
Sick or in health, in evil fame or good;
Hers will I be, and only with this thought
Content myself, although my chance be naught.

A PRAISE OF HIS LOVE WHEREIN HE RE-PROVETH THEM THAT COMPARE THEIR LADIES WITH HIS

GIVE place, ye lovers, here before
That spent your boasts and brags in vain;
My lady's beauty passeth more
The best of yours, I dare well sayn, [1]
Than doth the sun the candle light,
Or brightest day the darkest night.

And thereto hath a troth [2] as just
As had Penelope the fair;
For what she saith, ye may it trust
As it by writing sealèd were: 10
And virtues hath she many mo
Than I with pen have skill to show.

I could rehearse, if that I would,
The whole effect of Nature's plaint,
When she had lost the perfect mold,
The like to whom she could not paint:
With wringing hands, how she did cry,
And what she said, I know it, I.

[1] say   [2] fidelity

I know she swore with raging mind,
Her kingdom only set apart,
There was no loss by law of kind [1]
That could have gone so near her heart.
And this was chiefly all her pain:
She could not make the like again.

                                20

Sith Nature thus gave her the praise,
To be the chiefest work she wrought;
In faith, methink, some better ways
On your behalf might well be sought,
Than to compare, as ye have done,
To match the candle with the sun.

                                30

THE MEANS TO ATTAIN HAPPY LIFE

Martial, the things that do attain
The happy life, be these, I find:
The riches left, not got with pain,
The fruitful ground, the quiet mind;

The equal friend, no grudge, no strife,
No charge of rule, nor governance,
Without disease the healthful life,
The household of continuance;

The mean diet, no delicate fare,
True wisdom joined with simpleness,
The night dischargèd of all care,
Where wine the wit may not oppress;

                                10

The faithful wife, without debate,
Such sleeps as may beguile the night:

[1] nature

Contented with thine own estate,
Ne wish for death, ne fear his might.

OF THE DEATH OF SIR T[HOMAS] W[YATT]

W. RESTETH here, that quick [1] could never rest;
Whose heavenly gifts encreasèd by disdain,
And virtue sank the deeper in his breast;
Such profit he by envy could obtain.

A head, where wisdom mysteries did frame,
Whose hammers beat still in that lively brain,
As on a stithe,[2] where that some work of fame
Was daily wrought, to turn to Britain's gain.

A visage stern and mild, where both did grow,
Vice to contemn, in virtue to rejoice;   10
Amid great storms, whom grace assurèd so,
To live upright and smile at fortune's choice.

A hand that taught what might be said in rime,
That reft Chaucer the glory of his wit,
A mark, the which (unperfected, for time)
Some may approach, but never none shall hit.

A tongue that served in foreign realms his king,
Whose courteous talk to virtue did enflame
Each noble heart, a worthy guide to bring
Our English youth by travail unto fame.   20

An eye, whose judgment none affect could blind,
Friends to allure, and foes to reconcile,
Whose piercing look did represent a mind
With virtue fraught, reposèd, void of guile.

[1] alive   [2] anvil

A heart, where dread was never so imprest,
To hide the thought that might the truth advance,
In neither fortune lost nor yet represt,
To swell in wealth or yield unto mischance.

A valiant corse, where force and beauty met,
Happy, alas, too happy, but for foes, 30
Livèd, and ran the race that Nature set,
Of manhood's shape, where she the mold did lose.

But to the heavens that simple soul is fled,
Which left, with such as covet Christ to know,
Witness of faith that never shall be dead,
Sent for our health, but not receivèd so.

Thus, for our guilt, this jewel have we lost;
The earth his bones, the heavens possess his ghost.

HOW NO AGE IS CONTENT WITH HIS OWN ESTATE, AND HOW THE AGE OF CHILDREN IS THE HAPPIEST, IF THEY HAD SKILL TO UNDERSTAND IT

LAID in my quiet bed, in study as I were,
I saw within my troubled head a heap of thoughts appear;
And every thought did show so lively in mine eyes,
That now I sighed, and then I smiled, as cause of thought doth rise.
I saw the little boy in thought, how oft that he
Did wish of God to scape the rod, a tall young man to be;
The young man eke that feels his bones with pains opprest,

How he would be a rich old man, to live and lie at rest;
The rich old man that sees his end draw on so sore,
How he would be a boy again, to live so much the
    more.   10
Whereat full oft I smiled, to see how all these three,
From boy to man, from man to boy, would chop and
    change degree.
And musing thus I think, the case is very strange,
That man from wealth, to live in woe, doth ever seek
    to change.
Thus thoughtful as I lay, I saw my withered skin,
How it doth shew my dented chews,[1] the flesh was worn
    so thin.
And eke my toothless chaps, the gates of my right way,
That opes and shuts as I do speak, do thus unto me say:
'Thy white and hoarish hairs, the messengers of age,
That shew, like lines of true belief, that this life doth
    assuage,   20
Bid thee lay hand, and feel them hanging on thy chin,
The which do write two ages past, the third now com-
    ing in.
Hang up therefore the bit of thy young wanton time,
And thou that therein beaten art, the happiest life
    define.'
Whereat I sighed and said: 'Farewell, my wonted joy,
Truss up thy pack, and trudge from me to every little
    boy,
And tell them thus from me, their time most happy is,
If, to their time, they reason had, to know the truth
    of this.'

[1] checks

JOHN HEYWOOD (1497-1578?)

GREEN WILLOW

Refrain:
>   All a green willow, willow, willow,
>   All a green willow is my garland.

ALAS, by what mean may I make ye to know
The unkindness for kindness that to me doth grow?
That one who most kind love on me should bestow
Most unkind unkindness to me she doth show,
    For all a green willow is my garland.

To have love and hold love, where love is so sped,
Oh delicate food to the lover so fed!
From love won to love lost, where lovers be led,   10
Oh desperate dolor, the lover is dead!
    For all a green willow is his garland.

She said she did love me, and would love me still,
She sware above all men I had her good will;
She said and she sware she would my will fulfil:
The promise all good, the performance all ill;
    For all a green willow is my garland.

Now woe worth the willow, and woe worth the wight
That windeth the willow, willow garland to dight,
That dole dealt in almès, is all amiss quite   20
Where lovers are beggars for almès in sight;
    No lover doth beg for this willow garland.

Of this willow garland the burden seems small,
But my break-neck burden I may it well call;
Like the sow of lead on my head it doth fall,

Break head, and break neck, back, bones, brains, heart
    and all;
  All parts pressed in pieces [for this willow garland].

Too ill for her, think I, best things may be had;
Too good for me, think she, things being most bad;
All I do present her that may make her glad,   30
All she doth present me that may make me sad;
  This equity have I with this willow garland.

Could I forget thee, as thou canst forget me,
That were my sound fault, which cannot nor shall be;
Though thou like the soaring hawk, every way flee,
I will be the turtle most steadfast to thee,
  And patiently wear this green willow garland.

All ye that have had love, and have my like wrong,
My like truth and patience plant you among,
When feminine fancies for new love do long,   40
Old love cannot hold them, new love is so strong,
  For all a green willow is my garland.

LONG HAVE I BEEN A SINGING MAN

Long have I been a singing man,
  And sundry parts oft I have sung,
Yet one part since I first began
  I could nor can sing, old or young;
The mean, I mean, which part shows well
Above all parts most to excel.

The bass and treble are extremes,
  The tenor standeth sturdily,
The counter reigneth then meseems;
  The mean must make our melody.   10

This is the mean, who means it well,
The part of parts that doth excel.

Of all our parts, if any jar,
    Blame not the mean being sung true;
The mean must make, it may not mar;
    Lacking the mean, our mirth adieu:
Thus shows the mean not meanly well,
Yet doth the mean in this excel.

Mark well the manner of the mean,
    And thereby time and tune your song;   20
Unto the mean where all parts lean,
    All parts are kept from singing wrong.
Though singing men take this not well,
Yet doth the mean in this excel.

The mean in compass is so large
    That every part must join thereto;
It hath an oar in every barge,
    To say, to sing, to think, to do.
Of all these parts no part doth well
Without the mean, which doth excel.   30

Too high, too low, too loud, too soft,
    Too few, too many at a part alone,
The mean is more melodious [oft]
    Than other parts lacking that one:
Whereby the mean compareth well
Among all parts most to excel.

The mean in loss, the mean in gain,
    In wealth or in adversity;
The mean in health, the mean in pain,
    The mean means always equity.   40

The mean thus meant may mean full well,
Of all other parts most to excel.

To me and mine with all the rest,
   Good Lord, grant grace, with hearty voice
To sing the mean that meaneth best,
   All parts in the best for to rejoice:
Which mean in meaning meaneth well,
The mean of means that doth excel.

A PRAISE OF HIS LADY

GIVE place, you ladies, and begone,
   Boast not yourselves at all;
For here at hand approacheth one
   Whose face will stain you all.

The virtue of her lively looks
   Excels the precious stone;
I wish to have none other books
   To read or look upon.

In each of her two crystal eyes
   Smileth a naked boy;   10
It would you all in heart suffice
   To see that lamp of joy.

I think nature hath lost the mold,
   Where she her shape did take;
Or else I doubt if nature could
   So fair a creature make.

She may be well compared
   Unto the Phœnix kind,

Whose like was never seen or heard,
   That any man can find.   20

In life she is Diana chaste,
   In truth Penelope,
In word and eke in deed steadfast
   What will you more we say?

If all the world were sought so far,
   Who could find such a wight?
Her beauty twinketh like a star
   Within the frosty night.

Her rosial color comes and goes
   With such a comely grace,   30
More redier too than doth the rose,
   Within her lively face.

At Bacchus' feast none shall her meet,
   Ne at no wanton play,
Nor gazing in an open street,
   Nor gadding as a stray.

The modest mirth that she doth use
   Is mixt with shamefastness;
All vice she doth wholly refuse,
   And hateth idleness.   40

O Lord, it is a world to see
   How virtue can repair,
And deck in her such honesty,
   Whom nature made so fair!

Truly she doth as far exceed
   Our women now-a-days

As doth the gilli-flower [1] a weed,
  And more a thousand ways.

How might I do to get a graff [2]
  Of this unspotted tree?   50
For all the rest are plain but chaff,
  Which seem good corn to be.

This gift alone I shall her give,
  When Death doth what he can:
Her honest fame shall ever live
  Within the mouth of man.

THOMAS, LORD VAUX (1510-1556)

OF A CONTENTED MIND

WHEN all is done and said,
  In the end thus shall you find,
He most of all doth bathe in bliss
  That hath a quiet mind,
And, clear from worldly cares,
  To deem can be content
The sweetest time in all his life
  In thinking to be spent.

The body subject is
  To fickle Fortune's power,   10
And to a million of mishaps
  Is casual every hour;
And death in time doth change
  It to a clod of clay,
Whenas the mind, which is divine,
  Runs never to decay.

[1] carnation   [2] shoot, for grafting

Companion none is like
  Unto the mind alone;
For many have been harmed by speech;
  Through thinking few or none: 20
Fear oftentimes restraineth words,
  But makes not thought to cease,
And he speaks best that hath the skill
  When for to hold his peace.

Our wealth leaves us at death;
  Our kinsmen at the grave;
But virtues of the mind unto
  The heavens with us we have.
Wherefore, for virtue's sake,
  I can be well content   30
The sweetest time of all my life
  To deem in thinking spent.

THE AGED LOVER RENOUNCETH LOVE

I LOATHE that I did love,
  In youth that I thought sweet,
As time requires for my behove,
  Methinks they are not meet.

My lusts they do me leave,
  My fancies all be fled,
And tract of time begins to weave
  Grey hairs upon my head.

For age with stealing steps
  Hath clawed me with his crutch,   10
And lusty life away she leaps
  As there had been none such.

My Muse doth not delight
    Me as she did before;
My hand and pen are not in plight,
    As they have been of yore.

For reason me denies
    This youthly idle rhyme;
And day by day to me she cries,
    'Leave off these toys in time.'   20

The wrinkles in my brow,
    The furrows in my face,
Say, limping age will lodge him now
    Where youth must give him place.

The harbinger of death,
    To me I see him ride,
The cough, the cold, the gasping breath
    Doth bid me to provide

A pickaxe and a spade,
    And eke a shrouding sheet,   30
A house of clay for to be made
    For such a guest most meet.

Methinks I hear the clark
    That knolls the careful knell,
And bids me leave my woeful wark,
    Ere nature me compel.

My keepers knit the knot
    That youth did laugh to scorn,
Of me that clean shall be forgot
    As I had not been born.   40

Thus must I youth give up,
  Whose badge I long did wear;
To them I yield the wanton cup
  That better may it bear.

Lo, here the barèd skull,
  By whose bald sign I know
That stooping age away shall pull
  Which youthful years did sow.

For beauty with her band
  These crooked cares hath wrought,   50
And shippèd me into the land
  From whence I first was brought.

And ye that bide behind,
  Have ye none other trust:
As ye of clay were cast by kind,
  So shall ye waste to dust.

THOMAS NORTON (1532-1584)

AGAINST WOMEN EITHER GOOD OR BAD

A MAN may live thrice Nestor's life,
  Thrice wander out Ulysses' race,
Yet never find Ulysses' wife:
  Such change hath chancèd in this case.

Less age will serve than Paris had,
  Small pain—if none be small enough—
To find good store of Helen's trade:
  Such sap, the root doth yield the bough.

For one good wife Ulysses slew
  A worthy knot of gentle blood;   10
For one ill wife Greece overthrew
  The town of Troy. Sith bad and good

Work mischief, Lord, let be thy will
To keep me free from either ill!

ANONYMOUS (before 1558)

THE LOVER PRAYETH PITY, SHOWING THAT NATURE HATH TAUGHT HIS DOG AS IT WERE TO SUE FOR THE SAME BY KISSING HIS LADY'S HANDS

NATURE that taught my silly dog, God wat;
Even for my sake to like where I do love,
Enforcèd him whereas my lady sat
With humble suit before her falling flat.
As in his sort he might her pray and move
To rue upon his lord, and not forget
The steadfast faith he beareth her and love,
Kissing her hand, whom she could not remove
Away that would, for frowning nor for threat,
As though he would have said in my behalf,   10
'Pity my lord, your slave, that doth remain,
Lest by his death you guiltless slay us twaine.'

OF A NEW MARRIED STUDENT

A STUDENT at his book, so placed
  That wealth he might have won,
From book to wife did fleet in haste,
  From wealth to woe did run.
Now, who hath played a feater cast,

Since juggling first begun?
In knitting of himself so fast,
Himself he hath undone.

AN OLD LOVER TO A YOUNG GENTLEWOMAN

YE ARE too young to bring me in,
And I too old to gape for flies;
I have too long a lover been,
If such young babes should blear mine eyes.
But trill the ball before my face,
I am content to make you play;
I will not see, I hide my face,
And turn my back and run away.

But if you follow on so fast
And cross the ways where I should go,   10
Ye may wax weary at the last
And then at length yourself o'erthrow:
I mean, where you and all your flock
Devise to pen men in the pound,
I know a key can pick your lock
And make you run yourselves on ground.

Some birds can eat the strawy corn
And flee the lime the fowlers set,
And some are feared of every thorn
And so thereby they scape the net;   20
But some do light and never look
And see not who doth stand in wait,
As fish that swallow up the hook
And is beguilèd through the bait.

But men can look before they leap
And be at price [1] for every ware,
And pennyworths cast to buy good cheap,
And in each thing have eye and care;
But he that bluntly runs on head
And seeth not what the race shall be   30
Is like to bring a fool to bed,
And thus ye get no more of me.

IF EVER I MARRY, I'LL MARRY A MAID

If ever I marry, I'll marry a maid;
To marry a widow, I am sore afraid:
For maids they are simple, and never will grutch,
But widows full oft, as they say, know too much.

A maid is so sweet, and so gentle of kind,
That a maid is the wife I will choose to my mind.
A widow is froward, and never will yield;
Or if such there be, you will meet them but seeld. [2]

A maid ne'er complaineth, do what so you will;
But what you mean well, a widow takes ill: 10
A widow will make you a drudge and a slave,
And, cost ne'er so much, she will ever go brave [3]

A maid is so modest, she seemeth a rose
When it first beginneth the bud to unclose;
But a widow full-blowen full often deceives,
And the next wind that bloweth shakes down all her
          leaves.

The widows be lovely, I never gainsay,
But too well all their beauty they know to display;

[1] know the price   [2] seldom   [3] elaborately dressed

But a maid hath so great hidden beauty in store,
She can spare to a widow, yet never be poor. **20**

Then, if ever I marry, give me a fresh maid,
If to marry with any I be not afraid;
But to marry with any, it asketh much care;
And some bachelors hold they are best as they are.

FROM SACKVILLE TO MARLOWE

Thomas Sackville

John Foxe

Roger Ascham

Ralph Holinshed

John Lyly

Philip Sidney

Edmund Spenser

Walter Raleigh

Christopher Marlowe

THOMAS SACKVILLE, LORD BUCKHURST
(1536-1608)

THE INDUCTION TO A MIRROR FOR MAGISTRATES

The wrathful Winter, 'proaching on apace,
With blustering blasts had all ybared the treen,[1]
And old Saturnus, with his frosty face,
With chilling cold had pierced the tender green;
The mantles rent, wherein enwrappèd been
The gladsome groves that now lay overthrown,
The tapets torn, and every bloom down blown.

The soil, that erst [2] so seemly was to seen,
Was all despoilèd of her beauty's hue;
And soote fresh flowers, wherewith the summer's queen
Had clad the earth, now Boreas' blasts down blew;   11
And small fowls flocking, in their song did rue
The winter's wrath, wherewith each thing defaced
In woeful wise bewailed the summer past.

Hawthorn had lost his motley livery,
The naked twigs were shivering all for cold,
And dropping down the tears abundantly;
Each thing, methought, with weeping eye me told
The cruel season, bidding me withhold
Myself within; for I was gotten out   20
Into the fields, whereas [3] I walked about.

¹ trees   ² once   ³ where

33

When lo, the night with misty mantles spread,
Gan dark the day, and dim the azure skies;
And Venus in her message Hermes sped
To bloody Mars, to will him not to rise,
While she herself approached in speedy wise;
And Virgo hiding her disdainful breast,
With Thetis now had laid her down to rest.

Whiles Scorpio dreading Sagittarius' dart,
Whose bow prest bent in fight, the string had slipped, 30
Down slid into the ocean flood apart,
The Bear, that in the Irish seas had dipped
His grisly feet, with speed from thence he whipped:
For Thetis, hasting from the Virgin's bed,
Pursued the Bear, that ere she came was fled.

And Phaeton now, near reaching to his race
With glist'ring beams, gold streaming where they bent,
Was prest to enter in his resting place:
Erythius, that in the cart first went,
Had even now attained his journey's stent [1]　　　　40
And, fast declining, hid away his head,
While Titan couched him in his purple bed.

And pale Cynthea, with her borrowed light,
Beginning to supply her brother's place
Was past the noonstead [2] six degrees in sight,
When sparkling stars amid the heaven's face,
With twinkling light shone on the earth apace,
That, while they brought about the nightès chare, [3]
The dark had dimmed the day ere I was ware.

And sorrowing I to see the summer flowers, 50
The lively green, the lusty leas forlorn,
[1] finish　　[2] zenith　　[3] chariot

The sturdy trees so shattered with the showers,
The fields so fade, that flourished so beforn,
It taught me well, all earthly things be born
To die the death, for naught long time may last;
The summer's beauty yields to winter's blast.

Then looking upward to the heaven's leams,[1]
With nightès stars thick powdered everywhere,
Which erst so glistened with the golden streams
That cheerful Phœbus spread down from his sphere,   60
Beholding dark oppressing day so near:
The sudden sight reducèd to my mind,
The sundry changes that in earth we find.

That musing on this worldly wealth in thought,
Which comes, and goes, more faster than we see
The flickering flame that with the fire is wrought,
My busy mind presented unto me
Such fall of peers as in this realm had be;
That oft I wished some would their woes descrive,[2]
To warn the rest whom fortune left alive.   70

And straight forth stalking with redoubled pace,
For that I saw the night drew on so fast,
In black all clad, there fell before my face
A piteous wight,[3] whom woe had all forewaste;[4]
Forth from her eyen the crystal tears out brast;[5]
And sighing sore, her hands she wrung and fold,
Tare all her hair, that ruth was to behold.

Her body small, forewithered,[6] and forespent,[7]
As is the stalk that summer's drought oppressed;
Her welkèd[8] face with woeful tears besprent;[9]   80

---

[1] rays   [2] describe   [3] person   [4] wasted away   [5] burst
[6] completely withered   [7] worn out   [8] shrunken   [9] besprinkled

Her color pale; and, as it seemed her best,
In woe and plaint reposèd was her rest:
And, as the stone that drops of water wears,
So dented were her cheeks with fall of tears.

Her eyes swollen with flowing streams afloat,
Wherewith, her looks thrown up full piteously,
Her forceless hands together oft she smote,
With doleful shrieks, that echoed in the sky;
Whose plaint such sighs did straight accompany,
That, in my doom [1] was never man did see   90
A wight but half so woe-begone as she.

I stood aghast, beholding all her plight,
'Tween dread and dolor, so distrained in heart,
That, while my hairs upstarted with the sight,
The tears outstreamed for sorrow of her smart:
But, when I saw no end that could apart
The deadly dewle [2] which she so sore did make,
With doleful voice then thus to her I spake:

'Unwrap thy woes, whatever wight thou be,
And stint in time to spill [3] thyself with plaint: 100
Tell what thou art, and whence, for well I see
Thou canst not dure, with sorrow thus attaint:'
And, with that word of sorrow, all forefaint
She lookèd up, and, prostrate as she lay,
With piteous sound, lo, thus she gan to say:

'Alas, I wretch, whom thus thou seest distrained
With wasting woes, that never shall aslake,
Sorrow I am, in endless torments pained
Among the Furies in the infernal lake,
Where Pluto, god of hell, so grisly black,   110

[1] judgment   [2] sorrow   [3] destroy

Doth hold his throne, and Lethe's deadly taste
Doth reave remembrance of each thing forepast:

'Whence come I am, the dreary destiny
And luckless lot for to bemoan of those
Whom fortune, in this maze of misery,
Of wretched chance, most woeful mirrors chose;
That, when thou seest how lightly they did lose
 Their pomp, their power, and that they thought most
   sure.
Thou mayst soon deem no earthly joy may dure.'

Whose rueful voice no sooner had out brayed 120
Those woeful words wherewith she sorrowed so,
But out, alas, she shright,[1] and never stayed,
Fell down, and all to-dashed herself for woe:
 The cold pale dread my limbs gan overgo,
And I so sorrowed at her sorrows eft,[2]
That, what with grief and fear, my wits were reft.

I stretched myself, and straight my heart revives,
That dread and dolor erst did so appale;
Like him that with the fervent fever strives,
When sickness seeks his castle health to scale; 130
 With gathered spirits so forced I fear to avale:[3]
And, rearing her, with anguish all foredone,
My spirits returned, and then I thus begun:

'O Sorrow, alas, sith Sorrow is thy name,
And that to thee this drear [4] doth well pertain,
In vain it were to seek to cease the same:
But, as a man himself with sorrow slain,
So I, alas, do comfort thee in pain,
  [1] shrieked [2] again [3] abate [4] dreariness

That here in sorrow art foresunk so deep,
That at thy sight I can but sigh and weep.'   140

I had no sooner spoken of a stike,[1]
But that the storm so rumbled in her breast,
As Æölus could never roar the like:
And showers down rainèd from her eyen so fast,
That all bedrent[2] the place, till at the last,
Well easèd they the dolor of her mind,
As rage of rain doth swage the stormy wind:

For forth she pacèd in her fearful tale:
'Come, come,' quoth she, 'and see what I shall show,
Come, hear the plaining and the bitter bale   150
Of worthy men by Fortune overthrow:
Come thou, and see them ruing all in row,
They were but shades that erst in mind thou rolled:
Come, come with me, thine eyes shall them behold.'

What could these words but make me more aghast,
To hear her tell whereon I mused whilere?[3]
So was I mazed therewith, till, at the last,
Musing upon her words, and what they were,
All suddenly well lessoned was my fear;
For to my mind returnèd, how she telled   160
Both what she was, and where her won[4] she held.

Whereby I knew that she a goddess was,
And, therewithal, resorted to my mind
My thought, that late presented me the glass
Of brittle state, of cares that here we find,
Of thousand woes to silly men assigned:

  [1] verse or stanza   [2] bedrenched   [3] formerly   [4] dwelling

And how she now bid me come and behold,
To see with eye that erst in thought I rolled.

Flat down I fell, and with all reverence
Adorèd her, perceiving now that she,   170
A goddess, sent by godly providence,
In earthly shape thus showed herself to me,
To wail and rue this world's uncertainty:
And, while I honored thus her godhead's might
With plaining voice these words to me she shright:

'I shall thee guide first to the grisly lake,
And thence unto the blissful place of rest,
Where thou shalt see, and hear, the plaint they make
That whilom here bare swing [1] among the best:
This shalt thou see: but great is the unrest   180
That thou must bide, before thou canst attain
Unto the dreadful place where these remain.'

And, with these words, as I upraisèd stood,
And gan to follow her that straight forth paced,
Ere I was ware, into a desert wood
We now were come, where, hand in hand embraced,
She led the way, and through the thick so traced,
As, but I had been guided by her might,
It was no way for any mortal wight.

But lo, while thus amid the desert dark   190
We passèd on with steps and pace unmeet,
A rumbling roar, confused with howl and bark
Of dogs, shook all the ground under our feet,
And struck the din within our ears so deep,
As, half distraught, unto the ground I fell,
Besought return, and not to visit hell.

[1] formerly here bore sway

But she, forthwith, uplifting me apace,
Removed my dread, and, with a steadfast mind,
Bade me come on; for here was now the place,
The place where we our travail end should find: 200
Wherewith I rose, and to the place assigned
Astoined [1] I stalk, when straight we approached near
The dreadful place, that you will dread to hear.

An hideous hole all vast, withouten shape,
Of endless depth, o'erwhelmed with ragged stone,
With ugly mouth, and grisly jaws doth gape,
And to our sight confounds itself in one:
Here entered we, and yeding [2] forth, anon
An horrible loathly lake we might discern,
As black as pitch, that clepèd is Avern: 210

A deadly gulf, where naught but rubbish grows,
With foul black swelth [3] in thickened lumps that lies,
Which up in th' air such stinking vapors throws,
That over there may fly no fowl but dies,
Choked with the pestilent savors that arise:
Hither we come; whence forth we still did pace,
In dreadful fear amid the dreadful place:

And, first, within the porch and jaws of hell,
Sat deep Remorse of Conscience, all besprent
With tears, and to herself oft would she tell   220
Her wretchedness, and cursing never stent
To sob and sigh; but ever thus lament,
With thoughtful care, as she that, all in vain,
Would wear, and waste continually in pain.

Her eyes unsteadfast, rolling here and there,
Whirled on each place, as place that vengeance brought,
        [1] astonished   [2] going   [3] overflow

So was her mind continually in fear,
Tossed and tormented with the tedious thought
Of those detested crimes which she had wrought:
With dreadful cheer, and looks thrown to the sky,   230
Wishing for death, and yet she could not die.

Next saw we Dread, all trembling how he shook,
With foot uncertain, proffered here and there:
Benumbed of speech, and, with a ghastly look
Searched every place, all pale and dead for fear,
His cap borne up with staring of his hair,
'Stoined and amazed at his own shade for dread,
And fearing greater dangers than was need.

And next, within the entry of this lake,
Sat fell Revenge, gnashing her teeth for ire   240
Devising means how she may vengeance take,
Never in rest, till she have her desire:
But frets within so far forth with the fire
Of wreaking flames, that now determines she
To die by death, or venged by death to be.

When fell Revenge, with bloody foul pretence
Had showed herself, as next in order set,
With trembling limbs we softly parted thence,
Till in our eyes another sight we met:
When from my heart a sigh forthwith I fet,[1]   250
Ruing, alas! upon the woeful plight
Of Misery, that next appeared in sight.

His face was lean, and somedeal [2] pined away,
And eke his hands consumèd to the bone,
But what his body was, I cannot say,
For on his carcass raiment had he none,

          [1] fetched   [2] somewhat

Save clouts and patches, piecèd one by one;
With staff in hand, and scrip on shoulders cast,
His chief defence against the winter's blast.

His food, for most, was wild fruits of the tree,   260
Unless sometimes some crumbs fell to his share,
Which in his wallet long, God wot, kept he,
As on the which full daint'ly would he fare:
His drink, the running stream: his cup, the bare
Of his palm closed; his bed, the hard cold ground:
To this poor life was Misery ybound.

Whose wretched state when we had well beheld,
With tender ruth on him, and on his fears,
In thoughtful cares forth then our pace we held;
And, by and by, another shape appears,   270
Of greedy Care, still brushing up the breres,
His knuckles knobbed, his flesh deep dented in,
With tawed [1] hands, and hard ytannèd skin.

The morrow gray no sooner hath begun
To spread his light, even peeping in our eyes,
When he is up, and to his work yrun:
But let the night's black misty mantles rise,
And with foul dark never so much disguise
The fair bright day, yet ceaseth he no while,
But hath his candles to prolong his toil.   280

By him lay heavy Sleep, the cousin of Death,
Flat on the ground, and still as any stone,
A very corpse, save yielding forth a breath:
Small keep [2] took he, whom Fortune frownèd on,
Or whom she lifted up into the throne

[1] beaten, hardened   [2] care

Of high renown; but, as a living death,
So, dead alive, of life he drew the breath.

The body's rest, the quiet of the heart,
The travail's ease, the still night's fear was he,
And of our life in earth the better part;   290
Reaver [1] of sight, and yet in whom we see
Things oft that tide,[2] and oft that never be;
Without respect, esteeming equally
King Crœsus' pomp, and Irus' poverty.

And next, in order sad, Old Age we found:
His beard all hoar, his eyes hollow and blind,
With drooping cheer still poring on the ground,
As on the place where Nature him assigned
To rest, when that the Sisters had untwined
His vital thread, and ended with their knife   300
The fleeting course of fast declining life.

There heard we him with broke and hollow plaint
Rue with himself his end approaching fast,
And all for naught his wretched mind torment
With sweet remembrance of his pleasures past,
And fresh delights of lusty youth forewaste;
Recounting which, how would he sob and shriek,
And to be young again of Jove beseek!

But and [3] the cruel fates so fixèd be,
That time forepast cannot return again,   310
This one request of Jove yet prayèd he:
That, in such withered plight, and wretched pain,
As eld, accompanied with his loathsome train,
Had brought on him, all were it woe and grief,
He might a while yet linger forth his life,

[1] depriver   [2] occur   [3] although

And not so soon descend into the pit,
Where Death, when he the mortal corpse hath slain,
With reckless hand in grave doth cover it,
Thereafter never to enjoy again
The gladsome light, but in the ground ylain,   320
In the depth of darkness waste and wear to naught,
As he had never into the world been brought.

But who had seen him sobbing, how he stood
Unto himself, and how he would bemoan
His youth forepast, as though it wrought him good
To talk of youth, all were his youth foregone,
He would have mused, and marveled much, whereon
This wretched Age should life desire so fain,
And knows full well life doth but length his pain.

Crookbacked he was, tooth-shaken, and blear-eyed,   330
Went on three feet, and sometimes crept on four,
With old lame bones that rattled by his side,
His scalp all pilled,[1] and he with eld forlore:
His withered fist still knocking at Death's door.
Fumbling, and driveling, as he draws his breath:
For [2] brief, the shape and messenger of Death.

And fast by him pale Malady was placed,
Sore sick in bed, her color all foregone,
Bereft of stomach, savor, and of taste,
Ne could she brook no meat, but broths alone;   340
Her breath corrupt, her keepers every one
Abhorring her, her sickness past recure,
Detesting physic, and all physic's cure.

But, oh, the doleful sight that then we see!
We turned our look, and, on the other side,

---

[1] bare   [2] in

A grisly shape of Famine might we see,
With greedy looks, and gaping mouth that cried
And roared for meat, as she should there have died;
Her body thin and bare as any bone,
Whereto was left naught but the case alone.   350

And that, alas, was gnawn on every where,
All full of holes, that I ne might refrain
From tears, to see how she her arms could tear,
And with her teeth gnash on the bones in vain,
When, all for naught, she fain would so sustain
Her starven corpse, that rather seemed a shade,
Than any substance of a creature made.

Great was her force, whom stone wall could not stay,
Her tearing nails snatching at all she saw;
With gaping jaws, that by no means ymay   360
Be satisfied from hunger of her maw,
But eats herself as she that hath no law:
Gnawing, alas, her carcass all in vain,
Where you may count each sinew, bone, and vein.

On her while we thus firmly fixed our eyes,
That bled for ruth of such a dreary sight,
Lo, suddenly she shrieked in so huge wise,
As made hell-gates to shiver with the might:
Wherewith, a dart we saw, how it did light
Right on her breast, and, therewithal, pale Death   370
Enthrilling it, to reave her of her breath.

And by and by, a dumb dead corpse we saw,
Heavy and cold, the shape of Death aright,
That daunts all earthly creatures to his law;
Against whose force in vain it is to fight:
Ne peers, ne princes, nor no mortal wight,

No towns, ne realms, cities, ne strongest tower,
But all, perforce, must yield unto his power.

His dart, anon, out of the corpse he took,
And in his hand (a dreadful sight to see) 380
With great triumph eftsoons [1] the same he shook,
That most of all my fears affrayèd me:
His body dight with naught but bones, pardé.
The naked shape of man there saw I plain,
All save the flesh, the sinew, and the vein.

Lastly, stood War, in glittering arms yclad,
With visage grim, stern looks, and blackly hued;
In his right hand a naked sword he had,
That to the hilts was all with blood imbrued;
And in his left (that kings and kingdoms rued) 390
Famine and fire he held, and therewithal
He razèd towns, and threw down towers and all.

Cities he sacked, and realms that whilom flowered
In honor, glory, and rule, above the best,
He overwhelmed, and all their fame devoured,
Consumed, destroyed, wasted and never ceased,
Till he their wealth, their name, and all oppressed:
His face forehewed [2] with wounds, and by his side
There hung his targe, with gashes deep and wide.

In mids of which, depainted there, we found 400
Deadly Debate, all full of snaky hair,
That with a bloody fillet was ybound,
Out breathing naught but discord everywhere:
And round about were portrayed, here and there,
The hugy hosts, Darius and his power,
His kings, princes, his peers, and all his flower,

[1] immediately [2] cut to pieces

Whom great Macedo vanquished there in sight,
With deep slaughter, despoiling all his pride
Pierced through his realms, and daunted all his might:
Duke Hannibal beheld I there beside,   410
In Canna's field, victor how he did ride,
And woeful Romans that in vain withstood,
And consul Paulus covered all in blood.

Yet saw I more the fight at Thrasimene,
And Treby field, and eke when Hannibal
And worthy Scipio last in arms were seen
Before Carthago gate, to cry for all
The world's empire, to whom it should befall:
There saw I Pompey and Cæsar clad in arms,
Their hosts allied and all their civil harms: 420

With conquerors' hands, forebathed in their own blood,
And Cæsar weeping over Pompey's head;
Yet saw I Sulla and Marius where they stood,
Their great cruelty, and the deep bloodshed
Of friends: Cyrus I saw and his host dead,
And how the queen with great despite hath flung
His head in blood of them she overcome.

Xerxes, the Persian king, yet saw I there,
With his huge host, that drank the rivers dry,
Dismounted hills, and made the vales uprear,   430
His host and all yet saw I slain, pardé:
Thebës I saw, all razed how it did lie
In heaps of stones, and Tyrus put to spoil,
With walls and towers flat evened with the soil.

But Troy, alas, methought, above them all,
It made mine eyes in very tears consume:
When I beheld the woeful word befall,

That by the wrathful will of gods was come:
And Jove's unmovèd sentence and foredoom
On Priam king, and on his town so bent, 440
I could not lin,[1] but I must there lament.

And that the more, sith destiny was so stern
As, force perforce, there might no force avail,
But she must fall: and, by her fall, we learn,
That cities, towers, wealth, world, and all shall quail:
No manhood might, nor nothing might prevail;
All were there pressed full many a prince, and peer,
And many a knight that sold his death full dear.

Not worthy Hector, worthiest of them all,
Her hope, her joy, his force is now for naught: 450
O Troy, Troy, Troy, there is no boot[2] but bale,
The hugy horse within thy walls is brought;
Thy turrets fall, thy knights, that whilom fought
In arms amid the field, are slain in bed,
Thy gods defiled, and all thy honor dead.

The flames up spring, and cruelly they creep
From wall to roof, till all to cinders waste:
Some fire the houses where the wretches sleep,
Some rush in here, some run in there as fast;
In every where or sword or fire they taste: 460
The walls are torn, the towers whirled to the ground;
There is no mischief but may there be found.

Cassandra yet there saw I how they haled
From Pallas' house, with spercled[3] tress undone,
Her wrists fast bound, and with Greeks' rout empaled:
And Priam eke, in vain how he did run
To arms, whom Pyrrhus with despite hath done

---

[1] withhold [2] remedy [3] disheveled

To cruel death, and bathed him in the baign [1]
Of his son's blood, before the altar slain.

But how can I describe the doleful sight,   470
That in the shield so livelike fair did shine?
Sith in this world, I think was never wight
Could have set forth the half, not half so fine:
I can no more, but tell how there is seen
Fair Ilium fall in burning red gledes down,
And, from the soil, great Troy, Neptunus' town.

Herefrom when scarce I could mine eyes withdraw,
That filled with tears as doth the springing well,
We passèd on so far forth till we saw
Rude Acheron, a loathsome lake to tell,   480
That boils and bubs up swelth as black as hell;
Where grisly Charon, at their fixèd tide,
Still ferries ghosts unto the farther side.

The agèd God no sooner Sorrow spied,
But, hasting straight unto the bank apace,
With hollow call unto the rout he cried,
To swerve apart, and give the goddess place:
Straight it was done, when to the shore we pace,
Where, hand in hand as we then linkèd fast,
Within the boat we are together placed.   490

And forth we launch full fraughted to the brink:
When, with the unwonted weight, the rusty keel
Began to crack as if the same should sink:
We hoist up mast and sail, that in a while
We fetched the shore, where scarcely we had while
For to arrive, but that we heard anon
A three-sound bark confounded all in one.

[1] bath

We had not long forth passed, but that we saw
Black Cerberus, the hideous hound of hell,
With bristles reared, and with a three-mounted jaw   500
Foredinning the air with his horrible yell,
Out of the deep dark cave where he did dwell.
The goddess straight he knew, and by and by,
He peased [1] and couched, while that we passèd by.

Thence come we to the horror and the hell,
The large great kingdoms, and the dreadful reign
Of Pluto in his throne where he did dwell,
The wide waste places, and the hugy plain,
The wailings, shrieks, and sundry sorts of pain,
The sighs, the sobs, the deep and deadly groan;   510
Earth, air, and all, resounding plaint and moan.

Here puled the babes, and here the maids unwed
With folded hands their sorry chance bewailed;
Here wept the guiltless slain, and lovers dead,
That slew themselves when nothing else availed;
A thousand sorts of sorrows here, that wailed
With sighs, and tears, sobs, shrieks, and all yfear, [2]
That, of, alas, it was a hell to hear.

We staid us straight and with a rueful fear,
Beheld this heavy sight; while from mine eyes   520
The vapored tears down stillèd [3] here and there,
And Sorrow eke, in far more woeful wise,
Took on with plaint, upheaving to the skies
Her wretched hands, that, with her cry, the rout
Gan all in heaps to swarm us round about.

'Lo here' quoth Sorrow, 'princes of renown,
That whilom sat on top of Fortune's wheel,

    [1] was appeased   [2] together   [3] distilled

Now laid full low; like wretches whirlèd down,
Even with one frown, that stayed but with a smile:
And now behold the thing that thou, ere-while,   530
Saw only in thought; and, what thou now shalt hear,
Recount the same to kesar,[1] king, and peer.'

(1563)

JOHN FOXE (1516-1587)

ACTS AND MONUMENTS OF THESE LATTER AND PERILOUS DAYS
(*Book of Martyrs*)

THE BEHAVIOR OF DR. RIDLEY AND MASTER LATIMER AT THE TIME OF THEIR DEATH

Upon the north side of the town, in the ditch over against the Balliol College, the place of execution was appointed; and for fear of any tumult that might arise, to let[2] the burning of them, the Lord Williams was commanded by the Queen's letters and the householders of the city, to be there assistant, sufficiently appointed. And when every thing was in a readiness, the prisoners were brought forth by the mayor and the bailiffs. Master Ridley had a fair black gown furred, and faced with foins,[3] such as he was wont to wear being bishop, and a tippet of velvet, furred likewise, about his neck, a velvet night-cap upon his head, and a corner cap upon the same, going in a pair of slippers to the stake, and going between the mayor and an alderman, etc. After him came Master Latimer in a poor Bristol frieze [4] frock all worn, with his buttoned cap, and a kerchief on his head all ready to the fire, a new long shroud

[1] kaiser, emperor   [2] hinder   [3] marten fur trimmings
[4] coarse wool cloth

hanging over his hose down to the feet; which at the first sight stirred men's hearts to rue upon them, beholding on the one side the honor they sometime had, and on the other, the calamity whereunto they were fallen.

Master Doctor Ridley, as he passed toward Bocardo, looked up where Master Cranmer did lie, hoping belike to have seen him at the glass window, and to have spoken unto him. But then Master Cranmer was busy with Friar Soto and his fellows, disputing together, so that he could not see him through that occasion. Then Master Ridley, looking back, espied Master Latimer coming after, unto whom he said, "Oh, be ye there?" "Yea," said Master Latimer, "have after as fast as I can follow." So he following a pretty way off, at length they came both to the stake, the one after the other, where first Dr. Ridley entering the place, marvellous earnestly holding up both his hands, looked towards heaven. Then shortly after espying Master Latimer, with a wondrous cheerful look he ran to him, embraced and kissed him; and, as they that stood near reported, comforted him saying, "Be of good heart, brother, for God will either assuage the fury of the flame, or else strengthen us to abide it." With that went he to the stake, kneeled down by it, kissed it, and most effectuously prayed, and behind him Master Latimer kneeled, as earnestly calling upon God as he. After they arose, the one talked with the other a little while, till they which were appointed to see the execution, removed themselves out of the sun. What they said I can learn of no man.

Then Dr. Smith, of whose recantation in King Edward's time ye heard before, began his sermon to them upon this text of St. Paul in the 13 chap. of the first epistle to the Corinthians: *Si corpus meum tradam igni, charitatem autem non habeam, nihil inde utilitatis capio,* that is, "If I yield my body to the fire to be burnt, and have not charity, I shall gain nothing thereby." Wherein he alleged that the goodness of the cause, and not the order of death, maketh the holiness of the person; which he confirmed by the examples of Judas, and of a woman in Oxford that of late hanged herself, for that they, and such like as he recited, might then be adjudged righteous, which desperately sundered their lives from their bodies, as he feared that those men that stood before him would do. But he cried still to the people to beware of them, for they were heretics, and died out of the church. And on the other side, he declared their diversities in opinions, as Lutherians, Œcolampadians, Zwinglians, of which sect they were, he said, and that was the worst: but the old church of Christ and the catholic faith believed far otherwise. At which place they lifted up both their hands and eyes to heaven, as it were calling God to witness of the truth; the which countenance they made in many other places of his sermon, whereas they thought he spake amiss. He ended with a very short exhortation to them to recant, and come home again to the church, and save their lives and souls, which else were condemned. His sermon was scant in all a quarter of an hour.

Doctor Ridley said to Master Latimer, "Will you begin to answer the sermon, or shall I?" Master Latimer said: "Begin you first, I pray you." "I will," said Master Ridley.

Then the wicked sermon being ended, Dr. Ridley and Master Latimer kneeled down upon their knees towards my Lord Williams of Tame, the vice-chancellor of Oxford, and divers other commissioners appointed for that purpose, which sat upon a form [1] thereby. Unto whom

[1] bench

Master Ridley said: "I beseech you, my lord, even for Christ's sake, that I may speak but two or three words." And whilst my lord bent his head to the mayor and vice-chancellor, to know (as it appeared) whether he might give him leave to speak, the bailiffs and Dr. Marshall, vice-chancellor, ran hastily unto him, and with their hands stopped his mouth, and said: "Master Ridley, if you will revoke your erroneous opinions, and recant the same, you shall not only have liberty so to do, but also the benefit of a subject, that is, have your life." "Not otherwise?" said Master Ridley. "No," quoth Dr. Marshall. "Therefore if you will not so do, then there is no remedy but you must suffer for your deserts." "Well," quoth Master Ridley, "so long as the breath is in my body, I will never deny my Lord Christ, and his known truth: God's will be done in me!" And with that he rose up and said with a loud voice: "Well then, I commit our cause to almighty God, which shall indifferently [1] judge all." To whose saying, Master Latimer added his old posie,[2] "Well! there is nothing hid but it shall be opened." And he said, he could answer Smith well enough, if he might be suffered.

Incontinently [3] they were commanded to make them ready, which they with all meekness obeyed. Master Ridley took his gown and his tippet, and gave it to his brother-in-law, Master Shepside, who all his time of imprisonment, although he might not be suffered to come to him, lay there at his own charges to provide him necessaries, which from time to time he sent him by the sergeant that kept him. Some other of his apparel that was little worth, he gave away; other the bailiffs took. He gave away besides divers other small things to gentlemen standing by, and divers of them pitifully weeping, as to Sir Henry Lea he gave a new groat; and to

[1] impartially   [2] motto   [3] immediately

divers of my Lord Williams gentlemen some napkins, some nutmegs, and races [1] of ginger; his dial, and such other things as he had about him, to every one that stood next him. Some plucked the points of his hose. Happy was he that might get any rag of him. Master Latimer gave nothing, but very quickly suffered his keeper to pull off his hose, and his other array, which to look unto was very simple: and being stripped into his shroud, he seemed as comely a person to them that were there present as one should lightly see; and whereas in his clothes he appeared a withered and crooked silly old man, he now stood bolt upright, as comely a father as one might lightly behold.

Then Master Ridley, standing as yet in his truss, [2] said to his brother: "It were best for me to go in my truss still." "No," quoth his brother, "it will put you to more pain: and the truss will do a poor man good." Whereunto Master Ridley said: "Be it, in the name of God;" and so unlaced himself. Then being in his shirt, he stood upon the foresaid stone, and held up his hand and said: "O heavenly Father, I give unto thee most hearty thanks, for that thou hast called me to be a professor of thee, even unto death. I beseech thee, Lord God, take mercy upon this realm of England, and deliver the same from all her enemies."

Then the smith took a chain of iron, and brought the same about both Dr. Ridley's and Master Latimer's middles; and as he was knocking in a staple, Dr. Ridley took the chain in his hand, and shaked the same, for it did gird in his belly, and looking aside to the smith, said: "Good fellow, knock it in hard, for the flesh will have his course." Then his brother did bring him gunpowder in a bag, and would have tied the same about his neck. Master Ridley asked what it was. His brother

[1] roots [2] padded jacket

said, "Gunpowder." "Then," said he, "I take it to be sent of God; therefore I will receive it as sent of him. And have you any," said he, "for my brother?" meaning Master Latimer. "Yea, sir, that I have," quoth his brother. "Then give it unto him," said he "betime;[1] lest ye come too late." So his brother went, and carried of the same gunpowder unto Master Latimer.

In the meantime Dr. Ridley spake unto my Lord Williams, and said: "My lord, I must be a suitor unto your lordship in the behalf of divers poor men, and specially in the cause of my poor sister; I have made a supplication to the Queen's Majesty in their behalves. I beseech your lordship for Christ's sake, to be a mean to her Grace for them. My brother here hath the supplication, and will resort to your lordship to certify you hereof. There is nothing in all the world that troubleth my conscience, I praise God, this only excepted. While I was in the see of London divers poor men took leases of me, and agreed with me for the same. Now I hear say the bishop that now occupieth the same room will not allow my grants unto them made, but contrary unto all law and conscience hath taken from them their livings, and will not suffer them to enjoy the same. I beseech you, my lord, be a mean for them; you shall do a good deed, and God will reward you."

Then they brought a faggot, kindled with fire, and laid the same down at Dr. Ridley's feet. To whom Master Latimer spoke in this manner: "Be of good comfort, Master Ridley, and play the man. We shall this day light such a candle, by God's grace, in England, as I trust shall never be put out."

And so the fire being given unto them, when Dr. Ridley saw the fire flaming up towards him, he cried with a wonderful loud voice: *"In manus tuas, Domine,*

[1] quickly

*commendo spiritum meum; Domine, recipe spiritum
meum.*" And after, repeated this latter part often in
English, "Lord, Lord, receive my spirit;" Master Latimer crying as vehemently on the other side, "O Father
of heaven, receive my soul!" who received the flame as
it were embracing of it. After that he had stroked his
face with his hands, and as it were bathed them a little
in the fire, he soon died (as it appeared) with very
little pain or none. And thus much concerning the end
of this old and blessed servant of God, Master Latimer,
for whose laborious travails, fruitful life, and constant
death the whole realm hath cause to give great thanks
to almighty God.

But Master Ridley, by reason of the evil making of
the fire unto him, because the wooden faggots were
laid about the gosse [1] and over-high built, the fire burned
first beneath, being kept down by the wood; which when
he felt, he desired them for Christ's sake to let the fire
come unto him. Which when his brother-in-law heard,
but not well understood, intending to rid him out of
his pain (for the which cause he gave attendance), as
one in such sorrow not well advised what he did, heaped
faggots upon him, so that he clean covered him, which
made the fire more vehement beneath, that it burned
clean all his nether parts, before it once touched the
upper; and that made him leap up and down under
the faggots, and often desire them to let the fire come
unto him, saying, "I cannot burn." Which indeed appeared well; for, after his legs were consumed by reason
of his struggling through the pain (whereof he had no
release, but only his contentation in God), he showed
that side toward us clean, shirt and all untouched with
flame. Yet in all this torment he forgot not to call
unto God still, having in his mouth, "Lord have mercy

[1] gorse, brush

upon me," intermedling this cry, "Let the fire come
unto me, I cannot burn." In which pains he labored
till one of the standers by with his bill [1] pulled off the
faggots above, and where he saw the fire flame up, he
wrested himself unto that side. And when the flame
touched the gunpowder, he was seen to stir no more,
but burned on the other side, falling down at Master
Latimer's feet. Which some said happened by reason
that the chain loosed; others said that he fell over the
chain by reason of the poise of his body, and the weakness of the nether limbs.

Some said that before he was like to fall from the
stake, he desired them to hold him to it with their bills.
However it was, surely it moved hundreds to tears,
in beholding the horrible sight; for I think there was
none that had not clean exiled all humanity and mercy,
which would not have lamented to behold the fury of
the fire so to rage upon their bodies. Signs there were
of sorrow on every side. Some took it grievously to
see their deaths, whose lives they held full dear: some
pitied their persons, that thought the souls had no need
thereof. His brother moved many men, seeing his
miserable case, seeing (I say) him compelled to such
infelicity, that he thought then to do him best service
when he hastened his end. Some cried out of the luck,
to see his endeavor (who most dearly loved him, and
sought his release) turn to his greater vexation and increase of pain. But whoso considered their preferments
in time past, the places of honor that they some time
occupied in this common wealth, the favor they were
in with their princes, and the opinion of learning they
had in the university where they studied, could not
choose but sorrow with tears to see so great dignity,
honor, and estimation, so necessary members sometime

[1] spiked staff

accounted, so many godly virtues, the study of so many years, such excellent learning, to be put into the fire and consumed in one moment. Well! dead they are, and the reward of this world they have already. What reward remaineth for them in heaven, the day of the Lord's glory, when he cometh with his saints, shall shortly, I trust, declare. (1563)

ROGER ASCHAM (1515-1568)

THE SCHOOLMASTER
(from Book I)

SIR RICHARD SACKVILLE, that worthy gentleman of worthy memory, as I said in the beginning, in the Queen's privy chamber at Windsor, after he had talked with me, for the right choice of a good wit in a child for learning, and of the true difference betwixt quick and hard wits, of alluring young children by gentleness to love learning, and of the special care that was to be had, to keep young men from licentious living, he was most earnest with me, to have me say my mind also, what I thought, concerning the fancy that many young gentlemen of England have to travel abroad, and namely to lead a long life in Italy. His request, both for his authority and good will toward us, was a sufficient commandment unto me, to satisfy his pleasure, with uttering plainly my opinion in that matter. Sir, quoth I, I take going thither, and living there, for a young gentleman, that doth not go under the keep and guard of such a man, as both, by wisdom can, and authority dare rule him, to be marvelous dangerous. And why I said so then, I will declare at large now: which I said then privately, and write now openly, not because I do condemn, either the knowledge of strange and diverse tongues, and namely the Italian tongue, which next the Greek and Latin tongue, I like and love above all other: or else because I do despise the learning that is gotten, or the experience that is gathered in strange countries: or for any private malice that I bear to Italy: which country, and in it, namely Rome, I have always specially honored: because, time was, when Italy and Rome, have been, to the great good of us that now live, the best breeders and bringers up, of the worthiest men, not only for wise speaking, but also for well doing, in all civil affairs, that ever was in the world. But now, that time is gone, and though the place remain, yet the old and present manners, do differ as far, as black and white, as virtue and vice. Virtue once made that country mistress over all the world. Vice now maketh that country slave to them, that before, were glad to serve it. All man seeth it: they themselves confess it, namely such, as be best and wisest among them. For sin, by lust and vanity, hath and doth breed up every where, common contempt of God's word, private contention in many families, open factions in every city: and so, making themselves bound to vanity and vice at home, they are content to bear the yoke of serving strangers abroad. Italy now, is not that Italy, that it was wont to be: and therefore now, not so fit a place, as some do count it, for young men to fetch either wisdom or honesty from thence. For surely, they will make others but bad scholars, that be so ill masters to themselves. Yet, if a gentleman will needs travel into Italy, he shall do well, to look on the life of the wisest traveller that ever travelled thither, set out by the wisest writer that ever spake with tongue, God's doctrine only excepted: and that is Ulysses in Homer. Ulysses, and his travel, I wish our travellers to look upon, not so much to fear them, with the great dangers, that he many times suffered, as to instruct them, with his excellent wisdom, which he always and everywhere used. Yea even those, that be learned and witty travellers, when they be disposed to praise travelling, as a great commendation, and the best scripture they have for it, they gladly recite the third verse of Homer, in his first book of Odyssey, containing a great praise of Ulysses, for the wit he gathered, and wisdom he used in travelling.

Which verse, because, in my opinion, it was not made at the first, more naturally in Greek by Homer, nor after turned more aptly into Latin by Horace, than it was a good while ago, in Cambridge, translated into English, both plainly for the sense, and roundly for the verse, by one of the best scholars, that ever St. Johns College bred, Mr. Watson, my old friend, sometime Bishop of Lincoln, therefore, for their sake, that have lust to see, how our English tongue, in avoiding barbarous riming, may as well receive, right quantity of syllables, and true order of versifying (of which matter more at large hereafter) as either Greek or Latin, if a cunning man have it in the handling, I will set forth that one verse in all three tongues, for an example to good wits, that shall delight in like learned exercise.

Homerus.

πολλῶν δ' ἀνθρώπων ἴδεν ἄστεα καὶ νόον ἔγνω

Horatius.

Qui mores hominum multorum vidit et urbes.

Mr. Watson.

All travellers do gladly report great praise of Ulysses, For that he knew many men's manners, and saw many cities.

And yet is not Ulysses commended, so much, nor so oft, in Homer, because he was πολύτροπος, that is, skillful in many men's manners and fashions, as because he was πολύμητις, that is, wise in all purposes, and wary in all places: which wisdom and wariness will not serve neither a traveller, except Pallas be always at his elbow, that is God's special grace from heaven, to keep him in God's fear, in all his doings, in all his journey. For, he shall not always in his absence out of England, light upon the gentle Alcinous, and walk in his fair gardens full of all harmless pleasures: but he shall sometimes, fall, either into the hands of some cruel Cyclops, or into the lap of some wanton and dallying Dame Calypso: and so suffer the danger of many a deadly den, not so full of perils, to destroy the body, as, full of vain pleasures, to poison the mind. Some siren shall sing him a song, sweet in tune, but sounding in the end, to his utter destruction. If Scylla drown him not, Charybdis may fortune swallow him. Some Circe shall make him, of a plain English man, a right Italian. And at length to hell, or to some hellish place, is he likely to go: from whence is hard returning, although one Ulysses, and that by Pallas' aid, and good counsel of Tiresias once escaped that horrible den of deadly darkness.

Therefore, if wise men will needs send their sons into Italy, let them do it wisely, under the keep and guard of him, who, by his wisdom and honesty, by his example and authority, may be able to keep them safe and sound, in the fear of God, in Christ's true religion, in good order and honesty of living: except they will have them run headlong into overmany jeopardies, as Ulysses had done many times, if Pallas had not always governed him: if he had not used, to stop his ears with wax: to bind himself to the mast of his ship: to feed daily, upon that sweet herb Moly with the black root and white flower, given unto him by Mercury, to avoid all enchantments of Circe. Whereby, the divine poet Homer meant covertly (as wise and godly men do judge) that love of honesty, and hatred of ill, which David more plainly doth call the fear of God: the only remedy against all enchantments of sin.

I know diverse noble personages, and many worthy gentlemen of England, whom all the siren songs of Italy, could never untwine from the mast of God's word: nor no enchantment of vanity, overturn them, from the fear of God, and love of honesty.

But I know as many, or more, and some, sometime my dear friends, for whose sake I hate going into that country the more, who, parting out of England fervent in the love of Christ's doctrine, and well furnished with the fear of God, returned out of Italy worse transformed, than ever were any in Circe's court. I know diverse, that went out of England, men of innocent life, men of excellent learning, who returned out of Italy, not only with worse manners, but also with less learning: neither so willing to live orderly, nor yet so able to speak learnedly, as they were at home, before they went abroad. And why? Plato, that wise writer, and worthy traveller himself, telleth the cause why. He went into Sicily, a country, no nigher Italy by site of place, than Italy that is now, is like Sicily that was then, in all corrupt manners and licentiousness of life. Plato found in Sicily, every city full of vanity, full of factions, even as Italy is now. And as Homer, like a learned poet, doth feign, that Circe, by pleasant enchantments, did turn men into beasts, some into swine, some into asses, some into foxes, some into wolves etc., even so, Plato, like a wise philosopher, doth plainly declare, that pleasure, by licentious vanity, that sweet and perilous poison of all youth, doth engender in all those that yield up themselves to her, four notorious properties.

1. λήθην
2. δυσμαθίαν
3. ἀφροσύνην
4. ὕβριν

The first, forgetfulness of all good things learned before: the second, dulness to receive either learning or honesty ever after: the third, a mind embracing lightly the worse opinion, and barren of discretion to make true difference betwixt good and ill, betwixt truth, and vanity, the fourth, a proud disdainfulness of other good men, in all honest matters. Homer and Plato, have both one meaning, look both to one end. For, if a man englut himself with vanity, or welter [1] in filthiness like a swine, all learning, all goodness, is soon forgotten: then, quickly shall he become a dull ass, to understand either learning or honesty: and yet shall he be as subtle as a fox, in breeding of mischief, in bringing in misorder, with a busy head, a discoursing tongue, and a factious heart, in every private affair, in all matters of state, with this pretty property, always glad to commend the worse party, and ever ready to defend the falser opinion. And why? For, where will is given from goodness to vanity, the mind is soon carried from right judgment to any fond opinion, in religion, in philosophy, or any other kind of learning. The fourth fruit of vain pleasure, by Homer and Plato's judgment, is pride in themselves, contempt of others, the very badge of all those that serve in Circe's court. The true meaning of both Homer and Plato, is plainly declared in one short sentence of the holy prophet of

[1] wallow

God, Jeremiah, crying out of the vain and vicious life of the Israelites. This people (saith he) be fools and dull-heads to all goodness, but subtle, cunning and bold, in any mischief, etc.

The true medicine against the enchantments of Circe, the vanity of licentious pleasure, the enticements of all sin, is, in Homer, the herb Moly, with the black root, and white flower, sour at the first, but sweet in the end: which, Hesiod termeth the study of virtue, hard and irksome in the beginning, but in the end, easy and pleasant. And that, which is most to be marvelled at, the divine poet Homer saith plainly that this medicine against sin and vanity is not found out by man, but given and taught by God. And for some [one's] sake, that will have delight to read that sweet and godly verse, I will recite the very words of Homer and also turn them into rude English meter.

χαλεπὸν δέ τ' ὀρύσσειν
ἀνδράσι γε θνητοῖσι, θεοὶ δέ πάντα δύναντι.

In English thus:

No mortal man, with sweat of brow, or toil of mind,
But only God, who can do all, that herb doth find.

Plato also, that divine philosopher, hath many godly medicines against the poison of vain pleasure, in many places, but specially in his Epistles to Dionysius the tyrant of Sicily: yet against those, that will needs become beasts, with serving of Circe, the prophet David, crieth most loud, *Nolite fieri sicut eques et mulus:* and by and by giveth the right medicine, the true herb Moly, *In camo et freno maxillas eorum constringe,* that is to say, let God's grace be the bit, let God's fear be the bridle, to stay them from running headlong into vice, and to turn them into the right way again. David in the second Psalm after, giveth the same medicine, but in these plainer words, *Diverte a malo et fac bonum.* But I am afraid that over-many of our travelers into Italy do not eschew the way to Circe's Court, but go and ride, and run, and fly thither; they make great haste to come to her; they make great suit to serve her; yea, I could point out some with my finger that never had gone out of England but only to serve Circe in Italy. Vanity and vice and any licence to ill living in England was counted stale and rude unto them. And so, being mules and horses before they went, returned very swine and asses home again; yet everywhere very foxes with subtle and busy heads; and where they may, very wolves with cruel malicious hearts. A marvelous monster, which, for filthiness of living, for dulness to learning himself, for wiliness in dealing with others, for malice in hurting without cause, should carry at once, in one body, the belly of a swine, the head of an ass, the brain of a fox, the womb of a wolf. If you think we judge amiss and write too sore against you, hear what the Italian saith of the Englishman, what the master reporteth of the scholar; who uttereth plainly what is taught by him, and what is learned by you, saying, '*Inglese Italianato è un diabolo incarnato,*' that is to say, you remain men in shape and fashion, but become devils in life and condition. This is not the opinion of one for some private spite, but the judgment of all in a common proverb, which riseth of that learning and those manners which you gather in Italy: a good schoolhouse of wholesome doctrine, and worthy masters of commendable scholars, where the master had rather defame himself for his teaching, than not shame his scholar for his learning. A good nature of the master, and fair conditions of the scholars. And now choose you, you Italian Englishmen, whether you will be angry with us for calling you monsters, or with the Italians for calling you devils, or else with your own selves that take so much pains and go so far to make yourselves both. If some yet do not well understand what is an Englishman Italianated, I will plainly tell him. He that by living and traveling in Italy bringeth home into England out of Italy the religion, the learning, the policy, the experience, the manners of Italy. That is to say, for religion, papistry or worse; for learning, less, commonly, than they carried out with them; for policy, a factious heart, a discoursing head, a mind to meddle in all men's matters; for experience, plenty of new mischiefs never known in England before; for manners, variety of vanities and change of filthy living. These be the enchantments of Circe, brought out of Italy to mar men's manners in England; much by example of ill life, but more by precepts of fond books of late translated out of Italian into English, sold in every shop in London, commended by honest titles, the sooner to corrupt honest manners; dedicated over-boldly to virtuous and honorable personages, the easier to beguile simple and innocent wits. It is pity that those which have authority and charge to allow and disallow books to be printed, be no more circumspect herein than they are. Ten sermons at Paul's Cross do not so much good for moving men to true doctrine, as one of those books do harm with enticing men to ill living. Yea, I say farther, those books tend not so much to corrupt honest living, as they do to subvert true religion. More papists be made by your merry books of Italy than by your earnest books of Louvain. And because our great physicians do wink at the matter, and make no count of this sore, I, though not admitted one of their fellowship, yet having been many years a prentice to God's true religion, and trust to continue a poor journeyman therein all

days of my life, for the duty I owe and love I bear
both to true doctrine and honest living, though I have
no authority to amend the sore myself, yet I will declare my good-will to discover the sore to others.

St. Paul saith that sects and ill opinions be the works
of the flesh and fruits of sin. This is spoken no more
truly for the doctrine than sensible for the reason. And
why? For ill doings breed ill thinkings. And of corrupted manners spring perverted judgments. And how?
There be in man two special things: man's will, man's
mind. Where will inclineth to goodness, the mind is
bent to truth. Where will is carried from goodness to
vanity, the mind is soon drawn from truth to false
opinion. And so the readiest way to entangle the mind
with false doctrine is first to entice the will to wanton
living. Therefore, when the busy and open papists
abroad could not by their contentious books turn men in
England fast enough from truth and right judgment in
doctrine, then the subtle and secret papists at home
procured bawdy books to be translated out of the Italian
tongue, whereby over-many young wills and wits, allured
to wantonness, do now boldly contemn all severe books
that sound to honesty and godliness. In our forefather's
time, when papistry, as a standing pool, covered and
overflowed all England, few books were read in our
tongue, saving certain books [of] chivalry, as they
said, for pastime and pleasure, which, as some say, were
made in monasteries by idle monks or wanton canons:
as one, for example, *Morte Arthur,* the whole pleasure
of which book standeth in two special points—in open
manslaughter and bold bawdry. In which book those
be counted the noblest knights that do kill most men
without any quarrel, and commit foulest adulteries by
subtlest shifts: as Sir Lancelot with the wife of King
Arthur, his master; Sir Tristram with the wife of King

Mark, his uncle; Sir Lamerock with the wife of King Lot, that was his own aunt. This is good stuff for wise men to laugh at, or honest men to take pleasure at! Yet I know when God's Bible was banished the court, and *Morte Arthur* received into the prince's chamber. What toys the daily reading of such a book may work in the will of a young gentleman or a young maid that liveth wealthily and idly, wise men can judge and honest men do pity. And yet ten *Morte Arthurs* do not the tenth part so much harm as one of these books made in Italy and translated in England. They open not fond and common ways to vice, but such subtle, cunning, new, and diverse shifts to carry young wills to vanity and young wits to mischief, to teach old bawds new school-points, as the simple head of an Englishman is not able to invent, nor never was heard of in England before; yea, when papistry overflowed all. Suffer these books to be read, and they shall soon displace all books of godly learning. For they, carrying the will to vanity and marring good manners, shall easily corrupt the mind with ill opinions and false judgment in doctrine: first, to think nothing of God himself—one special point that is to be learned in Italy and Italian books. And that which is most to be lamented, and therefore more needful to be looked to, there be more of these ungracious books set out in print within these few months than have been seen in England many score years before. And because our Englishmen made Italians cannot hurt but certain persons and in certain places, therefore these Italian books are made English to bring mischief enough openly and boldly to all states, great and mean, young and old, everywhere.

And thus you see how will enticed to wantonness doth easily allure the mind to false opinions; and how corrupt manners in living, breed false judgment in doctrine; how sin and fleshliness bring forth sects and heresies. And, therefore, suffer not vain books to breed vanity in men's wills, if you would have God's truth take root in men's minds.

That Italian that first invented the Italian proverb against our Englishmen Italianated, meant no more their vanity in living than their lewd opinion in religion. For in calling them devils, he carrieth them clean from God; and yet he carrieth them no farther than they willingly go themselves—that is, where they may freely say their minds—to the open contempt of God and all godliness, both in living and doctrine.

And how? I will express how, not by a fable of Homer, nor by the philosophy of Plato, but by a plain truth of God's Word, sensibly uttered by David thus: 'These men, *abominabiles facti in studiis suis,* think verily and sing gladly the verse before, *Dixit insipiens in corde suo, non est Deus'*—that is to say, they giving themselves up to vanity, shaking off the motions of grace, driving from them the fear of God, and running headlong into all sin, first lustily contemn God, then scornfully mock his Word, and also spitefully hate and hurt all well-willers thereof. Then they have in more reverence the *Triumphs* of Petrarch than the *Genesis* of Moses. They make more account of *Tully's Offices* than St. Paul's *Epistles;* of a tale in Boccaccio than a story of the Bible. Then they count as fables the holy mysteries of Christian religion. They make Christ and his Gospel only serve civil policy. Then neither religion cometh amiss to them. In time they be promoters of both openly: in place, again, mockers of both privily, as I wrote once in a rude rime:—

Now new, now old, now both, now neither,
To serve the world's course, they care not with whether.

For where they dare, in company where they like, they boldly laugh to scorn both protestant and papist. They care for no Scripture; they make no count of general councils; they contemn the consent of the church; they pass for no doctors; they mock the Pope; they rail on Luther; they allow neither side; they like none, but only themselves. The mark they shoot at, the end they look for, the heaven they desire, is only their own present pleasure and private profit; whereby they plainly declare of whose school of what religion they be—that is, epicures in living and ἄθεοι in doctrine. This last word is no more unknown now to plain Englishmen than the person was unknown some time in England, until some Englishman took pains to fetch that devilish opinion out of Italy. These men, thus Italianated abroad, cannot abide our godly Italian church at home; they be not of that parish; they be not of that fellowship; they like not that preacher; they hear not his sermons, except sometimes for company they come thither to hear the Italian tongue naturally spoken, not to hear God's doctrine truly preached.

And yet these men in matters of divinity openly pretend a great knowledge, and have privately to themselves a very compendious understanding of all, which, nevertheless, they will utter when and where they list. And that is this: all the mysteries of Moses, the whole law and ceremonies, the Psalms and prophets, Christ and his Gospel, God and the devil, heaven and hell, faith, conscience, sin, death, and all they shortly wrap up they quickly expound with this one half verse of Horace:

Credat Judæus Apella.

Yet though in Italy they may freely be of no religion, as they are in England in very deed too, nevertheless, returning home into England, they must countenance the profession of the one or the other, however inwardly they laugh to scorn both. And though for their private matters they can follow, fawn, and flatter noble personages contrary to them in all respects, yet commonly they ally themselves with the worst papists, to whom they be wedded, and do well agree together in three proper opinions: in open contempt of God's Word; in a secret security of sin; and in a bloody desire to have all taken away by sword and burning that be not of their faction. They that do read with indifferent judgment Pygius and Machiavelli, two indifferent patriarchs of these two religions, do know full well what I say true.

Ye see what manners and doctrine our Englishmen fetch out of Italy. For, finding no other there, they can bring no other hither. And, therefore, many godly and excellent learned Englishmen, not many years ago, did make a better choice, when open cruelty drove them out of this country, to place themselves there where Christ's doctrine, the fear of God, punishment of sin, and discipline of honesty were had in special regard.

I was once in Italy myself; but I thank God my abode there was but nine days. And yet I saw in that little time, in one city, more liberty to sin than ever I heard tell of in our noble city of London in nine years. I saw it was there as free to sin not only without all punishment, but also without any man's marking, as it is free in the city of London to choose without all blame whether a man lust to wear shoe or pantofle.[1] And good cause why; for, being unlike in truth of religion, they must needs be unlike in honesty of living. For blessed be Christ, in our city of London commonly the command-

¹ slipper

ments of God be more diligently taught, and the service of God more reverently used, and that daily in many private men's houses, than they be in Italy once a week in their common churches; where making ceremonies to delight the eye, and vain sounds to please the ear, do quite thrust out of the churches all service of God in spirit and truth. Yea, the Lord Mayor of London, being but a civil officer, is commonly, for his time, more diligent in punishing sin, the bent enemy against God and good order, than all the bloody inquisitors in Italy be in seven years. For their care and charge is not to punish sin, not to amend manners, not to purge doctrine, but only to watch and oversee that Christ's true religion set no sure footing where the Pope hath any jurisdiction. I learned, when I was at Venice, that there it is counted good policy, when there be four or five brethren of one family, one only to marry, and all the rest to welter with as little shame in open lechery as swine do here in the common mire. Yea, there be as fair houses of religion, as great provision, as diligent officers to keep up this misorder, as Bridewell is and all the masters there to keep down misorder. And, therefore, if the Pope himself do not only grant pardons to further these wicked purposes abroad in Italy, but also (although this present Pope in the beginning made some show of misliking thereof) assign both meed and merit to the maintenance of stews and brothel-houses at home in Rome, then let wise men think Italy a safe place for wholesome doctrine and godly manners, and a fit school for young gentlemen of England to be brought up in!

Our Italians bring home with them other faults from Italy, though not so great as this of religion, yet a great deal greater than many good men can well bear. For commonly they come home common contemners of marriage and ready persuaders of all others to the same; not because they love virginity, nor yet because they hate pretty young virgins, but, being free in Italy to go whithersoever lust will carry them, they do not like that law and honesty should be such a bar to their like liberty at home in England. And yet they be the greatest makers of love, the daily dalliers, with such pleasant words, with such smiling and secret countenances, with such signs, tokens, wagers, purposed to be lost before they were purposed to be made, with bargains of wearing colors, flowers, and herbs, to breed occasion of ofter meeting of him and her, and bolder talking of this and that, etc. And although I have seen some, innocent of all ill and staid in all honesty, that have used these things without all harm, without all suspicion of harm, yet these knacks were brought first into England by them that learned them before in Italy in Circe's court; and how courtly courtesies soever they be counted now, yet, if the meaning and manners of some that do use them were somewhat amended, it were no great hurt neither to themselves nor to others.

Another property of this our English Italians is to be marvelous singular in all their matters; singular in knowledge; ignorant of nothing; so singular in wisdom (in their own opinion) as scarce they count the best counselor the prince hath comparable with them; common discoursers of all matters; busy searchers of most secret affairs; open flatterers of great men; privy mislikers of good men; fair speakers, with smiling countenances and much courtesy openly to all men; ready backbiters, sore nippers, and spiteful reporters privily of good men. And being brought up in Italy in some free city, as all cities be there, where a man may freely discourse against what he will, against whom he lust, against any prince, against any government, yea, against God himself and his whole religion; where he must be either Guelph or Ghibelin, either French or Spanish, and always compelled to be of some party, of some faction, he shall never be compelled to be of any religion; and if he meddle not over-much with Christ's true religion, he shall have free liberty to embrace all religions, and become, if he lust, at once, without any let or punishment, Jewish, Turkish, papish, and devilish.

A young gentleman thus bred up in this goodly school, to learn the next and ready way to sin, to have a busy head, a factious heart, a talkative tongue, fed with discoursing of factions, led to contemn God and his religion, shall come home into England but very ill taught, either to be an honest man himself, a quiet subject to his prince, or willing to serve God under the obedience of true doctrine, or within the order of honest living.

I know none will be offended with this my general writing, but only such as find themselves guilty privately therein: who shall have good leave to be offended with me, until they begin to amend themselves. I touch not them that be good; and I say too little of them that be not; and so, though not enough for their deserving, yet sufficiently for this time, and more else when if occasion so require.

And thus far have I wandered from my first purpose of teaching a child, yet not altogether out of the way, because this whole talk hath tended to the only advancement of truth in religion and honesty of living; and hath been wholly within the compass of learning and good manners, the special points belonging in the right bringing up of youth.

But to my matter, as I began plainly and simply with my young scholar, so will I not leave him, God willing, until I have brought him a perfect scholar out of the school, and placed him in the university, to become a fit student for logic and rhetoric: and so after to physic, law, or divinity, as aptness of nature, advice of friends, and God's disposition shall lead him.

(1570)

RALPH HOLINSHED (?-1580?)

CHRONICLES OF ENGLAND, SCOTLAND, AND IRELAND

MACBETH AND THE WEIRD SISTERS

SHORTLY after happened a strange and uncouth wonder, which afterward was the cause of much trouble in the realm of Scotland, as ye shall after hear. It fortuned as Macbeth and Banquo journeyed towards Fores, where the king then lay, they went sporting by the way together without other company, save only themselves, passing through the woods and fields, when suddenly in the midst of a land, there met them three women in strange and wild apparel, resembling creatures of elder [1] world, whom when they attentively beheld, wondering much at the sight, the first of them spake and said: 'All hail Macbeth, thane of Glammis' (for he had lately entered into that dignity and office by the death of his father Sinell). The second of them said: 'Hail Macbeth, thane of Cawdor.' But the third said: 'All hail Macbeth, that hereafter shalt be king of Scotland.'

Then Banquo; 'What manner of women (saith he)
[1] spirit

are you, that seem so little favorable unto me, whereas to my fellow here, besides high offices, ye assign also the kingdom, appointing forth nothing for me at all?' 'Yes (saith the first of them) we promise greater benefits unto thee, than unto him, for he shall reign indeed, but with an unlucky end: neither shall he leave any issue behind him to succeed in his place, where contrarily thou indeed shalt not reign at all, but of thee those shall be born which shall govern the Scottish kingdom by long order of continual descent.' Herewith the foresaid women vanished immediately out of their sight. This was reputed at the first but some vain fantastical illusion by Macbeth and Banquo, insomuch that Banquo would call Macbeth in jest, king of Scotland; and Macbeth again would call him in sport likewise, the father of many kings. But afterwards the common opinion was, that these women were either the weird sisters, that is (as ye would say) the goddesses of destiny, or else some nymphs or fairies, indued with knowledge of prophecy by their necromantical science, because everything came to pass as they had spoken. For shortly after, the thane of Cawdor being condemned at Fores of treason against the king committed; his lands, livings, and offices were given of the king's liberality to Macbeth.

The same night after, at supper, Banquo jested with him and said; 'Now Macbeth, thou hast obtained those things which the two former sisters prophesied, there remaineth only for thee to purchase that which the third said should come to pass.' Whereupon Macbeth revolving the thing in his mind, began even then to devise how he might attain to the kingdom: but yet he thought with himself that he must tarry a time, which should advance him thereto (by the divine providence) as it had come to pass in his former preferment. But shortly after it chanced that king Duncan, having two sons by his wife, which was the daughter of Siward earl of Northumberland, he made the elder of them called Malcolm Prince of Cumberland, as it were thereby to appoint him his successor in the kingdom, immediately after his decease. Macbeth sore troubled herewith, for that he saw by this means his hope sore hindered (where, by the old laws of the realm, the ordinance was, that if he that should succeed were not of able age to take the charge upon himself, he that was next of blood unto him should be admitted) he began to take counsel how he might usurp the kingdom by force, having a just quarrel so to do (as he took the matter) for that Duncan did what in him lay to defraud him of all manner of title and claim, which he might in time to come, pretend unto the crown.

The words of the three weird sisters also (of whom before ye have heard) greatly encouraged him hereunto, but specially his wife lay sore upon him to attempt the thing, as she that was very ambitious, burning in unquenchable desire to bear the name of a queen. At length therefore, communicating his purposed intent with his trusty friends, amongst whom Banquo was the chiefest, upon confidence of their promised aid, he slew the king at Envernes, or (as some say) at Botgoswane, in the sixth year of his reign. Then having a company about him of such as he had made privy to his enterprise, he caused himself to be proclaimed king, and forthwith went unto Scone, where (by common consent) he received the investure of the kingdom according to the accustomed manner. The body of Duncan was first conveyed unto Elgin, and there buried in kingly wise; but afterwards it was removed and conveyed unto Colmkill, and there laid in a sepulture amongst his predecessors, in the year after the birth of our Saviour, 1046.

OF KING RICHARD, THE FIRST, AND HIS JOURNEY
TO THE HOLY LAND

RICHARD THE FIRST of that name, and second son of Henry the Second, began his reign over England the sixth day of July, in the year of our Lord 1189. He received the crown with all due and accustomed solemnity, at the hands of Baldwin, the archbishop of Canterbury, the third day of September.

Upon this day of King Richard's coronation, the Jews that dwelt in London and in other parts of the realm, being there assembled, had but sorry hap, as it chanced. For they meaning to honor the same coronation with their presence, and to present to the king some honorable gift, whereby they might declare themselves glad for his advancement, and procure his friendship towards them, for the confirming of their privileges and liberties; he of a zealous mind to Christ's religion, abhorring their nation (and doubting some sorcery by them to be practised) commanded that they should not come within the church when he should receive the crown, nor within the palace whilst he was at dinner.

But at dinner-time, among other that pressed in at the palace gate, divers of the Jews were about to thrust in, till one of them was stricken by a Christian, who alleging [1] the king's commandment, kept them back from coming within the palace. Which some of the unruly people, perceiving, and supposing it had been done by the king's commandment, took lightly occasion thereof, and falling upon the Jews with staves, bats,

[1] citing

and stones, beat them and chased them home to their houses and lodgings. Then did they set fire on the houses, and the Jews within were either smoldered and burned to death within, or else at their coming forth most cruelly received upon the points of spears, bills, and swords of their adversaries that watched for them very diligently. This great riot well deserved sore and grievous punishment, but yet it passed over without correction, because of the hatred generally conceived against the obstinate frowardness of the Jews. Finally, after the tumult was ceased, the king commanded that no man should hurt or harm any of the Jews, and so they were restored to peace after they had sustained infinite damage.

No great while after this his coronation, the king sought to prepare himself to journey to the holy land, and to this end he had great need of money. Therefore he made such sale of things appertaining to him, as well in right of the crown, as otherwise, that it seemed to divers that he made his reckoning never to return again, in so much that some of his councillors told him plainly, that he did not well in making things away so freely; unto whom he answered "that in time of need it was no evil policy for a man to help himself with his own," and further, "that if London at that time of need would be bought, he would surely sell it, if he might meet with a convenient merchant that were able to give him money enough for it."

Then all things being ready, King Richard set forth, and, after great hindrance by tempests, and at the hands of the men of Cyprus, who warred against him and were overcome, he came to the city of Acres, which then was besieged by the Christian army. Such was the valiancy of King Richard shown in manful constraining [1] of the

[1] besieging

city, that his praise was greatly bruited both amongst the Christians and also the Saracens.

At last, on the twelfth date of July, in the year of grace 1192, the city of Acres was surrendered into the Christian men's hands. These things being concluded, the French King Philip, upon envy and malice conceived against King Richard (although he pretended sickness for excuse) departed homewards. Now touching this departure, divers occasions are remembered by writers of the emulation [1] and secret spite which he should bear towards King Richard. But, howsoever, it came to pass, partly through envy (as hath been thought) conceived at the great deeds of King Richard, whose mighty power and valiantness he could not well abide, and partly for other respects him moving, he took the sea with three galleys of the Genoese, and returned into Italy, and so home into France, having promised first unto King Richard in the holy land, and after to pope Celestine at Rome, that he would not attempt any hurtful enterprise against the English dominions, till King Richard should be returned out of the holy land. But this promise was not kept, for he sought to procure Earl John, King Richard's brother, to rebel against him, though he then sought it in vain.

Yet were matters nowise peaceful within the realm of England, and because of this, and likewise because the froward humours [2] of the French so greatly hindered him in waring against the Saracens, King Richard determined fully to depart homewards, and at last there was a peace concluded with Saladin. But on his journey homewards the King had but sorry hap, for he made shipwreck on the coast of Istria, and then fell into captivity.

[1] rivalry   [2] hostile feelings

OF GOOD QUEEN ELIZABETH, AND HOW SHE CAME INTO HER KINGDOM

AFTER all the stormy, tempestuous, and blustering windy weather of Queen Mary was overblown, the darksome clouds of discomfort dispersed, the palpable fogs and mists of most intolerable misery consumed, and the dashing showers of persecution overpast, it pleased God to send England a calm and quiet season, a clear and lovely sunshine, and a world of blessings by good Queen Elizabeth, into whose gracious reign we are now to make an happy entrance as followeth.

On her entering the city of London, she was received of the people with prayers, wishes, welcomings, cries, and tender words, all which argued a wonderful earnest love of most obedient subjects towards their sovereign. And on the other side, her grace, by holding up her hands, and merry countenance to such as stood far off, and most tender and gentle language to those that stood nigh unto her grace, did declare herself no less thankfully to receive her people's good will, than they lovingly offered it to her. And it was not only to those her subjects who were of noble birth that she showed herself thus very gracious, but also to the poorest sort. How many nosegays did her grace receive at poor women's hands! How oftentimes stayed she her chariot, when she saw any simple body offer to speak to her grace! A branch of rosemary given her grace with a supplication about Fleetbridge, was seen in her chariot till her grace came to Westminster, not without the marvellous wondering of such as knew the presenter, and noted the queen's most gracious receiving and keeping the same. Therefore may the poor and needy look for great hope at her grace's hand, who hath shown so loving a carefulness for them.

Moreover, because princes be set in their seat by God's appointing, and they must therefore first and chiefly tender the glory of Him from whom their glory issueth; it is to be noted in her grace that for so much as God hath so wonderfully placed her in the seat of government of this realm, she in all her doings doth show herself most mindful of His goodness and mercy shewed unto her. And one notable sign thereof her grace gave at the very time of her passage through London, for in the Tower, before she entered her chariot, she lifted up her eyes to Heaven and saith as followeth:

"O Lord Almighty and everlasting God, I give Thee most hearty thanks that Thou hast been so merciful unto me as to spare me to behold this joyful day. And I acknowledge that Thou hast dealt as wonderfully and as mercifully with me as Thou didst with Thy true and faithful servant Daniel Thy prophet, whom Thou deliveredst out of the den from the cruelty of the greedy and raging lions; even so was I overwhelmed, and only by Thee delivered. To Thee, therefore, only be thanks, honor, and praise, for ever. Amen."

On Sunday, the five and twentieth day of January, her majesty was with great solemnity crowned at Westminster, in the Abbey church there, by doctor Oglethorpe bishop of Carlisle. She dined in Westminster hall, which was richly hung, and everything ordered in such royal manner, as to such a regal and most solemn feast appertained. In the meantime, whilst her grace sat at dinner, Sir Edward Dimmock, knight, her champion by office, came riding into the hall in fair complete armour, mounted upon a beautiful courser, richly trapped in cloth of gold, and in the midst of the hall cast down his gauntlet, with offer to fight in her quarrel with any man that should deny her to be the righteous and lawful queen of this realm. The queen, taking a cup of gold full of wine, drank to him thereof, and sent it to him for his fee. Finally, this feast being celebrated with all due and fitting royal ceremonies, took end with great joy and contentation to all the beholders.

Yet, though there was thus an end of the ceremonies befitting the queen's coronation, her majesty was everywhere received with brave shows, and with pageants, all for the love and respect that her subjects bare her. Thus on Whitsunday, in the first year of her reign, the citizens of London set forth a muster before the queen's majesty at Greenwich in the park there, of the number of 1,400 men, whereof 800 were pikes, armed in fine corselets,[1] 400 shot in shirts of mail, and 200 halberdiers armed in Almaine rivets; these were furnished forth by the crafts and companies of the city. To every hundred two wifflers [2] were assigned, richly appointed and apparelled for the purpose. There were also twelve wardens of the best companies mounted on horseback in coats of black velvet, to conduct them, with drums and fifes, and six ensigns all in jerkins [3] of white satin of Bridges, cut and lined with black sarsenet, and caps, hosen, and scarfs according. The sergeant-majors, Captain Constable, and Captain Sanders, brought them in order before the queen's presence, placing them in battle array, even as they should have fought; so the show was very fair, the emperor's and the French king's ambassadors being present.

Verily the queen hath ever shown herself forward and most willing that her faithful subjects should be ready and skilful in war as in peace. Thus in the fourteenth year of her reign, by order of her council, the citizens of London, assembling in their several halls,

[1] body-armor   [2] heralds, buglers   [3] jackets

the masters chose out the most likely and active persons
of their companies to be pikemen and shot. To these
were appointed divers valiant captains, who to train
them up in warlike feats, mustered them thrice every
week, sometimes in the artillery yard, teaching the gun-
ners to handle their pieces, sometimes at the Miles End,
and in Saint George's field, teaching them to skirmish.

In the arts of peace likewise, she is greatly pleased
with them who are good craftsmen, and shows them favor. In government we have peace and security, and
do not greatly fear those who may stir up wicked rebellion within our land, or may come against us from
beyond the sea.

In brief, they of Norwich did say well, when the
queen's majesty came thither, and in a pageant in her
honor, one spake these words:

"Dost thou not see the joy of all this flock?
  Vouchsafe to view their passing gladsome cheer,
Be still (good queen) their refuge and their rock,
  As they are thine to serve in love and fear;
So fraud, nor force, nor foreign foe may stand
  Against the strength of thy most puissant hand."
                                                    (1577)

JOHN LYLY (1554?-1606)

EUPHUES,
THE ANATOMY OF WIT

VERY pleasant for all Gentlemen to read, and most
necessary to remember: wherein are contained the delights that Wit followeth in his youth by the pleasant-

ness of Love, and the happiness he reapeth in age by
the perfectness of Wisdom.

A COOLING CARD FOR PHILAUTUS AND ALL FOND LOVERS.

Musing with myself, being idle, how I might be well
employed, friend Philautus, I could find nothing either
more fit to continue our friendship, or of greater force
to dissolve our folly, than to write a remedy for that
which many judge past cure; for love, Philautus, with
the which I have been so tormented that I have lost my
time, thou so troubled that thou hast forgot reason, both
so mangled with repulse, inveigled by deceit, and almost
murdered by disdain, that I can neither remember our
miseries without grief, nor redress our mishaps without
groans. How wantonly, yea, and how willingly have
we abused our golden time and misspent our gotten
treasure! How curious were we to please our lady, how
careless to displease our Lord! How devout in serving
our goddess, how desperate in forgetting our God! Ah,
my Philautus, if the wasting of our money might not
dehort us, yet the wounding of our minds should deter
us; if reason might nothing persuade us to wisdom, yet
shame should provoke us to wit. If Lucilla read this
trifle, she will straight proclaim Euphues for a traitor,
and, seeing me turn my tippet, will either shut me out
for a wrangler, or cast me off for a wiredrawer,[1] either
convince me of malice in bewraying their sleights, or condemn me of mischief in arming young men against fleeting minions. And what then? Though Curio be as hot
as a toast, yet Euphues is as cold as a clock; though
he be a cock of the game, yet Euphues is content to be
craven and cry creek;[2] though Curio be old huddle, and
twang *"ipse, he,"* yet Euphues had rather shrink in the

[1] finicky person　　[2] admit defeat

wetting than waste in the wearing. I know Curio to be steel to the back, standard-bearer in Venus's camp, sworn to the crew, true to the crown, knight marshal to Cupid, and heir apparent to his kingdom. But by that time that he hath eaten but one bushel of salt with Lucilla, he shall taste ten quarters [1] of sorrow in his love; then shall he find for every pint of honey a gallon of gall, for every dram of pleasure an ounce of pain, for every inch of mirth an ell of moan. And yet, Philautus, if there be any man in despair to obtain his purpose, or so obstinate in his opinion that, having lost his freedom by folly, would also lose his life for love, let him repair hither, and he shall reap such profit as will either quench his flames or assuage his fury; either cause him to renounce his lady as most pernicious, or redeem his liberty as most precious. Come, therefore, to me, all ye lovers that have been deceived by fancy, the glass of pestilence, or deluded by women, the gate to perdition; be as earnest to seek a medicine as you were eager to run into a mischief; the earth bringeth forth as well endive to delight the people as hemlock to endanger the patient; as well the rose to distill as the nettle to sting; as well the bee to give honey as the spider to yield poison.

If my lewd life, gentlemen, have given you offence, let my good counsel make amends; if by my folly any be allured to lust, let them by my repentance be drawn to continency. Achilles's spear could as well heal as hurt; the Scorpion, though he sting, yet he stints the pain; though the herb Nerius poison the sheep, yet is it a remedy to man against poison; though I have infected some by example, yet I hope I shall comfort many by repentance. Whatsoever I speak to men, the same also I speak to women; I mean not to run with the hare and

[1] quarter-ton measures

hold with the hound, to carry fire in the one hand and water in the other; neither to flatter men as altogether faultless, neither to fall out with women as altogether guilty; for, as I am not minded to pick a thank with the one, so am I not determined to pick a quarrel with the other; if women be not perverse, they shall reap profit by remedy of pleasure. If Phyllis were now to take counsel, she would not be so foolish to hang herself, neither Dido so fond to die for Æneas, neither Pasiphaë so monstrous to love a bull, nor Phedra so unnatural to be enamored of her son.

This is, therefore, to admonish all young imps and novices in love not to blow the coals of fancy with desire, but to quench them with disdain. When love tickleth thee, decline it, lest it stifle thee; rather fast than surfeit; rather starve than strive to exceed. Though the beginning of love bring delight, the end bringeth destruction. For, as the first draught of wine doth comfort the stomach, the second inflame the liver, the third fume into the head, so the first sip of love is pleasant, the second perilous, the third pestilent. If thou perceive thyself to be enticed with their wanton glances or allured with their wicked guiles, either enchanted with their beauty or enamored with their bravery, enter with thyself into this meditation: What shall I gain if I obtain my purpose? nay, rather, what shall I lose in winning my pleasure? If my lady yield to be my lover, is it not likely she will be another's leman? [1] and if she be a modest matron, my labor is lost. This, therefore, remaineth; that either I must pine in cares or perish with curses.

If she be chaste, then is she coy; if light, then is she impudent; if a grave matron, who can woo her? if a lewd minion, who would wed her? if one of the Vestal

[1] mistress

Virgins, they have vowed virginity; if one of Venus's court, they have vowed dishonesty. If I love one that is fair, it will kindle jealousy; if one that is foul, it will convert me into frenzy. If fertile to bear children, my care is increased; if barren, my curse is augmented; if honest, I shall fear her death; if immodest, I shall be weary of her life.

To what end, then, shall I live in love, seeing always it is a life more to be feared than death? for all my time wasted in sighs and worn in sobs, for all my treasure spent on jewels and spilled in jollity, what recompense shall I reap besides repentance? What other reward shall I have than reproach? What other solace than endless shame? But haply thou wilt say, "If I refuse their courtesy I shall be accounted a mecock,[1] a milksop, taunted and retaunted with check and checkmate, flouted and reflouted with intolerable glee."

Alas, fond fool, art thou so pinned to their sleeves that thou regardest more their babble than thine own bliss, more their frumps than thine own welfare? Wilt thou resemble the kind spaniel, which, the more he is beaten the fonder he is, or the foolish eyas,[2] which will never away? Dost thou not know that women deem none valiant unless he be too venturous?—that they account one a dastard if he be not desperate, a pinch-penny if he be not prodigal; if silent, a sot, if full of words, a fool? Perversely do they always think of their lovers and talk of them scornfully, judging all to be clowns which be no courtiers, and all to be pinglers[3] that be not coursers.

Seeing therefore the very blossom of love is sour, the bud cannot be sweet. In time prevent danger, lest untimely thou run into a thousand perils. Search the wound while it is green; too late cometh the salve when the

---

[1] timid weakling   [2] unfledged bird   [3] dabblers

sore festereth, and the medicine bringeth double care when the malady is past cure.

Beware of delays. What less than the grain of mustard seed?—in time, almost what thing is greater than the stalk thereof? The slender twig groweth to a stately tree, and that which with the hand might easily have been pulled up will hardly with the ax be hewn down. The least spark, if it be not quenched, will burst into a flame; the least moth in time eateth the thickest cloth; and I have read that, in a short space, there was a town in Spain undermined with conies, in Thessaly with moles, with frogs in France, in Africa with flies. If these silly worms in tract of time overthrow so stately towns, how much more will love, which creepeth secretly into the mind (as the rust doth into the iron and is not perceived), consume the body, yea, and confound the soul. Defer not from hour to day, from day to month, from month to year, and always remain in misery.

He that to-day is not willing will to-morrow be more willful. But, alas, it is no less common than lamentable to behold the tottering estate of lovers, who think by delays to prevent dangers, with oil to quench fire, with smoke to clear the eyesight. They flatter themselves with a feinting farewell, deferring ever until to-morrow, whenas their morrow doth always increase their sorrow. Let neither their amiable countenances, neither their painted protestations, neither their deceitful promises, allure thee to delays. Think this with thyself, that the sweet songs of Calypso were subtle snares to entice Ulysses; that the crab then catcheth the oyster when the sun shineth; that hyena, when she speaketh like a man, deviseth most mischief; that women when they be most pleasant pretend most treachery.

Follow Alexander, which, hearing the commendation and singular comeliness of the wife of Darius, so courageously withstood the assaults of fancy that he would not so much as take a view of her beauty. Imitate Cyrus, a king endued with such continency that he loathed to look on the heavenly hue of Panthea; and, when Araspus told him that she excelled all mortal wights in amiable show, "By so much the more," said Cyrus, "I ought to abstain from her sight; for if I follow thy counsel in going to her, it may be I shall desire to continue with her, and by my light affection neglect my serious affairs." Learn of Romulus to refrain from wine, be it never so delicate; of Agesilaus to despise costly apparel, be it never so curious; of Diogenes to detest women, be they never so comely. He that toucheth pitch shall be defiled; the sore eye infecteth the sound; the society with women breedeth security in the soul, and maketh all the senses senseless. Moreover, take this counsel as an article of thy creed, which I mean to follow as the chief argument of my faith, that idleness is the only nurse and nourisher of sensual appetite, the sole maintenance of youthful affection, the first shaft that Cupid shooteth into the hot liver of a heedless lover. I would to God I were not able to find this for a truth by mine own trial, and I would the example of others' idleness had caused me rather to avoid that fault than experience of mine own folly. How dissolute have I been in striving against good counsel, how resolute in standing in mine own conceit, how forward to wickedness, how wanton with too much cockering,[1] how wayward in hearing correction! Neither was I much unlike these abbey lubbers in my life (though far unlike them in belief) which labored till they were cold, ate till they sweat, and lay in bed till their bones ached. Hereof cometh it, gentlemen,

[1] coddling

that love creepeth into the mind by privy craft, and keepeth his hold by main courage.

The man being idle, the mind is apt to all uncleanness; the mind being void of exercise, the man is void of honesty. Doth not the rust fret the hardest iron if it be not used? Doth not the moth eat the finest garment if it be not worn? Doth not moss grow on the smoothest stone if it be not stirred? Doth not impiety infect the wisest wit if it be given to idleness? Is not the standing water sooner frozen than the running stream? Is not he that sitteth more subject to sleep than he that walketh? Doth not common experience make this common unto us, that the fattest ground bringeth forth nothing but weeds if it be not well tilled, that the sharpest wit inclineth only to wickedness if it be not exercised? Is it not true which Seneca reporteth, that as too much bending breaketh the bow, so too much remission spoileth the mind? Besides this, immoderate sleep, immodest play, unsatiable swilling of wine doth so weaken the senses and bewitch the soul that, before we feel the motion of love, we are resolved into lust. Eschew idleness, my Philautus, so shalt thou easily unbend the bow and quench the brands of Cupid. Love gives place to labor; labor, and thou shalt never love. Cupid is a crafty child, following those at an inch that study pleasure, and flying those swiftly that take pains. Bend thy mind to the law, whereby thou mayest have understanding of old and ancient customs; defend thy clients; enrich thy coffers; and carry credit in thy country. If law seem loathsome unto thee, search the secrets of physic, whereby thou mayest know the hidden natures of herbs; whereby thou mayest gather profit to thy purse and pleasure to thy mind. What can be more exquisite in human affairs than for every fever, be it never so hot, for every palsy, be it never so cold, for every infection, be it never so strange, to give a remedy? The old verse standeth as yet in his old virtue: That Galen giveth goods, Justinian honors. If thou be so nice that thou canst no way brook the practice of physic, or so unwise that thou wilt not beat thy brains about the institutes of the law, confer all thy study, all thy time, all thy treasure to the attaining of the sacred and sincere knowledge of divinity; by this mayest thou bridle thine incontinency, rein thine affections, restrain thy lust. Here shalt thou behold, as it were in a glass, that all the glory of man is as the grass; all things under heaven are but vain; that our life is but a shadow, a warfare, a pilgrimage, a vapor, a bubble, a blast; of such shortness that David saith it is but a span long; of such sharpness that Job noteth it replenished with all miseries; of such uncertainty that we are no sooner born but we are subject to death; the one foot no sooner on the ground but the other ready to slip into the grave. Here shalt thou find ease for thy burden of sin, comfort for the conscience pined with vanity, mercy for thine offences by the martyrdom of thy sweet Savior. By this thou shalt be able to instruct those that be weak, to confute those that be obstinate, to confound those that be erroneous, to confirm the faithful, to comfort the desperate, to cut off the presumptuous, to save thine own soul by thy sure faith, and edify the hearts of many by thy sound doctrine. If this seems too strait a diet for thy straining disease, or too holy a profession for so hollow a person, then employ thyself to martial feats, to jousts, to tourneys, yea, to all torments, rather than to loiter in love and spend thy life in the laps of ladies; what more monstrous can there be than to see a young man abuse those gifts to his own shame which God hath given him for his own preferment? What greater infamy than to confer the sharp

wit to the making of lewd sonnets, to the idolatrous
worshiping of their ladies, to the vain delights of fancy,
to all kind of vice, as it were against kind and course
of nature? Is it not folly to show wit to women, which
are neither able nor willing to receive fruit thereof?
Dost thou not know that the tree Silvacenda beareth no
fruit in Pharos? That the Persian trees in Rhodes do
only wax green but never bring forth apple?

That amomus and nardus will only grow in India,
balsamum only in Syria; that in Rhodes no eagle will
build her nest, no owl live in Crete, no wit spring in the
will of women? Mortify, therefore, thy actions, and
force not nature against nature to strive in vain. Go
into the country, look to thy grounds, yoke thine oxen,
follow thy plow, graft thy trees, behold thy cattle, and
devise with thyself how the increase of them may
increase thy profit. In autumn pull thine apples, in
summer ply thy harvest, in the spring trim thy gardens,
in the winter, thy woods, and thus, beginning to delight
to be a good husband, thou shalt begin to detest to be
in love with an idle housewife; when profit shall begin
to fill thy purse with gold, then pleasure shall have no
force to defile thy mind with love. For honest recreation after thy toil, use hunting or hawking; either rouse
the deer, or unperch the pheasant; so shalt thou root
out the remembrance of thy former love, and repent
thee of thy foolish lust. And, although thy sweetheart
bind thee by oath always to hold a candle at her shrine,
and to offer thy devotion to thine own destruction, yet go,
run, fly into the country; neither water thou thy plants,[1]
in that thou departest from thy pigsny,[2] neither stand in
a mammering [3] whether it be best to depart or not; but
by how much the more thou art unwilling to go, by so
much the more hasten thy steps, neither feign for thyself

---

[1] weep   [2] sweetheart   [3] perplexity

any sleeveless excuse whereby thou mayest tarry.
Neither let rain nor thunder, neither lightning nor tempest, stay thy journey; and reckon not with thyself
how many miles thou hast gone—that showeth weariness; but how many thou hast to go—that proveth manliness. But foolish and frantic lovers will deem my
precepts hard, and esteem my persuasions haggard,[1] I
must of force confess that it is a corrosive to the stomach of a lover, but a comfort to a godly liver to run
through a thousand pikes to escape ten thousand perils.
Sour potions bring sound health; sharp purgations make
short diseases; and the medicine, the more bitter it is,
the more better it is in working. To heal the body we
try physic, search cunning, prove sorcery, venture
through fire and water, leaving nothing unsought that
may be gotten for money, be it never so much or procured by any means, be they never so unlawful. How
much more ought we to hazard all things for the safeguard of mind, and quiet of conscience! And, certes,
easier will the remedy be when the reason is espied;
do you not know the nature of women, which is grounded
only upon extremities?

Do they think any man to delight in them unless he
dote on them? Any to be zealous except they be jealous? Any to be fervent in case he be not furious? If
he be cleanly, then term they him proud; if mean in
apparel, a sloven; if tall, a longis; if short, a dwarf;
if bold, blunt; if shamefaced, a coward; insomuch as
they have neither mean in their frumps, nor measure
in their folly. But at the first the ox wieldeth not the
yoke, nor the colt the snaffle, nor the lover good counsel;
yet time causeth the one to bend his neck, the other to
open his mouth, and should enforce the third to yield

[1] unsociable

his right to reason. Lay before thine eyes the slights
and deceits of thy lady, her snatching in jest and keeping in earnest, her perjury, her impiety, the countenance
she showeth to thee of course, the love she beareth to
others of zeal, her open malice, her dissembled mischief.

O, I would in repeating their vices thou couldst be as
eloquent as in remembering them thou oughtst to be
penitent! Be she never so comely, call her counterfeit;
be she never so straight, think her crooked. And
wrest all parts of her body to the worst, be she never
so worthy. If she be well set, then call her a boss; if
slender, a hazel twig; if nutbrown, as black as a coal;
if well colored, a painted wall; if she be pleasant,
then is she a wanton; if sullen, a clown; if honest, then
is she coy; if impudent, a harlot.

Search every vein and sinew of their disposition; if
she have no sight in descant, desire her to chant it; if
no cunning to dance, request her to trip it; if no skill in
music, proffer her the lute; if an ill gait, then walk with
her; if rude in speech, talk with her; if she be jag-
toothed, tell her some merry jest to make her laugh; if
pink-eyed, some doleful history to cause her to weep: in
the one her grinning will show her deformed; in the
other her whining, like a pig half roasted.

It is a world to see how commonly we are blinded with
the collusions of women, and more enticed by their ornaments being artificial than their proportion being natural. I loathe almost to think on their ointments and
apothecary drugs, the sleeking of their faces, and all
their slibber sauces [1] which bring queasiness to the
stomach and disquiet to the mind.

Take from them their periwigs, their paintings, their
jewels, their rolls, their bolsterings, and thou shalt

[1] disgusting ointments

soon perceive that a woman is the least part of herself. When they be once robbed of their robes, then will they appear so odious, so ugly, so monstrous, that thou wilt rather think them serpents than saints; and so like hags that thou wilt fear rather to be enchanted than enamored. Look in their closets, and there shalt thou find an apothecary's shop of sweet confections, a surgeon's box of sundry salves, a pedlar's pack of new fangles. Besides all this, their shadows,[1] their spots,[2] their lawns, their lyfkies,[3] their ruffs, their rings, show them rather cardinals' courtesans than modest matrons, and more carnally affected than moved in conscience. If every one of these things severally be not of force to move thee, yet all of them jointly shall mortify thee.

Moreover, to make thee the more stronger to strive against these sirens, and more subtle to deceive these tame serpents, my counsel is that thou have more strings to thy bow than one; it is safe riding at two anchors; a fire divided in twain burneth slower; a fountain running into many rivers is of less force; the mind enamored on two women is less affected with desire and less infected with despair: one love expelleth another, and the remembrance of the latter quencheth the concupiscence of the first.

Yet, if thou be so weak, being bewitched with their wiles that thou hast neither will to eschew nor wit to avoid their company, if thou be either so wicked that thou wilt not, or so wedded that thou canst not abstain from their glances, yet at the least dissemble thy grief. If thou be as hot as the mount Etna, feign thyself as cold as the hill Caucasus; carry two faces in one hood; cover thy flaming fancy with feigned ashes; show

[1] hat brims   [2] patches   [3] bodices

thyself sound when thou art rotten; let thy hue be merry when thy heart is melancholy; bear a pleasant countenance with a pined [1] conscience, a painted sheath with a leaden dagger. Thus, dissembling thy grief, thou mayest recure thy disease. Love creepeth in by stealth, and by stealth slideth away.

If she break promise with thee in the night, or absent herself in the day, seem thou careless, and then will she be careful; if thou languish, then will she be lavish of her honor, yea, and of the other strange beast, her honesty. Stand thou on thy pantofles, and she will veil bonnet. Lie thou aloof, and she will seize on the lure; if thou pass by her door and be called back, either seem deaf and not to hear, or desperate, and not to care. Fly the places, the parlors, the portals wherein thou hast been conversant with thy lady; yea, Philautus, shun the street where Lucilla doth dwell, lest the sight of her window renew the sum of thy sorrow.

Yet, although I would have thee precise in keeping these precepts, yet would I have thee to avoid solitariness—that breeds melancholy; melancholy, madness; madness, mischief and utter desolation. Have ever some faithful fere [2] with whom thou mayest communicate thy counsels: some Pylades to encourage Orestes, some Damon to release Pythias, some Scipo to recure [3] Lælius. Phyllis in wandering the woods hanged herself; Asiarchus, forsaking company, spoiled himself with his own bodkin. [4] Biarus, a Roman, more wise than fortunate, being alone, destroyed himself with a potsherd. Beware solitariness. But, although I would have thee use company for thy recreation, yet would I have thee always to leave the company of those that accompany thy lady; yea, if she have any jewel of thine in her

---

[1] tortured   [2] companion   [3] recover   [4] poniard

custody, rather lose it than go for it, lest in seeking to recover a trifle thou renew thine old trouble. Be not curious to curl thy hair, nor careful to be neat in thine apparel; be not prodigal of thy gold nor precise in thy going; be not like the Englishman, which preferreth every strange fashion before the use of his country; be thou dissolute,[1] lest thy lady think thee foolish in framing thyself to every fashion for her sake. Believe not their oaths and solemn protestations, their exorcisms and conjurations, their tears which they have at commandment, their alluring looks, their treading on the toe, their unsavory toys.

Let every one loathe his lady and be ashamed to be her servant. It is riches and ease that nourisheth affection; it is play, wine, and wantonness that feedeth a lover as fat as a fool; refrain from all such meats as shall provoke thine appetite to lust, and all such means as may allure thy mind to folly. Take clear water for strong wine, brown bread for fine manchet,[2] beef and brewis [3] for quails and partridge; for ease, labor; for pleasure, pain; for surfeiting, hunger; for sleep, watching; for the fellowship of ladies, the company of philosophers. If thou say to me, "Physician, heal thyself," I answer that I am meetly well purged of that disease; and yet was I never more willing to cure myself than to comfort my friend. And, seeing the cause that made in me so cold a devotion should make in thee also as frozen a desire, I hope thou wilt be as ready to provide a salve as thou wast hasty in seeking a sore. And yet, Philautus, I would not that all women should take pepper in the nose,[4] in that I have disclosed the legerdemains of a few, for well I know none will wince unless she be galled, neither any be offended

[1] negligent   [2] white bread   [3] broth   [4] offense

unless she be guilty. Therefore I earnestly desire thee
that thou show this cooling card to none except thou
show also this my defence to them all. For, although
I weigh nothing the ill will of light housewives, yet
would I be loath to lose the good will of honest matrons.
Thus, being ready to go to Athens, and ready there to
entertain thee whensoever thou shalt repair thither, I
bid thee farewell, and fly women.

Thine ever,

Euphues.

(1578)

SONGS FROM PLAYS

CUPID AND CAMPASPE

(From *Alexander and Campaspe*)

Cupid and my Campaspe played
At cards for kisses; Cupid paid.
He stakes his quiver, bows and arrows,
His mother's doves and team of sparrows;
Loses them too; then down he throws
The coral of his lip, the rose
Growing on's cheek (but none knows how);
With these, the crystal of his brow,
And then the dimple of his chin;
All these did my Campaspe win.   10
At last he set her both his eyes;
She won, and Cupid blind did rise.
O Love, has she done this to thee?
What shall, alas! become of me?

(1580?)

SPRING'S WELCOME

(From *Alexander and Campaspe*)

WHAT bird so sings, yet so does wail?
O 'tis the ravished nightingale.
'Jug, jug, jug, jug, tereu,' she cries,
And still her woes at midnight rise.
Brave prick-song! who is 't now we hear?
None but the lark so shrill and clear;
Now at heaven's gates she claps her wings,
The morn not waking till she sings.
Hark, hark, with what a pretty throat
Poor robin redbreast tunes his note!   10
Hark how the jolly cuckoos sing,
'Cuckoo,' to welcome in the spring!
'Cuckoo,' to welcome in the spring!

(1580?)

CUPID'S INDICTMENT

(From *Galathea*)

O YES, O yes! if any maid
Whom leering Cupid has betrayed
To frowns of spite, to eyes of scorn,
And would in madness now see torn
The boy in pieces,—let her come
Hither, and lay on him her doom.

O yes, O yes! has any lost
A heart which many a sigh hath cost?
Is any cozened of a tear
Which as a pearl disdain does wear?   10

Here stands the thief,—let her but come
Hither, and lay on him her doom.

Is any one undone by fire,
And turned to ashes through desire?
Did ever any lady weep,
Being cheated of her golden sleep
Stolen by sick thoughts?—the pirate's found,
And in her tears he shall be drowned.

Read his indictment, let him hear
What he's to trust to. Boy, give ear!   20

(1585)

DAPHNE

(From *Midas*)

My DAPHNE's hair is twisted gold,
Bright stars a-piece her eyes do hold,
My Daphne's brow enthrones the graces,
My Daphne's beauty stains all faces;
On Daphne's cheek grow rose and cherry,
On Daphne's lip a sweeter berry;
Daphne's snowy hand but touched does melt,
And then no heavenlier warmth is felt;
My Daphne's voice tunes all the spheres,
My Daphne's music charms all ears.   10
Fond am I thus to sing her praise;
These glories now are turned to bays.

(1589)

O CUPID! MONARCH OVER KINGS

(From *Mother Bombie*)

O CUPID! monarch over kings,
Wherefore hast thou feet and wings?
It is to show how swift thou art,
When thou wound'st a tender heart!
Thy wings being clipped, and feet held still,
Thy bow so many could not kill.

It is all one, in Venus' school,
Who highest sits, the wise man or the fool.
   Fools in love's college
   Have far more knowledge   10
   To read a woman over,
   Than a neat prating lover:
   Nay, 'tis confessed
     That fools please women best.

(1590)

SIR PHILIP SIDNEY (1554-1586)

From THE DEFENSE OF POESIE

Now then go we to the most important imputations
laid to the poor poets; for aught I can yet learn, they
are these. First, that there being many other more
fruitful knowledges, a man might better spend his time
in them than in this. Secondly, that it is the mother
of lies. Thirdly, that it is the nurse of abuse, infect-
ing us with many pestilent desires; with a siren's sweetness, drawing the mind to the serpent's tale of sinful

fancy. And herein, especially, Comedies give the larg st field to ere,[1] as Chaucer saith: how both in other nations and in ours, before poets did soften us, we were full of courage, given to martial exercises, the pillars of man-like liberty, and not lulled asleep in shady idleness with poets' pastimes. And lastly, and chiefly, they cry out with an open mouth, as if they out-shot Robin Hood, that Plato banished them out of his common-wealth. Truly, this is much, if there be much truth in it. First to the first: that a man might better spend his time is a reason indeed: but it doth (as they say) but *petere principium:* for if it be, as I affirm, that no learning is so good as that which teacheth and moveth to virtue, and that none can both teach and move thereto so much as poetry, then is the conclusion manifest that ink and paper cannot be to a more profit-able purpose employed. And certainly, though a man should grant their first assumption, it should follow (me thinks) very unwillingly, that good is not good because better is better. But I still and utterly deny that there is sprung out of earth a more fruitful knowledge. To the second therefore, that they should be the principal liars, I answer paradoxically, but, truly, I think truly, that of all writers under the sun the poet is the least liar, and, though he would, as a poet can scarcely be a liar. The astronomer, with his cousin the geometrician, can hardly escape, when they take upon them to meas-ure the height of the stars. How often, think you, do the physicians lie, when they argue things good for sicknesses, which afterwards send Charon a great number of souls drowned in a potion before they come to his ferry? And no less of the rest, which take upon them to affirm. Now, for the poet, he nothing affirms, and therefore never lieth. For, as I take it, to lie is to

[1] plow

affirm that to be true which is false. So as the other artists, and especially the historian, affirming many things, can, in the cloudy knowledge of mankind, hardly escape from many lies. But the poet (as I said before) never affirmeth. The poet never maketh any circles about your imagination, to conjure you to believe for true what he writes. He citeth not authorities of other histories, but even for his entry calleth the sweet muses to inspire into him a good invention; in troth, not labouring to tell you what is, or is not, but what should or should not be: and therefore, though he recount things not true, yet because he telleth them not for true, he lieth not, without we will say that Nathan lied in his speech, before alleged, to David. Which as a wicked man durst scarce say, so think I none so simple would say that Æsop lied in the tales of his beasts: for who thinks that Æsop writ it for actually true were well worthy to have his name chronicled among the beasts he writeth of. What child is there that, coming to a play, and seeing *Thebes* written in great letters upon an old door, doth believe that it is Thebes? If then a man can arrive, at that child's age, to know that the poet's persons and doings are but pictures what should be, and not stories what have been, they will never give the lie to things not affirmatively but allegorically and figuratively written. And therefore, as in history, looking for truth, they go away full fraught with falsehood, so in poesy, looking for fiction, they shall use the narration but as an imaginative groundplot of a profitable invention.

But hereto is replied, that the poets give names to men they write of, which argueth a conceit of an actual truth, and so, not being true, proves a falsehood. And doth the lawyer lie then, when under the names of *John a stile* and *John a noakes* he puts his case? But

that is easily answered. Their naming of men is but
to make their picture the more lively, and not to build
any history; painting men, they cannot leave men name-
less. We see we cannot play at chess but that we must
give names to our chessmen; and yet, me thinks, he
were a very partial champion of truth that would say
we lied for giving a piece of wood the reverend title
of bishop. The poet nameth Cyrus or Æneas no other
way than to show what men of their fames, fortunes,
and estates should do.

Their third is, how much it abuseth men's wit, training it to wanton sinfulness and lustful love: for indeed
that is the principal, if not the only abuse I can hear
alleged. They say the comedies rather teach than repre-
hend amorous conceits. They say the lyric is larded
with passionate sonnets: the elegiac weeps the want
of his mistress: and that even to the heroical Cupid
hath ambitiously climbed. Alas, Love, I would thou
couldst as well defend thyself as thou canst offend
others. I would those, on whom thou dost attend, could
either put thee away, or yield good reason why they
keep thee. But grant love of beauty to be a beastly
fault (although it be very hard, since only man, and no
beast, hath that gift to discern beauty). Grant that
lovely name of Love to deserve all hateful reproaches
(although even some of my masters the philosophers
spent a good deal of their lamp-oil in setting forth
the excellence of it). Grant, I say, whatsoever they
will have granted; that not only love, but lust, but
vanity, but (if they list) scurrility, possesseth many
leaves of the poets' books: yet think I, when this is
granted, they will find their sentence may with good
manners put the last words foremost, and not say that
poetry abuseth man's wit, but that man's wit abuseth
poetry.

For I will not deny but that man's wit may make poesy (which should be *Eikastike,* which some learned have defined, figuring forth good things) to be *Phantastike:* which doth, contrariwise, infect the fancy with unworthy objects. As the painter, that should give to the eye either some excellent perspective, or some fine picture, fit for building or fortification, or containing in it some notable example, as Abraham sacrificing his son Isaac, Judith killing Holofernes, David fighting with Goliath, may leave those, and please an ill-pleased eye with wanton shows of better hidden matters. But what, shall the abuse of a thing make the right use odious? Nay truly, though I yield that poesy may not only be abused, but that being abused, by the reason of his sweet charming force, it can do more hurt than any other army of words, yet shall it be so far from concluding that the abuse should give reproach to the abused, that contrariwise it is a good reason, that whatsoever, being abused, doth most harm, being rightly used (and upon the right use each thing conceiveth his title), doth most good.

Do we not see the skill of physic (the best rampire [1] to our often-assaulted bodies) being abused, teach poison, the most violent destroyer? Doth not knowledge of law, whose end is to even and right all things being abused, grow the crooked fosterer of horrible injuries? Doth not (to go to the highest) God's word abused breed heresy? and his Name abused become blasphemy? Truly, a needle cannot do much hurt, and as truly (with leave of ladies be it spoken) it cannot do much good. With a sword thou may kill thy father, and with a sword thou may defend thy prince and country. So that, as in their calling poets the fathers of

[1] defense

lies they say nothing, so in this their argument of abuse they prove the commendation.

They allege herewith, that before poets began to be in price our nation hath set their hearts' delight upon action, and not upon imagination: rather doing things worthy to be written, than writing things fit to be done. What that before [1] time was, I think scarcely Sphinx can tell: since no memory is so ancient that hath the precedence of poetry. And certain it is that, in our plainest homeliness, yet never was the Albion nation without poetry. Marry, this argument, though it be levelled against poetry, yet is it indeed a chain-shot against all learning, or bookishness, as they commonly term it. Of such mind were certain Goths, of whom it is written that, having in the spoil of a famous city taken a fair library, one hangman (belike fit to execute the fruits of their wits), who had murdered a great number of bodies, would have set fire on it: 'no,' said another very gravely, 'take heed what you do, for while they are busy about these toys, we shall with more leisure conquer their countries.'

This indeed is the ordinary doctrine of ignorance, and many words sometimes I have heard spent in it: but because this reason is generally against all learning, as well as poetry, or rather, all learning but poetry; because it were too large a digression to handle, or at least too superfluous (since it is manifest that all government of action is to be gotten by knowledge, and knowledge best by gathering many knowledges, which is reading), I only, with Horace, to him that is of that opinion,

Jubeo stultum esse libenter:

for as for poetry itself, it is the freest from this objection. For poetry is the companion of the camps.

[1] earlier

I dare undertake, *Orlando Furioso,* or honest *King Arthur,* will never displease a soldier: but the quiddity [1] of *Ens* and *Prima materia* will hardly agree with a corslet: and therefore, as I said in the beginning, even Turks and Tartars are delighted with poets. Homer, a Greek, flourished before Greece flourished. And if to a slight conjecture a conjecture may be opposed, truly it may seem, that as by him their learned men took almost their first light of knowledge, so their active men received their first motions of courage. Only Alexander's example may serve, who by Plutarch is accounted of such virtue, that fortune was not his guide but his foot-stool; whose acts speak for him, though Plutarch did not; indeed the Phœnix of warlike princes. This Alexander left his schoolmaster, living Aristotle, behind him, but took dead Homer with him: he put the philosopher Calisthenes to death for his seeming philosophical, indeed mutinous, stubbornness; but the chief thing he ever was heard to wish for was that Homer had been alive. He well found he received more bravery of mind by the pattern of Achilles than by hearing the definition of fortitude; and therefore, if Cato disliked Fulvius for carrying Ennius with him to the field, it may be answered that, if Cato disliked it, the noble Fulvius liked it, or else he had not done it: for it was not the excellent Cato Uticensis (whose authority I would much more have reverenced), but it was the former, in truth a bitter punisher of faults, but else a man that had never well sacrificed to the graces. He disliked and cried out upon all Greek learning, and yet, being eighty years old, began to learn it; belike fearing that Pluto understood not Latin. Indeed, the Roman laws allowed no person to be carried to the wars but he that was in the soldiers' roll: and therefore, though Cato

[1] trifling subtlety

disliked his unmustered person, he disliked not his work. And if he had, Scipio Nasica, judged by common consent the best Roman, loved him. Both the other Scipio brothers, who had by their virtues no less surnames than of Asia and Africa, so loved him that they caused his body to be buried in their sepulchre. So as Cato's authority being but against his person, and that answered with so far greater than himself, is herein of no validity.

But now indeed my burthen is great; now Plato's name is laid upon me, whom, I must confess, of all philosophers I have ever esteemed most worthy of reverence, and with great reason, since of all philosophers he is the most poetical. Yet if he defile the fountain out of which his flowing streams have proceeded, let us boldly examine with what reasons he did it. First truly, a man might maliciously object that Plato, being a philosopher, was a natural enemy of poets: for indeed, after the philosophers had picked out of the sweet mysteries of poetry the right discerning true points of knowledge, they forthwith, putting it in method, and making a school-art of that which the poets did only teach by a divine delightfulness, beginning to spurn at their guides, like ungrateful apprentices, were not content to set up shops for themselves, but sought by all means to discredit their masters. Which by the force of delight being barred them, the less they could overthrow them, the more they hated them. For indeed, they found for Homer seven cities strove who should have him for their citizen; where many cities banished philosophers as not fit members to live among them. For only repeating certain of Euripides verses, many Athenians had their lives saved of the Syracusians; when the Athenians themselves thought many philosophers unworthy to live. Certain poets, as Simonides and Pindar, had so prevailed with Hiero the first, that of a tyrant they made him a just king, where Plato could do so little with Dionysius, that he himself of a philosopher was made a slave. But who should do thus, I confess, should requite the objections made against poets with like cavillation against philosophers, as likewise one should do that should bid one read *Phædrus* or *Symposium* in Plato, or the discourse of love in Plutarch, and see whether any poet do authorize abominable filthiness, as they do. Again, a man might ask out of what Common-wealth Plato did banish them? insooth, thence where he himself alloweth community of women. So as belike this banishment grew not for effeminate wantonness, since little should poetical sonnets be hurtful when a man might have what woman he listed. But I honor philosophical instructions, and bless the wits which bred them: so as they be not abused, which is likewise stretched to poetry.

S. Paul himself, who (yet for the credit of poets) allegeth [1] twice two poets, and one of them by the name of a prophet, setteth a watch-word upon philosophy, indeed upon the abuse. So doth Plato upon the abuse, not upon poetry. Plato found fault that the poets of his time filled the world with wrong opinions of the gods, making light tales of that unspotted essence; and, therefore, would not have the youth depraved with such opinions. Herein may much be said: let this suffice: the poets did not induce such opinions, but did imitate those opinions already induced. For all the Greek stories can well testify that the very religion of that time stood upon many, and many-fashioned, gods, not taught so by the poets, but followed according to their nature of imitation. Who list may read in Plutarch the discourses of *Isis* and *Osiris*, of the cause why oracles ceased, of the divine providence, and see whether

[1] cites

the theology of that nation stood not upon such dreams which the poets indeed superstitiously observed, and truly (since they had not the light of Christ) did much better in it than the philosophers, who, shaking off superstition, brought in atheism. Plato therefore (whose authority I had much rather justly conster [1] than unjustly resist) meant not in general of poets, in those words of which Julius Scaliger saith, *Qua authoritate barbari quidam atque hispidi abuti velint ad poetas e republica exigendos;* but only meant to drive out those wrong opinions of the deity (whereof now, without further law, Christianity hath taken away all the hurtful belief), perchance (as I thought) nourished by the then esteemed poets. And a man need go no further than to Plato himself to know his meaning: who, in his dialogue called *Ion,* giveth high and rightly divine commendation to poetry. So as Plato, banishing the abuse, not the thing, not banishing it, but giving due honor unto it, shall be our patron and not our adversary. For indeed I had much rather (since truly I may do it) show their mistaking of Plato (under whose lion's skin they would make an ass-like braying against poesy) than go about to overthrow his authority, whom the wiser a man is the more just cause he shall find to have in admiration; especially since he attributeth unto poesy more than myself do, namely, to be a very inspiring of a divine force, far above man's wit, as in the afore-named dialogue is apparent.

Of the other side, who would show the honors have been by the best sort of judgments granted them, a whole sea of examples would present themselves: Alexanders, Cæsars, Scipios, all favorers of poets; Lelius, called the Roman Socrates, himself a poet, so as part of *Heautontimorumenos* in Terence was supposed to be

[1] construe

made by him. And even the Greek Socrates, whom
Apollo confirmed to be the only wise man, is said to
have spent part of his old time in putting Æsop's fables
into verses. And therefore, full evil should it become
his scholar Plato to put such words in his master's mouth
against poets. But what need more? Aristotle writes
the *Art of Poesy:* and why, if it should not be written?
Plutarch teacheth the use to be gathered of them, and
how, if they should not be read? And who reads Plutarch's either history or philosophy shall find he trim-
meth both their garments with gards [1] of poesy. But I
list not to defend poesy with the help of her underling
historiography. Let it suffice that it is a fit soil for
praise to dwell upon; and what dispraise may set upon
it, is either easily overcome, or transformed into just
commendation. So that, since the excellencies of it may
be so easily and so justly confirmed, and the low-creep-
ing objections so soon trodden down; it not being an
art of lies, but of true doctrine; not of effeminateness,
but of notable stirring of courage; not of abusing man's
wit, but of strengthening man's wit; not banished, but
honored by Plato; let us rather plant more laurels for to
engarland our poets' heads (which honor of being lau-
reate, as besides them only triumphant captains wear,
is a sufficient authority to show the price they ought to
be had in) than suffer the ill-favoring breath of such
wrong-speakers once to blow upon the clear springs of
poesy.

But since I have run so long a career in this matter,
methinks, before I give my pen a full stop, it shall be
but a little more lost time to inquire, why England, the
mother of excellent minds, should be grown so hard a
step-mother to poets, who certainly in wit ought to pass
all others, since all only proceeds from their wit, being,

[1] ornamental trimming

indeed, makers of themselves, not takers of others. How can I but exclaim,

Musa, mihi causas memora, quo numine læso?

Sweet poesy! that hath anciently had kings, emperors, senators, great captains, such as besides a thousand others, David, Adrian, Sophocles, Germanicus, not only to favor poets, but to be poets; and of our nearer times can present for her patrons a Robert, King of Sicily; the great King Francis of France: King James of Scotland; such cardinals as Bembus and Bibiena; such famous preachers and teachers as Beza and Melancthon; so learned philosophers as Fracastorius and Scaliger; so great orators as Pontanus and Muretus; so piercing wits as George Buchanan; so grave councilors as, besides many, but before all, that Hospital of France, than whom, I think, that realm never brought forth a more accomplished judgment, more firmly builded upon virtue; I say these, with numbers of others, not only to read others' poesies, but to poetize for others' reading: that poesy, thus embraced in all other places, should only find in our time a hard welcome in England, I think the very earth laments it, and therefore decks our soil with fewer laurels than it was accustomed. For heretofore poets have in England also flourished; and, which is to be noted, even in those times when the trumpet of Mars did sound loudest. And now that an overfaint quietness should seem to strew the house for poets, they are almost in as good reputation as the mountebanks at Venice. Truly, ever that, as of the one side it giveth great praise to poesy, which, like Venus (but to better purpose), had rather be troubled in the net with Mars, than enjoy the homely quiet of Vulcan; so serves it for a piece of a reason why they are less grateful to idle England, which now can scarce endure the

pain of a pen. Upon this necessarily followeth that
base men with servile wits undertake it, who think it
enough if they can be rewarded of the printer; and so
as Epaminondas, is said, with the honor of his virtue,
to have made an office by exercising it, which before
was contemptible, to become highly respected; so these
men, no more but setting their names to it, by their
own disgracefulness, disgrace the most graceful poesy.
For now, as if all the Muses were got with child, to bring
forth bastard poets, without any commission, they do
post over the banks of Helicon, until they make their
readers more weary than post-horses; while, in the
meantime, they,

Queis meliore luto finxit præcordia Titan,

are better content to suppress the outflowings of their
wit than by publishing them to be accounted knights
of the same order.

But I that, before ever I durst aspire unto the dignity,
am admitted into the company of the paper-blurrers, do
find the very true cause of our wanting estimation is
want of desert, taking upon us to be poets in despite
of Pallas. Now, wherein we want desert, were a thank-
worthy labor to express. But if I knew, I should have
mended myself; but as I never desired the title, so have
I neglected the means to come by it; only, overmastered
by some thoughts, I yielded an inky tribute unto them.
Marry, they that delight in poesy itself, should seek to
know what they do, and how they do, and, especially,
look themselves in an unflattering glass of reason, if
they be inclinable unto it.

For poesy must not be drawn by the ears, it must
be gently led, or rather it must lead; which was partly
the cause that made the ancient learned affirm it was a
divine gift, and no human skill, since all other knowl-

edges lie ready for any that have strength of wit; a poet no industry can make, if his own genius be not carried into it. And therefore is it an old proverb, *Orator fit, poeta nascitur*. Yet confess I always, that, as the fertilest ground must be manured, so must the highest flying wit have a Dædalus to guide him. That Dædalus, they say, both in this and in other, hath three wings to bear itself up into the air of due commendation; that is, art, imitation, and exercise. But these, neither artificial rules, nor imitative patterns, we much cumber ourselves withal. Exercise, indeed, we do, but that very fore-backwardly; for where we should exercise to know, we exercise as having known; and so is our brain delivered of much matter which never was begotten by knowledge. For there being two principal parts, matter to be expressed by words, and words to express the matter, in neither we use art or imitation rightly. Our matter is *quodlibet* indeed, although wrongly, performing Ovid's verse,

Quicquid conabor dicere, versus erit;

never marshaling it into any assured rank, that almost the readers cannot tell where to find themselves.

Chaucer, undoubtedly, did excellently in his *Troilus and Criseyde;* of whom, truly, I know not whether to marvel more, either that he in that misty time could see so clearly, or that we in this clear age go so stumblingly after him. Yet had he great wants, fit to be forgiven in so reverend antiquity. I account the *Mirror for Magistrates* meetly furnished of beautiful parts. And in the Earl of Surrey's lyrics, many things tasting of a noble birth, and worthy of a noble mind. The *Shepherd's Calendar* hath much poetry in its eclogues, indeed, worthy the reading, if I be not deceived. That same framing of its style to an old rustic language, I dare not allow; since neither Theocritus in Greek, Virgil in Latin, nor Sannazaro in Italian, did affect it. Besides these, I do not remember to have seen but few (to speak boldly) printed that have poetical sinews in them. For proof whereof, let but most of the verses be put in prose, and then ask the meaning, and it will be found that one verse did but beget another, without ordering at the first what should be at the last; which becomes a confused mass of words, with a tinkling sound of rime, barely accompanied with reason.

Our tragedies and comedies (not without cause, cried out against) observing rules neither of honest civility nor of skilful poetry, excepting *Gorboduc* (again I say of those that I have seen), which notwithstanding, as it is full of stately speeches and well-sounding phrases, climbing to the height of Seneca's style, and as full of notable morality, which it does most delightfully teach, and so obtain the very end of poesy; yet, in truth, it is very defectious in the circumstances, which grieves me, because it might not remain as an exact model of all tragedies. For it is faulty both in place and time, the two necessary companions of all corporal actions. For where the stage should always represent but one place, and the uttermost time presupposed in it should be, both by Aristotle's precept, and common reason, but one day, there is both many days and many places inartificially imagined.

But if it be so in *Gorboduc,* how much more in all the rest? where you shall have Asia of the one side, and Afric of the other, and so many other under kingdoms, that the player, when he comes in, must ever begin with telling where he is, or else the tale will not be conceived. Now you shall have three ladies walk to gather flowers, and then we must believe the stage to be a garden. By and by, we hear news of shipwreck in the same place, and then we are to blame if we accept it not for a rock. Upon the back of that comes out a hideous monster, with fire and smoke, and then the miserable beholders are bound to take it for a cave; while, in the meantime, two armies fly in, represented with four swords and bucklers, and then, what hard heart will not receive it for a pitched field?

Now, of time they are much more liberal; for ordinary it is, that two young princes fall in love; after many traverses [1] she is got with child; delivered of a fair boy; he is lost, groweth a man, falls in love, and is ready to get another child; and all this in two hours' space; which, how absurd it is in sense, even sense may imagine; and art hath taught and all ancient examples justified, and at this day the ordinary players in Italy will not err in. Yet will some bring in an example of the *Eunuch* in Terence, that containeth matter of two days, yet far short of twenty years. True it is, and so was it to be played in two days, and so fitted to the time it set forth. And though Plautus have in one place done amiss, let us hit it with him, and not miss with him.

But they will say, How then shall we set forth a story which contains both many places and many times? And do they not know that a tragedy is tied to the laws of poesy, and not of history; not bound to follow the story, but having liberty either to feign a quite new matter, or to frame the history to the most tragical conveniency? Again, many things may be told, which cannot be showed: if they know the difference betwixt reporting and representing. As, for example, I may speak, though I am here, of Peru, and in speech digress from that to the description of Calicut; but in action I cannot represent it without Pacolet's horse. And so

_____
[1] difficulties

was the manner the ancients took, by some *Nuntius* to recount things done in former time, or other place.

Lastly, if they will represent an history, they must not, as Horace saith, begin *ab ovo,* but they must come to the principal point of that one action which they will represent. By example this will be best expressed. I have a story of young Polydorus, delivered, for safety's sake, with great riches, by his father Priamus to Polymnestor, King of Thrace, in the Trojan war time. He, after some years, hearing the overthrow of Priamus, for to make the treasure his own, murdereth the child; the body of the child is taken up by Hecuba; she, the same day, findeth a sleight to be revenged most cruelly of the tyrant. Where, now, would one of our tragedy-writers begin, but with the delivery of the child? Then should he sail over into Thrace, and so spend I know not how many years, and travel numbers of places. But where doth Euripides? Even with the finding of the body; leaving the rest to be told by the spirit of Polydorus. This needs no further to be enlarged; the dullest wit may conceive it.

But, besides these gross absurdities, how all their plays be neither right tragedies nor right comedies, mingling kings and clowns, not because the matter so carrieth it, but thrust in clowns by head and shoulders to play a part in majestical matters, with neither decency nor discretion; so as neither the admiration and commiseration, nor the right sportfulness, is by their mongrel tragi-comedy obtained. I know Apuleius did somewhat so, but that is a thing recounted with space of time, not represented in one moment: and I know the ancients have one or two examples of tragi-comedies, as Plautus hath *Amphitruo.* But, if we mark them well, we shall find that they never, or very daintily, match hornpipes and funerals. So falleth it out, that, having, indeed, no right comedy in that comical part of our tragedy, we have nothing but scurrility, unworthy of any chaste ears; or some extreme show of doltishness, indeed fit to lift up a loud laughter, and nothing else; where the whole tract of a comedy should be full of delight as the tragedy should be still maintained in a well-raised admiration.

But our comedians think there is no delight without laughter, which is very wrong; for though laughter may come with delight, yet cometh it not of delight, as though delight should be the cause of laughter; but well may one thing breed both together. Nay, in themselves, they have, as it were, a kind of contrariety. For delight we scarcely do, but in things that have a conveniency to ourselves, or to the general nature. Laughter almost ever cometh of things most disproportioned to ourselves and nature: delight hath a joy in it, either permanent or present; laughter hath only a scornful tickling. For example: we are ravished with delight to see a fair woman, and yet are far from being moved to laughter; we laugh at deformed creatures, wherein certainly we cannot delight; we delight in good chances; we laugh at mischances; we delight to hear the happiness of our friends or country, at which he were worthy to be laughed at that would laugh: we shall, contrarily, laugh sometimes to find a matter quite mistaken, and go down the hill against the bias, in the mouth of some such men, as for the respect of them, one shall be heartily sorry, yet he cannot choose but laugh, and so is rather pained than delighted with laughter. Yet deny I not, but that they may go well together; for, as in Alexander's picture well set out, we delight without laughter, and in twenty mad antics we laugh without delight: so in Hercules, painted with his great beard and furious countenance, in a woman's attire, spinning at

Omphale's commandment, it breedeth both delight and laughter; for the representing of so strange a power in love procures delight, and the scornfulness of the action stirreth laughter.

But I speak to this purpose, that all the end of the comical part be not upon such scornful matters as stir laughter only, but mix with it that delightful teaching which is the end of poesy. And the great fault, even in that point of laughter, and forbidden plainly by Aristotle, is, that they stir laughter in sinful things, which are rather execrable than ridiculous; or in miserable, which are rather to be pitied than scorned. For what is it to make folks gape at a wretched beggar, and a beggarly clown; or against the law of hospitality, to jest at strangers, because they speak not English so well as we do? what do we learn? since it is certain,

> *Nil habet infelix paupertas durius in se,*
> *Quam quod ridiculos, homines facit.*

But rather a busy loving courtier, a heartless threatening Thraso; a self-wise-seeming schoolmaster; a wry-transformed traveler: these, if we saw walk in stage names, which we play naturally, therein were delightful laughter, and teaching delightfulness: as in the other, the tragedies of Buchanan do justly bring forth a divine admiration.

But I have lavished out too many words of this play matter; I do it, because, as they are excelling parts of poesy, so is there none so much used in England, and none can be more pitifully abused; which, like an unmannerly daughter, showing a bad education, causeth her mother Poesy's honesty to be called in question.

Other sorts of poetry, almost have we none, but that lyrical kind of songs and sonnets, which, if the Lord gave us so good minds, how well it might be employed, and with how heavenly fruits, both private and public in singing the praises of the immortal beauty, the immortal goodness of that God, who giveth us hands to write, and wits to conceive; of which we might well want words, but never matter; of which we could turn our eyes to nothing, but we should ever have new budding occasions. But, truly, many of such writings as come under the banner of irresistible love, if I were a mistress, would never persuade me they were in love; so coldly they apply fiery speeches, as men that had rather read lovers' writings, and so caught up certain swelling phrases, which hang together—like a man which once told me, 'the wind was at northwest and by south,' because he would be sure to name winds enough—than that, in truth, they feel those passions, which easily, as I think, may be bewrayed by the same forcibleness, or *energia* (as the Greeks call it), of the writer. But let this be a sufficient, though short note, that we miss the right use of the material point of poesy.

Now for the outside of it, which is words, or, as I may term it, diction, it is even well worse; so is that honey-flowing matron Eloquence, appareled, or rather disguised, in a courtesan-like painted affectation. One time with so far-fetched words, that may seem monsters, but must seem strangers to any poor Englishman: another time with coursing of a letter, as if they were bound to follow the method of a dictionary: another time with figures and flowers, extremely winter-starved.

But I would this fault were only peculiar to versifiers, and had not as large possession among prose printers: and, which is to be marveled, among many scholars, and, which is to be pitied, among some preachers. Truly, I could wish (if at least I might be so bold to wish, in a thing beyond the reach of my capacity) the diligent imitators of Tully and Demosthenes, most worthy to be imitated, did not so much keep Nizolian paperbooks of their figures and phrases, as by attentive translation, as it were, devour them whole, and make them wholly theirs. For now they cast sugar and spice upon every dish that is served to the table: like those Indians, not content to wear earrings at the fit and natural place of the ears, but they will thrust jewels through their nose and lips, because they will be sure to be fine. Tully, when he was to drive out Catiline, as it were with a thunderbolt of eloquence, often used the figure of repetition.

Vivit. Vivit? imo in Senatum venit, etc.

Indeed, inflamed with a well-grounded rage, he would have his words, as it were, double out of his mouth; and so do that artificially which we see men do in choler naturally. And we, having noted the grace of those words, hale them in sometimes to a familiar epistle, when it were too much choler to be choleric.

How well, store of 'similiter cadences' doth sound with the gravity of the pulpit, I would but invoke Demosthenes' soul to tell, who with a rare daintiness useth them. Truly, they have made me think of the sophister, that with too much subtlety would prove two eggs three, and, though he might be counted a sophister, had none for his labor. So these men bringing in such a kind of eloquence, well may they obtain an opinion of a seeming fineness, but persuade few, which should be the end of their fineness.

Now for similitudes in certain printed discourses, I think all herbalists, all stories of beasts, fowls, and fishes are rifled up, that they come in multitudes to wait upon any of our conceits, which certainly is as absurd a surfeit to the ears as is possible. For the force of a similitude not being to prove anything to a contrary disputer, but only to explain to a willing hearer: when that is done, the rest is a most tedious prattling, rather overswaying the memory from the purpose whereto they were applied, than any whit informing the judgment, already either satisfied, or by similitudes not to be satisfied.

For my part, I do not doubt, when Antonius and Crassus, the great forefathers of Cicero in eloquence, the one (as Cicero testified of them) pretended not to know art, the other not to set by it, because with a plain sensibleness they might win credit of popular ears, which credit is the nearest step to persuasion (which persuasion is the chief mark of oratory); I do not doubt, I say, but that they used these knacks very sparingly; which who doth generally use, any man may see, doth dance to his own music; and so to be noted by the audience, more careful to speak curiously than to speak truly. Undoubtedly (at least to my opinion, undoubtedly) I have found in divers small-learned courtiers a more sound style than in some professors of learning; of which I can guess no other cause, but that the courtier following that which by practice he findeth fittest to nature, therein (though he know it not) doth according to art, though not by art: where the other, using art to show art, and not to hide art (as in these cases he should do), flieth from nature, and indeed abuseth art.

But what! methinks I deserve to be pounded for straying from poetry to oratory: but both have such an affinity in the wordish considerations, that I think this digression will make my meaning receive the fuller understanding: which is not to take upon me to teach poets how they should do, but only finding myself sick among the rest, to show some one or two spots of the common infection grown among the most part of writers; that, acknowledging ourselves somewhat awry, we may bend to the right use both of matter and manner: whereto our language giveth us great occasion, being, indeed, capable of any excellent exercising of it. I know some will say, it is a mingled language: and why not so much the better, taking the best of both the other? Another will say, it wanteth grammar. Nay, truly, it hath that praise, that it wanteth not grammar; for grammar it might have, but it needs it not; being so easy in itself, and so void of those cumbersome differences of cases, genders, moods, and tenses; which, I think, was a piece of the Tower of Babylon's curse, that a man should be put to school to learn his mother tongue. But for the uttering sweetly and properly the conceits of the mind, which is the end of speech, that hath it equally with any other tongue in the world, and is particularly happy in compositions of two or three words together, near the Greek, far beyond the Latin; which is one of the greatest beauties can be in a language.

Now, of versifying there are two sorts, the one ancient, the other modern; the ancient marked the quantity of each syllable, and according to that, framed its verse; the modern, observing only number, with some regard of the accent, the chief life of it standeth in that like sounding of the words, which we call rime. Whether of these be the more excellent, would bear many speeches; the ancient, no doubt more fit for music, both words and tune observing quantity; and more fit lively to express divers passions, by the low and lofty sound of the well-weighed syllable. The latter, likewise, with his rime striketh a certain music to the ear; and, in fine, since it doth delight, though by another way, it obtains the same purpose; there being in either, sweetness, and wanting in neither, majesty. Truly the English, before any other vulgar language I know, is fit for both sorts;

for, for the ancient, the Italian is so full of vowels, that it must ever be cumbered with elisions. The Dutch so of the other side with consonants, that they cannot yield the sweet sliding fit for a verse. The French, in his whole language, hath not one word that hath its accent in the last syllable, saving two, called antepenultima; and little more hath the Spanish; and, therefore, very gracelessly may they use dactyls. The English is subject to none of these defects.

Now for rime, though we do not observe quantity, yet we observe the accent very precisely, which other languages either cannot do, or will not do so absolutely. That cæsura, or breathing-place, in the midst of the verse, neither Italian nor Spanish have, the French and we never almost fail of. Lastly, even the very rime itself the Italian cannot put in the last syllable, by the French named the masculine rime, but still in the next to the last, which the French call the female; or the next before that, which the Italians term *sdrucciola:* the example of the former is, *buono, suono;* of the *sdrucciola* is, *femina, semina.* The French, of the other side, hath both the male, as *bon, son,* and the female, as *plaise, taise;* but the *sdrucciola* he hath not; where the English hath all three, as 'due,' 'true,' 'father,' 'rather,' 'motion,' 'potion,' with much more which might be said, but that I find already the triflingness of this discourse is much too much enlarged.

So that since the ever praiseworthy poesy is full of virtue-breeding delightfulness, and void of no gift that ought to be in the noble name of learning; since the blames laid against it are either false or feeble; since the cause why it is not esteemed in England is the fault of poet-apes, not poets; since, lastly, our tongue is most fit to honor poesy, and to be honored by poesy: I conjure you all that have had the evil luck to read this ink-

wasting toy of mine, even in the name of the Nine
Muses, no more to scorn the sacred mysteries of poesy;
no more to laugh at the name of poets, as though they
were next inheritors to fools; no more to jest at the
reverend title of a rimer; but to believe, with Aristotle,
that they were the ancient treasurers of the Grecians'
divinity; to believe, with Bembus, that they were the
first bringers in of all civility; to believe, with Scaliger,
that no philosopher's precepts can sooner make you an
honest man, than the reading of Virgil; to believe,
with Clauserus, the translator of Cornutus, that it
pleased the heavenly deity by Hesiod and Homer, under
the veil of fables, to give us all knowledge, logic, rhetoric, philosophy natural and moral, and *Quid non?* to
believe, with me, that there are many mysteries contained in poetry, which of purpose were written darkly,
lest by profane wits it should be abused; to believe, with
Landin, that they are so beloved of the gods that whatsoever they write proceeds of a divine fury. Lastly, to
believe themselves, when they tell you they will make
you immortal by their verses.

Thus doing, your names shall flourish in the printers'
shops: thus doing, you shall be of kin to many a poetical
preface: thus doing, you shall be most fair, most rich,
most wise, most all: you shall dwell upon superlatives:
thus doing, though you be *Libertino patre natus,* you
shall suddenly grow *Herculea proles,*

Si quid mea Carmina possunt:

Thus doing, your soul shall be placed with Dante's
Beatrice, or Virgil's Anchises.

But if (fie of such a but!) you be born so near the
dull-making cataract of Nilus, that you cannot hear the
planet-like music of poetry; if you have so earth-creep-
ing a mind, that it cannot lift itself up to look to the sky

of poetry, or rather, by a certain rustical disdain, will become such a Mome, as to be a Momus of poetry; then, though I will not wish unto you the ass's ears of Midas, nor to be driven by a poet's verses, as Bubonax was, to hang himself; nor to be rimed to death, as is said to be done in Ireland; yet thus much curse I must send you in behalf of all poets; that while you live, you live in love, and never get favor, for lacking skill of a sonnet; and when you die, your memory die from the earth for want of an epitaph.

(1583?)

(printed 1595)

SONNETS FROM ASTROPHEL AND STELLA

1

Loving in truth, and fain in verse my love to show,
That she, dear she, might take some pleasure of my pain,—
Pleasure might cause her read, reading might make
    her know,
Knowledge might pity win, and pity grace obtain,—
I sought fit words to paint the blackest face of woe,
Studying inventions fine, her wits to entertain,
Oft turning others' leaves, to see if thence would flow
Some fresh and fruitful showers upon my sunburnt brain.
But words came halting forth, wanting Invention's stay;
Invention, Nature's child, fled step-dame Study's blows;
And others' feet [1] still seemed but strangers' in my way.
Thus, great with child to speak, and helpless in my throes,
Biting my truant pen, beating myself for spite;
'Fool,' said my Muse to me, 'look in thy heart, and write.'

[1] poetic feet

3

Let dainty wits cry on the Sisters nine,
That, bravely masked, their fancies may be told;
Or Pindar's apes flaunt in their phrases fine,
Enam'ling with pied flowers their thoughts of gold;
Or else let them in stately glory shine,
Ennobling new-found tropes with problems old;
Or with strange similes enrich each line,
Of herbs or beasts which Inde or Afric hold.
For me, in sooth, no Muse but one I know;
Phrases and problems from my reach do grow   10
And strange things cost too dear for my poor sprites:
How then? even thus,—in Stella's face I read
What Love and Beauty be; then all my deed
But copying is, what in her Nature writes.

31

With how sad steps, O Moon, thou climb'st the skies!
How silently, and with how wan a face!
What, may it be that even in heavenly place
That busy archer his sharp arrows tries!
Sure, if that long-with-love-acquainted eyes
Can judge of love, thou feel'st a lover's case,
I read it in thy looks; thy languished grace,
To me that feel the like, my state descries.
Then, even of fellowship, O Moon, tell me,
Is constant love deemed there but want of wit?   10
Are beauties there as proud as here they be?
Do they above love to be loved, and yet
Those lovers scorn whom that love doth possess?
Do they call virtue there ungratefulness?

41

Having this day my horse, my hand, my lance
Guided so well that I obtained the prize,
Both by the judgment of the English eyes
And of some sent from that sweet enemy France;
Horsemen my skill in horsemanship advance,
Town folks my strength; a daintier judge applies
His praise to sleight which from good use doth rise;
Some lucky wits impute it but to chance;
Others, because of both sides I do take
My blood from them who did excel in this,   10
Think Nature me a man-at-arms did make.
How far they shot awry! the true cause is,
Stella looked on, and from her heavenly face
Sent forth the beams which made so fair my race.

90

Stella, think not that I by verse seek fame,
Who seek, who hope, who love, who live but thee;
Thine eyes my pride, thy lips my history:
If thou praise not, all other praise is shame.
Nor so ambitious am I, as to frame
A nest for my young praise in laurel tree:
In truth, I swear I wish not there should be
Graved in my epitaph a Poet's name.
Nor, if I would, could I just title make,
That any laud thereof to me should grow,   10
Without my plumes from others' wings I take:
For nothing from my wit or will doth flow,
Since all my words thy beauty doth endite,
And Love doth hold my hand, and makes me write.

(1580?)

LYRICS FROM ARCADIA

WHO HATH HIS FANCY PLEASED

WHO hath his fancy pleasèd
  With fruits of happy sight,
Let here his eyes be raisèd
  On Nature's sweetest light;
A light which doth dissever
  And yet unite the eyes;
A light which, dying never,
  Is cause the looker dies.

She never dies, but lasteth
  In life of lover's heart;   10
He ever dies that wasteth
  In love his chiefest part:
Thus is her life still guarded
  In never-dying faith;
Thus is his death rewarded,
  Since she lives in his death.

Look, then, and die: the pleasure
  Doth answer well the pain:
Small loss of mortal treasure
  Who may immortal gain.   20
Immortal be her graces,
  Immortal is her mind:
They, fit for heavenly places;
  This, heaven in it doth bind.

But eyes these beauties see not,
  Nor sense that grace descries;

Yet eyes deprivèd be not
    From sight of her fair eyes—
Which as of inward glory
    They are the outward seal,   30
So may they live still sorry,
    Which die not in that weal.

But who hath fancies pleasèd
    With fruits of happy sight,
Let here his eyes be raisèd
    On Nature's sweetest light!

SONG: THE NIGHTINGALE

THE nightingale, as soon as April bringeth
Unto her rested sense a perfect waking,
While late bare earth, proud of new clothing, springeth,
Sings out her woes, a thorn her song-book making,
    And mournfully bewailing,
    Her throat in tunes expresseth
    What grief her breast oppresseth
For Tereus' force on her chaste will prevailing.

O Philomela fair, O take some gladness,
    That here is juster cause of painful sadness: 10
    Thine earth now springs, mine fadeth;
    Thy thorn without, my thorn my heart invadeth.

Alas! she hath no other cause of anguish
But Tereus' love, on her by strong hand wroken;[1]
Wherein she suffering, all her spirits languish,
Full womanlike complains her will was broken.
    But I, who, daily craving,
    Can not have to content me,

[1] compelled

Have more cause to lament me,
Since wanting is more woe than too much having.   20

O Philomela fair! etc.

A FAREWELL

OFT have I mused, but now at length I find,
Why those that die, men say they do depart.
Depart!—a word so gentle, to my mind,
Weakly did seem to paint death's ugly dart.
But now the stars, with their strange course, do bind
Me one to leave, with whom I leave my heart;
I hear a cry of spirits, faint and blind,
That, parting thus, my chiefest part I part.
Part of my life, the loathèd part to me,
Lives to impart my weary clay some breath;   10
But that good part, wherein all comforts be,
Now dead, doth show departure is a death—
Yea, worse than death: death parts both woe and joy:
From joy I part, still living in annoy.

LOVE IS DEAD

RING out your bells, let mourning shows be spread;
     For Love is dead:
     All Love is dead, infected
With plague of deep disdain:
     Worth, as naught worth, rejected,
And Faith fair scorn doth gain.
     From so ungrateful fancy,
     From such a female franzie,
     From them that use men thus,
     Good Lord, deliver us!   10

Weep, neighbors, weep; do you not hear it said
  That Love is dead?
  His death-bed, peacock's folly;
His winding-sheet is shame;
  His will, false-seeming holy;
His sole exec'tor, blame.
   From so ungrateful fancy,
   From such a female franzie,
   From them that use men thus,
   Good Lord, deliver us!   20

Let dirge be sung, and trentals rightly read
  For Love is dead;
  Sir Wrong his tomb ordaineth
My mistress' marble heart;
  Which epitaph containeth,
'Her eyes were once his dart.'
   From so ungrateful fancy,
   From such a female franzie,
   From them that use men thus,
   Good Lord, deliver us!   30

Alas, I lie: rage hath this error bred;
  Love is not dead;
  Love is not dead, but sleepeth
In her unmatchèd mind,
  Where she his counsel keepeth,
Till due deserts she find.
   Therefore from so vile fancy,
   To call such wit a franzie,
   Who Love can temper thus,
   Good Lord, deliver us!   40

LEAVE ME, O LOVE!

LEAVE me, O Love, which reachest but to dust,
And thou, my mind, aspire to higher things;
Grow rich in that which never taketh rust:
Whatever fades, but fading pleasure brings.
Drag in thy beams, and humble all thy might
To that sweet yoke where lasting freedoms be,
Which breaks the clouds and opens forth the light
That doth both shine and give us sight to see.
Oh, take fast hold! Let that light be thy guide
In this small course which birth draws out to death, 10
And think how evil becometh him to slide
Who seeketh heaven, and comes of heavenly breath.
Then, farewell, world! thy uttermost I see.
Eternal Love, maintain thy life in me!

                                        (Before 1585)

EDMUND SPENSER (1552?-1599)

THE FAERIE QUEENE

A LETTER OF THE AUTHOR'S,
EXPOUNDING his whole intention in the course of this
worke: which, for that it giveth great light to the
reader, for the better understanding is hereunto an-
nexed.

To the Right Noble and Valorous SIR WALTER RALEIGH,
KNIGHT; Lord Wardein of the Stanneryes, and Her
Majesties Lieftenaunt of the County of Cornewayll.

SIR, knowing how doubtfully all allegories may be
construed, and this booke of mine, which I have entituled

the *Faery Queene,* being a continued allegory, or darke conceit, I have thought good, as well for avoyding of gealous opinions and misconstructions, as also for your better light in reading thereof (being so by you commanded), to discover unto you the general intention and meaning, which in the whole course thereof I have fashioned, without expressing of any particular purposes, or by-accidents therein occasioned. The generall end therefore of all the booke is to fashion a gentleman or noble person in vertuous and gentle discipline: which for that I conceived shoulde be most plausible and pleasing, being coloured with an historicall fiction, the which the most part of men delight to read, rather for variety of matter than for profite of the ensample, I chose the historye of King Arthure, as most fitte for the excellency of his person, being made famous by many men's former workes, and also furthest from the daunger of envy, and suspition of present time. In which I have followed all the antique Poets historicall: first Homere, who in the Persons of Agamemnon and Ulysses hath ensampled a good governour and a vertuous man, the one in his Ilias, the other in his Odysseis; then Virgil, whose like intention was to doe in the person of Æneas; after him Ariosto comprised them both in his Orlando: and lately Tasso dissevered them againe, and formed both parts in two persons, namely that part which they in Philosophy call Ethice, or vertues of a private man, coloured in his Rinaldo; the other named Politice in his Godfredo. By ensample of which excellente poets, I labour to pourtraict in Arthure, before he was king, the image of a brave knight, perfected in the twelve private morall vertues, as Aristotle hath devised; the which is the purpose of these first twelve bookes: which if I finde to be well accepted, I may be perhaps encoraged to frame the other part of polliticke vertues in his person, after that hee came to be king.

To some, I know, this methode will seeme displeasaunt, which had rather have good discipline delivered plainly in way of precepts, or sermoned at large, as they use, than thus clowdily enwrapped in Allegoricall devises. But such, me seeme, should be satisfide with the use of these dayes, seeing all things accounted by their showes, and nothing esteemed of, that is not delightfull and pleasing to commune sence. For this cause is Xenophon preferred before Plato, for that the one, in the exquisite depth of his judgement, formed a commune welth, such as it should be; but the other in the person of Cyrus, and the Persians, fashioned a governement, such as might best be: so much more profitable and gratious is doctrine by ensample, than by rule. So have I laboured to doe in the person of Arthure: whome I conceive, after his long education by Timon, to whom he was by Merlin delivered to be brought up, so soone as he was borne of the Lady Igrayne, to have seene in a dreame or vision the Faery Queen, with whose excellent beauty ravished, he awaking resolved to seeke her out; and so being by Merlin armed, and by Timon thoroughly instructed, he went to seeke her forth in Faerye Land. In that Faery Queene I meane glory in my generall intention, but in my particular I conceive the most excellent and glorious person of our soveraine the Queene, and her kingdome in Faery Land. And yet, in some places els, I doe otherwise shadow her. For considering she beareth two persons, the one of a most royall queene or empresse, the other of a most vertuous and beautifull Lady, this latter part in some places I doe expresse in Belphœbe, fashioning her name according to your owne excellent conceipt of Cynthia (Phœbe and

Cynthia being both names of Diana). So in the person
of Prince Arthure I sette forth magnificence in particular, which vertue, for that (according to Aristotle and
the rest) it is the perfection of all the rest, and con-
teineth in it them all, therefore in the whole course I
mention the deedes of Arthure applyable to that vertue
which I write of in that booke. But of the xii. other
vertues, I make xii. other knights the patrones, for the
more variety of the history: of which these three bookes
contayn three.   The first of the Knight of the Redcrosse, in whome I expresse Holynes: The seconde of
Sir Guyon, in whome I sette forth Temperaunce: The
third of Britomartis, a lady knight, in whome I picture
Chastity.   But, because the beginning of the whole
worke seemeth abrupte, and as depending upon other
antecedents, it needs that ye know the occasion of these
three knights severall adventures. For the methode of a
poet historical is not such as of an historiographer. For
an historiographer discourseth of affayres orderly as
they were donne, accounting as well the times as the
actions; but a poet thrusteth into the middest, even
where it most concerneth him, and there recoursing
to the thinges forepaste, and divining of thinges to
come, maketh a pleasing analysis of all.

The beginning therefore of my history, if it were to be
told by an historiographer, should be the twelfth booke,
which is the last; where I devise that the Faery Queene
kept her annuall feaste xii. dayes; upon which xii. severall dayes, the occasions of the xii. severall adventures
happed, which, being undertaken by xii. several knights,
are in these xii. books severally handled and discoursed.
The first was this.   In the beginning of the feast, there
presented himselfe a tall clownishe younge man, who,
falling before the Queene of Fairies, desired a boone

(as the manner then was) which during that feast she might not refuse: which was that hee might have the atchievement of any adventure, which during that feaste should happen: that being graunted, he rested him on the floore, unfitte through his rusticity for a better place.   Soone after entred a faire ladye in mourning weedes, riding on a white asse, with a dwarfe behind her leading a warlike steed, that bore the armes of a knight, and his speare in the dwarfes hand.   Shee, falling before the Queene of Faeries, complayned that her father and mother, an ancient king and queene, had bene by an huge dragon many years shut up in a brasen castle, who thence suffred them not to yssew; and therefore besought the Faery Queene to assygne her some one of her knights to take on him that exployt.   Presently that clownish person, upstarting, desired that adventure: whereat the Queene much wondering, and the lady much gainesaying, yet he earnestly importuned his desire.   In the end the lady told him, that unlesse that armour which she brought, would serve him (that is, the armour of a Christian man specified by Saint Paul, vi. Ephes.), that he could not succeed in that enterprise: which being forthwith put upon him with dewe furnitures thereunto, he seemed the goodliest man in al that company, and was well liked of the lady. And eftesoones taking on him knighthood, and mounting on that straunge courser, he went forth with her on that adventure: where beginneth the first booke, viz.,

A gentle knight was pricking on the playne, etc.

The second day there came in a palmer, bearing an infant with bloody hands, whose parents he complained to have bene slayn by an enchaunteresse called Acrasia; and therefore craved of the Faery Queene, to appoint him some knight to performe that adventure; which being assigned to Sir Guyon, he presently went forth with that same palmer: which is the beginning of the second booke and the whole subject thereof. The third day there came in a groome, who complained before the Faery Queene, that a vile enchaunter, called Busirane, had in hand a most faire lady, called Amoretta, whom he kept in most grievous torment, because she would not yield him the pleasure of her body. Whereupon Sir Scudamour, the lover of that lady, presently tooke on him that adventure. But being unable to performe it by reason of the hard enchauntments, after long sorrow, in the end met with Britomartis, who succoured him, and reskewed his love.

But by occasion hereof many other adventures are intermedled, but rather as accidents then intendments: as the love of Britomart, the overthrow of Marinell, the misery of Florimell, the vertuousness of Belphœbe, the lasciviousnes of Hellenora, and many the like.

Thus much, Sir, I have briefly overronne, to direct your understanding to the welhead of the history, that from thence gathering the whole intention of the conceit ye may, as in a handfull, gripe al the discourse, which otherwise may happily seeme tedious and confused. So, humbly craving the continuance of your honourable favour towards me, and th' eternall establishment of your happiness, I humbly take leave.

23 January, 1589.

Yours most humbly affectionate,

ED. SPENSER.

THE FIRST BOOKE OF THE FAERIE QUEENE

CONTAYNING
THE LEGENDE OF THE KNIGHT OF THE RED-CROSSE, OR OF HOLINESSE

1

Lo I the man, whose Muse whilome did maske,
As time her taught, in lowly Shepheards weeds,
Am now enforst a far unfitter taske,
For trumpets sterne to chaunge mine Oaten reeds,
And sing of Knights and Ladies gentle deeds;
Whose prayses having slept in silence long,
Me, all too meane, the sacred Muse areeds [1]
To blazon broad emongst her learnèd throng:
Fierce warres and faithfull loves shall moralize my song.

2

Helpe then, O holy Virgin chiefe of nine,   10
Thy weaker Novice to performe thy will,
Lay forth out of thine everlasting scryne [2]
The antique rolles, which there lye hidden still,
Of Faerie knights and fairest *Tanaquill,*
Whom that most noble Briton Prince so long
Sought through the world, and suffered so much ill,
That I must rue his undeservèd wrong:
O helpe thou my weake wit, and sharpen my dull tong.

3

And thou most dreaded impe of highest *Jove,*
Faire *Venus* sonne, that with thy cruell dart   20

[1] advises   [2] writing cabinet

At that good knight so cunningly didst rove,[1]
That glorious fire it kindled in his hart,
Lay now thy deadly Heben [2] bow apart,
And with thy mother milde come to mine ayde:
Come both, and with you bring triumphant *Mart*,[3]
In loves and gentle jollities arrayd,
After his murderous spoiles and bloudy rage allayd.

4

And with them eke, O Goddesse heavenly bright,
Mirrour of grace and Majestie divine,
Great Lady of the greatest Isle, whose light　　30
Like *Phœbus* lampe throughout the world doth shine,
Shed thy faire beames into my feeble eyne,
And raise my thoughts too humble and too vile,
To thinke of that true glorious type of thine,
The argument of mine afflicted stile:
The which to heare, vouchsafe, O dearest dred a-while.

CANTO I

The Patron of true Holinesse,
Foule Errour doth defeate:
Hypocrisie him to entrape,
Doth to his home entreate.

1

A Gentle Knight was pricking [4] on the plaine,
Y-cladd in mightie armes and silver shielde,
Wherein old dints of deepe wounds did remaine,
The cruell markes of many a bloudy fielde;
Yet armes till that time did he never wield:
　[1] shoot an arrow　　[2] ebony　　[3] Mars　　[4] spurring

His angry steede did chide his foming bitt,
As much disdayning to the curbe to yield:
Full jolly knight he seemed, and faire did sitt,
As one for knightly giusts and fierce encounters fitt.

2

But on his brest a bloudie Crosse he bore,   10
The deare remembrance of his dying Lord,
For whose sweete sake that glorious badge he wore,
And dead as living ever him ador'd:
Upon his shield the like was also scor'd,
For soveraine hope, which in his helpe he had:
Right faithfull true he was in deede and word,
But of his cheere did seeme too solemne sad;
Yet nothing did he dread, but ever was ydrad.

3

Upon a great adventure he was bond,
That greatest *Gloriana* to him gave,   20
That greatest Glorious Queene of *Faerie* lond,
To winne him worship, and her grace to have,
Which of all earthly things he most did crave;
And ever as he rode, his hart did earne
To prove his puissance in battell brave
Upon his foe, and his new force to learne;
Upon his foe, a Dragon horrible and stearne.

4

A lovely Ladie rode him faire beside,
Upon a lowly Asse more white than snow,
Yet she much whiter, but the same did hide   30
Under a vele, that wimpled was full low,

And over all a blacke stole she did throw,
As one that inly mournd: so was she sad,
And heavie sat upon her palfrey slow;
Seemèd in heart some hidden care she had,
And by her in a line a milke white lambe she lad.

5

So pure and innocent, as that same lambe,
She was in life and every vertuous lore,
And by descent from Royall lynage came
Of ancient Kings and Queenes, that had of yore　　40
Their scepters stretcht from East to Westerne shore,
And all the world in their subjection held;
Till that infernall feend with foule uprore
Forwasted all their land, and them expeld:
Whom to avenge, she had this Knight from far compeld.

6

Behind her farre away a Dwarfe did lag,
That lasie seemed in being ever last,
Or wearièd with bearing of her bag
Of needments at his backe. Thus as they past,
The day with cloudes was suddeine overcast,　　50
And angry *Jove* an hideous storme of raine
Did poure into his Lemans lap so fast,
That every wight to shrowd [1] it did constrain,
And this fair couple eke to shroud themselves were fain.

7

Enforst to seeke some covert nigh at hand,
A shadie grove not far away they spide,

[1] take shelter

That promist ayde the tempest to withstand:
Whose loftie trees yclad with sommers pride,
Did spred so broad, that heavens light did hide,
Not perceable with power of any starre: 60
And all within were pathes and alleies wide,
With footing worne, and leading inward farre:
Faire harbour that them seemes; so in they entred arre.

8

And foorth they passe, with pleasure forward led,
Joying to heare the birdes sweete harmony,
Which therein shrouded from the tempest dred,
Seemd in their song to scorne the cruell sky.
Much can they prayse the trees so straight and hy,
The sayling Pine, the Cedar proud and tall,
The vine-prop Elme, the Poplar never dry,   70
The builder Oake, sole king of forrests all,
The Aspine good for staves, the Cypresse funerall.

9

The Laurell, meed of mightie Conquerours
And Poets sage, the Firre that weepeth still,
The Willow worne of forlorne Paramours,
The Eugh [1] obedient to the benders will,
The Birch for shaftes, the Sallow for the mill,
The Mirrhe sweete bleeding in the bitter wound,
The warlike Beech, the Ash for nothing ill,
The fruitful Olive, and the Platane round,   80
The carver Holme, the Maple seeldom inward sound.

[1] yew

10

Led with delight, they thus beguile the way,
Untill the blustring storme is overblowne;
When weening to returne, whence they did stray,
They cannot finde that path, which first was showne,
But wander too and fro in wayes unknowne,
Furthest from end then, when they neerest weene,
That makes them doubt, their wits be not their owne:
So many pathes, so many turnings seene,
That which of them to take, in diverse doubt they
　　　been.　　　　　　　　　　　　　　　　　90

11

At last resolving forward still to fare,
Till that some end they finde or in or out,
That path they take, that beaten seemed most bare,
And like to lead the labyrinth about; [1]
Which when by tract they hunted had throughout,
At length it brought them to a hollow cave,
Amid the thickest woods.　The Champion stout
Eftsoones dismounted from his courser brave,
And to the Dwarfe awhile his needlesse spere he gave.

12

Be well aware, quoth then that Ladie milde,　　100
Least suddaine mischiefe ye too rash provoke:
The danger hid, the place unknowne and wilde,
Breedes dreadfull doubts: Oft fire is without smoke,
And perill without show: therefore your stroke

[1] out of

Sir knight with-hold, till further triall made.
Ah Ladie (said he) shame were to revoke,
The forward footing for an hidden shade;[1]
Vertue gives her selfe light, through darkenesse for to
    wade.

13

Yea but (quoth she) the perill of this place
I better wot then you, though now too late,   110
To wish you backe returne with foule disgrace,
Yet wisedome warnes, whilest foot is in the gate,
To stay the steppe, ere forcèd to retrate.
This is the wandring wood, this *Errours den,*
A monster vile, whom God and man does hate:
Therefore I read beware. Fly fly (quoth then
The fearefull Dwarfe:) this is no place for living men.

14

But full of fire and greedy hardiment,
The youthful knight could not for ought be staide,
But forth unto the darksome hole he went,   120
And lookèd in: his glistring armor made
A little glooming light, much like a shade,
By which he saw the ugly monster plaine,
Halfe like a serpent horribly displaide,
But th'other halfe did womans shape retaine,
Most lothsom, filthie, foule, and full of vile disdaine.

15

And as she lay upon the durtie ground,
Her huge long taile her den all overspred,

[1] imaginary danger

Yet was in knots and many boughtes ¹ upwound,
Pointed with mortall sting. Of her there bred   130
A thousand yong ones, which she dayly fed,
Sucking upon her poisonous dugs, each one
Of sundry shapes, yet all ill favorèd:
Soone as that uncouth light upon them shone,
Into her mouth they crept, and suddain all were gone.

16

Their dam upstart, out of her den effraide,
And rushèd forth, hurling her hideous taile
About her cursèd head, whose folds displaid
Were stretcht now forth at length without entraile.
She lookt about, and seeing one in mayle   140
Armèd to point, sought backe to turne againe;
For light she hated as the deadly bale,
Ay wont in desert darknesse to remaine,
Where plaine none might her see, nor she see any plaine.

17

Which when the valiant Elfe perceiv'd, he lept
As Lyon fierce upon the flying pray,
And with his trenchand blade her boldly kept
From turning backe, and forcèd her to stay:
Therewith enrag'd she loudly gan to bray,
And turning fierce, her speckled taile advaunst,   150
Threatning her angry sting, him to dismay:
Who nought aghast, his mightie hand enhaunst:
The stroke down from her head unto her shoulder
        glaunst.

¹ coils

18

Much daunted with that dint, her sence was dazd,
Yet kindling rage, her selfe she gathered round,
And all attonce her beastly body raizd
With doubled forces high above the ground:
Tho wrapping up her wrethed sterne arownd,
Lept fierce upon his shield, and her huge traine
All suddenly about his body wound,   160
That hand or foot to stirre he strove in vaine:
God helpe the man so wrapt in *Errours* endlesse traine.

19

His Lady sad to see his sore constraint,
Cride out, Now now Sir Knight, shew what ye bee,
Add faith unto your force, and be not faint:
Strangle her, else she sure will strangle thee.
That when he heard, in great perplexitie,
His gall did grate [1] for griefe and high disdaine,
And knitting all his force got one hand free,
Wherewith he grypt her gorge with so great paine,   170
That soone to loose her wicked bands did her constraine.

20

Therewith she spewd out of her filthy maw
A floud of poyson horrible and blacke,
Full of great lumpes of flesh and gobbets raw,
Which stunck so vildly, that it forst him slacke
His grasping hold, and from her turne him backe:
Her vomit full of bookes and papers was,
With loathly frogs and toades, which eyes did lacke,

[1] anger did grow

And creeping sought way in the weedy gras:
Her filthy parbreake all the place defilèd has.   180

21

As when old father *Nilus* gins to swell
With timely pride above the *Ægyptian* vale,
His fattie waves do fertile slime outwell,
And overflow each plaine and lowly dale:
But when his later spring gins to avale,[1]
Huge heapes of mudd he leaves, wherein there breed
Ten thousand kindes of creatures, partly male
And partly female of his fruitfull seed;
Such ugly monstrous shapes elswhere may no man reed.

22

The same so sore annoyèd has the knight,   190
That welnigh chokèd with the deadly stinke,
His forces faile, ne can no longer fight.
Whose corage when the feend perceiv'd to shrinke,
She pourèd forth out of her hellish sinke
Her fruitfull cursèd spawne of serpents small,
Deformèd monsters, fowle, and blacke as inke,
Which swarming all about his legs did crall,
And him encombred sore, but could not hurt at all.

23

As gentle Shepheard in sweete even-tide,
When ruddy *Phœbus* gins to welke in west,   200
High on an hill, his flocke to vewen wide,
Markes which do byte their hasty supper best;
A cloud of combrous gnattes do him molest,

[1] subside

All striving to infixe their feeble stings,
That from their noyance he no where can rest,
But with his clownish hands their tender wings
He brusheth oft, and oft doth mar their murmurings.

24

Thus ill bestedd, and fearefull more of shame,
Then of the certaine perill he stood in,
Halfe furious unto his foe he came,   **210**
Resolv'd in minde all suddenly to win,
Or soone to lose, before he once would lin;
And strooke at her with more then manly force,
That from her body full of filthie sin
He raft her hatefull head without remorse;
A streame of cole black bloud forth gushèd from her
      corse.

25

Her scattred brood, soone as their Parent deare
They saw so rudely falling to the ground,
Groning full deadly, all with troublous feare,
Gathred themselves about her body round,   220
Weening their wonted entrance to have found
At her wide mouth: but being there withstood
They flockèd all about her bleeding wound,
And suckèd up their dying mothers blood,
Making her death their life, and eke her hurt their good.

26

That detestable sight him much amazde,
To see th'unkindly Impes of heaven accurst,

Devoure their dam; on whom while so he gazd,
Having all satisfied their bloudy thurst,
Their bellies swolne he saw with fulnesse burst,   230
And bowels gushing forth: well worthy end
Of such as drunke her life, the which them nurst;
Now needeth him no lenger labour spend,
His foes have slaine themselves, with whom he should
     contend.

27

His Ladie seeing all, that chaunst, from farre
Approcht in hast to greet his victorie,
And said, Faire knight, borne under happy starre,
Who see your vanquisht foes before you lye:
Well worthy be you of that Armorie
Wherein ye have great glory wonne this day,   240
And proov'd your strength on a strong enimie,
Your first adventure: many such I pray,
And henceforth ever wish, that like succeed it may.

28

Then mounted he upon his Steede againe,
And with the Lady backward sought to wend;
That path he kept, which beaten was most plaine.
Ne ever would to any by-way bend,
But still did follow one unto the end,
The which at last out of the wood them brought.
So forward on his way (with God to frend)   250
He passeth forth, and new adventure sought;
Long way he travellèd, before he heard of ought.

29

At length they chaunst to meet upon the way
An agèd Sire, in long blake weedes yclad,
His feete all bare, his beard all hoarie gray,
And by his belt his booke he hanging had;
Sober he seemde, and very sagely sad,
And to the ground his eyes were lowly bent,
Simple in shew, and voyde of malice bad,
And all the way he prayèd, as he went,   260
And often knockt his brest, as one that did repent.

30

He faire the knight saluted, louting low,
Who faire him quited, as that courteous was:
And after askèd him, if he did know
Of straunge adventures, which abroad did pas.
Ah my deare Sonne (quoth he) how should, alas,
Silly old man, that lives in hidden cell,
Bidding his beades all day for his trespas,
Tydings of warre and worldly trouble tell?
With holy father fits not with such things to mell.   270

31

But if of daunger which hereby doth dwell,
And homebred evill ye desire to heare,
Of a straunge man I can you tidings tell,
That wasteth all this countrey farre and neare.
Of such (said he) I chiefly do inquere,
And shall you well reward to shew the place,
In which that wicked wight his dayes doth weare

For to all knighthood it is foule disgrace,
That such a cursèd creature lives so long a space.

32

Far hence (quoth he) in wastfull wildernesse   280
His dwelling is, by which no living wight
May ever passe, but thorough great distresse.
Now (sayd the Lady) draweth toward night,
And well I wote, that of your later fight
Ye all forwearied be: for what so strong,
But wanting rest will also want of might?
The Sunne that measures heaven all day long,
At night doth baite his steedes the *Ocean* waves emong.

33

Then with the Sunne take Sir, your timely rest,
And with new day new worke at once begin: 290
Untroubled night they say gives counsell best.
Right well Sir knight ye have advisèd bin,
(Quoth then that aged man;) the way to win
Is wisely to advise: now day is spent;
Therefore with me ye may take up your In
For this same night. The knight was well content:
So with that godly father to his home they went.

34

A little lowly Hermitage it was,
Downe in a dale, hard by a forests side,
Far from resort of people, that did pas   300
In travell to and froe: a little wyde [1]
There was an holy Chappell edifyde,
  [1] distance apart

Wherein the Hermite dewly wont to say
His holy things each morne and eventyde:
Thereby a Christall streame did gently play,
Which from a sacred fountaine wellèd forth alway.

35

Arrivèd there, the little house they fill,
Ne looke for entertainement, where none was:
Rest is their feast, and all things at their will;
The noblest mind the best contentment has.   310
With faire discourse the evening so they pas:
For that old man of pleasing wordes had store,
And well could file his tongue as smooth as glas;
He told of Saintes and Popes, and evermore
He strowd an *Ave-Mary* after and before.

36

The drouping Night thus creepeth on them fast,
And the sad humour loading their eye liddes,
As messenger of *Morpheus* on them cast
Sweet slombring deaw, the which to sleepe them biddes.
Unto their lodgings then his guestes he riddes: 320
Where when all drownd in deadly sleepe he findes,
He to his study goes, and there amiddes
His Magick bookes and artes of sundry kindes,
He seekes out mighty charmes, to trouble sleepy mindes.

37

Then choosing out few wordes most horrible,
(Let none them read) thereof did verses frame,
With which and other spelles like terrible,
He bad awake blacke *Plutoes* griesly Dame,

And cursèd heaven, and spake reproachfull shame
Of highest God, the Lord of life and light;   330
A bold bad man, that dar'd to call by name
Great *Gorgon,* Prince of darknesse and dead night,
At which *Cocytus* quakes, and *Styx* is put to flight.

38

And forth he cald out of deepe darknesse dred
Legions of Sprights, the which like little flyes
Fluttering about his ever damnèd hed,
A-waite whereto their service he applyes,
To aide his friends, or fray his enimies:
Of those he chose out two, the falsest twoo,
And fittest for to forge true-seeming lyes;   340
The one of them he gave a message too,
The other by him selfe staide other worke to doo.

39

He making speedy way through spersèd ayre,
And through the world of waters wide and deepe,
To *Morpheus* house doth hastily repaire.
Amid the bowels of the earth full steepe,
And low, where dawning day doth never peepe,
His dwelling is; there *Tethys* his wet bed
Doth ever wash, and *Cynthia* still doth steepe
In silver deaw his ever-drouping hed,   350
Whiles sad Night over him her mantle black doth spred.

40

Whose double gates he findeth lockèd fast,
The one faire fram'd of burnisht Yvory,
The other all with silver overcast;

And wakefull dogges before them farre do lye,
Watching to banish Care their enimy,
Who oft is wont to trouble gentle sleepe.
By them the Sprite doth passe in quietly,
And unto *Morpheus* comes, whom drownèd deepe
In drowsie fit he findes: of nothing he takes keepe. 360

41

And more, to lulle him in his slumber soft,
A trickling streame from high rocke tumbling downe
And ever-drizling raine upon the loft,
Mixt with a murmuring winde, much like the sowne
Of swarming Bees, did cast him in a swowne:
No other noyse, nor peoples troublous cryes,
As still are wont t'annoy the walled towne,
Might there be heard: but carelesse Quiet lyes,
Wrapt in eternall silence farre from enemyes.

42

The messenger approaching to him spake,   370
But his wast wordes returned to him in vaine:
So sound he slept, that nought mought him awake.
Then rudely he him thrust, and pusht with paine,
Whereat he gan to stretch: but he againe
Shooke him so hard, that forcèd him to speake.
As one then in a dreame, whose dryer braine
Is tost with troubled sights and fancies weake,
He mumbled soft, but would not all his silence breake.

43

The Sprite then gan more boldly him to wake,
And threatned unto him the dreaded name   380

Of *Hecate;* whereat he gan to quake,
And lifting up his lumpish head, with blame
Halfe angry askèd him, for what he came.
Hither (quoth he) me *Archimago* sent,
He that the stubborne Sprites can wisely tame,
He bids thee to him send for his intent
A fit false dreame, that can delude the sleepers sent.

44

The God obayde, and calling forth straight way
A diverse dreame out of his prison darke,
Delivered it to him, and downe did lay   390
His heavie head, devoide of carefull carke,[1]
Whose sences all were straight benumbd and starke.
He backe returning by the Yvorie dore,
Remounted up as light as chearefull Larke,
And on his litle winges the dreame he bore
In hast unto his Lord, where he him left afore.

45

Who all this while with charmes and hidden artes,
Had made a Lady of that other Spright,
And fram'd of liquid ayre her tender partes
So lively, and so like in all mens sight,   400
That weaker sence it could have ravisht quight:
The maker selfe for all his wondrous witt,
Was nigh beguilèd with so goodly sight:
Her all in white he clad, and over it
Cast a blake stole, most like to seeme for *Una* fit.

[1] worry

46

Now when that ydle dreame was to him brought,
Unto that Elfin knight he bad him fly,
Where he slept soundly void of evill thought,
And with false shewes abuse his fantasy,
In sort as he him schoolèd privily: 410
And that new creature borne without her dew,[1]
Full of the makers guile, with usage sly
He taught to imitate that Lady trew,
Whose semblance she did carrie under feignèd hew.

47

Thus well instructed, to their worke they hast,
And comming where the knight in slumber lay,
The one upon his hardy head him plast,
And made him dreame of loves and lustfull play,
That night his manly hart did melt away,
Bathèd in wanton blis and wicked joy: 420
Then seemèd him his Lady by him lay,
And to him playnd, how that false wingèd boy,
Her chast hart had subdewd, to learne Dame pleasures
        toy.

48

And she her selfe of beautie soveraigne Queene,
Faire Venus seemde unto his bed to bring
Her, whom he waking evermore did weene,
To be the chastest flowre, that ay did spring
On earthly braunch, the daughter of a king,
Now a loose Leman to vile service bound:
[1] born unnaturally

And eke the *Graces* seemèd all to sing,   430
Hymen Iö Hymen, dauncing all around,
Whilst freshest *Flora* her with Yvie girlond crownd.

49

In this great passion of unwonted lust,
Or wonted feare of doing ought amis,
He started up, as seeming to mistrust,
Some secret ill, or hidden foe of his:
Lo there before his face his Lady is,
Under blake stole hyding her bayted hooke,
And as halfe blushing offred him to kis,
With gentle blandishment and lovely looke,   440
Most like that virgin true, which for her knight him
    took.

50

All cleane dismayd to see so uncouth sight,
And halfe enragèd at her shamelesse guise,
He thought have slaine her in his fierce despight:
But hasty heat tempring with sufferance wise,
He stayde his hand, and gan himselfe advise
To prove his sense, and tempt her faignèd truth.
Wringing her hands in wemens pitteous wise,
Tho can she weepe, to stirre up gentle ruth,
Both for her noble bloud, and for her tender youth. 450

51

And said, Ah Sir, my liege Lord and my love,
Shall I accuse the hidden cruell fate,
And mightie causes wrought in heaven above,
Or the blind God, that doth me thus amate,[1]
    [1] dismay

For hopèd love to winne me certaine hate?
Yet thus perforce he bids me do, or die.
Die is my dew: yet rew my wretched state
You, whom my hard avenging destinie
Hath made judge of my life or death indifferently.

52

Your owne deare sake forst me at first to leave   460
My Fathers kingdome, There she stopt with teares;
Her swollen hart her speach seemd to bereave,
And then againe begun, My weaker yeares
Captiv'd to fortune and frayle worldly feares,
Fly to your faith for succour and sure ayde:
Let me not dye in languor and long teares.
Why Dame (quoth he) what hath ye thus dismayd?
What frayes ye, that were wont to comfort me affrayd?

53

Love of your selfe, she said, and deare constraint
Lets me not sleepe, but wast the wearie night   470
In secret anguish and unpittied plaint,
Whiles you in carelesse sleepe are drownèd quight.
Her doubtfull words made that redoubted knight
Suspect her truth: yet since no'untruth he knew,
Her fawning love with foule disdainefull spight
He would not shend, but said, Deare dame I rew,
That for my sake unknowne such griefe unto you grew.

54

Assure your selfe, it fell not all to ground;
For all so deare as life is to my hart,
I deeme your love, and hold me to you bound;   480

Ne let vaine feares procure your needlesse smart,
Where cause is none, but to your rest depart.
Not all content, yet seemed she to appease
Her mournefull plaintes, beguilèd of her art,
And fed with words, that could not chuse but please,
So slyding softly forth, she turnd as to her ease.

55

Long after lay he musing at her mood,
Much griev'd to thinke that gentle Dame so light,
For whose defence he was to shed his blood.
At last dull wearinesse of former fight　　　490
Having yrockt asleepe his irkesome spright,
That troublous dreame gan freshly tosse his braine,
With bowres, and beds, and Ladies deare delight:
But when he saw his labour all was vaine,
With that misformèd spright he backe returnd againe.

CANTO II

The guilefull great Enchaunter parts
The Redcrosse Knight from Truth:
Into whose stead faire falshood steps,
And workes him wofull ruth.

1

By this the Northerne wagoner had set
His sevenfold teme behind the stedfast starre,
That was in Ocean waves yet never wet,
But firme is fixt, and sendeth light from farre
To all, that in the wide deepe wandring arre:
And chearefull Chauntclere with his note shrill
Had warnèd once, that *Phœbus* fiery carre

In hast was climbing up the Easterne hill,
Full envious that night so long his roome did fill.

2

When those accursèd messengers of hell,   10
That feigning dreame, and that faire-forgèd Spright
Came to their wicked maister, and gan tell
Their bootelesse paines, and ill succeeding night:
Who all in rage to see his skilfull might
Deluded so, gan threaten hellish paine
And sad *Proserpines* wrath, them to affright.
But when he saw his threatning was but vaine,
He cast about, and searcht his balefull bookes againe.

3

Eftsoones he tooke that miscreated faire,
And that false other Spright, on whom he spred   20
A seeming body of the subtile aire,
Like a young Squire, in loves and lusty-hed
His wanton dayes that ever loosely led,
Without regard of armes and dreaded fight:
Those two he tooke, and in a secret bed,
Covered with darknesse and misdeeming night,
Them both together laid, to joy in vaine delight.

4

Forthwith he runnes with feignèd faithfull hast
Unto his guest, who after troublous sights
And dreames, gan now to take more sound repast,   30
Whom suddenly he wakes with fearefull frights,
As one aghast with feends or damnèd sprights,
And to him cals, Rise rise unhappy Swaine,

That here wex old in sleepe, whiles wicked wights
Have knit themselves in *Venus* shamefull chaine;
Come see, where your false Lady doth her honour staine.

5

All in amaze he suddenly up start
With sword in hand, and with the old man went;
Who soone him brought into a secret part,
Where that false couple were full closely ment [1]   40
In wanton lust and lewd embracèment:
Which when he saw, he burnt with gealous fire,
The eye of reason was with rage yblent [2]
And would have slaine them in his furious ire,
But hardly was restreinèd of that agèd sire.

6

Returning to his bed in torment great,
And bitter anguish of his guiltie sight,
He could not rest, but did his stout heart eat,
And wast his inward gall with deepe despight,
Yrkesome of life, and too long lingring night.   50
At last faire *Hesperus* in highest skie
Had spent his lampe, and brought forth dawning light,
Then up he rose, and clad him hastily;
The Dwarfe him brought his steed: so both away do fly.

7

Now when the rosy-fingred Morning faire,
Weary of agèd *Tithones* saffron bed,
Had spred her purple robe through deawy aire,
And the high hils *Titan* discoverèd,

[1] mingled   [2] blinded

The royall virgin shooke off drowsy-hed,
And rising forth out of her baser bowre,   60
Lookt for her knight, who far away was fled,
And for her Dwarfe, that wont to wait each houre;
Then gan she waile and weepe, to see that woefull
      stowre.

8

And after him she rode with so much speede
As her slow beast could make, but all in vaine;
For him so far had borne his light-foot steede,
Prickèd with wrath and fiery fierce disdaine,
That him to follow was but fruitlesse paine;
Yet she her weary limbes would never rest,
But every hill and dale, each wood and plaine   70
Did search, sore grievèd in her gentle brest,
He so ungently left her, whom she lovèd best.

9

But subtill *Archimago,* when his guests
He saw divided into double parts,
And *Una* wandring in woods and forrests,
Th'end of his drift, he praisd his divelish arts,
That had such might over true meaning harts;
Yet rests not so, but other meanes doth make,
How he may worke unto her further smarts:
For her he hated as the hissing snake,   80
And in her many troubles did most pleasure take.

10

He then devisde himself how to disguise;
For by his mightie science he could take

As many formes and shapes in seeming wise,
As ever *Proteus* to himselfe could make:
Sometime a fowle, sometime a fish in lake,
Now like a foxe, now like a dragon fell,
That of himselfe he oft for feare would quake,
And oft would flie away. O who can tell
The hidden power of herbes, and might of Magicke
    spell? 90

11

But now seemde best, the person to put on
Of that good knight, his late beguilèd guest:
In mighty armes he was yclad anon:
And silver shield: upon his coward brest
A bloudy crosse, and on his craven crest
A bounch of haires discolourd diversly:
Full jolly knight he seemde, and well addrest,
And when he sate upon his courser free,
Saint George himself ye would have deemèd him to be.

12

But he the knight, whose semblaunt he did beare, 100
The true *Saint George* was wandred far away,
Still flying from his thoughts and gealous feare;
Will was his guide, and griefe led him astray.
At last him chaunst to meete upon the way
A faithlesse Sarazin all arm'd to point,
In whose great shield was writ with letters gay
Sans foy: full large of limbe and every joint
He was, and carèd not for God or man a point.

13

He had a faire companion of his way,
A goodly Lady clad in scarlot red,   110
Purfled with gold and pearle of rich assay,
And like a *Persian* mitre on her hed.
She wore, with crownes and owches garnishèd,
The which her lavish lovers to her gave;
Her wanton palfrey all was overspred
With tinsell trappings, woven like a wave,
Whose bridle rung with golden bels and bosses brave.

14

With faire disport and courting dalliaunce
She intertainde her lover all the way:
But when she saw the knight his speare advaunce,   120
She soone left off her mirth and wanton play,
And bad her knight addresse him to the fray:
His foe was nigh at hand. He, prikt with pride
And hope to winne his Ladies heart that day,
Forth spurrèd fast: adowne his coursers side
The red bloud trickling staind the way, as he did ride.

15

The knight of the *Redcrosse* when him he spide,
Spurring so hote with rage dispiteous,
Gan fairely couch his speare, and towards ride:
Soone meete they both, both fell and furious,   130
That daunted with their forces hideous,
Their steeds do stagger, and amazèd stand,
And eke themselves too rudely rigorous,

Astonied with the stroke of their owne hand,
Do backe rebut, and each to other yeeldeth land.

16

As when two rams stird with ambitious pride,
Fight for the rule of the rich fleecèd flocke,
Their hornèd fronts so fierce on either side
Do meete, that with the terrour of the shocke
Astonied both, stand sencelesse as a blocke,   140
Forgetfull of the hanging victory:
So stood these twaine, unmovèd as a rocke,
Both staring fierce, and holding idely,
The broken reliques of their former cruelty.

17

The *Sarazin* sore daunted with the buffe
Snatcheth his sword, and fiercely to him flies;
Who well it wards, and quyteth cuff with cuff:
Each others equall puissaunce envies,
And through their iron sides with cruelties
Does seeke to perce: repining courage yields   150
No foote to foe. The flashing fier flies
As from a forge out of their burning shields,
And streames of purple bloud new dies the verdant
        fields.

18

Curse on that Crosse (quoth then the *Sarazin*)
That keepes thy body from the bitter fit; [1]
Dead long ygoe I wote thou haddest bin,
Had not that charme from thee forwarnèd it:
        [1] death agony

But yet I warne thee now assurèd sitt,
And hide thy head.   Therewith upon his crest
With rigour so outrageous he smitt,   160
That a large share it hewd out of the rest,
And glauncing downe his shield, from blame him fairely
     blest.

19

Who thereat wondrous wroth, the sleeping spark
Of native vertue gan eftsoones revive,
And at his haughtie helmet making mark,
So hugely stroke, that it the steele did rive,
And cleft his head.   He tumbling downe alive,
With bloudy mouth his mother earth did kis,
Greeting his grave: his grudging ghost did strive
With the fraile flesh; at last it flitted is,   170
Whither the soules do fly of men, that live amis.

20

The Lady when she saw her champion fall,
Like the old ruines of a broken towre,
Staid not to waile his woefull funerall,
But from him fled away with all her powre;
Who after her as hastily gan scowre,
Bidding the Dwarfe with him to bring away
The *Sarazins* shield, signe of the conqueroure.
Her soone he overtooke, and bad to stay,
For present cause was none of dread her to dismay.   180

21

She turning backe with ruefull countenaunce,
Cride, Mercy mercy Sir vouchsafe to show

On silly Dame, subject to hard mischaunce,
And to your mighty will. Her humblesse low
In so ritch weedes and seeming glorious show,
Did much emmove his stout heroïcke heart,
And said, Deare dame, your suddein overthrow
Much rueth me; but now put feare apart,
And tell, both who ye be, and who that tooke your part.

22

Melting in teares, then gan she thus lament;⠀⠀⠀⠀⠀190
The wretched woman, whom unhappy howre
Hath now made thrall to your commandement,
Before that angry heavens list to lowre,
And fortune false betraide me to your powre,
Was (O what now availeth that I was!)
Borne the sole daughter of an Emperour,
He that the wide West under his rule has,
And high hath set his throne, where *Tiberis* doth pas.

23

He in the first flowre of my freshest age,
Betrothèd me unto the onely haire⠀⠀⠀⠀⠀200
Of a most mighty king, most rich and sage;
Was never Prince so faithfull and so faire,
Was never Prince so meeke and debonaire;
But ere my hopèd day of spousall shone,
My dearest Lord fell from high honours staire,
Into the hands of his accursèd fone,[1]
And cruelly was slaine, that shall I ever mone.

---

[1] foes

24

His blessèd body spoild of lively breath,
Was afterward, I know not how, convaid
And from me hid: of whose most innocent death   210
When tidings came to me unhappy maid,
O how great sorrow my sad soule assaid.
Then forth I went his woefull corse to find,
And many yeares throughout the world I straid,
A virgin widow, whose deepe wounded mind
With love, long time did languish as the stricken hind.

25

At last it chancèd this proud *Sarazin*,
To meete me wandring, who perforce me led
With him away, but yet could never win
The Fort, that Ladies hold in soveraigne dread.   220
There lies he now with foule dishonour dead,
Who whiles he liv'de, was callèd proud *Sans foy*,
The eldest of three brethren, all three bred
Of one bad sire, whose youngest is *Sans joy*,
And twixt them both was borne the bloudy bold *Sans loy*.

26

In this sad plight, friendlesse, unfortunate,
Now miserable I *Fidessa* dwell,
Craving of you in pitty of my state,
To do none ill, if please ye not do well.
He in great passion all this while did dwell,   230
More busying his quicke eyes, her face to view,
Then his dull eares, to heare what she did tell;

And said, faire Lady hart of flint would rew
The undeservèd woes and sorrowes, which ye shew.

27

Henceforth in safe assuraunce may ye rest,
Having both found a new friend you to aid,
And lost an old foe, that did you molest:
Better new friend then an old foe is said.
With chaunge of cheare the seeming simple maid
Let fall her eyen, as shamefast to the earth,   240
And yeelding soft, in that she nought gain-said,
So forth they rode, he feining seemely merth,
And she coy lookes: so dainty they say maketh derth.

28

Long time they thus together traveilèd,
Till weary of their way, they came at last,
Where grew two goodly trees, that faire did spred
Their armes abroad, with gray mosse overcast,
And their greene leaves trembling with every blast,
Made a calme shadow far in compasse round:
The fearefull Shepheard often there aghast   250
Under them never sat, ne wont there sound
His mery oaten pipe, but shund th'unlucky ground.

29

But this good knight soone as he them can spie,
For the coole shade him thither hastly got:
For golden *Phœbus* now ymounted hie,
From fiery wheeles of his faire chariot
Hurlèd his beame so scorching cruell hot,
That living creature mote it not abide;

And his new Lady it endurèd not.

There they alight, in hope themselves to hide   260
From the fierce heat, and rest their weary limbs a tide.

30

Faire seemely pleasaunce each to other makes,
With goodly purposes there as they sit:
And in his falsèd fancy he her takes
To be the fairest wight, that livèd yit;
Which to expresse, he bends his gentle wit,
And thinking of those braunches greene to frame
A girlond for her dainty forehead fit,
He pluckt a bough: out of whose rift there came
Small drops of gory bloud, that trickled downe the
          same.   270

31

Therewith a piteous yelling voyce was heard,
Crying, O spare with guilty hands to teare
My tender sides in this rough rynd embard,[1]
But fly, ah fly far hence away, for feare
Least to you hap, that happened to me heare,
And to this wretched Lady, my deare love,
O too deare love, love bought with death too deare.
Astond he stood, and up his haire did hove,
And with that suddein horror could no member move.

32

At last whenas the dreadfull passion   280
Was overpast, and manhood well awake,
Yet musing at the straunge occasion,
  [1] confined

And doubting much his sence, he thus bespake;
What voyce of damnèd Ghost from *Limbo* lake,
Or guilefull spright wandring in empty aire,
Both which fraile men do oftentimes mistake,
Sends to my doubtfull eares these speaches rare,
And ruefull plaints, me bidding guiltlesse bloud to spare?

33

Then groning deepe, Nor damnèd Ghost (quoth he),
Nor guilefull sprite to thee these wordes doth speake, 290
But once a man *Fradubio,* now a tree,
Wretched man, wretched tree; whose nature weake,
A cruell witch her cursèd will to wreake,
Hath thus transformd, and plast in open plaines,
Where *Boreas* doth blow full bitter bleake,
And scorching Sunne does dry my secret vaines:
For though a tree I seeme, yet cold and heat me paines.

34

Say on *Fradubio* then, or man, or tree,
Quoth then the knight, by whose mischievous arts
Art thou misshapèd thus, as now I see?   300
He oft finds med'cine, who his griefe imparts;
But double griefs afflict concealing harts,
As raging flames who striveth to suppresse.
The author then (said he) of all my smarts,
Is one *Duessa* a false sorceresse,
That many errant knights hath brought to wretched-
        nesse.

35

In prime of youthly yeares, when corage hot
The fire of love and joy of chevalree

First kindled in my brest, it was my lot
To love this gentle Lady, whom ye see,   310
Now not a Lady, but a seeming tree;
With whom as once I rode accompanyde,
Me chauncèd of a knight encountred bee,
That had a like faire Lady by his syde,
Like a faire Lady, but did fowle *Duessa* hyde.

36

Whose forgèd beauty he did take in hand,[1]
All other Dames to have exceeded farre;
I in defence of mine did likewise stand,
Mine, that did then shine as the Morning starre:
So both to battell fierce arraungèd arre,   320
In which his harder fortune was to fall
Under my speare: such is the dye of warre:
His Lady left as a prise martiall,
Did yield her comely person, to be at my call.

37

So doubly lov'd of Ladies unlike faire,
Th'one seeming such, the other such indeede,
One day in doubt I cast for to compare,
Whether [2] in beauties glorie did exceede;
A Rosy girlond was the victors meede:
Both seemde to win, and both seemde won to bee,   330
So hard the discord was to be agreede.
Frœlissa was as faire, as faire mote bee,
And ever false *Duessa* seemde as faire as shee.

    [1] maintain   [2] which of two

38

The wicked witch now seeing all this while
The doubtfull ballaunce equally to sway,
What not by right, she cast to win by guile,
And by her hellish science raisd streightway
A foggy mist, that overcast the day,
And a dull blast, that breathing on her face,
Dimmèd her former beauties shining ray,   340
And with foule ugly forme did her disgrace:
Then was she faire alone, when none was faire in place.

39

Then cride she out, Fye, fye, deformèd wight,
Whose borrowed beautie now appeareth plaine
To have before bewitchèd all mens sight;
O leave her soone, or let her soone be slaine.
Her loathly visage viewing with disdaine,
Eftsoones I thought her such, as she me told,
And would have kild her; but with faignèd paine,
The false witch did my wrathfull hand withhold;   350
So left her, where she now is turnd to treen mould.[1]

40

Thenceforth I tooke *Duessa* for my Dame,
And in the witch unweening joyd long time,
Ne ever wist, but that she was the same,
Till on a day (that day is every Prime,[2]
When Witches wont do penance for their crime)
I chaunst to see her in her proper hew,
Bathing her selfe in origane and thyme:

___

[1] form of a tree   [2] Springtime

A filthy foule old woman I did vew,
That ever to have toucht her, I did deadly rew. 360

41

Her neather partes misshapen, monstruous,
Were hidd in water, that I could not see,
But they did seeme more foule and hideous,
Then womans shape man would beleeve to bee.
Thenceforth from her most beastly companie
I gan refraine, in minde to slip away,
Soone as appeard safe opportunitie:
For danger great, if not assur'd decay
I saw before mine eyes, if I were knowne to stray.

42

The divelish hag by chaunges of my cheare 370
Perceiv'd my thought, and drownd in sleepie night,
With wicked herbes and ointments did besmeare
My bodie all, through charmes and magicke might,
That all my senses were bereavèd quight:
Then brought she me into this desert waste,
And by my wretched lovers side me pight,
Where now enclosd in wooden wals full faste,
Banisht from living wights, our wearie dayes we waste.

43

But how long time, said then the Elfin knight,
Are you in this misformèd house to dwell? 380
We may not chaunge (quoth he) this evil plight,
Till we be bathèd in a living well;
That is the terme prescribèd by the spell.

O how, said he, mote I that well out find,
That may restore you to your wonted well? [1]
Time and suffisèd fates to former kynd
Shall us restore, none else from hence may us unbynd.

44

The false *Duessa,* now *Fidessa* hight,
Heard how in vaine *Fradubio* did lament,
And knew well all was true. But the good knight 390
Full of sad feare and ghastly dreriment,
When all this speech the living tree had spent,
The bleeding bough did thrust into the ground,
That from the bloud he might be innocent,
And with fresh clay did close the wooden wound:
Then turning to his Lady, dead with feare her found.

45

Her seeming dead he found with feignèd feare,
As all unweeting of that well she knew,
And paynd himselfe with busie care to reare
Her out of carelesse swowne. Her eylids blew 400
And dimmèd sight with pale and deadly hew
At last she up gan lift: with trembling cheare
Her up he tooke, too simple and too trew,
And oft her kist. At length all passèd feare,
He set her on her steede, and forward forth did beare.
   [1] accustomed well-being

CANTO III

Forsaken Truth long seekes her love,
And makes the Lyon mylde,
Marres blind Devotions mart, and fals
In hand of leachour vylde.

1

Nought is there under heav'ns wide hollownesse,
That moves more deare compassion of mind,
Then beautie brought t'unworthy wretchednesse
Through envies snares or fortunes freakes unkind:
I, whether lately through her brightnesse blind,
Or through alleageance and fast fealtie,
Which I do owe unto all woman kind,
Feele my heart perst with so great agonie,
When such I see, that all for pittie I could die.

2

And now it is empassionèd so deepe,   10
For fairest *Unaes* sake, of whom I sing,
That my fraile eyes these lines with teares do steepe,
To thinke how she through guilefull handeling,
Though true as touch, though daughter of a king,
Though faire as ever living wight was faire,
Though nor in word nor deede ill meriting,
Is from her knight divorcèd in despaire
And her due loves deriv'd to that vile witches share.

3

Yet she most faithfull Ladie all this while
Forsaken, wofull, solitarie mayd   20
Farre from all peoples prease, as in exile,

In wildernesse and wastfull deserts strayd,
To seeke her knight; who subtilly betrayd
Through that late vision, which th'Enchaunter wrought,
Had her abandoned. She of nought affrayd,
Through woods and wastnesse wide him daily sought;
Yet wishèd tydings none of him unto her brought.

4

One day nigh wearie of the yrkesome way,
From her unhastie beast she did alight,
And on the grasse her daintie limbes did lay   30
In secret shadow, farre from all mens sight:
From her faire head her fillet she undight,
And laid her stole aside. Her angels face
As the great eye of heaven shynèd bright,
And made a sunshine in the shadie place;
Did never mortall eye behold such heavenly grace.

5

It fortunèd out of the thickest wood
A ramping Lyon rushèd suddainly,
Hunting full greedie after salvage blood;
Soone as the royall virgin he did spy,   40
With gaping mouth at her ran greedily,
To have attonce devour'd her tender corse:
But to the pray when as he drew more ny,
His bloudie rage asswagèd with remorse,
And with the sight amazd, forgot his furious forse.

6

In stead thereof he kist her wearie feet,
And lickt her lilly hands with fawning tong,
As he her wrongèd innocence did weet.
O how can beautie maister the most strong,

And simple true subdue avenging wrong!   50
Whose yeelded pride and proud submission,
Still dreading death, when she had markèd long,
Her hart gan melt in great compassion,
And drizling teares did shed for pure affection.

7

The Lyon Lord of every beast in field
Quoth she, his princely puissance doth abate,
And mightie proud to humble weake does yield,
Forgetfull of the hungry rage, which late
Him prickt, in pittie of my sad estate:
But he my Lyon, and my noble Lord   60
How does he find in cruell hart to hate
Her that him lov'd, and ever most adord,
As the God of my life? why hath he me abhord?

8

Redounding teares did choke th'end of her plaint,
Which softly ecchoed from the neighbour wood;
And sad to see her sorrowfull constraint
The kingly beast upon her gazing stood;
With pittie calmd, downe fell his angry mood.
At last in close hart shutting up her paine,
Arose the virgin borne of heavenly brood,   70
And to her snowy Palfrey got againe,
To seeke her strayèd Champion, if she might attaine.

9

The Lyon would not leave her desolate,
But with her went along, as a strong gard

Of her chast person, and a faithfull mate
Of her sad troubles and misfortunes hard:
Still when she slept, he kept both watch and ward,
And when she wakt, he waited diligent,
With humble service to her will prepard:
From her faire eyes he tooke commaundement,   80
And ever by her lookes conceivèd her intent.

10

Long she thus traveilèd through deserts wyde,
By which she thought her wandring knight shold pas,
Yet never shew of living wight espyde;
Till that at length she found the troden gras,
In which the tract of peoples footing was,
Under the steepe foot of a mountaine hore;
The same she followes, till at last she has
A damzell spyde slow footing her before,
That on her shoulders sad a pot of water bore.   90

11

To whom approaching she to her gan call,
To weet, if dwelling place were nigh at hand;
But the rude wench her answer'd nought at all,
She could not heare, nor speake, nor understand;
Till seeing by her side the Lyon stand,
With suddaine feare her pitcher downe she threw,
And fled away: for never in that land
Face of faire Ladie she before did vew,
And that dread Lyons looke her cast in deadly hew.

12

Full fast she fled, ne ever lookt behynd,   100
As if her life upon the wager lay,

And home she came, whereas her mother blynd
Sate in eternall night: nought could she say,
But suddaine catching hold, did her dismay
With quaking hands, and other signes of feare:
Who full of ghastly fright and cold affray,
Gan shut the dore. By this arrivèd there
Dame *Una,* wearie Dame, and entrance did requere.

13

Which when none yeelded, her unruly Page
With his rude clawes the wicket open rent,   110
And let her in; where of his cruell rage
Nigh dead with feare, and faint astonishment,
She found them both in darkesome corner pent;
Where that old woman day and night did pray
Upon her beades devoutly penitent;
Nine hundred *Pater nosters* every day,
And thrise nine hundred *Aves* she was wont to say.

14

And to augment her painefull pennance more,
Thrise every weeke in ashes she did sit,
And next her wrinkled skin rough sackcloth wore,   120
And thrise three times did fast from any bit:
But now for feare her beads she did forget.
Whose needlesse dread for to remove away,
Faire *Una* framèd words and count'nance fit:
Which hardly doen, at length she gan them pray,
That in their cotage small, that night she rest her may.

15

The day is spent, and commeth drowsie night,
When every creature shrowded is in sleepe;

Sad *Una* downe her laies in wearie plight,
And at her feet the Lyon watch doth keepe: 130
In stead of rest, she does lament, and weepe
For the late losse of her deare lovèd knight,
And sighes, and grones, and evermore does steepe
Her tender brest in bitter teares all night,
All night she thinks too long, and often lockes for light.

16

Now when *Aldeboran* was mounted hie
Above the shynie *Cassiopeias* chaire,
And all in deadly sleepe did drownèd lie,
One knockèd at the dore, and in would fare;
He knockèd fast, and often curst, and sware,   140
That readie entrance was not at his call:
For on his backe a heavy load he bare
Of nightly stelths and pillage severall,
Which he had got abroad by purchase [1] criminall.

17

He was to weet a stout and sturdie thiefe,
Wont to robbe Churches of their ornaments,
And poore mens boxes of their due reliefe,
Which given was to them for good intents;
The holy Saints of their rich vestiments
He did disrobe, when all men carelesse slept,   150
And spoild the Priests of their habiliments,
Whiles none the holy things in safety kept;
Then he by cunning sleights in at the window crept.

[1] contrivance

18

And all that he by right or wrong could find,
Unto this house he brought, and did bestow
Upon the daughter of this woman blind,
Abessa daughter of *Corceca* slow,
With whom he whoredome usd, that few did know,
And fed her fat with feast of offerings,
And plentie, which in all the land did grow;   160
Ne sparèd he to give her gold and rings:
And now he to her brought part of his stolen things.

19

Thus long the dore with rage and threats he bet,
Yet of those fearefull women none durst rize,
The Lyon frayèd them, him in to let:
He would no longer stay him to advize,
But open breakes the dore in furious wize,
And entring is; when that disdainfull beast
Encountring fierce, him suddaine doth surprize,
And seizing cruell clawes on trembling brest,   170
Under his Lordly foot him proudly hath supprest.

20

Him booteth [1] not resist, nor succour call,
His bleeding hart is in the vengers hand,
Who streight him rent in thousand peeces small,
And quite dismembred hath: the thirstie land
Drunke up his life; his corse left on the strand.
His fearefull friends weare out the wofull night,
Ne dare to weepe, nor seeme to understand

[1] profits

The heavie hap, which on them is alight,
Affraid, least to themselves the like mishappen might. 180

21

Now when broad day the world discoverèd has,
Up *Una* rose, up rose the Lyon eke,
And on their former journey forward pas,
In wayes unknowne, her wandring knight to seeke,
With paines farre passing that long wandring *Greeke,*
That for his love refusèd deitie;
Such were the labours of this Lady meeke,
Still seeking him, that from her still did flie,
Then furthest from her hope, when most she weenèd
      nie.

22

Soone as she parted thence, the fearefull twaine,   190
That blind old woman and her daughter deare
Came forth, and finding *Kirkrapine* there slaine,
For anguish great they gan to rend their heare,
And beat their brests, and naked flesh to teare.
And when they both had wept and wayld their fill,
Then forth they ranne like two amazèd deare,
Halfe mad through malice, and revenging will,
To follow her, that was the causer of their ill.

23

Whom overtaking, they gan loudly bray,
With hollow howling, and lamenting cry,   200
Shamefully at her rayling all the way,
And her accusing of dishonesty,
That was the flowre of faith and chastity;

And still amidst her rayling, she did pray,
That plagues, and mischiefs, and long misery
Might fall on her, and follow all the way,
And that in endlesse error she might ever stray.

24

But when she saw her prayers nought prevaile,
She backe returnèd with some labour lost;
And in the way as she did weepe and waile,   210
A knight her met in mighty armes embost,
Yet knight was not for all his bragging bost,
But subtill *Archimag,* that *Una* sought
By traynes [1] into new troubles to have tost:
Of that old woman tydings he besought,
If that of such a Ladie she could tellen ought.

25

Therewith she gan her passion to renew,
And cry, and curse, and raile, and rend her heare,
Saying, that harlot she too lately knew,
That causd her shed so many a bitter teare,   220
And so forth told the story of her feare:
Much seemèd he to mone her haplesse chaunce,
And after for that Ladie did inquere;
Which being taught, he forward gan advaunce
His faire enchaunted steed, and eke his charmèd launce.

26

Ere long he came, where *Una* traveild slow,
And that wilde Champion wayting her besyde:
Whom seeing such, for dread he durst not show

[1] tricks

Himselfe too nigh at hand, but turnèd wyde
Unto an hill; from whence when she him spyde, 230
By his like seeming shield, her knight by name
She weend it was, and towards him gan ryde:
Approaching nigh, she wist it was the same,
And with faire fearefull humblesse towards him she
    came.

27

And weeping said, Ah my long lackèd Lord,
Where have ye bene thus long out of my sight?
Much fearèd I to have bene quite abhord,
Or ought have done, that ye displeasen might,
That should as death unto my deare hart light:
For since mine eye your joyous sight did mis, 240
My chearefull day is turnd to chearelesse night,
And eke my night of death the shadow is;
But welcome now my light, and shining lampe of bliss.

28

He thereto meeting said, My dearest Dame,
Farre be it from your thought, and fro my will,
To thinke that knighthood I so much should shame,
As you to leave, that have me lovèd still,
And chose in Faery court of meere goodwill,
Where noblest knights were to be found on earth:
The earth shall sooner leave her kindly skill 250
To bring forth fruit, and make eternall derth.
Then I leave you, my liefe, yborne of heavenly berth.

29

And sooth to say, why I left you so long,
Was for to seeke adventure in strange place,

Where *Archimago* said a felon strong
To many knights did daily worke disgrace;
But knight he now shall never more deface:
Good cause of mine excuse; that mote ye please
Well to accept, and evermore embrace
My faithfull service, that by land and seas   260
Have vowd you to defend, now then your plaint appease.

30

His lovely words her seemd due recompence
Of all her passèd paines: one loving howre
For many yeares of sorrow can dispence:
A dram of sweet is worth a pound of sowre:
She has forgot, how many a wofull stowre
For him she late endur'd; she speakes no more
Of past: true is, that true love hath no powre
To looken backe; his eyes be fixt before.
Before her stands her knight, for whom she toyld so
          sore.   270

31

Much like, as when the beaten marinere,
That long hath wandred in the *Ocean* wide.
Oft soust in swelling *Tethys* saltish teare,
And long time having tand his tawney hide
With blustring breath of heaven, that none can bide,
And scorching flames of fierce *Orions* hound,
Soone as the port from farre he has espide,
His chearefull whistle merrily doth sound,
And *Nereus* crownes with cups; his mates him pledg
          around.

32

Such joy made *Una,* when her knight she found;　　**280**
And eke th'enchaunter joyous seemd no lesse,
Then the glad marchant, that does vew from ground
His ship farre come from watrie wildernesse,
He hurles out vowes, and *Neptune* oft doth blesse:
So forth they past, and all the way they spent
Discoursing of her dreadfull late distresse,
In which he askt her, what the Lyon ment:
Who told her all that fell [1] in journey as she went.

33

They had not ridden farre, when they might see
One pricking towards them with hastie heat,　　**290**
Full strongly armd, and on a courser free,
That through his fiercenesse fomèd all with sweat,
And the sharpe yron did for anger eat,
When his hot ryder spurd his chauffèd side;
His looke was sterne, and seemèd still to threat
Cruell revenge, which he in hart did hyde,
And on his shield *Sans loy* in bloudie lines was dyde.

34

When nigh he drew unto this gentle payre
And saw the Red-crosse, which the knight did beare,
He burnt in fire, and gan eftsoones prepare　　**300**
Himselfe to battell with his couchèd speare.
Loth was that other, and did faint through feare,
To taste th'untryèd dint of deadly steele;
But yet his Lady did so well him cheare,

[1] *i. e.* all that befell her

That hope of new goodhap he gan to feele;
So bent his speare, and spurnd his horse with yron
    heele.

35

But that proud Paynim forward came so fierce,
And full of wrath, that with his sharp-head speare
Through vainely crossèd shield he quite did pierce,
And had his staggering steede not shrunke for feare, 310
Through shield and bodie eke he should him beare:
Yet so great was the puissance of his push,
That from his saddle quite he did him beare:
He tombling rudely downe to ground did rush,
And from his gorèd wound a well of bloud did gush.

36

Dismounting lightly from his loftie steed,
He to him lept, in mind to reave his life,
And proudly said, Lo there the worthie meed
Of him, that slew *Sansfoy* with bloudie knife;
Henceforth his ghost freed from repining strife,   320
In peace may passen over *Lethe* lake,
When morning altars purgd with enemies life,
The blacke infernall *Furies* doen aslake:
Life from *Sansfoy* thou tookst, *Sansloy* shall from thee
    take.

37

Therewith in haste his helmet gan unlace,
Till *Una* cride, O hold that heavie hand,
Deare Sir, what ever that thou be in place:
Enough is, that thy foe doth vanquisht stand
Now at thy mercy: Mercie not withstand:

For he is one the truest knight alive, 330
Though conquered now he lie on lowly land,
And whilest him fortune favourd, faire did thrive
In bloudie field: therefore of life him not deprive.

38

Her piteous words might not abate his rage,
But rudely rending up his helmet, would
Have slaine him straight: but when he sees his age,
And hoarie head of *Archimago* old,
His hastie hand he doth amazèd hold,
And halfe ashamèd, wondred at the sight:
For the old man well knew he, though untold, 340
In charmes and magicke to have wondrous might,
Ne ever wont in field, ne in round lists to fight.

39

And said, Why *Archimago*, lucklesse syre,
What doe I see? what hard mishap is this,
That hath thee hither brought to taste mine yre?
Or thine the fault, or mine the error is,
In stead of foe to wound my friend amis?
He answered nought, but in a traunce still lay,
And on those guilefull dazèd eyes of his
The cloud of death did sit. Which doen away, 350
He left him lying so, ne would no lenger stay.

40

But to the virgin comes, who all this while
Amasèd stands, her selfe so mockt to see
By him, who has the guerdon of his guile,
For so misfeigning her true knight to bee:

Yet is she now in more perplexitie,
Left in the hand of that same Paynim bold,
From whom her booteth not at all to flie;
Who by her cleanly garment catching hold,
Her from her Palfrey pluckt, her visage to behold. 360

41

But her fierce servant full of kingly awe
And high disdaine, when as his soveraine Dame
So rudely handled by her foe he sawe,
With gaping jawes full greedy at him came,
And ramping on his shield, did weene the same
Have reft away with his sharpe rending clawes:
But he was stout, and lust did now inflame
His corage more, that from his griping pawes
He hath his shield redeem'd, and foorth his swerd he
        drawes.

42

O then too weake and feeble was the forse   370
Of salvage beast, his puissance to withstand:
For he was strong, and of so mightie corse,
As ever wielded speare in warlike hand,
And feates of armes did wisely understand.
Eftsoones he percèd through his chaufèd chest
With thrilling [1] point of deadly yron brand,
And launcht his Lordly hart: with death opprest
He roar'd aloud, whiles life forsooke his stubborne brest.

43

Who now is left to keepe the forlorne maid
From raging spoile of lawlesse victors will?   380

[1] piercing

Her faithfull gard remov'd, her hope dismaid,
Her selfe a yeelded pray to save or spill.
He now Lord of the field, his pride to fill,
With foule reproches, and disdainfull spight
Her vildly entertaines, and will or nill,
Beares her away upon his courser light:
Her prayers nought prevaile, his rage is more of might.

44

And all the way, with great lamenting paine,
And piteous plaints she filleth his dull eares,
That stony hart could riven have in twaine,   390
And all the way she wets with flowing teares:
But he enrag'd with rancor, nothing heares.
Her servile beast yet would not leave her so,
But followes her farre off, ne ought he feares,
To be partaker of her wandering woe,
More mild in beastly kind, then that her beastly foe.

CANTO IV

To sinfull house of Pride, Duessa
guides the faithfull knight,
Where brothers death to wreak Sansjoy
doth chalenge him to fight.

1

Young knight, whatever that dost armes professe,
And through long labours huntest after fame,
Beware of fraud, beware of ficklenesse,
In choice, and change of thy deare lovèd Dame,
Least thou of her beleeve too lightly blame,
And rash misweening doe thy hart remove:

For unto knight there is no greater shame,
Then lightnesse and inconstancie in love;
That doth this *Redcrosse* knights ensample plainly
    prove.

2

Who after that he had faire *Una* lorne,   10
Through light misdeeming of her loialtie,
And false *Duessa* in her sted had borne,
Callèd *Fidess'*, and so supposed to bee;
Long with her traveild, till at last they see
A goodly building, bravely garnishèd,
The house of mightie Prince it seemed to bee:
And towards it a broad high way that led,
All bare through peoples feet, which thither traveilèd.

3

Great troupes of people traveild thitherward
Both day and night, of each degree and place,   20
But few returnèd, having scapèd hard,
With balefull beggerie, or foule disgrace,
Which ever after in most wretched case,
Like loathsome lazars, by the hedges lay.
Thither *Duessa* bad him bend his pace:
For she is wearie of the toilesome way,
And also nigh consumèd is the lingring day.

4

A stately Pallace built of squarèd bricke,
Which cunningly was without morter laid,
Whose wals were high, but nothing strong, nor thick,   30
And golden foile all over them displaid,
That purest skye with brightnesse they dismaid:

High lifted up were many loftie towres,
And goodly galleries farre over laid,
Full of faire windowes, and delightfull bowres;
And on the top a Diall told the timely howres.

5

It was a goodly heape for to behould,
And spake the praises of the workmans wit;
But full great pittie, that so faire a mould
Did on so weake foundation ever sit: 40
For on a sandie hill, that still did flit,
And fall away, it mounted was full hie,
That every breath of heaven shakèd it:
And all the hinder parts, that few could spie,
Were ruinous and old, but painted cunningly.

6

Arrivèd there they passèd in forth right;
For still to all the gates stood open wide,
Yet charge of them was to a Porter hight
Cald *Malvenù,* who entrance none denide:
Thence to the hall, which was on every side   50
With rich array and costly arras dight:
Infinite sorts of people did abide
There waiting long, to win the wishèd sight
Of her, that was the Lady of that Pallace bright.

7

By them they passe, all gazing on them round,
And to the Presence mount; whose glorious vew
Their frayle amazèd senses did confound:
In living Princes court none ever knew

Such endlesse richesse, and so sumptuous shew;
Ne *Persia* selfe, the nourse of pompous pride   60
Like ever saw.   And there a noble crew
Of Lordes and Ladies stood on every side,
Which with their presence faire, the place much beau-
               tifide.

8

High above all a cloth of State was spred,
And a rich throne, as bright as sunny day,
On which there sate most brave embellishèd
With royall robes and gorgeous array,
A mayden Queene, that shone as *Titans* ray,
In glistring gold, and peerelesse pretious stone:
Yet her bright blazing beautie did assay   70
To dim the brightnesse of her glorious throne,
As envying her selfe, that too exceeding shone.

9

Exceeding shone, like *Phœbus* fairest childe,
That did presume his fathers firie wayne,
And flaming mouthes of steedes unwonted wilde
Through highest heaven with weaker hand to rayne;
Proud of such glory and advancement vaine,
While flashing beames do daze his feeble eyen,
He leaves the welkin way most beaten plaine,
And rapt with whirling wheeles, inflames the skyen,   80
With fire not made to burne, but fairely for to shyne.

10

So proud she shynèd in her Princely state,
Looking to heaven, for earth she did disdayne;
And sitting high, for lowly she did hate:

Lo underneath her scornefull feete, was layne
A dreadfull Dragon with an hideous trayne,
And in her hand she held a mirrhour bright,
Wherein her face she often viewèd fayne,
And in her selfe-lov'd semblance tooke delight;
For she was wondrous faire, as any living wight.　　90

11

Of griesly *Pluto* she the daughter was,
And sad *Proserpina* the Queene of hell;
Yet did she thinke her pearelesse worth to pas
That parentage, with pride so did she swell,
And thundring *Jove,* that high in heaven doth dwell,
And wield the world, she claymèd for her syre,
Or if that any else did *Jove* excell:
For to the highest she did still aspyre,
Or if ought higher were then that, did it desyre.

12

And proud *Lucifera* men did her call,　　100
That made her selfe a Queene, and crowned to be,
Yet rightfull kingdome she had none at all,
Ne heritage of native soveraintie,
But did usurpe with wrong and tyrannie
Upon the scepter, which she now did hold:
Ne ruld her Realmes with lawes, but pollicie,
And strong advizement of six wizards old,
That with their counsels bad her kingdome did uphold.

13

Soone as the Elfin knight in presence came,
And false *Duessa* seeming Lady faire,　　110

A gentle Husher, *Vanitie* by name
Made rowme, and passage for them did prepaire:
So goodly brought them to the lowest staire
Of her high throne, where they on humble knee
Making obeysaunce, did the cause declare,
Why they were come, her royall state to see,
To prove the wide report of her great Majestee.

14

With loftie eyes, halfe loth to looke so low,
She thankèd them in her disdainefull wise,
Ne other grace vouchsafèd them to show   120
Of Princesse worthy, scarse them bad arise.
Her Lordes and Ladies all this while devise
Themselves to setten forth to straungers sight:
Some frounce their curlèd haire in courtly guise,
Some prancke their ruffes, and others trimly dight
Their gay attire: each others greater pride does spight.

15

Goodly they all that knight do entertaine,
Rightly glad with him to have increast their crew:
But to *Duess'* each one himselfe did paine
All kindnesse and faire courtesie to shew;   130
For in that court whylome her well they knew:
Yet the stout Faerie mongst the middest crowd
Thought all their glorie vaine in knightly vew,
And that great Princesse too exceeding prowd,
That to strange knight no better countenance allowd.

16

Suddein upriseth from her stately place
The royall Dame, and for her coche doth call:
All hurtlen forth, and she with Princely pace,
As faire *Aurora* in her purple pall,
Out of the East the dawning day doth call: 140
So forth she comes: her brightness brode doth blaze;
The heapes of people thronging in the hall,
Do ride each other, upon her to gaze:
Her glorious glitterand light doth all mens eyes amaze.

17

So forth she comes, and to her coche does clyme,
Adornèd all with gold, and girlonds gay,
That seemed as fresh as *Flora* in her prime,
And strove to match, in royall rich array,
Great *Junoes* golden chaire, the which they say
The Gods stand gazing on, when she does ride   150
To *Joves* high house through heavens bras-pavèd way
Drawne of faire Pecocks, that excell in pride,
And full of *Argus* eyes their tailes dispredden wide.

18

But this was drawne of six unequall beasts,
On which her six sage Counsellours did ryde,
Taught to obay their bestiall beheasts,
With like conditions to their kinds applyde:
Of which the first, that all the rest did guyde,
Was sluggish *Idlenesse* the nourse of sin;
Upon a slouthfull Asse he chose to ryde,   160

Arrayd in habit blacke, and amiss [1] thin,
Like to an holy Monck, the service to begin.

19

And in his hand his Portesse [2] still he bare,
That much was worne, but therein little red,
For of devotion he had little care,
Still drowned in sleepe, and most of his dayes ded;
Scarse could he once uphold his heavie hed,
To looken, whether it were night or day:
May seeme the wayne was very evill led,
When such an one had guiding of the way,   170
That knew not, whether right he went, or else astray.

20

From worldly cares himselfe he did esloyne,[3]
And greatly shunnèd manly exercise,
From every worke he chalengèd *essoyne*,[4]
For contemplation sake: yet otherwise,
His life he led in lawlesse riotise;
By which he grew to grievous malady;
For in his lustlesse limbs through evill guise
A shaking fever raignd continually:
Such one was *Idlenesse,* first of this company.   180

21

And by his side rode loathsome *Gluttony,*
Deformèd creature, on a filthie swyne,
His belly was up-blowne with luxury,
And eke with fatnesse swollen were his eyne,
And like a Crane his necke was long and fyne,

[1] amice   [2] prayer book   [3] withdraw   [4] excuse

With which he swallowd up excessive feast,
For want whereof poore people oft did pyne;
And all the way, most like a brutish beast,
He spuèd up his gorge, that all did him deteast.

22

In greene vine leaves he was right fitly clad;   190
For other clothes he could not weare for heat,
And on his head an yvie girland had,
From under which fast trickled downe the sweat:
Still as he rode, he somewhat still did eat,
And in his hand did beare a bouzing [1] can,
Of which he supt so oft, that on his seat
His dronken corse he scarse upholden can,
In shape and life more like a monster, than a man.

23

Unfit he was for any worldly thing,
And eke unhable once to stirre or go,   200
Not meet to be of counsell to a king,
Whose mind in meat and drinke was drownèd so,
That from his friend he seldome knew his fo:
Full of diseases was his carcas blew,
And a dry dropsie through his flesh did flow:
Which by misdiet daily greater grew:
Such one was *Gluttony*, the second of that crew.

24

And next to him rode lustfull *Lechery*,
Upon a bearded Goat, whose rugged haire,
And whally [2] eyes (the signe of gelosy)   210
    [1] drinking   [2] discolored

Was like the person selfe, whom he did beare:
Who rough, and blacke, and filthy did appeare,
Unseemely man to please faire Ladies eye;
Yet he of Ladies oft was lovèd deare,
When fairer faces were bid standen by:
O who does know the bent of womens fantasy?

25

In a greene gowne he clothèd was full faire,
Which underneath did hide his filthinesse,
And in his hand a burning hart he bare,
Full of vaine follies, and new fanglenesse: 220
For he was false, and fraught with ficklenesse,
And learnèd had to love with secret lookes,
And well could daunce, and sing with ruefulnesse,
And fortunes tell, and read in loving bookes,
And thousand other wayes, to bait his fleshly hookes.

26

Inconstant man, that lovèd all he saw,
And lusted after all, that he did love,
Ne would his looser life be tide to law,
But joyd weake wemens hearts to tempt and prove
If from their loyall loves he might them move;   230
Which lewdnesse fild him with reproachfull paine
Of that fowle evill, which all men reprove,
That rots the marrow, and consumes the braine:
Such one was *Lecherie,* the third of all this traine.

27

And greedy *Avarice* by him did ride,
Upon a Camell loaden all with gold;

Two iron coffers hong on either side,
With precious mettall full, as they might hold,
And in his lap an heape of coine he told;
For of his wicked pelfe his God he made,　　240
And unto hell him selfe for money sold;
Accursèd usurie was all his trade,
And right and wrong ylike in equall ballaunce waide.

28

His life was nigh unto deaths doore yplast,
And thred-bare cote, and cobled shoes he ware,
Ne scarse good morsell all his life did tast,
But both from backe and belly still did spare,
To fill his bags, and richesse to compare;[1]
Yet chylde ne kinsman living had he none
To leave them to; but thorough daily care　　250
To get, and nightly feare to lose his owne,
He led a wretched life unto him selfe unknowne.

29

Most wretched wight, whom nothing might suffise,
Whose greedy lust did lacke in greatest store,
Whose need had end, but no end covetise,
Whose wealth was want, whose plenty made him pore,
Who had enough, yet wishèd ever more;
A vile disease, and eke in foote and hand
A grievous gout tormented him full sore,
That well he could not touch, nor go, nor stand:　　260
Such was one *Avarice,* the fourth of this faire band.

[1] acquire

30

And next to him malicious *Envie* rode,
Upon a ravenous wolfe, and still did chaw
Between his cankred teeth a venemous tode,
That all the poison ran about his chaw;
But inwardly he chawèd his owne maw
At neighbours wealth, that made him ever sad;
For death it was, when any good he saw,
And wept, that cause of weeping none he had,
But when he heard of harme, he wexèd wondrous
          glad.   270

31

All in a kirtle of discoloured say[1]
He clothèd was, ypainted full of eyes;
And in his bosome secretly there lay
An hateful Snake, the which his taile uptyes
In many folds, and mortall sting implyes.
Still as he rode, he gnasht his teeth, to see
Those heapes of gold with griple[2] Covetyse,
And grudgèd at the great felicitie
Of proud *Lucifera,* and his owne companie.

32

He hated all good workes and vertuous deeds,   280
And him no lesse, that any like did use,
And who with gracious bread the hungry feeds,
His almes for want of faith he doth accuse;
So every good to bad he doth abuse:
And eke the verse of famous Poets witt

[1] serge   [2] grasping

He does backbite, and spightfull poison spues
From leprous mouth on all, that ever writt:
Such one vile *Envie* was, that fifte in row did sitt.

33

And him beside rides fierce revenging *Wrath*,
Upon a Lion, loth for to be led;   290
And in his hand a burning brond he hath,
The which he brandisheth about his hed;
His eyes did hurle forth sparkles fiery red,
And starèd sterne on all, that him beheld,
As ashes pale of hew and seeming ded;
And on his dagger still his hand he held,
Trembling through hasty rage, when choler in him sweld.

34

His ruffin raiment all was staind with blood,
Which he had spilt, and all to rage yrent,
Through unadvizèd rashnesse woxen wood [1]   300
For of his hands he had no government,
Ne car'd for bloud in his avengement;
But when the furious fit was overpast,
His cruell facts he often would repent;
Yet wilfull man he never would forecast,
How many mischieves should ensue his heedlesse hast.

35

Full many mischiefes follow cruell *Wrath*:
Abhorrèd bloudshed, and tumultuous strife,
Unmanly murder, and unthrifty scath,
Bitter despight, with rancours rusty knife,   310
[1] grown mad

And fretting griefe the enemy of life;
All these, and many evils moe haunt ire,
The swelling Splene, and Frenzy raging rife,
The shaking Palsey, and Saint *Fraunces* fire:
Such one was *Wrath,* the last of this ungodly tire.

36

And after all, upon the wagon beame
Rode *Satan,* with a smarting whip in hand,
With which he forward lasht the laesie teme,
So oft as *Slowth* still in the mire did stand.
Huge routs of people did about them band,   320
Showting for joy, and still before their way
A foggy mist had covered all the land;
And underneath their feet, all scattered lay
Dead sculs and bones of men, whose life had gone
          astray.

37

So forth they marchen in this goodly sort,
To take the solace of the open aire,
And in fresh flowring fields themselves to sport;
Emongst the rest rode that false Lady faire,
The fowle *Duessa,* next unto the chaire
Of proud *Lucifera,* as one of the traine: 330
But that good knight would not so nigh repaire,
Him selfe estraunging from their joyaunce vaine,
Whose fellowship seemed far unfit for warlike swaine.

38

So having solacèd themselves a space
With pleasaunce of the breathing fields yfed,

They backe returnèd to the Princely Place;
Whereas an errant knight in armes ycled,
And heathnish shield, wherein with letters red
Was writ *Sans joy,* they new arrivèd find:
Enflam'd with fury and fiers hardy-hed,　　　　340
He seemed in hart to harbour thoughts unkind,
And nourish bloudy vengeaunce in his bitter mind.

39

Who when the shamèd shield of slaine *Sans foy*
He spide with that same Faery champions page,
Bewraying him, that did of late destroy
His eldest brother, burning all with rage
He to him leapt, and that same envious gage
Of victors glory from him snatcht away:
But th' Elfin knight, which ought [1] that warlike wage,
Disdaind to loose the meed he wonne in fray,　　　　350
And him recountring fierce, reskewd the noble pray.

40

Therewith they gan to hurtlen greedily,
Redoubted battaile ready to darrayne, [2]
And clash their shields, and shake their swords on hy,
That with their sturre they troubled all the traine;
Till that great Queene upon eternal paine
Of high displeasure, that ensewen might,
Commaunded them their fury to refraine,
And if that either to that shield had right,
In equall lists they should the morrow next it fight.　　　360

　　[1] owned　　[2] prepare

41

Ah dearest Dame (quoth then the Paynim bold),
Pardon the errour of enragèd wight,
Whom great griefe made forget the raines to hold
Of reasons rule, to see this recreant knight,
No knight, but treachour full of false despight
And shamefull treason, who through guile hath slayn
The prowest knight, that ever field did fight,
Even stout *Sans foy* (O who can then refrayn?)
Whose shield he beares renverst, the more to heape dis-
        dayn.

42

And to augment the glorie of his guile,   370
His dearest love the faire *Fidessa* loe
Is there possessèd of the traytour vile,
Who reapes the harvest sowen by his foe,
Sowen in bloudy field, and bought with woe:
That brothers hand shall dearely well requight
So be, O Queene, you equall favour showe.
Him litle answered th'angry Elfin knight;
He never meant with words, but swords to plead his
        right.

43

But threw his gauntlet as a sacred pledge,
His cause in combat the next day to try: 380
So been they parted both, with harts on edge,
To be aveng'd each on his enimy.
That night they pas in joy and jollity,
Feasting and courting both in bowre and hall;

For Steward was excessive *Gluttonie,*
That of his plenty pourèd forth to all;
Which doen, the Chamberlain *Slowth* did to rest them
          call.

44

Now whenas darkesome night had all displayd
Her coleblacke curtein over brightest skye,
The warlike youthes on dayntie couches layd,   390
Did chace away sweet sleepe from sluggish eye,
To muse on meanes of hopèd victory.
But whenas *Morpheus* had with leaden mace
Arrested all that courtly company,
Up-rose *Duessa* from her resting place,
And to the Paynims lodging comes with silent pace.

45

Whom broad awake she finds, in troublous fit,
Forecasting, how his foe he might annoy,
And him amoves with speaches seeming fit:
Ah deare *Sans joy,* next dearest to *Sans foy,*   400
Cause of my new griefe, cause of my new joy,
Joyous, to see his ymage in mine eye,
And greev'd, to thinke how foe did him destroy,
That was the flowre of grace and chevalrye;
Lo his *Fidessa* to thy secret faith I flye.

46

With gentle wordes he can her fairely greet,
And bad say on the secret of her hart.
Then sighing soft, I learne that little sweet
Oft tempred is (quoth she) with muchell smart:

For since my brest was launcht with lovely dart   410
Of deare *Sansfoy,* I never joyèd howre,
But in eternall woes my weaker hart
Have wasted, loving him with all my powre,
And for his sake have felt full many an heavie stowre.

47

At last when perils all I weenèd past,
And hop'd to reape the crop of all my care,
Into new woes unweeting I was cast,
By this false faytor, who unworthy ware
His worthy shield, whom he with guilefull snare
Entrappèd slew, and brought to shamefull grave.   420
Me silly maid away with him he bare,
And ever since hath kept in darksome cave,
For that I would not yeeld, that to *Sans-foy* I gave.

48

But since faire Sunne hath sperst that lowring clowd,
And to my loathèd life now shewes some light,
Under your beames I will me safely shrowd,
From dreaded storme of his disdainfull spight:
To you th'inheritance belongs by right
Of brothers prayse, to you eke longs his love.
Let not his love, let not his restlesse spright   430
Be unreveng'd, that calles to you above
From wandring *Stygian* shores, where it doth endlesse
     move.

49

Thereto said he, faire Dame be nought dismaid
For sorrows past; their griefe is with them gone:

Ne yet of present peril be affraid;
For needlesse feare did never vantage none,
And helplesse hap it booteth not to mone,
Dead is *Sans-foy,* for his vitall paines are past,
Though greevèd ghost for vengeance deepe do grone:
He lives, that shall him pay his dewties last,   440
And guiltie Elfin bloud shall sacrifice in hast.

50

O but I feare the fickle freakes (quoth shee)
Of fortune false, and oddes of armes in field.
Why dame (quoth he) what oddes can ever bee,
Where both do fight alike, to win or yield?
Yea but (quoth she) he beares a charmèd shield,
And eke enchaunted armes, that none can perce,
Ne none can wound the man, that does them yield.
Charmd or enchaunted (answered he then ferce)
I no whit reck, ne you the like need to reherce.   450

51

But faire *Fidessa,* sithens fortunes guile,
Or enimies powre hath now captivèd you,
Returne from whence ye came, and rest a while
Till morrow next, that I the Elfe subdew,
And with *Sans-foyes* dead dowry you endew.
Ay me, that is a double death (she said)
With proud foes sight my sorrow to renew:
Where ever yet I be, my secret aid
Shall follow you, So passing forth she him obaid.

(Printed 1590)

AMORETTI

1

HAPPY ye leaves! when as those lilly hands,
Which hold my life in their dead doing might,
Shall handle you, and hold in loves soft bands,
Lyke captives trembling at the victors sight.
And happy lines! on which, with starry light,
Those lamping eyes will deigne sometimes to look,
And reade the sorrowes of my dying spright,
Written with teares in harts close bleeding book,
And happy rymes! bathed in the sacred brooke
Of Helicon, whence she derivèd is,   10
When ye behold that angels blessèd looke,
My soules long lackèd foode, my heavens blis.
Leaves, lines, and rymes, seeke her to please alone,
Whom if ye please, I care for other none.

15

Ye tradefull merchants, that with weary toyle
Do seeke most precious things to make your gain,
And both the Indias of their treasures spoile,
What needeth you to seeke so farre in vaine?
For loc! my love doth in her selfe containe
All this worlds riches that may farre be found:
If saphyres, loe! her eies be saphyres plaine;
If rubies, loe! her lips be rubies sound;
If pearls, her teeth be pearls both pure and round;
If yvorie, her forehead yvory weene;   10
If gold, her locks are finest gold on ground;
If silver, her faire hands are silver sheene:

But that which fairest is but few behold,
Her mind, adorned with vertues manifold.

33

Great wrong I doe, I can it not deny,
To that most sacred empresse, my dear dread,
Not finishing her Queene of Faëry,
That mote enlarge her living prayses, dead.
But Lodwick, this of grace to me aread:
Do ye not thinck th' accomplishment of it
Sufficient worke for one mans simple head,
All were it, as the rest, but rudely writ?
How then should I, without another wit,
Thinck ever to endure so tædious toyle,   10
Sins that this one is tost with troublous fit
Of a proud love, that doth my spirite spoyle?
Cease then, till she vouchsafe to grawnt me rest,
Or lend you me another living brest.

34

Lyke as a ship, that through the ocean wyde
By conduct of some star doth make her way,
Whenas a storme hath dimd her trusty guyde,
Out of her course doth wander far astray;
So I, whose star, that wont with her bright ray
Me to direct, with cloudes is overcast,
Doe wander now in darknesse and dismay,
Through hidden perils round about me plast.
Yet hope I well, that when this storme is past,
My Helice, the lodestar of my lyfe,   10
Will shine again, and looke on me at last,
With lovely light to cleare my cloudy grief.

Till then I wander carefull comfortlesse,
In secret sorrow and sad pensivenesse.

37

What guyle is this, that those her golden tresses
She doth attyre under a net of gold,
And with sly skill so cunningly them dresses,
That which is gold or heare may scarse be told?
Is it that mens frayle eyes, which gaze too bold,
She may entangle in that golden snare,
And being caught, may craftily enfold
Theyr weaker harts, which are not wel aware?
Take heed therefore, myne eyes, how ye doe stare
Henceforth too rashly on that guilefull net,   10
In which if ever ye entrapped are,
Out of her bands ye by no meanes shall get.
Fondnesse it were for any, being free,
To covet fetters, though they golden bee.

46

When my abodes prefixèd time is spent,
My cruell fayre streight bids me wend my way:
But then from heaven most hideous stormes are sent,
As willing me against her will to stay.
Whom then shall I, or heaven or her, obay?
The heavens know best what is the best for me:
But as she will, whose will my life doth sway,
My lower heaven, so it perforce must bee.
But ye high hevens, that all this sorrowe see,
Sith all your tempests cannot hold me backe,   10
Aswage your stormes, or else both you and she
Will both together me too sorely wrack.

Enough it is for one man to sustaine
The stormes which she alone on me doth raine.

62

The weary yeare his race now having run,
The new begins his compast course anew:
With shew of morning mylde he hath begun,
Betokening peace and plenty to ensew.
So let us, which this chaunge of weather vew,
Chaunge eeke our mynds, and former lives amend;
The old yeares sinnes forepast let us eschew,
And fly the faults with which we did offend.
Then shall the new yeares joy forth freshly send
Into the glooming world his gladsome ray;   10
And all these stormes, which now his beauty blend,
Shall turne to caulmes, and tymely cleare away.
So likewise, love, cheare you your heavy spright,
And chaunge old yeares annoy to new delight.

63

After long stormes and tempests sad assay,
Which hardly I endurèd heretofore,
In dread of death, and daungerous dismay,
With which my silly barke was tossèd sore,
I doe at length descry the happy shore,
In which I hope ere long for to arryve:
Fayre soyle it seemes from far, and fraught with store
Of all that deare and daynty is alyve.
Most happy he that can at last atchyve
The joyous safety of so sweet a rest;   10
Whose least delight sufficeth to deprive
Remembrance of all paines which him opprest.

All paines are nothing in respect of this,
All sorrowes short that gaine eternall blisse.

68

Most glorious Lord of lyfe, that on this day
Didst make thy triumph over death and sin,
And having harrowd hell, didst bring away
Captivity thence captive, us to win:
This joyous day, deare Lord, with joy begin,
And grant that we, for whom thou diddest dye,
Being with thy deare blood clene washt from sin,
May live for ever in felicity:
And that thy love we weighing worthily,
May likewise love thee for the same againe;   10
And for thy sake, that all lyke deare didst buy,
With love may one another entertayne.
So let us love, deare love, lyke as we ought:
Love is the lesson which the Lord us taught.

70

Fresh Spring, the herald of loves mighty king,
In whose cote-armour richly are displayd
All sorts of flowers the which on earth do spring,
In goodly colours gloriously arrayd,
Goe to my love, where she is carelesse layd,
Yet in her winters bowre, not well awake;
Tell her the joyous time wil not be staid,
Unlesse she doe him by the forelock take:
Bid her therefore her selfe soone ready make,
To wayt on Love amongst his lovely crew,   10
Where every one that misseth then her make
Shall be by him amearst with penance dew.

Make hast therefore, sweet love, whilest it is prime;
For none can call againe the passèd time.

72

Oft when my spirit doth spred her bolder winges,
In mind to mount up to the purest sky,
It down is weighd with thoght of earthly things,
And clogd with burden of mortality:
Where, when that soverayne beauty it doth spy,
Resembling heavens glory in her light,
Drawne with sweet pleasures bayt, it back doth fly,
And unto heaven forgets her former flight.
There my fraile fancy, fed with full delight,
Doth bath in blisse, and mantleth [1] most at ease: 10
Ne thinks of other heaven, but how it might
Her harts desire with most contentment please.
Hart need not wish none other happinesse,
But here on earth to have such hevens blisse.

75

One day I wrote her name upon the strand,
But came the waves and washèd it away:
Agayne I wrote it with a second hand,
But came the tyde, and made my paynes his pray.
Vayne man, sayd she, that doest in vaine assay
A mortall thing so to immortalize!
For I my selve shall lyke to this decay,
And eek my name bee wypèd out lykewize.
Not so, (quod I) let baser things devize
To dy in dust, but you shall live by fame: 10
My verse your vertues rare shall eternize,
And in the hevens wryte your glorious name;
___
[1] stretches

Where, whenas death shall all the world subdew,
Our love shall live, and later life renew.

82

Joy of my life, full oft for loving you
I blesse my lot, that was so lucky placed:
But then the more your owne mishap I rew,
That are so much by so meane love embased.
For had the equall hevens so much you graced
In this as in the rest, ye mote invent
Som hevenly wit, whose verse could have enchased
Your glorious name in golden moniment.
But since ye deignd so goodly to relent
To me your thrall, in whom is little worth,   10
That little that I am shall all be spent
In setting your immortall prayses forth:
Whose lofty argument, uplifting me,
Shall lift you up unto an high degree.

(1595)

EPITHALAMION

YE LEARNÈD sisters, which have oftentimes
Beene to me ayding, others to adorne,
Whom ye thought worthy of your gracefull rymes,
That even the greatest did not greatly scorne
To heare theyr names sung in your simple layes,
But joyèd in theyr praise;
And when ye list your owne mishaps to mourne,
Which death, or love, or fortunes wreck did rayse,
Your string could soone to sadder tenor turne,
And teach the woods and waters to lament   10
Your dolefull dreriment:
Now lay those sorrowfull complaints aside,

And having all your heads with girland crownd,
Helpe me mine owne loves prayses to resound;
Ne let the same of any be envide:
So Orpheus did for his owne bride:
So I unto my selfe alone will sing;
The woods shall to me answer, and my eccho ring.

Early, before the worlds light giving lampe
His golden beame upon the hils doth spred,   20
Having disperst the nights unchearefull dampe,
Doe ye awake, and, with fresh lustyhed,
Go to the bowre of my belovèd love,
My truest turtle dove:
Bid her awake; for Hymen is awake,
And long since ready forth his maske to move,
With his bright tead [1] that flames with many a flake,
And many a bachelor to waite on him,
In theyr fresh garments trim.
Bid her awake therefore, and soone her dight,   30
For lo! the wishèd day is come at last,
That shall, for al the paynes and sorrowes past,
Pay to her usury of long delight:
And whylest she doth her dight,
Doe ye to her of joy and solace sing,
That all the woods may answer, and your eccho ring.

Bring with you all the nymphes that you can heare,
Both of the rivers and the forrests greene,
And of the sea that neighbours to her neare,
Al with gay girlands goodly wel beseene.   40
And let them also with them bring in hand
Another gay girland,
For my fayre love, of lillyes and of roses,
Bound truelove wize with a blew silke riband.
    [1] torch

And let them make great store of bridale poses,
And let them eeke bring store of other flowers,
To deck the bridale bowers.
And let the ground whereas her foot shall tread,
For feare the stones her tender foot should wrong,
Be strewed with fragrant flowers, all along,   50
And diapred [1] lyke the discolored mead.[2]
Which done, doe at her chamber dore awayt,
For she will waken strayt;
The whiles doe ye this song unto her sing,
The woods shall to you answer, and your eccho ring.

Ye nymphes of Mulla, which with carefull heed
The silver scaly trouts doe tend full well,
And greedy pikes which use therein to feed,
(Those trouts and pikes all others doo excell)
And ye likewise which keepe the rushy lake,   60
Where none doo fishes take,
Bynd up the locks the which hang scatterd light,
And in his waters, which your mirror make,
Behold your faces as the christall bright,
That when you come whereas my love doth lie,
No blemish she may spie.
And eke ye lightfoot mayds which keepe the dere
That on the hoary mountayne use to towre,
And the wylde wolves, which seeke them to devoure,
With your steele darts doo chace from coming near,   70
Be also present heere,
To helpe to decke her, and to help to sing,
That all the woods may answer, and your eccho ring.

Wake now, my love, awake! for it is time:
The rosy Morne long since left Tithones bed,
All ready to her silver coche to clyme,

---

[1] variegated   [2] meadow

And Phœbus gins to shew his glorious hed.
Hark how the cheerefull birds do chaunt theyr laies,
And carroll of loves praise!
The merry larke hir mattins sings aloft,　　　　　80
The thrush replyes, the mavis descant playes,
The ouzell shrills, the ruddock warbles soft,
So goodly all agree, with sweet consent,
To this dayes merriment.
Ah! my deere love, why doe ye sleepe thus long,
When meeter were that ye should now awake,
T' awayt the comming of your joyous mate,
And hearken to the birds love-learnèd song,
The deawy leaves among?
For they of joy and pleasance to you sing,　　　90
That all the woods them answer, and theyr eccho ring.

My love is now awake out of her dreame,
And her fayre eyes, like stars that dimmèd were
With darksome cloud, now shew theyr goodly beams
More bright then Hesperus his head doth rere.
Come now, ye damzels, daughters of delight,
Helpe quickly her to dight.
But first come ye, fayre Houres, which were begot,
In Joves sweet paradice, of Day and Night,
Which doe the seasons of the year allot,　　　100
And al that ever in this world is fayre
Do make and still repayre.
And ye three handmayds of the Cyprian Queene.
The which doe still adorne her beauties pride,
Helpe to addorne my beautifullest bride:
And as ye her array, still throw betweene
Some graces to be seene:
And as ye use to Venus, to her sing,
The whiles the woods shal answer, and your eccho ring

Now is my love all ready forth to come: 110
Let all the virgins therefore well awayt,
And ye fresh boyes, that tend upon her groome,
Prepare your selves, for he is comming strayt.
Set all your things in seemly good aray,
Fit for so joyfull day,
The joyfulst day that ever sunne did see.
Faire Sun, shew forth thy favourable ray,
And let thy lifull heat not fervent be,
For feare of burning her sunshyny face,
Her beauty to disgrace.   120
O fayrest Phœbus, father of the Muse,
If ever I did honour thee aright,
Or sing the thing that mote thy mind delight,
Doe not thy servants simple boone refuse,
But let this day, let this one day be myne,
Let all the rest be thine.
Then I thy soverayne prayses loud wil sing,
That all the woods shal answer, and theyr eccho ring.

Harke how the minstrels gin to shrill aloud
Their merry musick that resounds from far,   130
The pipe, the tabor,[1] and the trembling croud,[2]
That well agree withouten breach or jar,
But most of all the damzels doe delite,
When they their tymbrels smyte,
And thereunto doe daunce and carrol sweet,
That all the sences they doe ravish quite,
The whyles the boyes run up and downe the street,
Crying aloud with strong confusèd noyce,
As if it were one voyce.
'Hymen, Iö Hymen, Hymen,' they do shout,   140
That even to the heavens theyr shouting shrill
Doth reach, and all the firmament doth fill;

    [1] small drum   [2] fiddle

To which the people, standing all about,
As in approvance doe thereto applaud,
And loud advaunce her laud,
And evermore they 'Hymen, Hymen' sing,
That al the woods them answer, and theyr eccho ring.

Loe! where she comes along with portly pace,
Lyke Phœbe, from her chamber of the east,
Arysing forth to run her mighty race,   150
Clad all in white, that seemes a virgin best.
So well it her beseemes, that ye would weene
Some angell she had beene.
Her long loose yellow locks lyke golden wyre,
Sprinckled with perle, and perling flowres atweene,
Doe lyke a golden mantle her attyre,
And being crownèd with a girland greene,
Seeme lyke some mayden queene.
Her modest eyes, abashèd to behold
So many gazers as on her do stare,   160
Upon the lowly ground affixèd are;
Ne dare lift up her countenance too bold,
But blush to heare her prayses sung so loud.
So farre from being proud.
Nathlesse doe ye still loud her prayses sing,
That all the woods may answer, and your eccho ring.

Tell me, ye merchants daughters, did ye see
So fayre a creature in your towne before,
So sweet, so lovely, and so mild as she,
Adornd with beautyes grace and vertues store?   170
Her goodly eyes lyke saphyres shining bright,
Her forehead yvory white,
Her cheekes lyke apples which the sun hath rudded,
Her lips lyke cherryes charming men to byte,
Her brest like to a bowle of creame uncrudded,

Her paps lyke lyllies budded,
Her snowie necke lyke to a marble towre,
And all her body like a pallace fayre,
Ascending uppe, with many a stately stayre,
To honors seat and chastities sweet bowre.   180
Why stand ye still, ye virgins, in amaze,
Upon her so to gaze,
While ye forget your former lay to sing,
To which the woods did answer, and your eccho ring.

But if ye saw that which no eyes can see,
The inward beauty of her lively spright,
Garnisht with heavenly guifts of high degree,
Much more than would ye wonder at that sight,
And stand astonisht lyke to those which red [1]
Medusaes mazeful hed.   190
There dwels sweet Love and constant Chastity,
Unspotted Fayth, and comely Womanhood,
Regard of Honour, and mild Modesty;
There Vertue raynes as queene in royal throne,
And giveth lawes alone,
The which the base affections doe obay,
And yeeld theyr services unto her will;
Ne thought of thing uncomely ever may
Thereto approach to tempt her mind to ill.
Had ye once seene these her celestial threasures, 200
And unrevealèd pleasures,
Then would ye wonder, and her prayses sing,
That al the woods should answer, and your echo ring.

Open the temple gates unto my love,
Open them wide that she may enter in,
And all the postes adorne as doth behove,
And all the pillours deck with girlands trim,

[1] saw

For to receyve this saynt with honour dew,
That commeth in to you.
With trembling steps and humble reverence,   210
She commeth in before th' Almighties vew:
Of her, ye virgins, learne obedience,
When so ye come into those holy places,
To humble your proud faces.
Bring her up to th' high altar, that she may
The sacred ceremonies there partake,
The which do endlesse matrimony make;
And let the roring organs loudly play
The praises of the Lord in lively notes,
The whiles with hollow throates   220
The choristers the joyous antheme sing,
That al the woods may answere, and their eccho ring.

Behold, whiles she before the altar stands,
Hearing the holy priest that to her speakes,
And blesseth her with his two happy hands,
How the red roses flush up in her cheekes,
And the pure snow with goodly vermill stayne,
Like crimsin dyde in grayne:
That even th' angels, which continually
About the sacred altare doe remaine,   230
Forget their service and about her fly,
Ofte peeping in her face, that seemes more fayre,
The more they on it stare.
But her sad eyes, still fastened on the ground.
Are governèd with goodly modesty,
That suffers not one looke to glaunce awry,
Which may let in a little thought unsownd.
Why blush ye, love, to give to me your hand,
The pledge of all our band? [1]

[1] bond

Sing, ye sweet angels, Alleluya sing,   240
That all the woods may answere, and your eccho ring.

Now al is done; bring home the bride againe,
Bring home the triumph of our victory,
Bring home with you the glory of her gaine,
With joyance bring her and with jollity.
Never had man more joyful day then this,
Whom heaven would heape with blis.
Make feast therefore now all this live long day;
This day for ever to me holy is;
Poure out the wine without restraint or stay,   250
Poure not by cups, but by the belly full,
Poure out to all that wull,
And sprinkle all the postes and wals with wine,
That they may sweat, and drunken be withal.
Crowne ye God Bacchus with a coronall.
And Hymen also crowne with wreathes of vine;
And let the Graces daunce unto the rest,
For they can doo it best:
The whiles the maydens doe theyr carroll sing,
The which the woods shal answer, and theyr eccho
    ring.   260

Ring ye the bels, ye yong men of the towne,
And leave your wonted labors for this day:
This day is holy; doe ye write it downe,
That ye for ever it remember may.
This day the sunne is in his chiefest hight,
With Barnaby the bright,
From whence declining daily by degrees,
He somewhat loseth of his heat and light,
When once the Crab behind his back he sees.
But for this time it ill ordainèd was,   270
To chose the longest day in all the yeare,

And shortest night, when longest fitter weare:
Yet never day so long, but late would passe.
Ring ye the bels, to make it weare away,
And bonfires make all day,
And daunce about them, and about them sing:
That all the woods may answer, and your eccho ring.

Ah! when will this long weary day have end,
And lende me leave to come unto my love?
How slowly do the houres theyr numbers spend!   280
How slowly does sad Time his feathers move!
Hast thee, O fayrest planet, to thy home
Within the westerne fome:
Thy tyrèd steedes long since have need of rest.
Long though it be, at last I see it gloome,
And the bright evening star with golden creast
Appeare out of the east.
Fayre childe of beauty, glorious lampe of love,
That all the host of heaven in rankes doost lead,
And guydest lovers through the nightès dread,   290
How chearefully thou lookest from above,
And seemst to laugh atweene thy twinkling light,
As joying in the sight
Of these glad many, which for joy doe sing,
That all the woods them answer, and their echo ring!

Now ceasse, ye damsels, your delights forepast;
Enough is it that all the day was youres:
Now day is doen, and night is nighing fast:
Now bring the bryde into the brydall boures.
The night is come, now soone her disaray,   300
And in her bed her lay;
Lay her in lillies and in violets,
And silken courteins over her display,
And odourd sheetes, and Arras coverlets.

Behold how goodly my faire love does ly,
In proud humility!
Like unto Maia, when as Jove her tooke
In Tempe, lying on the flowry gras,
Twixt sleepe and wake, after she weary was
With bathing in the Acidalian brooke.   310
Now it is night, ye damsels may be gon,
And leave my love alone,
And leave likewise your former lay to sing:
The woods no more shal answere, nor your echo ring.

Now welcome, night! thou night so long expected,
That long daies labour doest at last defray,
And all my cares, which cruell Love collected,
Hast sumd in one, and cancellèd for aye:
Spread thy broad wing over my love and me,
That no man may us see,   320
And in thy sable mantle us enwrap,
From feare of perrill and foule horror free.
Let no false treason seeke us to entrap,
Nor any dread disquiet once annoy
The safety of our joy:
But let the night be calme and quietsome,
Without tempestuous storms or sad afray:
Lyke as when Jove with fayre Alcmena lay,
When he begot the great Tirynthian groome:
Or lyke as when he with thy selfe did lie,   330
And begot Majesty.
And let the mayds and yongmen cease to sing:
Ne let the woods them answer, nor theyr eccho ring.

Let no lamenting cryes, nor dolefull teares,
Be heard all night within, nor yet without:
Ne let false whispers, breeding hidden feares,

Breake gentle sleepe with misconceivèd dout.
Let no deluding dreames, nor dreadful sights,
Make sudden sad affrights;
Ne let house-fyres, nor lightnings helplesse harmes, 340
Ne let the Pouke, nor other evill sprights,
Ne let mischivous witches with theyr charmes,
Ne let hob goblins, names whose sense we see not,
Fray us with things that be not.
Let not the shriech oule, nor the storke be heard,
Nor the night raven that still deadly yels,
Nor damnèd ghosts cald up with mighty spels,
Nor griesly vultures make us once affeard:
Ne let th' unpleasant quyre of frogs still croking
Make us to wish theyr choking. 350
Let none of these theyr drery accents sing;
Ne let the woods them answer, nor theyr eccho ring.

But let stil Silence trew night watches keepe,
That sacred Peace may in assurance rayne,
And tymely Sleep, when it is tyme to sleepe,
May poure his limbs forth on your pleasant playne,
The whiles an hundred little wingèd loves,
Like divers fethered doves,
Shall fly and flutter round about our bed,
And in the secret darke, that none reproves, 360
Their prety stealthes shall worke, and snares shal spread
To filch away sweet snatches of delight,
Conceald through covert night.
Ye sonnes of Venus, play your sports at will:
For greedy Pleasure, careless of your toyes,
Thinks more upon her paradise of joyes,
Then what ye do, albe it good or ill.
All night therefore attend your merry play,
For it will soone be day:

Now none doth hinder you, that say or sing,   370
Ne will the woods now answer, nor your eccho ring.

Who is the same which at my window peepes?
Or whose is that faire face that shines so bright?
Is it not Cinthia, she that never sleepes,
But walkes about high heaven al the night?
O fayrest goddesse, do thou not envy
My love with me to spy:
For thou likewise didst love, though now unthought,
And for a fleece of woll, which privily
The Latmian shephard once unto thee brought,   380
His pleasures with thee wrought.
Therefore to us be favorable now;
And sith of wemen's labours thou hast charge,
And generation goodly dost enlarge,
Encline thy will t' effect our wishfull vow,
And the chast wombe informe with timely seed,
That may our comfort breed:
Till which we cease our hopefull hap to sing,
Ne let the woods us answere, nor our eccho ring.

And thou, great Juno, which with awful might   390
The lawes of wedlock still dost patronize,
And the religion of the faith first plight
With sacred rites hast taught to solemnize,
And eeke for comfort often callèd art
Of women in their smart.
Eternally bind thou this lovely band,
And all thy blessings unto us impart.
And thou, glad Genius, in whose gentle hand
The bridale bowre and geniall bed remaine,
Without blemish or staine,   400
And the sweet pleasures of theyr loves delight

With secret ayde doest succour and supply,
Till they bring forth the fruitfull progeny,
Send us the timely fruit of this same night.
And thou, fayre Hebe, and thou, Hymen free,
Grant that it may so be.
Til which we cease your further prayse to sing,
Ne any woods shal answer, nor your eccho ring.

And ye high heavens, the temple of the gods,
In which a thousand torches flaming bright   410
Doe burne, that to us wretched earthly clods
In dreadfull darknesse lend desirèd light,
And all ye powers which in the same remayne,
More then we men can fayne,
Poure out your blessing on us plentiously,
And happy influence upon us raine,
That we may raise a large posterity,
Which from the earth, which they may long possesse
With lasting happinesse,
Up to your haughty pallaces may mount,   420
And for the guerdon of theyr glorious merit,
May heavenly tabernacles there inherit,
Of blessèd saints for to increase the count.
So let us rest, sweet love, in hope of this,
And cease till then our tymely joyes to sing:
The woods no more us answer, nor our eccho ring.

Song, made in lieu of many ornaments
With which my love should duly have bene dect,
Which cutting off through hasty accidents,
Ye would not stay your dew time to expect,   430
But promist both to recompens,
Be unto her a goodly ornament,
And for short time an endlesse moniment.

(1595)

SIR WALTER RALEIGH (1552?-1618)

THE FIGHT BETWIXT THE "REVENGE" AND AN ARMADA OF THE KING OF SPAIN

BECAUSE the rumors are diversely spread, as well in England as in the low countries and elsewhere, of this late encounter between her Majesty's ships and the Armada of Spain; and that the Spaniards according to their usual manner, fill the world with their vainglorious vaunts, making great appearance of victories, when on the contrary, themselves are most commonly and shamefully beaten and dishonored; thereby hoping to possess the ignorant multitude by anticipating and forerunning false reports: it is agreeable with all good reason, for manifestation of the truth, to overcome falsehood and untruth; that the beginning, continuance and success of this late honorable encounter of Sir Richard Grenville, and other her Majesty's captains, with the Armada of Spain; should be truly set down and published without partiality or false imaginations. And it is no marvel that the Spaniards should seek by false and slanderous pamphlets, advisos and letters, to cover their own loss, and to derogate from others their due honors, especially in this fight being performed far off: seeing they were not ashamed in the year 1588, when they purposed the invasion of this land, to publish in sundry languages, in print, great victories in words, which they pleaded to have obtained against this realm; and spread the same in a most false sort over all parts of France, Italy, and elsewhere. When shortly after it was happily manifested in very deed to all nations, how their navy which they termed invincible, consisting of two hundred and forty sail of ships, not only of their own kingdom, but strengthened by the greatest argosies, Portugal, Caracks, Florentines, and huge hulks of other countries, were by thirty of her Majesty's own ships of war, and a few of our own merchants, by the wise, valiant, and most advantageous conduction of the L. Charles Howard high Admiral of England, beaten and shuffled together; even from the Lizard in Cornwall first to Portland, where they shamefully left Don Pedro de Valdes, with his mighty ship; from Portland to Cales, where they lost Hugo de Moncado, with the gallies of which he was captain, and from Cales, driven with squibs [1] from their anchors, were chased out of the sight of England, round about Scotland and Ireland. Where for the sympathy of their barbarous religion, hoping to find succour and assistance, a great part of them were crushed against the rocks, and those other that landed, being very many in number, were notwithstanding broken, slain, and taken, and so sent from village to village coupled in halters, to be shipped into England. Where her Majesty of her princely and invincible disposition, disdaining to put them to death, and scorning either to retain or entertain them: they were all sent back again to their countries, to witness and recount the worthy achievements of their invincible and dreadful navy: of which the number of soldiers and fearful burthen of their ships, the commanders' names of every squadron, with all other their magazines of provisions, were put in print, as an army and navy unresistable, and disdaining prevention. With all which so great and terrible an ostentation, they did not in all their sailing round about England, so much as sink or take one ship, bark, pinnace, or cockboat of ours: or ever burnt so much as one sheepcote of this land. When as on the contrary, Sir Francis Drake, with only

[1] bombs

eight hundred soldiers not long before, landed in their Indies, and forced [1] Sant-Iago, Santo Domingo, Cartagena, and the forts of Florida.

And after that, Sir John Norris marched from Peniche in Portugal, with a handful of soldiers, to the gates of Lisbon, being above forty English miles. Where the Earl of Essex himself and other valiant gentlemen braved the city of Lisbon, encamped at the very gates; from whence, after many days abode, finding neither promised party, nor provision to batter, made retreat by land, in despite of all their garrisons, both of horse and foot. In this sort I have a little digressed from my first purpose, only by the necessary comparison of theirs and our actions: the one covetous of honor without vaunt or ostentation; the other so greedy to purchase the opinion of their own affairs, and by false rumors to resist the blasts of their own dishonors, as they will not only not blush to spread all manner of untruths: but even for the least advantage, be it but for the taking of one poor adventurer of the English, will celebrate the victory with bonfires in every town, always spending more in fagots than the purchase was worth they obtained. When as we never thought it worth the consumption of two billets,[2] when we have taken eight or ten of their Indian ships at one time, and twenty of the Brazil fleet. Such is the difference between true valor and ostentation: and between honorable actions and frivolous vainglorious vaunts. But now to return to my purpose.

The Lord Thomas Howard with six of her Majesty's ships, six victualers of London, the bark *Ralegh,* and two or three other pinnaces riding at anchor near unto Flores, one of the westerly islands of the Azores, the last of August in the afternoon, had intelligence by one

[1] captured   [2] sticks of firewood

Captain Middleton of the approach of the Spanish armada. Which Middleton being in a very good sailer, had kept them company three days before, of good purpose, both to discover their forces the more, as also to give advice to my Lord Thomas of their approach. He had no sooner delivered the news but the fleet was in sight; many of our ships' companies were on shore in the island; some providing ballast for their ships; others filling of water and refreshing themselves from the land with such things as they could either for money, or by force recover. By reason whereof our ships being all pestered and rummaging every thing out of order, very light for want of ballast, and that which was most to our disadvantage, the one half part of the men of every ship sick, and utterly unserviceable: for in the *Revenge* there were ninety diseased: in the *Bonaventure* not so many in health as could handle her mainsail. For had not twenty men been taken out of a bark of Sir George Carey's, his being commanded to be sunk, and those appointed to her, she had hardly ever recovered England. The rest, for the most part, were in little better state. The names of her Majesty's ships were these as followeth: the *Defiance,* which was admiral, the *Revenge,* viceadmiral, the *Bonaventure* commanded by Captain Cross, the *Lion* by George Fenner, the *Foresight* by M. Thomas Vavasour, and the *Crane* by Duffield. The *Foresight* and the *Crane* being but small ships; only the other were of the middle size; the rest, besides the bark *Ralegh,* commanded by Captain Thin, were victualers, and of small force or none. The Spanish fleet having shrouded their approach by reason of the island; were now so soon at hand, as our ships had scarce time to weigh their anchors, but some of them were driven to let slip their cables and set sail. Sir Richard Grenville was the last weighed, to recover the men that were

upon the island, which otherwise had been lost.   The
Lord Thomas with the rest very hardly recovered the
wind, which Sir Richard Grenville not being able to
do, was persuaded by the master and others to cut his
mainsail and cast about, and to trust to the sailing of
the ship; for the squadron of Seville were on his weather
bow.   But Sir Richard utterly refused to turn from
the enemy, alleging that he would rather choose to die,
than to dishonor himself, his country, and her Majesty's
ship, persuading his company that he would pass through
the two squadrons, in despite of them, and enforce
those of Seville to give him way.   Which he performed
upon divers of the foremost, who, as the mariners term
it, sprang their luff,[1] and fell under the lee of the
Revenge.   But the other course had been the better,
and might right well have been answered in so great an
impossibility of prevailing.   Notwithstanding out of the
greatness of his mind, he could not be persuaded.   In
the mean while as he attended those which were nearest
him, the great *San Philip* being in the wind of him,
and coming towards him, becalmed his sails in such
sort, as the ship could neither make way, nor feel the
helm; so huge and high carged[2] was the Spanish ship,
being of a thousand and five hundred tons.   Who after
laid the *Revenge* aboard.[3]   When he was thus bereft of
his sails, the ships that were under his lee luffing up,
also laid him aboard: of which the next was the admiral
of the Biscayans, a very mighty and puissant ship commanded by Brittandona.   The said *Philip* carried three
tier of ordnance on a side, and eleven pieces in every
tier.   She shot eight forth right out of her chase,[4] besides those of her stern ports.

After the *Revenge* was entangled with this *Philip*,

[1] steered into the wind   [2] carriaged, *i.e.* high-bodied   [3] came
close for attack   [4] bow

four others boarded her; two on her larboard, and two on her starboard. The fight thus beginning at three of the clock in the afternoon, continued very terrible all that evening. But the great *San Philip* having received the lower tier of the *Revenge,* discharged with crossbar shot, shifted herself with all diligence from her sides, utterly misliking her first entertainment. Some say that the ship foundered, but we cannot report it for truth, unless we were assured. The Spanish ships were filled with companies of soldiers: in some two hundred besides the mariners; in some five, in others eight hundred. In ours there were none at all beside the mariners, but the servants of the commanders and some few voluntary gentlemen only. After many interchanged volleys of great ordnance and small shot, the Spaniards deliberated to enter the *Revenge,* and made divers attempts, hoping to force her by the multitudes of their armed soldiers and musketeers, but were still repulsed again and again, and at all times beaten back into their own ships, or into the seas. In the beginning of the fight, the *George Noble* of London having received some shot through her by the armadas, fell under the lee of the *Revenge,* and asked Sir Richard what he would command him, being but one of the victualers and of small force: Sir Richard bade him save himself, and leave him to his fortune. After the fight had thus, without intermission, continued while the day lasted and some hours of the night, many of our men were slain and hurt, and one of the great galleons of the armada, and the admiral of the hulks both sunk, and in many other of the Spanish ships great slaughter was made. Some write that Sir Richard was very dangerously hurt almost in the beginning of the fight, and lay speechless for a time ere he recovered. But two of the *Revenge's* own company, brought home in a ship of Lima from the islands, examined by some of the lords and others, affirmed that he was never so wounded as that he forsook the upper deck, till an hour before midnight: and then being shot into the body with a musket as he was a-dressing, was again shot into the head, and withal [1] his surgeon wounded to death. This agreeth also with an examination taken by Sir Francis Godolphin, of four other mariners of the same ship being returned, which examination, the said Sir Francis sent unto Master William Killigrew, of her Majesty's privy chamber.

But to return to the fight, the Spanish ships which attempted to board the *Revenge,* as they were wounded and beaten off, so always others came in their places, she having never less than two mighty galleons by her sides, and aboard her: so that ere the morning, from three of the clock the day before, there had fifteen several armadas assailed her; and all so ill approved their entertainment, as they were by the break of day, far more willing to hearken to a composition [2] than hastily to make any more assaults or entries. But as the day increased, so our men decreased: and as the light grew more and more, by so much more grew our discomforts. For none appeared in sight but enemies, saving one small ship called the *Pilgrim,* commanded by Jacob Whiddon, who hovered all night to see the success: but in the morning bearing with the *Revenge,* was hunted like a hare amongst many ravenous hounds, but escaped.

All the powder of the *Revenge* to the last barrel was now spent, all her pikes broken, forty of her best men slain, and the most part of the rest hurt. In the beginning of the fight she had but one hundred free from sickness, and fourscore and ten sick, laid in hold upon the ballast. A small troop to man such a ship, and a weak garrison to resist so mighty an army. By those hundred

[1] in spite of the efforts of   [2] offer of peace

all was sustained, the volleys, boardings, and enterings of fifteen ships of war, besides those which beat her at large. On the contrary, the Spanish were always supplied with soldiers brought from every squadron: all manner of arms and powder at will. Unto ours there remained no comfort at all, no hope, no supply either of ships, men, or weapons; the masts all beaten overboard, all her tackle cut asunder, her upper work altogether razed, and in effect evened she was with the water, but the very foundation or bottom of a ship, nothing being left overhead either for flight or defense. Sir Richard finding himself in this distress, and unable any longer to make resistance, having endured in this fifteen hours' fight, the assault of fifteen several armadas, all by turns aboard him, and by estimation eight hundred shot of great artillery, besides many assaults and entries; and that himself and the ship must needs be possessed by the enemy, who were now all cast in a ring round about him. (The *Revenge* not able to move one way or other, but as she was moved with the waves and billow of the sea) commanded the master gunner, whom he knew to be a most resolute man, to split and sink the ship; that thereby nothing might remain of glory or victory to the Spaniards: seeing in so many hours fight, and with so great a navy they were not able to take her, having had fifteen hours time, fifteen thousand men, and fifty and three sail of men-of-war to perform it withal: and persuaded the company, or as many as he could induce, to yield themselves unto God, and to the mercy of none else; but as they had, like valiant resolute men, repulsed so many enemies, they should not now shorten the honor of their nation, by prolonging their own lives for a few hours, or a few days. The master gunner readily condescended and divers others; but the captain and the master were of another opinion, and besought Sir Richard to have care of them: alleging that the Spaniard would be as ready to entertain a composition, as they were willing to offer the same: and that there being divers sufficent and valiant men yet living, and whose wounds were not mortal, they might do their country and prince acceptable service hereafter. And (that where Sir Richard had alleged that the Spaniards should never glory to have taken one ship of her Majesty, seeing they had so long and so notably defended themselves); they answered, that the ship had six foot water in hold, three shot under water, which were so weakly stopped as with the first working of the sea, she must needs sink, and was besides so crushed and bruised, as she could never be removed out of the place.

And as the matter was thus in dispute, and Sir Richard refusing to hearken to any of those reasons: the master of the *Revenge* (while the captain won unto him the greater party) was convoyed aboard the General Don Alfonso Baçan. Who finding none over hasty to enter the *Revenge* again, doubting lest Sir Richard would have blown them up and himself, and perceiving by the report of the master of the *Revenge* his dangerous disposition, yielded that all their lives should be saved, the company sent for England, and the better sort to pay such reasonable ransom as their estate would bear, and in the mean season to be free from galley or imprisonment. To this he so much the rather condescended as well, as I have said, for fear of further loss and mischief to themselves, as also for the desire he had to recover Sir Richard Grenville; whom for his notable valor he seemed greatly to honor and admire.

When this answer was returned, and that safety of life was promised, the common sort being now at the end of their peril, the most drew back from Sir Richard and

the master gunner, being no hard matter to dissuade
men from death to life. The master gunner finding
himself and Sir Richard thus prevented and mastered
by the greater number, would have slain himself with
a sword, had he not been by force withheld and locked
into his cabin. Then the *General* sent many boats aboard
the *Revenge,* and divers of our men fearing Sir Richard's
disposition, stole away aboard the *General* and other
ships. Sir Richard thus overmatched, was sent unto
by Alfonso Baçan to remove out of the *Revenge,* the
ship being marvellous unsavory, filled with blood and
bodies of dead, and wounded men like a slaughter-house.
Sir Richard answered that he might do with his body
what he list, for he esteemed it not, and as he was carried out of the ship he swooned, and reviving again desired the company to pray for him. The General used
Sir Richard with all humanity, and left nothing unat-
tempted that tended to his recovery, highly commend-
ing his valor and worthiness, and greatly bewailed the
danger wherein he was, being unto them a rare spectacle, and a resolution seldom approved, to see one
ship turn toward so many enemies, to endure the charge
and boarding of so many huge armadas, and to resist and
repel the assaults and entries of so many soldiers. All
which and more is confirmed by a Spanish captain of
the same Armada, and a present actor in the fight, who
being severed from the rest in a storm, was by the *Lion*
of London, a small ship taken, and is now prisoner in
London.

The general commander of the Armada was Don
Alfonso Baçan, brother to the Marquis of Santa Cruz.
The admiral of the Biscayan squadron, was Britan
Dona. Of the squadron of Seville, the Marquis of
Arumburch. The Hulks [1] and Fly-boats [2] were com-

———

[1] transports   [2] light sailboats

manded by Luis Coutinho. There were slain and
drowned in this fight, well near two thousand of the
enemies, and two especial commanders Don Luis de Sant
John, and Don George de Prunaria de Malaga, as the
Spanish captain confesseth, besides divers others of special account, whereof as yet report is not made.

The Admiral of the Hulks and the *Ascension* of
Seville were both sunk by the side of the *Revenge;* one
other recovered the road of Saint Michaels, and sunk
also there; a fourth ran herself with the shore to save
her men. Sir Richard died, as it is said, the second or
third day aboard the *General,* and was by them greatly
bewailed. What became of his body, whether it was
buried in the sea or on the land we know not: the comfort that remaineth to his friends is, that he hath ended
his life honorably in respect of the reputation won to
his nation and country, and of the same to his posterity,
and that being dead, he hath not outlived his own
honor.

For the rest of her Majesty's ships that entered not
so far into the fight as the *Revenge,* the reasons and
causes were these. There were of them but six in all,
whereof two but small ships; the *Revenge* engaged
past recovery: the island of Flores was on the one side,
fifty-three sail of the Spanish, divided into sqadrons
on the other, all as full filled with soldiers as they could
contain: almost the one half of our men sick and not
able to serve: the ships grown foul, unrummaged, and
scarcely able to bear any sail for want of ballast, having
been six months at sea before. If all the rest had entered, all had been lost: for the very hugeness of the
Spanish fleet, if no other violence had been offered,
would have crushed them between them into shivers.
Of which the dishonor and loss to the Queen had been
far greater than the spoil or harm that the enemy

could any way have received. Notwithstanding it is very true, that the Lord Thomas would have entered between the squadrons, but the rest would not condescend; and the master of his own ship offered to leap into the sea, rather than to conduct that her Majesty's ship and the rest to be a prey to the enemy, where there was no hope nor possibility either of defense or victory. Which also in my opinion had ill sorted or answered the discretion and trust of a general, to commit himself and his charge to an assured destruction, without hope or any likelihood of prevailing: thereby to diminish the strength of her Majesty's navy, and to enrich the pride and glory of the enemy. The *Foresight* of the Queen's commanded by M. Thomas Vavasour performed a very great fight, and staid two hours as near the *Revenge* as the weather would permit him, not forsaking the fight, till he was like to be encompassed by the squadrons, and with great difficulty cleared himself. The rest gave divers volleys of shot, and entered as far as the place permitted, and their own necessities, to keep the weather gage [1] of the enemy, until they were parted by night. A few days after the fight was ended, and the English prisoners dispersed into the Spanish and Indian ships, there arose so great a storm from the west and northwest, that all the fleet was dispersed, as well the Indian fleet which were then come unto them, as the rest of the Armada which attended their arrival, of which, fourteen sail together with the *Revenge,* and in her two hundred Spaniards, were cast away from the isle of St. Michaels. So it pleased them to honor the burial of that renowned ship the *Revenge,* not suffering her to perish alone, for the great honor she achieved in her lifetime. On the rest of the islands there were cast

[1] to windward

away in this storm, fifteen or sixteen more of the ships of war: and of an hundred and odd sail of the Indian fleet, expected this year in Spain, what in this tempest, and what before in the bay of Mexico, and about the Bermudas, there were seventy and odd consumed and lost, with those taken by our ships of London, besides one very rich Indian ship, which set herself on fire, being boarded by the *Pilgrim,* and five other taken by master Watts his ships of London, between the Havana and Cape St. Antonio. The fourth of this month of November we received letters from the Tercera, affirming that there are three thousand bodies of men remaining in that island, saved out of the perished ships: and that by the Spaniards' own confession, there are ten thousand cast away in this storm, besides those that are perished between the islands and the main. Thus it hath pleased God to fight for us, and to defend the justice of our cause, against the ambitious and bloody pretenses of the Spaniard, who seeking to devour all nations, are themselves devoured. A manifest testimony how unjust and displeasing, their attempts are in the sight of God, who hath pleased to witness by the success of their affairs, his mislike of their bloody and injurious designs, purposed and practised against all Christian princes, over whom they seek unlawful and ungodly rule and empery.

One day or two before this wreck happened to the Spanish fleet, when as some of our prisoners desired to be set on shore upon the islands, hoping to be from thence transported into England, which liberty was formerly by the general promised: one Morice Fitz John, son of old John of Desmond, a notable traitor, cousin german to the late Earl of Desmond, was sent to the English from ship to ship, to persuade them to serve the King of Spain. The arguments he used to induce them were these. The increase of pay which he promised to be trebled: advancement to the better sort: and the exercise of the true Catholic Religion, and safety of their souls to all. For the first, even the beggarly and unnatural behavior of those English and Irish rebels, that served the King in that present action, was sufficient to answer that first argument of rich pay. For so poor and beggarly they were, as for want of apparel they stripped their poor countrymen prisoners out of their ragged garments, worn to nothing by six months' service, and spared not to despoil them even of their bloody shirts, from their wounded bodies, and the very shoes from their feet: a notable testimony of their rich entertainment and great wages. The second reason was hope of advancement if they served well, and would continue faithful to the King. But what man can be so blockishly ignorant ever to expect place or honor from a foreign King, having no other argument or persuasion than his own disloyalty; to be unnatural to his own country that bred him; to his parents that begat him, and rebellious to his true prince, to whose obedience he is bound by oath, by nature, and by religion? No, they are only assured to be employed in all desperate enterprises, to be held in scorn and disdain ever among those whom they serve. And that ever traitor was either trusted or advanced I could never yet read, neither can I at this time remember any example. And no man could have less become the place of an orator for such a purpose, than this Morice of Desmond. For the Earl his cousin being one of the greatest subjects in that kingdom of Ireland, having almost whole countries in his possession; so many goodly manors, castles, and lordships; the Count Palatine of Kerry, five hundred gentlemen of his own name and family to follow him, besides others, all which he possessed in peace for three or four hundred years, was in less than three years after his adhering to the Spaniards and rebellion, beaten from all his holds, not so many as ten gentlemen of his name left living, himself taken and beheaded by a soldier of his own nation, and his land given by a Parliament to her Majesty, and possessed by the English: his other cousin Sir John of Desmond taken by Master John Zouch, and his body hanged over the gates of his native city to be devoured by ravens: the third brother Sir James hanged, drawn, and quartered in the same place. If he had withal vaunted of this success of his own house, no doubt the argument would have moved much, and wrought great effect: which because, he for that present forgot, I thought it good to remember in his behalf. For matter of religion it would require a particular volume, if I should set down how irreligiously they cover their greedy and ambitious pretences, with that veil of piety. But sure I am, that there is no kingdom or commonwealth in all Europe, but if they be reformed,[1] they then invade it for religion sake: if it be, as they term Catholic, they pretend title; as if the Kings of Castile were the natural heirs of all the world: and so between both, no kingdom is unsought. Where they dare not with their own forces to invade, they basely entertain the traitors and vagabonds of all nations: seeking by those and by their runnagate Jesuits to win parts, and have by that mean ruined many noble houses and others in this land, and have extinguished both their lives and families. What good, honor, or fortune ever man yet by them achieved, is yet unheard of, or unwritten. And if our English Papists do but look into Portugal, against whom they have no pretence of religion, how the nobility are put to death, impris-

[1] become Protestants

oned, their rich men made a prey, and all sorts of people captived; they shall find that the obedience even of the Turk is easy and a liberty, in respect of the slavery and tyranny of Spain. What have they done in Sicily, in Naples, Milan, and in the low countries; who hath there been spared for religion at all? And it cometh to my remembrance of a certain Burger of Antwerp, whose house being entered by a company of Spanish soldiers, when they first sacked the city, he besought them to spare him and his goods, being a good Catholic, and one of their own party and faction. The Spaniards answered, that they knew him to be of a good conscience for himself, but his money, plate, jewels, and goods, were all heretical, and therefore good prize. So they abused and tormented the foolish Fleming, who hoped that an *Agnus Dei* had been a sufficient target against all force of that holy and charitable nation. Neither have they at any time as they protest invaded the kingdoms of the Indies and Peru, and elsewhere, but only led thereunto, rather to reduce the people to Christianity, than for either gold or empery. When as in one only island called Hispaniola, they have wasted thirty hundred thousand of the natural people, besides many millions else in other places of the Indies: a poor and harmless people created of God, and might have been won to his knowledge, as many of them were, and almost as many as ever were persuaded thereunto. The story whereof is at large written by a bishop of their own nation called Bartholomew de las Casas, and translated into English and many other languages, entitled *The Spanish Cruelties.* Who would therefore repose trust in such a nation of ravenous strangers, and especially in those Spaniards which more greedily thirst after English blood, than after the lives of any other people of Europe, for the many overthrows and dishonors they have received at our hands, whose weakness we have discovered to the world, and whose forces at home, abroad, in Europe, in India, by sea and land, we have even with handfuls of men and ships, overthrown and dishonored. Let not therefore any English man, of what religion soever, have other opinion of the Spaniards, but that those whom he seeketh to win of our nation, he esteemeth base and traitorous, unworthy persons, or unconstant fools: and that he useth his pretence of religion, for no other purpose but to bewitch us from the obedience of our natural prince, thereby hoping in time to bring us to slavery and subjection, and then none shall be unto them so odious, and disdained as the traitors themselves, who have sold their country to a stranger, and forsaken their faith and obedience contrary to nature and religion; and contrary to that human and general honor, not only of Christians, but of heathen and irreligious nations, who have always sustained what labor soever, and embraced even death itself, for their country, prince, or commonwealth. To conclude, it hath ever to this day pleased God to prosper and defend her Majesty, to break the purposes of malicious enemies, of forsworn traitors, and of unjust practices and invasions. She hath ever been honored of the worthiest kings, served by faithful subjects, and shall by the favor of God resist, repel, and confound all whatsoever attempts against her sacred person or kingdom. In the meantime let the Spaniard and traitor vaunt of their success, and we her true and obedient vassals, guided by the shining light of her virtues, shall always love her, serve her, and obey her to the end of our lives.

(1591)

LYRICS

REPLY TO MARLOWE'S PASSIONATE SHEPHERD

If ALL the world and love were young,
And truth in every shepherd's tongue,
These pretty pleasures might me move,
To live with thee and be thy love.

But time drives flocks from field to fold,
When rivers rage and rocks grow cold;
And Philomel becometh dumb;
The rest complains of cares to come.

The flowers do fade, and wanton fields
To wayward winter reckoning yields: 10
A honey tongue, a heart of gall,
Is fancy's spring, but sorrow's fall.

Thy gowns, thy shoes, thy beds of roses,
Thy cap, thy kirtle, and thy posies,
Soon break, soon wither, soon forgotten,
In folly ripe, in reason rotten.

Thy belt of straw and ivy buds,
Thy coral clasps and amber studs,—
All those in me no means can move,
To come to thee and be thy love.   20

But could youth last, and love still breed,
Had joys no date, nor age no need;
Then those delights my mind might move
To live with thee and be thy love.

(1589?)

A VISION UPON THIS CONCEIT
OF THE FAERY QUEEN

METHOUGHT I saw the grave where Laura lay,
Within that temple where the vestal flame
Was wont to burn: and, passing by that way,
To see that buried dust of living fame,
Whose tomb fair Love and fairer Virtue kept,
All suddenly I saw the Faery Queen;
At whose approach the soul of Petrarch wept,
And from thenceforth those graces were not seen,
For they this queen attended; in whose stead
Oblivion laid him down on Laura's hearse.   10
Hereat the hardest stones were seen to bleed,
And groans of buried ghosts the heavens did pierce:
Where Homer's sprite did tremble all for grief,
And cursed the access of that celestial thief.

                                        (1590)

A DESCRIPTION OF LOVE

Now what is love, I pray thee tell?
It is that fountain and that well
Where pleasure and repentance dwell.
It is perhaps that sauncing [1] bell
That tolls all into heaven or hell.
And this is love, as I hear tell.

Yet what is love, I pray thee say?
It is a work on holy day.
It is December matched with May,
When lusty bloods in fresh array   10
Hear ten months after of the play.

[1] holy

And this is love, as I hear say.

Yet what is love, I pray thee sain?
It is a sunshine mixed with rain.
It is a tooth-ache, or like pain;
It is a game where none doth gain:
The lass saith No, and would full fain,
And this is love, as I hear sain.

Yet what is love, I pray thee say?
It is a yea, it is a nay,   20
A pretty kind of sporting fray;
It is a thing will soon away:
Then take the vantage while you may.
And this is love, as I hear say.

Yet what is love, I pray thee show?
A thing that creeps, it cannot go;
A prize that passeth to and fro;
A thing for one, a thing for mo;
And he that proves must find it so.
And this is love, sweet friend, I trow.   30

                                        (1593)

THE SILENT LOVER

I

Our passions are most like to floods and streams,
    The shallow murmur, but the deep are dumb;
So, when affection yields discourse, it seems
    The bottom is but shallow whence they come.
They that are rich in words, must needs discover
That they are poor in that which makes a lover.

II

Wrong not, sweet empress of my heart,
   The merit of true passion,
With thinking that he feels no smart,
   That sues for no compassion   10
Since, if my plaints serve not to prove
   The conquest of your beauty,
They come not from defect of love,
   But from excess of duty.

For knowing that I sue to serve
   A saint of such perfection
As all desire—yet none deserve—
   A place in her affection,
I rather choose to want relief
   Than venture the revealing;   20
When glory recommends the grief,
   Despair distrusts the healing.

Thus those desires that aim too high
   For any mortal lover,
When reason cannot make them die,
   Discretion doth them cover.
Yet, when discretion doth bereave
   The plaints that they should utter,
Then your discretion may perceive
   That silence is a suitor.   30

Silence in love bewrays more woe
   Than words though ne'er so witty;
A beggar that is dumb, you know,
   Deserveth double pity.

Then misconceive not, dearest heart,
  My true, though secret passion;
He smarteth most that hides his smart,
  And sues for no compassion.

(1600?)

HIS PILGRIMAGE

Give me my scallop-shell of quiet,
  My staff of faith to walk upon,
My scrip [1] of joy, immortal diet,
  My bottle of salvation,
My gown of glory, hope's true gauge;
And thus I'll take my pilgrimage.

Blood must be my body's balmer;
  No other balm will there be given;
Whilst my soul, like a quiet palmer,
  Traveleth towards the land of heaven,   10
Over the silver mountains,
Where spring the nectar fountains.
    There will I kiss
    The bowl of bliss;
And drink mine everlasting fill
Upon every milken hill.
My soul will be a-dry before;
But, after, it will thirst no more.

Then by that happy blissful day
  More peaceful pilgrims I shall see,   20
That have cast off their rags of clay,
  And walk appareled fresh like me.
    I'll take them first,
    To quench their thirst
─────────────
[1] wallet

And taste of nectar suckets,[1]
   At those clear wells
   Where sweetness dwells,
Drawn up by saints in crystal buckets.

And when our bottles and all we
Are filled with immortality,   30
Then the blessèd paths we'll travel,
Strowed with rubies thick as gravel;
Ceilings of diamonds, sapphire floors,
High walls of coral, and pearly bowers.

From thence to heaven's bribeless hall,
Where no corruptèd voices brawl;
No conscience molten into gold;
No forged accuser bought or sold;
No cause deferred, no vain-spent journey,
For there Christ is the King's attorney,   40
Who pleads for all, without degrees,
And he hath angels but no fees.
   And when the grand twelve million jury
Of our sins, with direful fury,
Against our souls black verdicts give,
Christ pleads his death; and then we live.

Be Thou my speaker, taintless pleader!
Unblotted lawyer! true proceeder!
Thou giv'st salvation, even for alms,
Not with a bribèd lawyer's palms.   50

And this is mine eternal plea
To him that made heaven and earth and sea:
That, since my flesh must die so soon,
And want a head to dine next noon,

[1] delicacies

Just at the stroke, when my veins start and spread,
Set on my soul an everlasting head!

Then am I ready, like a palmer fit,
To tread those blest paths; which before I writ.

Of death and judgment, heaven and hell,
Who oft doth think, must needs die well.   60
                                        (1603)

THE CONCLUSION

EVEN such is time, that takes in trust
    Our youth, our joys, our all we have,
And pays us but with earth and dust;
    Who, in the dark and silent grave,
When we have wandered all our ways,
    Shuts up the story of our days;
But from this earth, this grave, this dust,
    My God shall raise me up, I trust!
                                        (1618)

CHRISTOPHER MARLOWE
(1564-1593)

HERO AND LEANDER

(From the First Sestiad)

ON HELLESPONT, guilty of true love's blood
In view and opposite two cities stood,
Sea-borderers, disjoined by Neptune's might;
The one Abydos, the other Sestos hight.
At Sestos Hero dwelt; Hero the fair,
Whom young Apollo courted for her hair,

And offered as a dower his burning throne,
Where she should sit, for men to gaze upon.
The outside of her garments were of lawn,
The lining purple silk, with gilt stars drawn: 10
Her wide sleeves green, and bordered with a grove,
Where Venus in her naked glory strove
To please the careless and disdainful eyes
Of proud Adonis, that before her lies;
Her kirtle blue, whereon was many a stain,
Made with the blood of wretched lovers slain.
Upon her head she ware a myrtle wreath,
From whence her veil reached to the ground beneath;
Her veil was artificial flowers and leaves
Whose workmanship both man and beast deceives.   20
Many would praise the sweet smell as she past,
When 'twas the odor which her breath forth cast;
And there, for honey, bees have sought in vain,
And, beat from thence, have lighted there again.
About her neck hung chains of pebble-stone,
Which, lightened by her neck, like diamonds shone.
She ware no gloves; for neither sun nor wind
Would burn or parch her hands, but, to her mind,
Or warm or cool them, for they took delight
To play upon those hands, they were so white.   30
Buskins [1] of shells, all silvered, uséd she,
And branched with blushing coral to the knee;
Where sparrows perched of hollow pearl and gold,
Such as the world would wonder to behold:
Those with sweet water oft her handmaid fills,
Which as she went, would chirrup through the bills.
Some say, for her the fairest Cupid pined,
And, looking in her face, was strooken blind.
But this is true; so like was one the other,
As he imagined Hero was his mother;   40

[1] high-laced shoes

And oftentimes into her bosom flew,
About her naked neck his bare arms threw,
And laid his childish head upon her breast,
And, with still panting rock, there took his rest.
So lovely-fair was Hero, Venus' nun,
As Nature wept, thinking she was undone,
Because she took more from her than she left,
And of such wondrous beauty her bereft:
Therefore, in sign her treasure suffered wrack,
Since Hero's time hath half the world been black.   50
    Amorous Leander, beautiful and young
(Whose tragedy divine Musæus sung),
Dwelt at Abydos; since him dwelt there none
For whom succeeding times make greater moan.
His dangling tresses, that were never shorn,
Had they been cut, and unto Colchos borne,
Would have allured the venturous youth of Greece
To hazard more than for the golden fleece.
Fair Cynthia wished his arms might be her sphere;
Grief makes her pale, because she moves not there.   60
His body was as straight as Circe's wand;
Jove might have sipt out nectar from his hand.
Even as delicious meat is to the taste,
So was his neck in touching, and surpast
The white of Pelops' shoulder: I could tell ye,
How smooth his breast was, and how white his belly;
And whose immortal fingers did imprint
That heavenly path with many a curious dint
That runs along his back; but my rude pen
Can hardly blazon forth the loves of men,   70
Much less of powerful gods: let it suffice
That my slack Muse sings of Leander's eyes;
Those orient cheeks and lips, exceeding his
That leapt into the water for a kiss
Of his own shadow, and, despising many,

Died ere he could enjoy the love of any.
Had wild Hippolytus Leander seen,
Enamored of his beauty had he been.
His presence made the rudest peasant melt,
That in the vast uplandish country dwelt;   80
The barbarous Thracian soldier, moved with naught,
Was moved with him, and for his favor sought.
Some swore he was a maid in man's attire,
For in his looks were all that men desire,—
A pleasant-smiling cheek, a speaking eye,
A brow for love to banquet royally;
And such as knew he was a man, would say,
'Leander, thou art made for amorous play;
Why art thou not in love, and loved of all?
Though thou be fair, yet be not thine own thrall.'   90
  The men of wealthy Sestos every year,
For his sake whom their goddess held so dear,
Rose-cheeked Adonis, kept a solemn feast.
Thither resorted many a wandering guest
To meet their loves; such as had none at all,
Came lovers home from this great festival;
For every street, like to a firmament,
Glistered with breathing stars, who, where they went,
Frightèd the melancholy earth, which deemed
Eternal heaven to burn, for so it seemed   100
As if another Phaëton had got
The guidance of the sun's rich chariot.
But, far above the loveliest, Hero shined,
And stole away th' enchanted gazer's mind;
For like sea-nymphs' inveigling harmony,
So was her beauty to the standers by;
Nor that night-wandering, pale, and watery star
(When yawning dragons draw her thirling car
From Latmus' mount up to the gloomy sky,

Where, crowned with blazing light and majesty,⠀⠀110
She proudly sits) more over-rules the flood
Than she the hearts of those that near her stood.
Even as, when gaudy nymphs pursue the chase,
Wretched Ixion's shaggy-footed race,
Incensed with savage heat, gallop amain
From steep pine-bearing mountains to the plain,
So ran the people forth to gaze upon her,
And all that viewed her were enamored on her.
And as, in fury of a dreadful fight,
Their fellows being slain or put to flight,⠀⠀120
Poor soldiers stand with fear of death dead-strooken,
So at her presence all surprised and tooken,
Await the sentence of her scornful eyes;
He whom she favors lives; the other dies.
There might you see one sigh; another rage;
And some, their violent passions to assuage,
Compile sharp satires; but, alas, too late!
For faithful love will never turn to hate.
And many, seeing great princes were denied,
Pined as they went, and thinking on her died.⠀⠀130
On this feast-day—O cursèd day and hour!—
Went Hero thorough Sestos, from her tower
To Venus' temple, where unhappily,
As after chanced, they did each other spy.
So fair a church as this had Venus none:
The walls were of discolored jasper-stone,
Wherein was Proteus carved; and overhead
A lively vine of green sea-agate spread,
Where by one hand light-headed Bacchus hung,
And with the other wine from grapes outwrung.⠀⠀140
Of crystal shining fair the pavement was;
The town of Sestos called it Venus' glass:
There might you see the gods in sundry shapes,

Committing heady riots, incest, rapes:
For know, that underneath this radiant flour
Was Danae's statue in a brazen tower;
Jove slily stealing from his sister's bed,
To dally with Idalian Ganymed,
And for his love Europa bellowing loud,
And tumbling with the Rainbow in a cloud;   150
Blood-quaffing Mars, heaving the iron net,
Which limping Vulcan and his Cyclops set:
Love kindling fire, to burn such towns as Troy:
Silvanus weeping for the lovely boy
That now is turned into a cypress-tree,
Under whose shade the wood-gods love to be.
And in the midst a silver altar stood:
There Hero, sacrificing turtles' blood,
Vailed to the ground, veiling her eyelids close;
And modestly they opened as she rose.   160
Thence flew Love's arrow with the golden head;
And thus Leander was enamorèd.
Stone-still he stood, and evermore he gazed,
Till with the fire that from his countenance blazed
Relenting Hero's gentle heart was strook:
Such force and virtue hath an amorous look.

  It lies not in our power to love or hate,
For will in us is over-ruled by fate.
When two are stript long ere the course begin,
We wish that one should lose, the other win;   170
And one especially do we affect
Of two gold ingots, like in each respect:
The reason no man knows, let it suffice,
What we behold is censured by our eyes.
Where both deliberate, the love is slight:
Who ever loved, that loved not at first sight?

*   *   *

(From the Second Sestiad)

*   *   *

Now had the Morn espied her lover's steeds;
Whereat she starts, puts on her purple weeds,
And, red for anger that he stay'd so long,
All headlong throws herself the clouds among.
And now Leander, fearing to be miss'd,
Embrac'd her suddenly, took leave, and kiss'd:
Long was he taking leave, and loathe to go,
And kiss'd again, as lovers use to do.
Sad Hero wrung him by the hand, and wept,
Saying, "Let your vows and promises be kept":   10
Then standing at the door, she turn'd about,
As loathe to see Leander going out.
And now the sun, that through th' horizon peeps,
As pitying these lovers, downward creeps;
So that in silence of the cloudy night,
Though it was morning, did he take his flight.
But what the secret trusty night conceal'd,
Leander's amorous habit soon reveal'd:
With Cupid's myrtle was his bonnet crown'd,
About his arms the purple riband wound,   20
Wherewith she wreath'd her largely-spreading hair;
Nor could the youth abstain, but he must wear
The sacred ring wherewith she was endow'd,
When first religious chastity she vow'd;
Which made his love through Sestos to be known,
And thence unto Abydos sooner blown
That he could sail; for incorporeal Fame,
Whose weight consists in nothing but her name,
Is swifter than the wind, whose tardy plumes
Are reeking water and dull earthly fumes.   30
    Home when he came, he seem'd not to be there,
But, like exiled air thrust from his sphere,

Set in a foreign place; and straight from thence,
Alcides-like, by mighty violence,
He would have chas'd away the swelling main,
That him from her unjustly did detain.
Like as the sun in a diameter
Fires and inflames objects removèd far,
And heateth kindly, shining laterally;
So beauty sweetly quickens when 'tis nigh,   40
But being separated and remov'd,
Burns where it cherish'd, murders where it lov'd.
Therefore even as an index to a book,
So to his mind was young Leander's look.
O, none but gods have power their love to hide!
Affection by the countenance is descried;
The light of hidden fire itself discovers,
And love that is conceal'd betrays poor lovers.
His secret flame apparently was seen:
Leander's father knew where he had been,   50
And for the same mildly rebuk'd his son,
Thinking to quench the sparkles new-begun.
But love resisted once, grows passionate,
And nothing more than counsel lovers hate;
For as a hot proud horse highly disdains
To have his head controll'd, but breaks the reins,
Spits forth the ringled bit, and with his hoves
Checks the submissive ground; so he that loves,
The more he is restrain'd, the worse he fares:
What is it now but mad Leander dares?   60
"O Hero, Hero!" thus he cried full oft;
And then he got him to a rock aloft,
Where having spied her tower, long star'd he on't,
And pray'd the narrow toiling Hellespont
To part in twain, that he might come and go;
But still the rising billows answer'd, "No."
With that, he stripp'd him to the ivory skin,

And, crying, "Love, I come" leap'd lively in:
Whereat the sapphire-visag'd god grew proud,
And made his capering Triton sound aloud,　　70
Imagining that Ganymede, displeas'd,
Had left the heavens; therefore on him he seiz'd.
Leander striv'd; the waves about him wound,
And pull'd him to the bottom, where the ground
Was strew'd with pearl, and in low coral groves
Sweet-singing mermaids sported with their loves
On heaps of heavy gold, and took great pleasure
To spurn in careless sort the shipwreck treasure;
For here the stately azure palace stood,
Where kingly Neptune and his train abode.　　80

* * *

(1593? printed 1598)

THE PASSIONATE SHEPHERD

COME live with me, and be my love;
And we will all the pleasures prove
That hills and valleys, dales and fields,
Woods, or steepy mountain yields.

And we will sit upon the rocks,
Seeing the shepherds feed their flocks
By shallow rivers, to whose falls
Melodious birds sing madrigals.

And I will make thee beds of roses,
And a thousand fragrant posies;　　10
A cap of flowers, and a kirtle
Embroidered all with leaves of myrtle;

A gown made of the finest wool
Which from our pretty lambs we pull;

Fair-linèd slippers for the cold,
With buckles of the purest gold;

A belt of straw and ivy-buds,
With coral clasps and amber studs:
And, if these pleasures may thee move,
Come live with me, and be my love.   20

The shepherd-swains shall dance and sing
For thy delight each May-morning:
If these delights thy mind may move,
Then live with me, and be my love.

(1589)

ELIZABETHAN LYRICS

ANONYMOUS

The proverb reporteth, no man can deny,
That wedding and hanging is destiny.

(From *Tom Tyler and His Wife*)

I AM a poor tiler in simple array,
And get a poor living, but eightpence a day,
My wife as I get it doth spend it away,
    And I cannot help it, she saith; wot we why?
    For wedding and hanging is destiny.

I thought, when I wed her, she had been a sheep,
At board to be friendly, to sleep when I sleep;
She loves so unkindly, she makes me to weep;
    But I dare say nothing, God wot! wot ye why?
    For wedding and hanging is destiny.   10

Besides this unkindness whereof my grief grows,
I think few tilers are matched with such shrows:
Before she leaves brawling, she falls to deal blows
    Which, early and late, doth cause me cry
    That wedding and hanging is destiny.

The more that I please her, the worse she doth like me;
The more I forbear her, the more she doth strike me;
The more that I get her, the more she doth glike[1] me;
    Woe worth this ill fortune that maketh me cry
    That wedding and hanging is destiny.

[1] mock

If I had been hanged when I had been married,
My torments had ended, though I had miscarried;
If I had been warned, then would I have tarried;
  But now all too lately I feel and cry
  That wedding and hanging is destiny.

                                        (1558-9)

ALE SONG

(From *Gammer Gurton's Needle*)

I CANNOT eat but little meat,
  My stomach is not good;
But, sure, I think that I can drink
  With him that wears a hood.
Though I go bare, take ye no care,
  I am nothing a-cold,
I stuff my skin so full within
  Of jolly good ale and old.

CHORUS—

  Back and side, go bare, go bare;
    Both foot and hand, go cold: 10
  But, belly, God send thee good ale enough,
    Whether it be new or old.

I love no roast, but a nut-brown toast
  And a crab laid in the fire;
A little bread shall do me stead,
  Much bread I not desire.
No frost nor snow, no wind, I trow,
  Can hurt me if I would,
I am so wrapt and throughly lapt
  Of jolly good ale and old.   20

And Tib my wife, that as her life
  Loveth well good ale to seek,
Full oft drinks she till ye may see
  The tears run down her cheek;
Then doth she trowl to me the bowl,
  Even as a malt-worm should,
And saith, 'Sweetheart, I took my part
  Of this jolly good ale and old.'

Now let them drink till they nod and wink,
  Even as good fellows should do;   30
They shall not miss to have the bliss
  Good ale doth bring men to.
And all poor souls that have scoured bowls,
  Or have them lustily trowled,
God save the lives of them and their wives,
  Whether they be young or old.

                                    (1575)

A NOSEGAY ALWAYS SWEET

*For lovers to send for tokens of love at New Year's
Tide, or for fairings*

A NOSEGAY, lacking flowers fresh,
  To you now I do send;
Desiring you to look thereon,
  When that you may intend:
For flowers fresh begin to fade,
  And Boreas in the field
Even with his hard congealed frost
  No better flowers doth yield.

But if that winter could have sprung
  A sweeter flower than this,   10

I would have sent it presently
   To you withouten miss:
Accept this then as time doth serve,
   Be thankful for the same,
Despise it not, but keep it well,
   And mark each flower his name.

Lavender is for lovers true,
   Which evermore be fain,
Desiring always for to have
   Some pleasure for their pain;   20
And when that they obtained have
   The love that they require,
Then have they all their perfect joy,
   And quenchèd is the fire.

Rosemary is for remembrance
   Between us day and night;
Wishing that I might always have
   You present in my sight.
And when I cannot have
   As I have said before,   30
Then Cupid with his deadly dart
   Doth wound my heart full sore.

Sage is for sustenance
   That should man's life sustain;
For I do still lie languishing
   Continually in pain,
And shall do still until I die,
   Except thou favor show:
My pain and all my grievous smart
   Full well you do it know.   40

Fennel is for flatterers,
  An evil thing it is sure:
But I have always meant truly,
  With constant heart most pure;
And will continue in the same
  As long as life doth last,
Still hoping for a joyful day
  When all our pains be past.

Violet is for faithfulness
  Which in me shall abide;   50
Hoping likewise that from your heart
  You will not let it slide;
And will continue in the same
  As you have now begun,
And then for ever to abide,
  Then you my heart have won.

Thyme is to try me,
  As each be trièd must,
Letting you know while life doth last
  I will not be unjust;   60
And if I should I would to God
  To hell my soul should bear,
And eke also that Belzebub
  With teeth he should me tear.

Roses is to rule me
  With reason as you will,
For to be still obedient
  Your mind for to fulfil;
And thereto will not disagree
  In nothing that you say,   70
But will content your mind truly
  In all things that I may.

Gillyflowers is for gentleness,
    Which in me shall remain,
Hoping that no sedition shall
    Depart our hearts in twain.
As soon the sun shall lose his course,
    The moon against her kind
Shall have no light, if that I do
    Once put you from my mind.   80

Carnations is for graciousness,
    Mark that now by the way,
Have no regard to flatterers,
    Nor pass not what they say:
For they will come with lying tales
    Your ears for to fulfil:
In any case do you consent
    Nothing unto their will.

Marigolds is for marriage,
    That would our minds suffice,   90
Lest that suspicion of us twain
    By any means should rise:
As for my part, I do not care,
    Myself I will still use
That all the women of the world
    For you I will refuse.

Pennyroyal is to print your love
    So deep within my heart,
That when you look this Nosegay on
    My pain you may impart;   100
And when that you have read the same,
    Consider well my woe,
Think ye then how to recompense
    Even him that loves you so.

Cowslips is for counsel,
    For secrets us between,
That none but you and I alone
    Should know the thing we mean:
And if you will thus wisely do,
    As I think to be best,   110
Then have you surely won the field
    And set my heart at rest.

I pray you keep this Nosegay well,
    And set by it some store:
And thus farewell! the gods thee guide
    Both now and evermore!
Not as the common sort do use,
    To set it in your breast,
That when the smell is gone away,
    On ground he takes his rest.   120

                  (1582?)

GEORGE GASCOIGNE (1535?-1577)

THE LULLABY OF A LOVER

    Sing lullaby, as women do,
Wherewith they bring their babes to rest,
And lullaby can I sing too,
    As womanly as can the best.
With lullaby they still the child,
And if I be not much beguiled,
Full many wanton babes have I,
Which must be stilled with lullaby.

    First, lullaby my youthful years,
It is now time to go to bed,   10
For crookèd age and hoary hairs,

Have won the haven within my head:
With lullaby then youth be still,
With lullaby content thy will,
Since courage quails and comes behind,
Go sleep, and so beguile thy mind.

Next lullaby my gazing eyes,
Which wonted were to glance apace;
For every glass may now suffice,
To shew the furrows in my face: 20
With lullaby then wink awhile,
With lullaby your looks beguile:
Let no fair face, nor beauty bright,
Entice you eft with vain delight.

And lullaby my wanton will,
Let Reason's rule now rein thy thought,
Since all too late I find by skill,
How dear I have thy fancies bought.
With lullaby now take thine ease,
With lullaby thy doubts appease: 30
For trust to this, if thou be still,
My body shall obey thy will.

      .   .   .   .   .   .

Thus lullaby my youth, mine eyes,
My will, my ware,¹ and all that was,
I can no more delays devise,
But welcome pain, let pleasure pass:
With lullaby now take your leave,
With lullaby your dreams deceive,
And when you rise with waking eye,
Remember then this lullaby.   40

                                      (1572)

¹ caution

ANTHONY MUNDAY (1553-1633)

I SERVE A MISTRESS

(From *Two Italian Gentlemen*)

I SERVE a mistress whiter than the snow,
  Straighter than cedar, brighter than the glass,
Finer in trip and swifter than the roe,
  More pleasant than the field of flowering grass;
More gladsome to my withering joys that fade
Than winter's sun or summer's cooling shade.

Sweeter than swelling grape of ripest wine,
  Softer than feathers of the fairest swan,
Smoother than jet, more stately than the pine,
  Fresher than poplar, smaller than my span,   10
Clearer than beauty's fiery-pointed beam,
Or icy crust of crystal's frozen stream.

Yet is she curster than the bear by kind,
  And harder-hearted than the agèd oak,
More glib than oil, more fickle than the wind,
  Stiffer than steel, no sooner bent but broke.
Lo, thus my service is a lasting sore;
Yet will I serve, although I die therefore.

(1584)

BEAUTY SAT BATHING BY A SPRING

(From *England's Helicon*)

BEAUTY sat bathing by a spring
  Where fairest shades did hide her;

The winds blew calm, the birds did sing,
　　The cool streams ran beside her.
My wanton thoughts enticed mine eye
　　To see what was forbidden:
But better memory said, fie!
　　So vain desire was chidden.
　　　　Hey nonny, nonny, &c.

Into a slumber then I fell,　　　　　　10
　　When fond imagination
Seemed to see, but could not tell
　　Her feature or her fashion.
But even as babes in dreams do smile,
　　And sometime fall a-weeping,
So I awaked, as wise this while
　　As when I fell a-sleeping.
　　　　Hey nonny, nonny, &c.

　　　　　　　　　　　　　　(1600)

SIR EDWARD DYER (1550?-1607)

MY MIND TO ME A KINGDOM IS

My MIND to me a kingdom is,
　　Such present joys therein I find,
That it excels all other bliss
　　That earth affords or grows by kind:
Though much I want which most would have,
Yet still my mind forbids to crave.

No princely pomp, no wealthy store,
　　No force to win the victory,
No wily wit to salve a sore,
　　No shape to feed a loving eye;　　　　10

To none of these I yield as thrall:
For why? My mind doth serve for all.

I see how plenty surfeits oft,
    And hasty climbers soon do fall;
I see that those which are aloft
    Mishap doth threaten most of all;
They get with toil, they keep with fear:
Such cares my mind could never bear.

Content to live, this is my stay;
    I seek no more than may suffice;   20
I press to bear no haughty sway;
    Look, what I lack my mind supplies:
Lo, thus I triumph like a king,
Content with that my mind doth bring.

Some have too much, yet still do crave;
    I little have, and seek no more.
They are but poor, though much they have,
    And I am rich with little store:
They poor, I rich; they beg, I give;
They lack, I leave; they pine, I live.   30

I laugh not at another's loss;
    I grudge not at another's pain;
No worldly waves my mind can toss;
    My state at one doth still remain:
I fear no foe, I fawn no friend;
I loathe not life, nor dread my end.

Some weigh their pleasure by their lust,
    Their wisdom by their rage of will;
Their treasure is their only trust;
    A cloakèd craft their store of skill: 40

But all the pleasure that I find
Is to maintain a quiet mind.

My wealth is health and perfect ease:
    My conscience clear my chief defense;
I neither seek by bribes to please,
    Nor by deceit to breed offense:
Thus do I live; thus will I die;
Would all did so as well as I!

(1588)

THE LOWEST TREES HAVE TOPS

THE lowest trees have tops; the ant her gall;
    The fly her spleen; the little sparks their heat:
The slender hairs cast shadows, though but small;
    And bees have stings, although they be not great.
Seas have their source, and so have shallow springs;
And love is love, in beggars as in kings.

Where rivers smoothest run, deep are the fords;
    The dial stirs, yet none perceives it move;
The firmest faith is in the fewest words;
    The turtles cannot sing, and yet they love.   10
True hearts have eyes and ears, no tongues to speak;
They hear and see, and sigh; and then they break.

(1599)

GEORGE PEELE (1558?-1598?)

FAIR AND FAIR

(From The Arraignment of Paris)

Oenone:	Fair and fair, and twice so fair,
	As fair as any may be;
	The fairest shepherd on our green,
	A love for any lady.
Paris:	Fair and fair, and twice so fair,
	As fair as any may be;
	Thy Love is fair for thee alone,
	And for no other lady.
Oenone:	My Love is fair, my Love is gay,
	As fresh as bin the flowers in May; 10
	And of my Love my roundelay
	My merry, merry, merry roundelay
	Concludes with Cupid's curse,—
	They that do change old love for new,
	Pray gods they change for worse.
Together:	They that do change old love for new,
	Pray gods they change for worse.
Oenone:	Fair and fair, and twice so fair,
	As fair as any may be:
	The fairest shepherd on our green,
	A Love for any lady. 20
Paris:	Fair and fair, and twice so fair,
	As fair as any may be;
	Thy Love is fair for thee alone,
	And for no other lady.
Oenone:	My Love can pipe, my Love can sing,
	My Love can many a pretty thing,

And of his lovely praises ring
  My merry, merry, merry roundelays.
    Amen to Cupid's curse,—
They that do change old love for new,   30
  Pray gods they change for worse.
Together: They that do change old love for new.
  Pray gods they change for worse.

                    (1584)

HIS GOLDEN LOCKS TIME HATH TO SILVER TURNED

(From *Polyhymnia*)

His golden locks time hath to silver turned;
  O time too swift, O swiftness never ceasing!
His youth 'gainst time and age hath ever spurned,
  But spurned in vain; youth waneth by increasing:
Beauty, strength, youth, are flowers but fading seen;
Duty, faith, love, are roots, and ever green.

His helmet now shall make a hive for bees;
  And, lovers' sonnets turned to holy psalms,
A man-at-arms must now serve on his knees,
  And feed on prayers, which are age his alms: 10
But though from court to cottage he depart,
His saint is sure of his unspotted heart.

And when he saddest sits in homely cell,
  He'll teach his swains this carol for a song,—
'Blest be the hearts that wish my sovereign well,
  Curst be the souls that think her any wrong.'
Goddess, allow this agèd man his right,
To be your beadsman now that was your knight.

                    (1590)

HARVESTMEN A-SINGING

(From *The Old Wives Tale*)

ALL ye that lovely lovers be,
Pray you for me:
Lo, here we come a-sowing, a-sowing,
And sow sweet fruits of love;
In your sweet hearts well may it prove!

Lo, here we come a-reaping, a-reaping,
To reap our harvest-fruit!
And thus we pass the year so long,
And never be we mute.

(1595)

THOMAS LODGE (1558?-1625)

ROSALIND'S MADRIGAL

(From *Rosalind*)

LOVE in my bosom like a bee
  Doth suck his sweet:
Now with his wings he plays with me,
  Now with his feet.
Within mine eyes he makes his nest,
His bed amidst my tender breast;
My kisses are his daily feast,
And yet he robs me of my rest.
    Ah, wanton, will ye?

And if I sleep, then percheth he   10
  With pretty flight,

And makes his pillow of my knee
   The livelong night.
Strike I my lute, he tunes the string,
He music plays if so I sing,
He lends me every lovely thing;
Yet cruel he my heart doth sting.
   Whist, wanton, still ye!

Else I with roses every day
   Will whip you hence,   20
And bind you, when you long to play,
   For your offense;
I'll shut mine eyes to keep you in,
I'll make you fast it for your sin,
I'll count your power not worth a pin.
Alas, what hereby shall I win,
   If he gainsay me?

What if I beat the wanton boy
   With many a rod?
He will repay me with annoy,   30
   Because a god.
Then sit thou safely on my knee,
And let thy bower my bosom be;
Lurk in mine eyes, I like of thee.
O Cupid, so thou pity me,
   Spare not, but play thee.

                   (1590)

ROSALIND'S DESCRIPTION

(From *Rosalind*)

LIKE to the clear in highest sphere
Where all imperial glory shines,

Of selfsame color is her hair,
Whether unfolded or in twines:
  Heigh ho, fair Rosalind!
Her eyes are sapphires set in snow,
Refining heaven by every wink;
The gods do fear whenas they glow,
And I do tremble when I think:
  Heigh ho, would she were mine!   10

Her cheeks are like the blushing cloud
That beautifies Aurora's face,
Or like the silver crimson shroud
That Phœbus' smiling looks doth grace:
  Heigh ho, fair Rosalind!
Her lips are like two budded roses,
Whom ranks of lilies neighbor nigh,
Within which bounds she balm encloses,
Apt to entice a deity:
  Heigh ho, would she were mine!   20

Her neck like to a stately tower
Where Love himself imprisoned lies,
To watch for glances every hour
From her divine and sacred eyes:
  Heigh ho, fair Rosalind!
Her paps are centres of delight,
Her breasts are orbs of heavenly frame,
Where Nature molds the dew of light,
To feed perfection with the same:
  Heigh ho, would she were mine!   30

With orient pearl, with ruby red,
With marble white, with sapphire blue,
Her body every way is fed,

Yet soft in touch, and sweet in view:
   Heigh ho, fair Rosalind!
Nature herself her shape admires,
The gods are wounded in her sight,
And Love forsakes his heavenly fires
And at her eyes his brand doth light:
   Heigh ho, would she were mine!   40

Then muse not, nymphs, though I bemoan
The absence of fair Rosalind,
Since for her fair there's fairer none,
Nor for her virtues so divine:
   Heigh ho, fair Rosalind!
Heigh ho, my heart! would God that she were
   mine!

                      (1590)

PHYLLIS

(From *Phyllis*)

MY PHYLLIS hath the morning sun
   At first to look upon her;
And Phyllis hath morn-waking birds
   Her risings for to honor.
My Phyllis hath prime-feathered flowers
   That smile when she treads on them;
And Phyllis hath a gallant flock
   That leaps since she doth own them.
But Phyllis hath so hard a heart—
   Alas that she should have it!—   10
As yields no mercy to desart,
   Nor grace to those that crave it.

Sweet sun, when thou lookest on,
Pray her regard my moan;
Sweet birds, when you sing to her,
To yield some pity, woo her;
Sweet flowers, whenas she treads on,
Tell her, her beauty deads one:
And if in life her love she nill agree me,
Pray her, before I die she will come see me.   20

(1593)

AN ODE

(From *Phyllis*)

Now I find thy looks were feignèd,
Quickly lost and quickly gainèd.
Soft thy skin like wool of wethers;
Heart unstable, light as feathers;
Tongue untrusty, subtle sighted;
Wanton will with change delighted;
   Siren pleasant, foe to reason,
   Cupid plague thee for this treason!

Of thine eyes I made my mirror,
From thy beauty came mine error;   10
All thy words I counted witty,
All thy smiles I deemèd pity;
Thy false tears that me aggrievèd
First of all my trust deceivèd.
   Siren pleasant, foe to reason,
   Cupid plague thee for this treason!

Feigned acceptance when I askèd,
Lovely words with cunning maskèd,
Holy vows but heart unholy,

Wretched man! my trust was folly.   20
Lily-white and pretty winking,
Solemn vows but sorry thinking.
   Siren pleasant, foe to reason,
   Cupid plague thee for this treason!

Now I see—oh, seemly cruel!—
Others warm them at my fuel.
Wit shall guide me in this durance
Since in love is no assurance.
Change thy pasture, take thy pleasure,
Beauty is a fading treasure.   30
   Siren pleasant, foe to reason,
   Cupid plague thee for this treason!

Prime youth lasts not, age will follow
And make white these tresses yellow;
Wrinkled face for looks delightful
Shall acquaint the dame despiteful;
And when time shall date thy glory
Then too late thou wilt be sorry.
   Siren pleasant, foe to reason,
   Cupid plague thee for thy treason!   40

(1593)

NICHOLAS BRETON (1545?-1626?)

PHYLLIDA AND CORYDON

In the merry month of May,
In a morn by break of day,
Forth I walked by the wood-side,
When as May was in her pride:
Then I spièd all alone
Phyllida and Corydon.

Much ado there was, God wot!
He would love and she would not.
She said, never man was true;
He said, none was false to you.   10
He said, he had loved her long;
She said, love should have no wrong.
Corydon would kiss her then;
She said, maids must kiss no men,
Till they did for good and all;
Then she made the shepherd call
All the heavens to witness truth:
Never loved a truer youth.
Thus with many a pretty oath,
Yea and nay, and faith and troth,   20
Such as silly shepherds use
When they will not love abuse,
Love, which had been long deluded,
Was with kisses sweet concluded;
And Phyllida, with garlands gay,
Was made the Lady of the May.

(1591)

THE MERRY COUNTRY LAD

(From *The Passionate Shepherd*)

Who can live in heart so glad
As the merry country lad?
Who upon a fair green balk [1]
May at pleasure sit and walk,
And amid the azure skies
See the morning sun arise,
While he hears in every spring
How the birds do chirp and sing:

[1] strip of land between plowed furrows

Or before the hounds in cry
See the hare go stealing by: 10
Or along the shallow brook,
Angling with a baited hook,
See the fishes leap and play
In a blessèd sunny day:
Or to hear the partridge call
Till she have her covey all:
Or to see the subtle fox,
How the villain plies the box: [1]
After feeding on his prey,
How he closely sneaks away,   20
Through the hedge and down the furrow
Till he gets into his burrow:
Then the bee to gather honey;
And the little black-haired coney,
On a bank for sunny place,
With her forefeet wash her face,—
Are not these, with thousands moe
Than the courts of kings do know,
The true pleasing spirit's sights
That may breed true love's delights?   30

*   *   *

(1604)

ROBERT SOUTHWELL (1561?-1595)

THE BURNING BABE

(From *Saint Peters' Complaint*)

As I in hoary winter's night stood shivering in the snow,
Surprised I was with sudden heat, which made my heart
        to glow;

[1] creeps beside the boxwood hedge

And lifting up a fearful eye to view what fire was near,
A pretty babe, all burning bright, did in the air appear,
Who, scorchèd with excessive heat, such floods of tears
    did shed,
As though his floods should quench his flames which
    with his tears were fed.
'Alas!' quoth he, 'but newly born in fiery heats I fry;
Yet none approach to warm their hearts or feel my
    fire but I!
My faultless breast the furnace is, the fuel, wounding
    thorns,
Love is the fire, and sighs the smoke, the ashes, shame
    and scorns.   10
The fuel Justice layeth on, and Mercy blows the coals,
The metal in this furnace wrought are men's defilèd
    souls,
For which, as now on fire I am, to work them to their
    good,
So will I melt into a bath to wash them in my blood.'
With this he vanished out of sight, and swiftly shrunk
    away;
And straight I callèd unto mind that it was Christmas-
    day.

                            (1595)

SAMUEL DANIEL (1562-1619)

SONNETS

(From *Delia*)

6

FAIR is my love, and cruel as she's fair;
Her brow shades frowns, although her eyes are sunny;

Her smiles are lightning, though her pride despair;
And her disdains are gall, her favors honey.
A modest maid, decked with a blush of honor;
Whose feet do tread green paths of youth and love!
The wonder of all eyes that look upon her:
Sacred on earth; designed a saint above!
Chastity and beauty, which were deadly foes,
Live reconcilèd friends within her brow: 10
And had she pity to conjoin with those;
Then who had heard the plaints I utter now?
For had she not been fair, and thus unkind,
My muse had slept, and none had known my mind.

38

Thou canst not die, whilst any zeal abound
In feeling hearts, that can conceive these lines:
Though thou, a Laura, hast no Petrarch found;
In base attire, yet, clearly, Beauty shines.
And I, though born within a colder clime,
Do feel mine inward heat as great, I know it.
He never had more faith, although more rime:
I love as well, though he could better show it.
But I may add one feather to thy fame,
To help her flight throughout the fairest Isle;   10
And if my pen could more enlarge thy name,
Then shouldst thou live in an immortal style.
For though that Laura better limnèd be,
Suffice, thou shalt be loved as well as she!

41

When men shall find thy flower, thy glory, pass,
And thou, with careful brow sitting alone,
Receivèd hast this message from thy glass,

That tells the truth and says that all is gone;
Fresh shalt thou see in me the wounds thou madest,
Though spent thy flame, in me the heat remaining:
I that have loved thee thus before thou fadest,
My faith shall wax when thou art in thy waning:
The world shall find this miracle in me,
That fire can burn when all the matter's spent: 10
Then, what my faith hath been thyself shalt see;
And that thou wast unkind thou mayst repent.
Thou mayst repent that thou hast scorned my tears,
When winter snows upon thy sable hairs.

42

When winter snows upon thy sable hairs,
And frost of age hath nipt thy beauties near;
When dark shall seem thy day that never clears,
And all lies withered that was held so dear:
Then take this picture which I here present thee,
Limned with a pencil not all unworthy:
Here see the gifts that God and Nature lent thee,
Here read thyself, and what I suffered for thee.
This may remain thy lasting monument,
Which happily posterity may cherish;   10
These colors with thy fading are not spent,
These may remain when thou and I shall perish.
If they remain, then thou shalt live thereby;
They will remain, and so thou can'st not die.

49

Care-charmer Sleep, son of the sable Night,
Brother to Death, in silent darkness born:
Relieve my anguish, and restore the light;
With dark forgetting of my care, return!

And let the day be time enough to mourn
The shipwreck of my ill-adventured youth:
Let waking eyes suffice to wail their scorn,
Without the torment of the night's untruth.
Cease, dreams, the images of day-desires,
To model forth the passions of the morrow;   10
Never let rising sun approve you liars,
To add more grief to aggravate my sorrow.
Still let me sleep, embracing clouds in vain;
And never wake to feel the day's disdain.

50

Let others sing of Knights and Paladins
In agèd accents and untimely words;
Paint shadows in imaginary lines
Which well the reach of their high wits records.
But I must sing of thee, and those fair eyes
Authentic shall my verse in time to come;
When yet th' unborn shall say, 'Lo, where she lies
Whose beauty made him speak that else was dumb.'
These are the arcs, the trophies I erect
That fortify thy name against old age;   10
And these thy sacred virtues must protect
Against the dark, and Time's consuming rage.
Though the error of my youth in them appear,
Suffice they show I lived and loved thee dear.

58

None other fame mine unambitious Muse
Affected ever, but t' eternize thee:
All other honors do my hopes refuse,
Which meaner-prized and momentary be.
For God forbid I should my papers blot

With mercenary lines, with servile pen;
Praising virtues in them that have them not,
Basely attending on the hopes of men.
No, no; my verse respects not Thames nor theaters;
Nor seeks it to be known unto the great: 10
But Avon, rich in fame though poor in waters,
Shall have my song; where Delia hath her seat.
Avon shall be my Thames, and she my song;
No other prouder brooks shall hear my wrong.

(1592)

LOVE

(From *Hymen's Triumph*)

Love is a sickness full of woes,
    All remedies refusing;
A plant that with most cutting grows,
    Most barren with best using.
            Why so?
More we enjoy it, more it dies;
If not enjoyed, it sighing cries,
            Heigh ho!

Love is a torment of the mind,
    A tempest everlasting;   10
And Jove hath made it of a kind
    Not well, nor full, nor fasting.
            Why so?
More we enjoy it, more it dies;
If not enjoyed, it sighing cries,
            Heigh ho!

(1615)

WILLIAM SHAKESPEARE (1564-1616)

SONGS FROM THE PLAYS

WHEN DAISIES PIED

(From *Love's Labor's Lost*)

WHEN daisies pied and violets blue,
    And lady-smocks all silver-white,
And cuckoo-buds of yellow hue
    Do paint the meadows with delight,
The cuckoo then, on every tree,
Mocks married men; for thus sings he,
Cuckoo, cuckoo!—O word of fear,
Unpleasing to a married ear!

When shepherds pipe on oaten straws,
    And merry larks are ploughmen's clocks,   10
When turtles tread, and rooks, and daws,
    And maidens bleach their summer smocks
The cuckoo then, on every tree,
Mocks married men; for thus sings he,
Cuckoo, cuckoo!—O word of fear,
Unpleasing to a married ear!

(1591)

WHEN ICICLES HANG BY THE WALL

(From *Love's Labor's Lost*)

WHEN icicles hang by the wall,
    And Dick the shepherd blows his nail,

And Tom bears logs into the hall,
    And milk comes frozen home in pail,
When blood is nipped and ways be foul,
    Then nightly sings the staring owl,
      "Tu-whit, tu-who!" a merry-note,
While greasy Joan doth keel [1] the pot.

When all aloud the wind doth blow,
    And coughing drowns the parson's saw,   **10**
And birds sit brooding in the snow,
    And Marian's nose looks red and raw,
When roasted crabs hiss in the bowl,
    Then nightly sings the staring owl,
      "Tu-whit, tu-who!" a merry-note,
While greasy Joan doth keel the pot.

                                    (1591)

WHO IS SYLVIA?

(From *Two Gentlemen of Verona*)

Who is Sylvia? what is she,
    That all our swains commend her?
Holy, fair, and wise is she;
    The heaven such grace did lend her,
That she might admiréd be.

Is she kind as she is fair?
    For beauty lives with kindness.
Love doth to her eyes repair
    To help him of his blindness,
And, being helped, inhabits there.   **10**

[1] cool by stirring

Then to Sȳlvia let us sing,
　That Sylvia is excelling;
She excels each mortal thing
　Upon the dull earth dwelling:
To her let us garlands bring.

(1591-2)

THE FAIRIES' LULLABY

(From *Mid-Summer Night's Dream*)

You spotted snakes with double tongue,
　Thorny hedgehogs, be not seen;
Newts and blind-worms do no wrong,
　Come not near our fairy queen.
　　Philomel, with melody,
　　Sing in our sweet lullaby:
Lulla, lulla, lullaby; lulla, lulla, lullaby!
　　Never harm, nor spell, nor charm,
　　Come our lovely lady nigh;
　　So, good night, with lullaby.　　10

Weaving spiders, come not here:
　Hence, you long-legged spinners, hence!
Beetles black, approach not near;
　Worm, nor snail, do no offense.
　　Philomel, with melody,
　　Sing in our sweet lullaby:
Lulla, lulla, lullaby; lulla, lulla, lullaby!
　　Never harm, nor spell, nor charm,
　　Come our lovely lady nigh;
　　So, good night, with lullaby.　　20

(1594-5)

TELL ME, WHERE IS FANCY BRED

(From *The Merchant of Venice*)

TELL me, where is fancy bred,
Or in the heart, or in the head?
How begot, how nourishèd?
 Reply, reply.
It is engendered in the eyes,
With gazing fed; and fancy dies
In the cradle where it lies:
Let us all ring fancy's knell;
I'll begin it,—Ding-dong, bell.
 Ding, dong, bell.   10

     (1595-6)

UNDER THE GREENWOOD TREE

(From *As You Like It*)

UNDER the greenwood tree
Who loves to lie with me,
And turn his merry note
Unto the sweet bird's throat,
Come hither! come hither! come hither!
Here shall he see
No enemy
But winter and rough weather.

Who doth ambition shun
And loves to live i' the sun,   10
Seeking the food he eats
And pleased with what he gets,

Come hither! come hither! come hither!
　　Here shall he see
　　No enemy
But winter and rough weather.

(1599)

BLOW, BLOW, THOU WINTER WIND

(From *As You Like It*)

Blow, blow, thou winter wind,
Thou art not so unkind
　　As man's ingratitude;
Thy tooth is not so keen,
Because thou art not seen,
　　Although thy breath be rude.
Heigh-ho! sing, heigh-ho! unto the green holly:
Most friendship is feigning, most loving mere folly.
　　Then heigh-ho! the holly!
　　This life is most jolly.　　　　　　　10

Freeze, freeze, thou bitter sky,
That dost not bite so nigh
　　As benefits forgot:
Though thou the waters warp,
Thy sting is not so sharp
　　As friend remembered not.
Heigh-ho! sing, heigh-ho! etc.

(1599)

IT WAS A LOVER AND HIS LASS

(From *As You Like It*)

It was a lover and his lass,
　　With a hey, and a ho, and a hey nonino,

That o'er the green corn-field did pass,
  In the spring time, the only pretty ring time,
When birds do sing, hey ding a ding, ding;
Sweet lovers love the spring.

Between the acres of the rye,
  With a hey, and a ho, and a hey nonino,
These pretty country folks would lie,
  In the spring time, etc.   10

This carol they began that hour,
  With a hey, and a ho, and a hey nonino,
How that a life was but a flower
  In the spring time, etc.

And therefore take the present time,
  With a hey, and a ho, and a hey nonino;
For love is crownèd with the prime
  In the spring time, etc.

(1599)

SIGH NO MORE

(From *Much Ado About Nothing*)

Sigh no more, ladies, sigh no more!
  Men were deceivers ever,
One foot in sea and one on shore,
  To one thing constant never:
Then sigh not so, but let them go,
  And be you blithe and bonny,
Converting all your sounds of woe
  Into Hey nonny, nonny!

Sing no more ditties, sing no moe
   Of dumps so dull and heavy!   10
The fraud of men was ever so,
   Since summer first was leafy:
Then sigh not so, but let them go,
   And be you blithe and bonny,
Converting all your sounds of woe
   Into Hey nonny, nonny!

                          (1599)

O MISTRESS MINE

(From *Twelfth Night*)

O MISTRESS mine, where are you roaming?
O, stay and hear; your true love's coming,
   That can sing both high and low:
Trip no further, pretty sweeting,
Journeys end in lovers meeting,
   Every wise man's son doth know.

What is love? 't is not hereafter;
Present mirth hath present laughter;
   What's to come is still unsure:
In delay there lies no plenty;   10
Then come kiss me, sweet and twenty,
   Youth's a stuff will not endure.   *cape diem*

                          (1601)

TAKE, O, TAKE THOSE LIPS AWAY

(From *Measure for Measure*)

TAKE, O, take those lips away,
   That so sweetly were forsworn;

And those eyes, the break of day,
  Lights that do mislead the morn:
But my kisses bring again,
              Bring again;
Seals of love, but sealed in vain,
              Sealed in vain!

(1603)

HARK, HARK! THE LARK

(From *Cymbeline*)

HARK, hark! the lark at heaven's gate sings,
  And Phœbus 'gins arise,
His steeds to water at those springs
  On chaliced flowers that lies;
And winking Mary-buds begin
  To ope their golden eyes:
With every thing that pretty is,
  My lady sweet, arise!
    Arise, arise!

(1610)

FEAR NO MORE THE HEAT O' THE SUN

(From *Cymbeline*)

FEAR no more the heat o' th' sun,
  Nor the furious winter's rages;
Thou thy worldly task hast done,
  Home art gone, and ta'en thy wages:
Golden lads and girls all must,
As chimney-sweepers, come to dust.

Fear no more the frown o' th' great;
   Thou art past the tyrant's stroke;
Care no more to clothe and eat;
   To thee the reed is as the oak: 10
The Scepters, Learning, Physic, must
All follow this, and come to dust.

Fear no more the lightning-flash,
   Nor th' all-dreaded thunder-stone;
Fear not slander, censure rash;
   Thou hast finished joy and moan:
All lovers young, all lovers must
Consign to thee, and come to dust.

No exorciser harm thee!
   Nor no witchcraft charm thee!   20
Ghost unlaid forbear thee!
   Nothing ill come near thee!
Quiet consummation have;
And renownèd be thy grave!

               (1610)

COME UNTO THESE YELLOW SANDS

(From *The Tempest*)

Come unto these yellow sands,
   And then take hands:
Courtsied when you have, and kissed, —
   The wild waves whist, —
Foot it featly here and there;
And sweet sprites, the burden bear.
     Hark, hark!
       Bow, wow.

The watch-dogs bark:
  Bow, wow.   10
Hark, hark! I hear
The strain of strutting Chanticleer
  Cock-a-diddle-dow.

(1611)

FULL FATHOM FIVE THY FATHER LIES

(From *The Tempest*)

FULL fathom five thy father lies;
  Of his bones are coral made:
Those are pearls that were his eyes:
  Nothing of him that doth fade,
But doth suffer a sea-change
Into something rich and strange.
Sea-nymphs hourly ring his knell;
                              Ding-dong.
Hark! now I hear them,—Ding-dong, bell.

(1611)

WHERE THE BEE SUCKS

(From *The Tempest*)

WHERE the bee sucks, there suck I
In a cowslip's bell I lie;
There I couch when owls do cry.
On the bat's back I do fly
After summer merrily:
  Merrily, merrily shall I live now
  Under the blossom that hangs on the bough.

(1611)

THE SONNETS

15

WHEN I consider every thing that grows
Holds in perfection but a little moment,
That this huge stage presenteth naught but shows
Whereon the stars in secret influence comment;
When I perceive that men as plants increase,
Cheerèd and checked even by the self-same sky,
Vaunt in their youthful sap, at height decrease,
And wear their brave state out of memory:
Then the conceit of this inconstant stay
Sets you most rich in youth before my sight,   10
Where wasteful Time debateth with Decay,
To change your day of youth to sullied night;
And all in war with Time for love of you,
As he takes from you, I engraft you new.

18

SHALL I compare thee to a summer's day?
Thou art more lovely and more temperate:
Rough winds do shake the darling buds of May,
And summer's lease hath all too short a date:
Sometime too hot the eye of heaven shines,
And often is his gold complexion dimmed;
And every fair from fair sometime declines,
By chance or nature's changing course untrimmed;
But thy eternal summer shall not fade
Nor lose possession of that fair thou owest;   10
Nor shall Death brag thou wander'st in his shade,
When in eternal lines to time thou growest:

So long as men can breathe or eyes can see,
So long lives this and this gives life to thee.

29

WHEN in disgrace with fortune and men's eyes, *disgrace*
I all alone beweep my outcast state,
And trouble deaf heaven with my bootless cries, *disap-*
And look upon myself, and curse my fate, *pointment*
Wishing me like to one more rich in hope,
Featured like him, like him with friends possessed,
Desiring this man's art, and that man's scope,
With what I most enjoy contented least; *hardship*
Yet in these thoughts myself almost despising,
Haply I think on thee,—and then my state,   10
Like to the lark at break of day arising
From sullen earth, sings hymns at heaven's gate;
For thy sweet love remembered such wealth brings
That then I scorn to change my state with kings.

30

WHEN to the sessions of sweet silent thought *not*
I summon up remembrance of things past, *having done*
I sigh the lack of many a thing I sought, *what should*
And with old woes new wail my dear time's waste: *have been*
Then can I drown an eye, unused to flow, *done,*
For precious friends hid in death's dateless night, *and me*
And weep afresh love's long since canceled woe, *converse*
And moan the expense [1] of many a vanished sight:
Then can I grieve at grievances foregone,
And heavily from woe to woe tell o'er   10
The sad account of fore-bemoanèd moan,
Which I new pay as if not paid before.

[1] loss

But if the while I think on thee, dear friend,
All losses are restored and sorrows end.

33

FULL many a glorious morning have I seen
Flatter the mountain-tops with sovereign eye,
Kissing with golden face the meadows green,
Gilding pale streams with heavenly alchemy;
Anon permit the basest clouds to ride
With ugly rack on his celestial face,
And from the forlorn world his visage hide,
Stealing unseen to west with this disgrace:
Even so my sun one early morn did shine,
With all-triumphant splendor on my brow;　　10
But, out! alack! he was but one hour mine,
The region cloud hath masked him from me now.
Yet him for this my love no whit disdaineth;
Suns of the world may stain when heaven's sun staineth.

55

NOT marble, nor the gilded monuments
Of princes, shall outlive this powerful rime;
But you shall shine more bright in these contents
Than unswept stone, besmeared with sluttish time.
When wasteful war shall statues overturn,
And broils root out the work of masonry,
Nor Mars his sword nor war's quick fire shall burn
The living record of your memory.
'Gainst death and all-oblivious enmity
Shall you pace forth; your praise shall still find room　10
Even in the eyes of all posterity
That wear this world out to the ending doom.

So, till the judgment that yourself arise,
You live in this, and dwell in lovers' eyes.

60

Like as the waves make towards the pebbled shore,
So do our minutes hasten to their end;
Each changing place with that which goes before,
In sequent toil all forwards do contend.
Nativity, once in the main of light,
Crawls to maturity, wherewith being crowned,
Crookèd eclipses 'gainst his glory fight,
And Time that gave doth now his gift confound.
Time doth transfix the flourish set on youth
And delves the parallels in beauty's brow,   10
Feeds on the rarities of nature's truth,
And nothing stands but for his scythe to mow:
And yet to times in hope my verse shall stand,
Praising thy worth, despite his cruel hand.

64

When I have seen by Time's fell hand defaced
The rich-proud cost of outworn buried age;
When sometime lofty towers I see down-razed
And brass eternal slave to mortal rage;
When I have seen the hungry ocean gain
Advantage on the kingdom of the shore,
And the firm soil win of the watery main,
Increasing store with loss, and loss with store;
When I have seen such interchange of state,
Or state itself confounded to decay;   10
Ruin hath taught me thus to ruminate —
That Time will come and take my love away.

This thought is as a death, which cannot choose
But weep to have that which it fears to lose.

71

No LONGER mourn for me when I am dead
Than you shall hear the surly sullen bell
Give warning to the world that I am fled
From this vile world, with vilest worms to dwell:
Nay, if you read this line, remember not
The hand that writ it; for I love you so
That I in your sweet thoughts would be forgot
If thinking on me then should make you woe.
O, if, I say, you look upon this verse
When I perhaps compounded am with clay,   10
Do not so much as my poor name rehearse,
But let your love even with my life decay.
Lest the wise world should look into your moan
And mock you with me after I am gone.

73

THAT time of year thou mayst in me behold
When yellow leaves, or none, or few, do hang
Upon those boughs which shake against the cold,
Bare ruined choirs, where late the sweet birds sang.
In me thou see'st the twilight of such day
As after sunset fadeth in the west,
Which by and by black night doth take away,
Death's second self, that seals up all in rest.
In me thou see'st the glowing of such fire
That on the ashes of his youth doth lie,   10
As the death-bed whereon it must expire,
Consumed with that which it was nourished by.

This thou perceiv'st, which makes thy love more strong,
To love that well which thou must leave ere long.

97

How like a winter hath my absence been
From thee, the pleasure of the fleeting year
What freezings have I felt, what dark days seen!
What old December's bareness everywhere!
And yet this time removed was summer's time,
The teeming autumn, big with rich increase,
Bearing the wanton burden of the prime,
Like widowed wombs after their lord's decease:
Yet this abundant issue seemed to me
But hope of orphans and unfathered fruit;   10
For summer and his pleasures wait on thee,
And, thou away, the very birds are mute;
Or, if they sing, 'tis with so dull a cheer
That leaves look pale, dreading the winter's near.

106

When in the chronicle of wasted time
I see descriptions of the fairest wights,
And beauty making beautiful old. rime
In praise of ladies dead and lovely knights,
Then, in the blazon of sweet beauty's best,
Of hand, of foot, of lip, of eye, of brow,
I see their antique pen would have expressed
Even such a beauty as you master now.
So all their praises are but prophecies
Of this our time, all you profiguring: 10
And, for they looked but with divining eyes,
They had not skill enough your worth to sing:

For we, which now behold these present days,
Have eyes to wonder, but lack tongues to praise.

110

Alas, 'tis true I have gone here and there
And made myself a motley to the view,
Gored mine own thoughts, sold cheap what is most dear,
Made old offenses of affections new;
Most true it is that I have looked on truth
Askance and strangely; but, by all above,
These blenches [1] gave my heart another youth,
And worse essays proved thee my best of love.
Now all is done, have what shall have no end:
Mine appetite I never more will grind   10
On newer proof, to try an older friend,
A god in love, to whom I am confined.
Then give me welcome, next my heaven the best,
Even to thy pure and most most loving breast.

116

Let me not to the marriage of true minds
Admit impediments. Love is not love
Which alters when it alteration finds,
Or bends with the remover to remove:
O, no! it is an ever-fixèd mark,
That looks on tempests and is never shaken;
It is the star to every wandering bark,
Whose worth's unknown, although his height be taken.
Love's not Time's fool, though rosy lips and cheeks
Within his bending sickle's compass come;   10
Love alters not with his brief hours and weeks,
But bears it out even to the edge of doom.

[1] side-glances

If this be error and upon me proved,
I never writ, nor no man ever loved.

127

IN THE old age black was not counted fair,
Or if it were, it bore not beauty's name;
But now is black beauty's successive heir,
And beauty slander'd with a bastard shame:
For since each hand hath put on nature's power,
Fairing the foul with art's false borrow'd face,
Sweet beauty hath no name, no holy bower,
But is profaned, if not lives in disgrace.
Therefore my mistress' eyes are raven black,
Her eyes so suited, and they mourners seem   10
At such who, not born fair, no beauty lack,
Slandering creation with a false esteem:
Yet so they mourn, becoming of their woe,
That every tongue says beauty should look so.

128

How oft, when thou, my music, music play'st,
Upon that blessèd wood whose motion sounds
With thy sweet fingers, when thou gently sway'st
The wiry concord that mine ear confounds,
Do I envy those jacks that nimble leap
To kiss the tender inward of thy hand,
Whilst my poor lips, which should that harvest reap,
At the wood's boldness by thee blushing stand!
To be so tickled, they would change their state
And situation with those dancing chips,   10
O'er whom thy fingers walk with gentle gait,
Making dead wood more blest than living lips.

Since saucy jacks [1] so happy are in this,
Give them thy fingers, me thy lips to kiss.

130

My mistress' eyes are nothing like the sun;
Coral is far more red than her lips' red;
If snow be white, why then her breasts are dun;
If hairs be wires, black wires grow on her head,
I have seen roses damasked, red and white,
But no such roses see I in her cheeks;
And in some perfumes is there more delight
Than in the breath that from my mistress reeks.
I love to hear her speak, yet well I know
That music hath a far more pleasing sound;   10
I grant I never saw a goddess go;
My mistress, when she walks, treads on the ground:
And yet, by heaven, I think my love as rare
As any she belied with false compare.

153

Cupid laid by his brand, and fell asleep.
A maid of Dian's this advantage found.
And his love-kindling fire did quickly steep
In a cold valley-fountain of that ground;
Which borrow'd from this holy fire of Love
A dateless lively heat, still to endure,
And grew a seething bath, which yet men prove
Against strange maladies a sovereign cure.
But at my mistress' eye Love's brand new-fired,
The boy for trial needs would touch my breast;   10
I, sick withal, the help of bath desired,
And thither hied, a sad distemper'd guest,

[1] keys of the instrument

But found no cure: the bath for my help lies
Where Cupid got new fire—my mistress' eyes.

154

THE little Love-god lying once asleep
Laid by his side his heart-inflaming brand,
Whilst many nymphs that vowed chaste life to keep
Came tripping by; but in her maiden hand
The fairest votary took up that fire
Which many legions of true hearts had warmed;
And so the general of hot desire
Was, sleeping, by a virgin hand disarmed.
This brand she quenchèd in a cool well by,
Which from Love's fire took heat perpetual,   10
Growing a bath and healthful remedy
For men diseased; but I, my mistress' thrall,
Came there for cure, and this by that I prove,
Love's fire heats water, water cools not love.

(1609)

THOMAS CAMPION

(?-1619)

A RENUNCIATION

(From *A Book of Airs*)

THOU art not fair, for all thy red and white,
    For all those rosy ornaments in thee,—
Thou art not sweet, though made of mere delight,
    Nor fair, nor sweet—unless thou pity me!
I will not soothe thy fancies; thou shalt prove
That beauty is no beauty without love.

Yet love not me, nor seek not to allure
  My thoughts with beauty, were it more divine:
Thy smiles and kisses I cannot endure,
  I'll not be wrapped up in those arms of thine: 10
Now show it, if thou be a woman right—
Embrace and kiss and love me, in despite!

(1601)

THE MAN OF LIFE UPRIGHT

(From A Book of Airs)

THE man of life upright,
  Whose guiltless heart is free
From all dishonest deeds,
  Or thought of vanity;

The man whose silent days,
  In harmless joys are spent,
Whom hopes cannot delude
  Nor sorrow discontent;

That man needs neither towers
  Nor armor for defense,   10
Nor secret vaults to fly
  From thunder's violence:

He only can behold
  With unaffrighted eyes
The horrors of the deep
  And terrors of the skies.

Thus, scorning all the cares
  That fate or fortune brings,
He makes the heaven his book,
  His wisdom heavenly things;   20

Good thoughts his only friends,
  His wealth a well-spent age,
And earth his sober inn
  And quiet pilgrimage.

(1601)

JACK AND JOAN THEY THINK NO ILL

(From *Two Books of Airs*)

JACK and Joan they think no ill,
But loving live, and merry still;
Do their week-days' work, and pray
Devoutly on the holy-day:
Skip and trip it on the green,
And help to choose the Summer Queen;
Lash out, at a country feast,
Their silver penny with the best.

Well can they judge of nappy ale,
And tell at large a winter tale;   10
Climb up to the apple loft,
And turn the crabs till they be soft.
Tib is all the father's joy,
And little Tom the mother's boy.
All their pleasure is content;
And care, to pay their yearly rent.

Joan can call by name her cows,
And deck her window with green boughs;
She can wreaths and tutties [1] make,
And trim with plums a bridal cake.   20
Jack knows what brings gain or loss,

[1] nosegays

And his long flail can stoutly toss:
Makes the hedge which others break;
And ever thinks what he doth speak.

Now, you courtly dames and knights,
That study only strange delights;
Though you scorn the homespun gray,
And revel in your rich array:
Though your tongues dissemble deep,
And can your heads from danger keep;   30
Yet, for all your pomp and train,
Securer lives the silly swain.

(1613)

THERE IS A GARDEN IN HER FACE

(From *A Fourth Book of Airs*)

THERE is a garden in her face,
Where roses and white lilies grow;
A heavenly paradise is that place,
Wherein all pleasant fruits do flow.
There cherries grow, which none may buy
Till 'Cherry ripe' themselves do cry.

Those cherries fairly do enclose
Of orient pearl a double row;
Which when her lovely laughter shows,
They look like rosebuds filled with snow.   10
Yet them nor peer nor prince can buy
Till 'Cherry ripe' themselves do cry.

Her eyes like angels watch them still;
Her brows like bended bows do stand,
Threatening with piercing frowns to kill

All that attempt, with eye or hand,
Those sacred cherries to come nigh
Till 'Cherry ripe' themselves do cry.

(1618)

MICHAEL DRAYTON (1563-1631)

SONNETS from IDEA

To the Reader of These Sonnets.

INTO these loves, who but for passion looks,
At this first sight, here let him lay them by,
And seek elsewhere in turning other books,
Which better may his labor satisfy.
No far-fetched sigh shall ever wound my breast;
Love from mine eye a tear shall never wring;
Nor in 'Ah me's!' my whining sonnets drest!
A libertine! fantasticly I sing!
My verse is the true image of my mind,
Ever in motion, still desiring change;   10
And as thus, to variety inclined,
So in all humors sportively I range!
My Muse is rightly of the English strain,
That cannot long one fashion entertain.

9

As OTHER men, so I myself, do muse
Why in this sort I wrest invention so?
And why these giddy metaphors I use,
Leaving the path the greater part do go?
I will resolve you. I am lunatic!
And ever this in madmen you shall find,

What they last thought of, when the brain grew sick,
In most distraction, they keep that in mind.
Thus talking idly, in this Bedlam fit,
Reason and I, you must conceive, are twain;   10
'Tis nine years now, since first I lost my wit.
Bear with me, then, though troubled be my brain!
With diet and correction, men distraught,
Not too far past, may to their wits be brought.

61

Since there's no help, come, let us kiss and part!
Nay, I have done; you get no more of me!
And I am glad, yea, glad, with all my heart,
That thus so cleanly I myself can free.
Shake hands for ever! Cancel all our vows!
And when we meet at any time again,
Be it not seen in either of our brows,
That we one jot of former love retain!
Now at the last gasp of Love's latest breath,
When, his pulse failing, Passion speechless lies;   10
When Faith is kneeling by his bed of death,
And Innocence is closing up his eyes,—
Now, if thou wouldst, when all have given him over,
From death to life thou might'st him yet recover!

(1619)

ODE TO THE VIRGINIAN VOYAGE

(From *The Ballad of Agincourt*)

You brave heroic minds,
Worthy your country's name,
    That honor still pursue;
    Go and subdue!

Whilst loitering hinds
Lurk here at home with shame.

Britons, you stay too long;
Quickly aboard bestow you!
  And with a merry gale
  Swell your stretched sail,   10
With vows as strong
As the winds that blow you!

Your course securely steer,
West-and-by-south forth keep!
  Rocks, lee-shores, nor shoals,
  When Eolus scowls,
You need not fear,
So absolute the deep.

And, cheerfully at sea,
Success you still entice,   20
  To get the pearl and gold;
  And ours to hold,
Virginia,
Earth's only Paradise.

Where Nature hath in store
Fowl, venison, and fish;
  And the fruitful'st soil,—
  Without your toil,
Three harvests more,
All greater than your wish.   30

And the ambitious vine
Crowns with his purple mass
  The cedar reaching high
  To kiss the sky,

The cypress, pine,
And useful sassafras.

To whom, the Golden Age
Still Nature's laws doth give:
   Nor other cares attend,
   But them to defend   40
From winter's rage,
That long there doth not live.

When as the luscious smell
Of that delicious land,
   Above the seas that flows,
   The clear wind throws,
Your hearts to swell,
Approaching the dear strand.

In kenning [1] of the shore
(Thanks to God first given!)   50
   O you, the happiest men,
   Be frolic then!
Let cannons roar,
Frightening the wide heaven!

And in regions far,
Such heroes bring ye forth
   As those from whom we came!
   And plant our name
Under that star
Not known unto our North!   60

[1] recognizing

And as there plenty grows
The laurel everywhere,
   Apollo's sacred tree
   You may it see
A poet's brows
To crown, that may sing there.

The Voyages attend,
Industrious Hakluyt!
   Whose reading shall inflame
   Men to seek fame;   70
And much commend
To after times thy wit.

                                    (1605)

THE BALLAD OF AGINCOURT

FAIR stood the wind for France,
When we our sails advance,
Nor now to prove our chance
   Longer will tarry;
But putting to the main
At Caux, the mouth of Seine,
With all his martial train
   Landed King Harry.

And taking many a fort,
Furnished in warlike sort,   10
Marcheth towards Agincourt
   In happy hour;
Skirmishing day by day
With those that stopped his way,
Where the French general lay
   With all his power.

Which, in his height of pride,
King Henry to deride,
His ransom to provide
  To the King sending;   20
Which he neglects the while,
As from a nation vile,
Yet, with an angry smile,
  Their fall portending.

And turning to his men,
Quoth our brave Henry then:
'Though they to one be ten
  Be not amazèd!
Yet have we well begun:
Battles so bravely won   30
Have ever to the sun
  By Fame been raisèd!

'And for myself,' quoth he,
'This my full rest shall be:
England ne'er mourn for me,
  Nor more esteem me!
Victor I will remain,
Or on this earth lie slain;
Never shall she sustain
  Loss to redeem me!   40

'Poitiers and Cressy tell,
When most their pride did swell,
Under our swords they fell.
  No less our skill is,
Than when our Grandsire great,
Claiming the regal seat,
By many a warlike feat
  Lopped the French lilies.'

The Duke of York so dread
The eager vanward led;   50
With the main, Henry sped
    Amongst his henchmen;
Exeter had the rear,
A braver man not there!
O Lord, how hot they were
    On the false Frenchmen!

They now to fight are gone;
Armor on armor shone;
Drum now to drum did groan:
    To hear, was wonder;   60
That, with the cries they make,
The very earth did shake;
Trumpet to trumpet spake;
    Thunder to thunder.

Well it thine age became,
O noble Erpingham,
Which didst the signal aim
    To our hid forces!
When, from a meadow by,
Like a storm suddenly,   70
The English archery
    Stuck the French horses.

With Spanish yew so strong;
Arrows a cloth-yard long,
That like to serpents stung,
    Piercing the weather.
None from his fellow starts;
But, playing manly parts,
And like true English hearts,
    Stuck close together.   80

When down their bows they threw,
And forth their bilboes [1] drew,
And on the French they flew:
   Not one was tardy.
Arms were from shoulders sent,
Scalps to the teeth were rent,
Down the French peasants went:
   Our men were hardy.

This while our noble King,
His broad sword brandishing,   90
Down the French host did ding,
   As to o'erwhelm it.
And many a deep wound lent;
His arms with blood besprent,
And many a cruel dent
   Bruisèd his helmet.

Gloucester, that duke so good,
Next of the royal blood,
For famous England stood
   With his brave brother.   100
Clarence, in steel so bright,
Though but a maiden knight,
Yet in that furious fight
   Scarce such another!

Warwick in blood did wade;
Oxford, the foe invade,
And cruel slaughter made,
   Still as they ran up.
Suffolk his axe did ply;
Beaumont and Willoughby   110

[1] swords

Bare them right doughtily;
  Ferrers, and Fanhope.

Upon Saint Crispin's Day
Fought was this noble fray;
Which Fame did not delay
  To England to carry.
O, when shall English men
With such acts fill a pen?
Or England breed again
  Such a King Harry?   120

(1605)

JOHN FLETCHER (1579-1625)

ASPATIA'S SONG

(From *The Maid's Tragedy*)

LAY a garland on my hearse
  Of the dismal yew;
Maidens, willow branches bear;
  Say I dièd true.

My love was false, but I was firm
  From my hour of birth:
Upon my buried body lie
  Lightly, gentle earth!

(1611)

WHAT IS LOVE?

(From *The Captain*)

Tell me, dearest, what is love?
'Tis a lightning from above;
'Tis an arrow, 't is a fire,
'Tis a boy they call Desire.
  'Tis a grave,
  Gapes to have
Those poor fools that long to prove.

Tell me more, are women true?
Yes, some are, and some as you.
Some are willing, some are strange,   10
Since you men first taught to change.
  And till troth
  Be in both,
All shall love, to love anew.

Tell me more yet, can they grieve?
Yes, and sicken sore, but live,
And be wise, and delay,
When you men are wise as they.
  Then I see,
  Faith will be,   20
Never till they both believe.

(1613)

CARE-CHARMING SLEEP

(From *Valentinian*)

CARE-CHARMING Sleep, thou easer of all woes,
Brother to Death, sweetly thyself dispose
On this afflicted prince; fall like a cloud,
In gentle showers; give nothing that is loud,
Or painful to his slumbers; easy, light,
And as a purling stream, thou son of Night,
Pass by his troubled senses; sing his pain,
Like hollow murmuring wind or silver rain;
Into this prince gently, O gently slide,
And kiss him into slumbers like a bride.   10

(1612?)

LOVE'S EMBLEMS

(From *Valentinian*)

Now the lusty spring is seen;
    Golden yellow, gaudy blue,
    Daintily invite the view.
Everywhere on every green,
Roses blushing as they blow,
    And enticing men to pull
Lilies whiter than the snow,
    Woodbines of sweet honey full:
    All love's emblems, and all cry,
    'Ladies, if not plucked, we die.'   10

Yet the lusty spring hath stayed;
    Blushing red and purest white
    Daintily to love invite

Every woman, every maid.
Cherries kissing as they grow,
    And inviting men to taste,
Apples even ripe below,
    Winding gently to the waist:
    All love's emblems, and all cry,
    'Ladies, if not plucked, we die.'   20

(1612?)

WEEP NO MORE

(From *The Queen of Corinth*)

WEEP no more, nor sigh, nor groan,
Sorrow calls no time that's gone;
Violets plucked the sweetest rain
Makes not fresh nor grow again;
Trim thy locks, look cheerfully;
Fate's hid ends eyes cannot see;
Joys as wingèd dreams fly fast,
Why should sadness longer last?
Grief is but a wound to woe;
Gentlest fair, mourn, mourn no mo.   10

(1617?)

JOHN DONNE (1573-1631)

SONG

Go AND catch a falling star,
  Get with child a mandrake root,
Tell me where all past years are,
  Or who cleft the devil's foot;
Teach me to hear mermaids singing,

Or to keep off envy's stinging,
      And find
      What wind
Serves to advance an honest mind.

If thou be'st born to strange sights,   10
  Things invisible go see,
Ride ten thousand days and nights
  Till Age snow white hairs on thee;
Thou, when thou return'st, wilt tell me
All strange wonders that befell thee,
      And swear
      No where
Lives a woman true and fair.

If thou find'st one, let me know;
  Such a pilgrimage were sweet.   20
Yet do not; I would not go,
  Though at next door we might meet.
Though she were true when you met her,
And last till you write your letter,
      Yet she
      Will be
False, ere I come, to two or three.

                (1598?)

THE INDIFFERENT

I CAN love both fair and brown;
Her whom abundance melts, and her whom want be-
    trays;
Her who loves loneness best, and her who masks and
    plays;
Her whom the country formed, and whom the town;
Her who believes, and her who tries;

Her who still weeps with spongy eyes,
And her who is dry cork and never cries.
I can love her, and her, and you, and you;
I can love any, so she be not true.

Will no other vice content you?　　　　　　　　　　10
Will it not serve your turn to do as did your mothers?
Or have you all old vices spent and now would find
　　　out others?
Or doth a fear that men are true torment you?
O we are not, be not you so;
Let me—and do you—twenty know;
Rob me, but bind me not, and let me go.
Must I, who came to travel thorough you,
Grow your fixed subject, because you are true?

Venus heard me sigh this song;
And by love's sweetest part, variety, she swore,　　　20
She heard not this till now; it should be so no more.
She went, examined, and returned ere long,
And said, 'Alas! some two or three
Poor heretics in love there be,
Which think to stablish dangerous constancy.
But I have told them, "Since you will be true,
You shall be true to them who 're false to you." '

(1598?)

LOVE'S DEITY

I LONG to talk with some old lover's ghost,
　　Who died before the god of Love was born:
I cannot think that he, who then loved most,
　　Sunk so low, as to love one who did scorn.
But since this god produced a destiny,

And that vice-nature, custom, lets it be,
  I must love her that loves not me.

Sure they, which made him god, meant not so much,
  Nor he in his young godhead practised it;
But when an even flame two hearts did touch,   10
  His office was indulgently to fit
Actives to passives, correspondency
Only his subject was; it cannot be
  Love, if I love who loves not me.

But every modern god will now extend
  His vast prerogative as far as Jove;
To rage, to lust, to write to, to commend,
  All is the purlieu of the god of Love.
Oh were we wakened by this tyranny
To ungod this child again, it could not be   20
  I should love her, who loves not me.

Rebel and atheist too, why murmur I
  As though I felt the worst that love could do?
Love may make me leave loving, or might try
  A deeper plague, to make her love me too,
Which, since she loves before, I'm loath to see;
Falsehood is worse than hate; and that must be,
  If she whom I love, should love me.

                                        (1598?)

THE GOOD-MORROW

I WONDER, by my troth, what thou and I
Did, till we loved: were we not weaned till then?
But sucked on country pleasures, childishly?
Or snorted we in the Seven Sleepers' den?

'Twas so; but this, all pleasures fancies be;
If ever any beauty I did see,
Which I desired, and got, 'twas but a dream of thee.

And now good-morrow to our waking souls,
Which watch not one another out of fear;
For love all love of other sights controls,
And makes one little room an everywhere.   10
Let sea-discoverers to new worlds have gone;
Let maps to other worlds on worlds have shown,
Let us possess one world; each hath one, and is one.

My face in thine eye, thine in mine appears,
And true plain hearts do in the faces rest;
Where can we find two better hemispheres
Without sharp north, without declining west?
What ever dies, was not mixed equally;
If our two loves be one, or thou and I   20
Love so alike that none do slacken, none can die.

                      (1602?)

LOVERS' INFINITENESS

If yet I have not all thy love,
Dear, I shall never have it all,
I cannot breathe one other sigh, to move,
Nor can intreat one other tear to fall,
And all my treasure, which should purchase thee,
Sigh, tears, and oaths, and letters, I have spent.
Yet no more can be due to me,
Than at the bargain made was meant;
If then thy gift of love were partial,
That some to me, some should to others fall,   10
    Dear, I shall never have thee all.

Or if then thou gavest me all,
All was but all, which thou hadst then;
But if in thy heart, since, there be or shall,
New love created be, by other men,
Which have their stocks entire, and can in tears,
In sighs, in oaths, and letters outbid me,
This new love may beget new fears,
For, this love was not vowed by thee;
And yet it was, thy gift being general,   20
The ground, thy heart is mine, what ever shall
   Grow there, dear; I should have it all.

Yet I would not have all yet;
He that hath all can have no more,
And since my love doth every day admit
New growth, thou shouldst have new rewards in store;
Thou canst not every day give me thy heart,
If thou canst give it, then thou never gavest it:
Love's riddles are, that though thy heart depart,
It stays at home, and thou with losing savest it: 30
But we will have a way more liberal,
Than changing hearts, to join them, so we shall
   Be one, and one another's all.

(1602?)

THE CANONIZATION

For God's sake hold your tongue, and let me love;
  Or chide my palsy, or my gout;
  My five gray hairs, or ruined fortune flout;
With wealth your state, your mind with arts improve;
    Take you a course, get you a place,
    Observe his Honor, or his Grace;
Or the king's real, or his stamped face

Contemplate; what you will, approve,
So you will let me love.

Alas! alas! who's injured by my love?   10
  What merchant's ships have my sighs drowned?
  Who says my tears have overflowed his ground?
When did my colds a forward spring remove?
    When did the heats which my veins fill
    Add one more to the plaguy bill?
Soldiers find wars, and lawyers find out still
  Litigious men, which quarrels move,
  Though she and I do love.

Call 's what you will, we are made such by love;
  Call her one, me another fly,   20
  We're tapers too, and at our own cost die,
And we in us find th' eagle and the dove.
    The phœnix riddle hath more wit
    By us; we two being one, are it;
So, to one neutral thing both sexes fit.
  We die and rise the same, and prove
  Mysterious by this love.

We can die by it, if not live by love,
  And if unfit for tomb or hearse
  Our legend be, it will be fit for verse;   30
And if no piece of chronicle we prove,
    We'll build in sonnets pretty rooms;
    As well a well-wrought urn becomes
The greatest ashes, as half-acre tombs,
  And by these hymns all shall approve
  Us canonized for love;

And thus invoke us, 'You, whom reverend love
  Made one another's hermitage;
   You, to whom love was peace, that now is rage;
Who did the whole world's soul contract, and drove   40
    Into the glasses of your eyes;
     So made such mirrors, and such spies,
That they did all to you epitomize—
  Countries, towns, courts beg from above
   A pattern of your love.'

(1602?)

THE COMPUTATION

FOR my first twenty years, since yesterday,
I scarce believed thou couldst be gone away;
For forty more I fed on favors past,
And forty on hopes, that thou wouldst they might last;
Tears drowned one hundred, and sighs blew out two;
A thousand I did neither think nor do.
Or not divide, all being one thought of you;
Or in a thousand more, forgot that too.
Yet call not this long life; but think that I
Am, by being dead, immortal; can ghosts die?   10

(1602?)

THE FUNERAL

WHOEVER comes to shroud me, do not harm
  Nor question much
That subtle wreath of hair about mine arm;
The mystery, the sign you must not touch,
  For 'tis my outward soul,
Viceroy to that which, unto heav'n being gone,
  Will leave this to control
And keep these limbs, her provinces, from dissolution.

For if the sinewy thread my brain lets fall
    Through every part   10
Can tie those parts, and make me one of all;
Those hairs which upward grew, and strength and art
    Have from a better brain,
Can better do't: except she meant that I
    By this should know my pain,
As prisoners then are manacled, when they're condemned
    to die.

Whate'er she meant by 't, bury it with me;
    For since I am
Love's martyr, it might breed idolatry
If into other hands these relics came;
    As 'twas humility   20
To afford to it all that a soul can do,
    So 'tis some bravery
That, since you would have none of me, I bury some
    of you.

                        (1602?)

HOLY SONNET

Death, be not proud, though some have callèd thee
Mighty and dreadful, for thou art not so;
For those whom thou think'st thou dost overthrow
Die not, poor Death; nor yet canst thou kill me.
From rest and sleep, which but thy picture be,
Much pleasure; then from thee much more must flow;
And soonest our best men with thee do go—
Rest of their bones and souls' delivery!
Thou'rt slave to fate, chance, kings, and desperate men,
And dost with poison, war, and sickness dwell;   10
And poppy or charms can make us sleep as well
And better than thy stroke. Why swell'st thou then?

One short sleep past, we wake eternally,
And Death shall be no more: Death, thou shalt die!

(1609?)

FORGET

IF POISONOUS minerals, and if that tree
Whose fruit threw death on else immortal us,
If lecherous goats, if serpents envious
Cannot be damned, alas! why should I be?
Why should intent or reason, born in me,
Make sins, else equal, in me more heinous?
And, mercy being easy and glorious
To God, in his stern wrath why threatens he?
But who am I, that dare dispute with thee?
O God, O! of thine only worthy blood   10
And my tears make a heavenly Lethean flood,
And drown in it my sin's black memory.
That thou remember them, some claim as debt;
I think it mercy if thou wilt forget.

(1615?)

A HYMN TO GOD THE FATHER

WILT thou forgive that sin where I begun,
  Which was my sin, though it were done before?
Wilt thou forgive that sin through which I run,
  And do run still, though still I do deplore?
When thou hast done, thou hast not done;
        For I have more.

Wilt thou forgive that sin which I have won
  Others to sin, and made my sins their door?
Wilt thou forgive that sin which I did shun
  A year or two, but wallowed in a score?   10

When thou hast done, thou hast not done;
     For I have more.

I have a sin of fear, that when I've spun
   My last thread, I shall perish on the shore;
But swear by thyself that at my death thy Son
   Shall shine as he shines now and heretofore;
And having done that, thou hast done;
     I fear no more.

                (1615?)

FROM GREENE TO JONSON

Robert Greene

Thomas Nashe

Thomas Dekker

Francis Bacon

Ben Jonson

ROBERT GREENE (1560?-1592)

A PLEASANT CONCEITED COMEDY OF GEORGE a GREENE, THE PINNER OF WAKEFIELD

Dramatis Personæ

Earl of Kendal, Henry Momford
Lord Bonfield ⎫
Sir Nicholas Mannering ⎬ rebel leaders
Sir Gilbert Armstrong ⎭
John Taylor, messenger
Justice Woodroffe
George a Greene
William Musgrove
Cuddie Musgrove, his son
Master Grime
Bettris, his daughter
James, King of Scots
Lord Humes
Ned, Jane a Barley's son
Jane a Barley
Jenkin, the clown
Wily, George a Greene's boy
A Shoemaker of Bradford
Edward, King of England
Lord Warwick
Robin Hood
Maid Marian
Scarlet

Much, the Miller

Townsmen, soldiers, shoemakers

　　Scene: Wakefield, Bradford, and vicinity.

GEORGE a GREENE, THE PINNER OF WAKEFIELD

Scene 1

Near the town of Bradford.

Enter the Earl of Kendal, with him the Lord Bonfield, Sir Nicholas Mannering, and Sir Gilbert Armstrong; and enter later John Taylor.

EARL OF KENDAL.　Welcome to Bradford, martial
　　gentlemen!
Lord Bonfield, and Sir Gilbert Armstrong both,
And all my troops, even to my basest groom,
Courage and welcome, for the day is ours!
Our cause is good—it is for the land's avail;
Then let us fight, and die for England's good!
　　OMNES.　We will, my lord!
　　KENDAL.　As I am Henry Momford, Kendal's Earl,
You honor me with this assent of yours.
And here upon my sword I make protest　　　　10
For to relieve the poor, or die myself.
And know, my lords, that James, the King of Scots,
Wars hard upon the borders of this land.

Enter John Taylor.

Here is his post.—Say, John Taylor,
What news with King James?
　　JOHN.　War, my lord! Tell; and good news, I trow;
For King Jamie vows to meet you the 26 of this month,
God willing; marry, doth he, sir.

KENDAL. My friends, you see what we have to win.—
Well, John, commend me to King James,   20
And tell him, I will meet him the 26 of this month,
And all the rest. And so, farewell.

Exit John.

Bonfield, why standst thou as a man in dumps?
Courage! for, if I win, I'll make thee duke.
I, Henry Momford, will be king myself;
And I will make thee Duke of Lancaster,
And Gilbert Armstrong, Lord of Doncaster.

BONFIELD. Nothing, my lord, makes me amazed at all,
But that our soldiers find our victuals scant.
We must make havoc of those country swains;   30
For so will the rest tremble and be afraid,
And humbly send provision to your camp.

GILB. My Lord Bonfield gives good advice.
They make a scorn, and stand upon the king;
So what is brought is sent from them perforce.
Ask Mannering else.

KEND. What sayest thou, Mannering?

MAN. When-as I showed your high commission,
They made this answer—
Only to send provision for your horses.   40

KEND. Well, hie thee to Wakefield; bid the town
To send me all provision that I want,
Lest I, like martial Tamberlaine, lay waste
Their bordering countries,
And leaving none alive that contradicts my commission.

MAN. Let me alone, my lord; I'll make them
Vail their plumes! For whatsoe'er he be,
The proudest knight, justice, or other, that gainsayeth
Your word, I'll clap him fast, to make the rest to fear.

KEND. Do so, Nick. Hie thee thither presently;   50
And let us hear of thee again tomorrow.

MAN. Will you not remove, my lord?

KEND. No; I will lie at Bradford all this night,
And all the next.—Come, Bonfield, let us go
And listen out [1] some bonny lasses here.

Exeunt omnes.

Scene 2

At Wakefield

*Enter the Justice, a Townsman, George a Greene, and
Sir Nicholas Mannering with his Commission.*

JUSTICE. Master Mannering, stand aside whilst we
confer what is best to do. *Mannering stands to one side.*
Townsmen of Wakefield, the Earl of Kendal here hath
sent for victuals; and in aiding him we show ourselves
no less than traitors to the King. Therefore let me [60
hear, townsmen, what is your consents.

TOWNES. Even as you please, we are all content.

JUSTICE. Then—Master Mannering, we are resolved.

Mannering advances.

MAN. As how?

JUSTICE. Marry, sir, thus. We will send the Earl
of Kendal no victuals, because he is a traitor to the king,
and in aiding him we show ourselves no less.

MAN. Why, men of Wakefield! are you waxen mad,
That present danger cannot whet your wits
Wisely to make provision of yourselves?   70
The earl is thirty thousand men strong in power,
And what town soever him resist,
He lays it flat and level with the ground.
Ye silly men, you seek your own decay!

[1] find out about

Therefore send my lord such provision as he wants,
So he will spare your town, and come no nearer
Wakefield than he is.

JUSTICE. Master Mannering, you have your answer.
You may be gone.

MAN. Well, Woodroffe—for so I guess is thy [80
name—I'll make thee curse thy overthwart [1] denial; and
all that sit upon the bench [2] this day shall rue the hour
they have withstood my lord's commission.

JUSTICE. Do thy worst, we fear thee not.

MAN. See you these seals? Before you pass the town
I will have all things that my lord doth want,
In spite of you!

GEORGE A GREENE. Proud dapper Jack, vail bonnet to
the bench
That represents the person of the king;
Or, sirra, I'll lay thy head before thy feet. 90

MAN. Why, who art thou?

GEORGE. Why, I am George a Greene,
True liegeman to my king,
Who scorns that men of such esteem as these
Should brook the braves of any traitorous squire.
You of the bench, and you, my fellow-friends,
Neighbors we, subjects all unto the king,
We are English born, and therefore Edward's friends,
Vowed unto him even in our mother's womb,
Our minds to God, our hearts unto our king. 100
Our wealth, our homage, and our carcasses,
Be all King Edward's. Then, sirra, we have
Nothing left for traitors but our swords,
Whetted to bathe them in your bloods, and die
Against you, before we send you any victuals.

JUSTICE. Well spoken, George a Greene!

TOWNES. Pray let George a Greene speak for us.

[1] arrogant [2] village officials

GEORGE. Sirra, you get no victuals here—
Not if a hoof of beef would save your lives.

MAN. Fellow, I stand amazed at thy presumption. 110
Why, what are thou that darest gainsay my lord,
Knowing his mighty puissance and his stroke?
Why, my friend, I come not barely of my self;
For, see, I have a large commission.

GEORGE. Let me see it, sirra. *Takes the Commission.* Whose seals be these?

MAN. This is the Earl of Kendal's seal-at-arms;
This, Lord Charnel Bonfield's;
And this, Sir Gilbert Armstrong's.

GEORGE. I tell thee, sirra, did good King Ed- [120
ward's son seal a commission against the king his father,
thus would I tear it in despite of him, being traitor to
my sovereign.

He tears the Commission.

MAN. What! hast thou torn my lord's commission?
Thou shalt rue it—and so shall all Wakefield.

GEORGE. What! are you in choler? I will give you
pills to cool your stomach! Seest thou these seals?
Now, by my father's soul, which was a yeoman when he
was alive, eat them, or eat my dagger's point, proud
squire!   130

MAN. But thou dost but jest, I hope.

GEORGE. Sure that shall you see before we two
part.

MAN. Well, and there be no remedy, so, George.
Swallows one of the seals. One is gone. I pray thee,
no more now.

GEORGE. O sir, if one be good, the others cannot hurt.
Mannering swallows the other seals. So, sir; now you
may go tell the Earl of Kendal, although I have rent

his large commission, yet of courtesy I have sent [140
all his seals back again by you.

MAN.   Well, sir, I will do your errand.

Exit Mannering.

GEORGE.   Now let him tell his lord that he hath
spoke with George a Greene, right pinner of merry
Wakefield town, that hath physic for a fool, pills for
a traitor that doth wrong his sovereign. Are you content with this that I have done?

JUSTICE.   Aye, content, George;
For highly hast thou honored Wakefield town
In cutting of proud Mannering so short.   150
Come; thou shalt be my welcome guest today;
For well thou hast deserved reward and favor.

Exeunt omnes.

Scene 3

Outside Sandon Castle, which Musgrove keeps.

Enter old Musgrove and young Cuddie his son.

CUDDIE.   Now, gentle father, list unto thy son;
And for my mother's love,
That erst was blithe and bonny in thine eye,
Grant one petition that I shall demand.

OLD MUSGROVE.   What is that, my Cuddie?

CUDDIE.   Father, you know the ancient enmity of late
Between the Musgroves and the wily Scots,
Whereof they have oath   160
Not to leave one alive that strides a lance.
O, Father, you are old, and, waning, age unto the grave.
Old William Musgrove, which whilom was thought
The bravest horseman in all Westmoreland,
Is weak, and forced to stay his arm upon a staff,

That erst could wield a lance.
Then, gentle father, resign the hold to me;
Give arms to youth, and honor unto age.

Mus. Avaunt, false hearted boy! My joints do quake
Even with anguish of thy very words! 170
Hath William Musgrove seen an hundred years?
Have I been feared and dreaded of the Scots
That when they heard my name in any road [1]
They fled away, and posted thence amain,
And shall I die with shame now in mine age?
No, Cuddie, no. Thus resolve I:—
Here have I lived, and here will Musgrove die.

Exeunt omnes.

Scene 4

Before Grime's house.

*Enter Lord Bonfield, Sir Gilbert Armstrong, Master
Grime, and Bettris his daughter.*

Bon. Now, gentle Grime, God-a-mercy for our good
cheer!
Our fare was royal, and our welcome great.
And sith so kindly thou hast entertained us, 180
If we return with happy victory
We will deal as friendly with thee in recompense.

Grime. Your welcome was but duty, gentle lord;
For wherefore have we given us our wealth
But to make our betters welcome when they come?
Aside. O, this goes hard when traitors must be flattered!
But life is sweet, and I cannot withstand it.
God, I hope, will revenge the quarrel of my king.

Gilb. What said you, Grime?

Grime. I say, Sir Gilbert, looking on my daughter 190
[1] raid, foray

I curse the hour that ere I got the girl;
For, sir, she may have many wealthy suitors,
And yet she disdains them all to have
Poor George a Greene unto her husband.

    BONFIELD.   On that, good Grime, I am talking with
        thy daughter;
But she in quirks and quiddities of love
Sets me to school, she is so overwise.—
But, gentle girl, if thou wilt forsake
The pinner and be my love, I will advance thee high.
To dignify those hairs of amber hue,   200
I'll grace them with a chaplet made of pearl,
Set with choice rubies, sparks, and diamonds,
Planted upon a velvet hood, to hide that head
Wherein two sapphires burn like sparkling fire.
This will I do, fair Bettris, and far more,
If thou wilt love the Lord of Doncaster.

    BETTRIS.   Heigh ho! my heart is in a higher place—
Perhaps on the earl, if that be he. *Pointing.*
See where he comes, or angry, or in love,
For why his color looketh discontent.   210

    KENDAL.   Come, Nick, follow me.

Enter the Earl of Kendal and Sir Nicholas Mannering.

    BONFIELD.   How now, my lord! what news?

    KENDAL.   Such news, Bonfield, as will make thee
        laugh
And fret thy fill to hear how Nick was used.
Why, the justices stand on their terms.
Nick, as you know, is haughty in his words;
He laid the law unto the justices
With threat'ning braves, that one looked on another
Ready to stoop, but that a churl came in,
One George a Greene, the pinner of the town,   220
And with his dagger drawn laid hands on Nick,
And by no beggars [1] swore that we were traitors,

[1] no trifling oaths

Rent our commission, and upon a brave
Made Nick to eat the seals or brook the stab.
Poor Mannering, afraid, came posting hither straight.

BETTRIS *aside.*   O lovely George, fortune be still thy
    friend!
And as thy thoughts be high, so be thy mind
In all accords, even to thy heart's desire!

BONFIELD.   What says fair Bettris?

GRIMES.   My Lord, she is praying for George a
    Greene.   230
He is the man, and she will none but him.

BONFIELD.   But him! why, look on me, my girl.
Thou knowest that yesternight I courted thee,
And swore at my return to wed with thee.
Then tell me, love, shall I have all thy fair?

BETTRIS.   I care not for earl, nor yet for knight,
Nor baron that is so bold;
For George a Greene, the merry pinner,
He hath my heart in hold.

BONFIELD.   Bootless, my lord, are many vain re-
    plies.   240
Let us hie us to Wakefield, and send her the pinners
    head.

KEND.   It shall be so.—Grime, gramercy.
Shut up thy daughter; bridle her affects;
Let me not miss her when I make return.
Therefore look to her as to thy life, good Grime.

GRIME.   I warrant you, my Lord.

KEND. *aside to Bettris.*   And, Bettris, leave a base
    pinner, for to love an earl.

Exeunt Grime and Bettris.

Fain would I see this pinner, George a Greene.
It shall be thus:

Nick Mannering shall lead on the battle,   250
And we three will go to Wakefield in some disguise.
But howsoever, I'll have his head today!

Exeunt omnes.

Scene 5

Before Sir John a Barley's castle.

*Enter the King of Scots, Lord Humes, with Soldiers,
and John.*

KING JAMES. Why, Johnny, then the Earl of Kendal
     is blithe,
And hath brave men that troop along with him?
   JOHN. Ay, marry, my liege, and hath good men
That come along with him;
And vows to meet you at Scrasblesea, God willing.
   KING JAMES. If good Saint Andrew lend King Jamie
     leave,
I will be with him at the pointed day.
But, soft!—Whose pretty boy art thou?   260

Enter Ned, Jane a Barley's son.

NED. Sir, I am son unto Sir John a Barley,
Eldest and all that ere my mother had;
Edward my name.
   K. JAMES. And whither art thou going, pretty Ned?
   NED. To seek some birds, and kill them, if I can.
And now my schoolmaster is also gone,
So have I liberty to ply my bow;
For when he comes, I stir not from my book.
   K. JAMES. Lord Humes, but mark the visage of this
     child!
By him I guess the beauty of his mother;   270
None but Leda could breed Helena.

Tell me, Ned, who is within with thy mother?

NED.   Nought but herself and household servants, sir.
If you would speak with her, knock at this gate.

K. JAMES.   Johnny, knock at that gate.

Enter Jane a Barley upon the walls.

JANE.   O, I am betrayed! What multitudes be these?

K. JAMES.   Fear not, fair Jane, for all these men are
    mine—
And all thy friends, if thou be friend to me.
I am thy lover, James, the King of Scots.
That oft have sued and wooed with many letters,   280
Painting my outward passions with my pen
When as my inward soul did bleed for woe.
Little regard was given to my suit,
But haply thy husband's presence wrought it.
Therefore, sweet Jane, I fitted me to time,
And, hearing that thy husband was from home,
Am come to crave what long I have desired.

NED.   Nay, soft you, sir! You get no entrance here,
That seek to wrong Sir John a Barley so,
And offer such dishonor to my mother.   290

K. JAMES.   Why, what dishonor, Ned?

NED.   Though young,
Yet often have I heard my father say,
"No greater wrong than to be made cuckold."
Were I of age, or were my body strong,
Were he ten kings, I would shoot him to the heart
That should attempt to give Sir John the horn.—
Mother, let him not come in.
I will go lie at Jockie Miller's house.

K. JAMES.   Stay him.   300

JANE.   Ay, well said, Ned! Thou hast given the king
His answer.
For were the ghost of Cæsar on the earth,

Wrapped in the wonted glory of his honor,
He should not make me wrong my husband so.
But good King James is pleasant,[1] as I guess,
And means to try what humor I am in;
Else would he never have brought an host of men
To have them witness of his Scottish lust.

   K. JAMES. Jane, in faith, Jane—   310
   JANE. Never reply; for I protest by the highest Holy
      God,
That doometh just revenge for things amiss,
King James, of all men, shall not have my love.

   K. JAMES. Then list to me: Saint Andrew be my
      boot,[2]
But I'll raze thy castle to the very ground,
Unless thou open the gate and let me in!

   JANE. I fear thee not, King Jamie. Do thy worst!
This castle is too strong for thee to scale;
Besides, tomorrow will Sir John come home.

   K. JAMES. Well, Jane, since thou disdainst King
      James's love,   320
I'll draw thee on with sharp and deep extremes;
For, by my father's soul, this brat of thine
Shall perish here before thine eyes,
Unless thou open the gate and let me in.

   JANE. O deep extremes! My heart begins to break!
My little Ned looks pale for fear.—
Cheer thee, my boy; I will do much for thee.

   NED. But not so much as to dishonor me.
   JANE. But if thou diest, I cannot live, sweet Ned.
   NED. Then die with honor, mother, dying chaste. 330
   JANE. I am armed.
My husband's love, his honor, and his fame,
Joins victory by virtue. Now, King James,

  [1] jesting   [2] help

If mother's tears cannot allay thine ire,
Then butcher him, for I will never yield.
The son shall die before I wrong the father.

    K. JAMES. Why, then, he dies.

Alarm within. Enter a Messenger.

    MESSENGER. My Lord, Musgrove is at hand.

    K. JAMES. Who? Musgrove! The devil he is! Come,
My horse!   340

Exeunt omnes. Skirmish within.
Enter old Musgrove with King James prisoner.

    MUS. Now, King James, thou art my prisoner.

    K. JAMES. Not thine, but Fortune's prisoner.

Enter Cuddie.

    CUDDIE. Father, the field is ours! Their colors we
      have seized,
And Humes is slain; I slew him hand to hand.

    MUS. God and Saint George!

    CUDDIE. O father, I am sore athirst!

    JANE. Come in, young Cuddie, come and drink thy
      fill.
Bring in King Jamie with you as a guest;
For all this broil was cause he could not enter.

Exeunt omnes.

Scene 6.

Near George a Greene's wheat field outside Wakefield.

Enter George a Greene alone.

    GEORGE. The sweet content of men that live in love [350
Breeds fretting humors in a restless mind;

And fancy, being checked by fortune's spite,
Grows too impatient in her sweet desires;—
Sweet to those men whom love leads on to bliss,
But sour to me, whose hap is still amiss.

Enter the Clown.

JENKIN.   Marry, amen, sir!

GEORGE.   Sir, what do you cry, "Amen" at?

JENKIN.   Why, did not you talk of love?

GEORGE.   How do you know that?

JENKIN.   Well, though I say it that should not [360
say it, there are few fellows in our parish so nettled with
love as I have been of late.

GEORGE.   Sirra, I thought no less when the other
morning you rose so early to go to your wenches. Sir, I
had thought you had gone about my honest business.

JENKIN.   Trow, you have hit it! For, master, be it
known to you, there is some good-will betwixt Madge,
the sousewife, and I. Marry, she hath another lover.

GEORGE.   Canst thou brook any rivals in thy love?

JENKIN.   A rider! no, he is a sow-gelder and [370
goes afoot. But Madge pointed to meet me in your
wheat close.

GEORGE.   Well, did she meet you there?

JENKIN.   Never make a question of that! And first I
saluted her with a green gown, and after fell as hard a
wooing as if the priest had been at our backs to have
married us.

GEORGE.   What, did she grant?

JENKIN.   Did she grant? Never make question of
that! And she gave me a shirt-collar wrought over [380
with no counterfeit stuff.

GEORGE.   What, was it gold?

JENKIN.   Nay, 'twas better than gold.

GEORGE. What was it?

JENKIN. Right Coventry-blue. We had no sooner come there but wot you who came by?

GEORGE. No; who?

JENKIN. Clim, the sow-gelder.

GEORGE. Came he by?

JENKIN. He spied Madge and I sit together. He [390 leapt from his horse, laid his hand on his dagger, and began to swear. Now I, seeing he had a dagger, and I nothing but this twig in my hand, I gave him fair words and said nothing. He comes to me and takes me by the bosom. "You whoreson slave," said he, "hold my horse; and look he take no cold in his feet." "No, marry, shall he, sir," quoth I; "I'll lay my cloak underneath him." I took my cloak, spread it all along, and his horse on the midst of it.

GEORGE. Thou clown! didst thou set his horse [400 upon thy cloak?

JENKIN. Ay; but mark how I served him. Madge and he was no sooner gone down into the ditch, but I plucked out my knife, cut four holes in my cloak, and made his horse stand on the bare ground.

GEORGE. 'Twas well done. Now, sir, go and survey my fields; if you find any cattle in the corn, to pound with them.

JENKIN. And if I find any in the pound, I shall turn them out.   410

Exit Jenkin

Enter the Earl of Kendal, Lord Bonfield, Sir Gilbert, all disguised, with a train of men in ambush.

KEND. Now we have put the horses in the corn, let us stand in some corner for to hear what braving terms the pinner will breathe when he spies our horses in the corn.

Enter Jenkin blowing of his horn.

JENKIN. O master, where are you? We have a prize.

GEORGE. A prize! what is it?

JENKIN. Three goodly horses in our wheat close.

GEORGE. Three horses in our wheat close! Whose be they?

JENKIN. Marry, that's a riddle to me. But [420 they are there—velvet horses, and I never saw such horses before. As my duty was, I put off my cap, and said as followeth: "My masters, what do you make in our close?" One of them, hearing me ask what he made there, held up his head and neighed, and, after his manner, laughed as heartily as if a mare had been tied to his girdle. "My masters," said I, "it is no laughing matter; for, if my master take you here, you go as round as a top to the pound." Another untoward jade, hearing me threaten him to the pound and to tell you of [430 them, cast up both his heels. . . . Now I put on my cap, blew my horn, called them all jades, and came to tell you.

GEORGE. Now, sir, go and drive me those three horses to the pound.

JENKIN. Do you hear? I were best to take a constable with me.

GEORGE. Why so?

JENKIN. Why, they, being gentlemen's horses, may stand on their reputation, and will not obey me.   440

GEORGE. Go do as I bid you, sir.

JENKIN. Well, I may go.

The Earl of Kendal, the Lord Bonfield, and Sir Gilbert Armstrong, meet them.

KEND. Whither away, sir?

JENKIN. Whither away? I am going to put the horses in the pound.

KEND. Sirra, those three horses belong to us, and we put them in; and they must tarry there, and eat their fill.

JENKIN. Stay, I will go tell my master.—Hear you, master; we have another prize! Those three horses [450 be in your wheat close still, and here be three geldings more.

GEORGE. What be these?

JENKIN. These are the masters of the horses.

GEORGE. Now, gentlemen—I know not your degrees, but more you cannot be unless you be kings—why wrong you us of Wakefield with your horses? I am the pinner, and before you pass you shall make good the trespass they have done.

KEND. Peace, saucy mate! Prate not to us: I [460 tell thee, pinner, we are gentlemen.

GEORGE. Why, sir, so may I, sir, although I give no arms.[1]

KEND. Thou! How art thou a gentleman?

JENKIN. And such is my master, and he may give as good arms as ever your great grandfather could give.

KEND. Pray thee, let me hear how.

JENKIN. Marry, my master may give for his arms the picture of April in a green jerkin, with a rook on one fist and an horn on the other: but my master gives [470 his arms the wrong way, for he gives the horn on his fist; and your grandfather, because he would not lose his arms, wears the horn on his own head.

KEND. Well, pinner, sith our horses be in, in spite of thee they now shall feed their fill, and eat until our leisures serve to go.

GEORGE. Now, by my father's soul, were good King Edward's horses in the corn, they shall amend the scath,

[1] have no coat-of-arms

or kiss the pound; much more yours, sir, whatsoever
you be!   480

KEND. Why, man, thou knowest not us. We do belong to Henry Momford, Earl of Kendal; men that,
before a month be full expired, will be King Edward's
betters in the land.

GEORGE. King Edward's betters! Rebel, thou liest!

George strikes him.

BONFIELD. Villain, what hast thou done. Thou hast
struck an earl.

GEORGE. Why, what care I? A poor man that is
true is better than an earl, if he be false. Traitors
reap no better favors at my hands.   490

KEND. Ay, so me thinks; but thou shall dear abide
this blow.—Now or never, lay hold on the pinner!

Enter all the ambush.

GEORGE. Stay, my lords. Let us parley on these
broils. "Not Hercules against two," the proverb is,
nor I against so great a multitude. *Aside.* Had not
your troops come marching as they did, I would have
stopped your passage unto London: but now I'll fly to
secret policy.

KEND. What dost thou murmur, George?

GEORGE. Marry, this, my lord: I muse, if thou [500
be Henry Momford, Kendal's Earl, that thou wilt do
poor George a Greene this wrong, ever to match me
with a troop of men.

KEND. Why dost thou strike me, then?

GEORGE. Why, my lord, measure me but by yourself:
had you a man had served you long, and heard your foe
misuse you behind your back and would not draw his
sword in your defense, you would cashier him. Much
more, King Edward is my king; and, before I'll hear

him so wronged, I'll die within this place, and [510 maintain good whatsoever I have said. And, if I speak not reason in this case, what I have said I'll maintain in this place.

Bon. A pardon, my lord, for this pinner; for, trust me, he speaketh like a man of worth.

Kend. Well, George, wilt thou leave Wakefield and with me, I'll freely put up all and pardon thee.

George. I, my lord, considering [1] me one thing— you will leave these arms and follow your good king.

Kend. Why, George, I rise not against King [520 Edward, but for the poor that is oppressed by wrong; and if King Edward will redress the same, I will not offer him disparagement, but otherwise; and so let this suffice. Thou hearest the reason why I rise in arms; now, wilt thou leave Wakefield and wend with me, I'll make thee captain of a hardy band, and, when I have my will, dub thee a knight.

George. Why, my lord, have you any hope to win?

Kend. Why, there is a prophecy doth say that [530 King James and I shall meet at London, and make the king vail bonnet to us both.

George. If this were true, my lord, this were a mighty reason.

Kend. Why, it is a miraculous prophecy, and cannot fail.

George. Well, my lord, you have almost turned me. —Jenkin, come hither.

Jenkin. Sir?

George. Go your ways home, sir, and drive me [540 those three horses home unto my house; and pour them down a bushel of good oats.

Jenkin. Well, I will. *Aside.* Must I give these scurvy horses oats?

[1] granting

Exit Jenkin.

GEORGE. Will it please you to command your train aside?

KEND. Stand aside.

Exit the train.

GEORGE. Now list to me: here in a wood, not far from hence, there dwells an old man in a cave alone, that can foretell what fortunes shall befall you, for he is [550 greatly skilful in magic art. Go you three to him early in the morning and question him: if he says good, why, then, my lord, I am the foremost man! We will march up with your camp to London.

KEND. George, thou honorest me in this. But where shall we find him out?

GEORGE. My man shall conduct you to the place. But, good my lords, tell me true what the wise man saith.

KEND. That will I, as I am Earl of Kendal.   560

GEORGE. Why, then, to honor George a Greene the more, vouchsafe a piece of beef at my poor house. You shall have wafer cakes your fill, a piece of beef hung up since Martinmas:—if that like you not, take what you bring, for me!

KEND. Gramercies, George.

Exeunt omnes.

Scene 7.

Before Grime's House.

Enter George a Greene's boy, Wily, disguised like a woman, to Master Grimes.

WILY. O, what is love! It is some mighty power, Else could it never conquer George a Greene.

Here dwells a churl that keeps away his love.
I know the worst—and if I be espied,   570
'Tis but a beating. And if I by this means
Can get fair Bettris forth her father's door,
It is enough.
Venus, for me, and all the gods above,
Be aiding to my wily enterprise!

He knocks at the door.

Enter Grime.

GRIME. How now! Who knocks there? What would
    you have?
From whence came you? Where do you dwell?
WILY. I am, forsooth, a seamster's maid hard by,
That hath brought work home to your daughter.
GRIME. Nay, are you not some crafty quean   580
That comes from George a Greene, that rascal,
With some letters to my daughter?
I will have you searched.
WILY. Alas, sir, it is Hebrew unto me
To tell me of George a Greene, or any other!
Search me, good sir,
And if you find a letter about me,
Let me have the punishment that is due.
GRIME. Why are you muffled? I like you the worse
For that.   590
WILY. I am not, sir, ashamed to show my face,
Yet loth I am my cheeks should take the air—
Not that I am chary of my beauty's hue,
But that I am troubled with the tooth-ache sore.

Bares his face.

GRIME. A pretty wench, of smiling countenance!
Old men can like, although they cannot love—

Ay, and love, though not so brief as young men can.
Well, go in, my wench, and speak with my daughter.

Exit Wily.

I wonder much at the Earl of Kendal,
Being a mighty man, as still he is,   600
Yet for to be a traitor to his king
Is more than God or man will well allow.
But what a fool am I to talk of him!
My mind is more here of the pretty lass.
Had she brought some forty pounds to town
I could be content to make her my wife.
Yet I have heard it in a proverb said,
"He that is old and marries with a lass,
Lies but at home, and proves himself an ass."

Enter Bettris in Wily's apparel, to Grime.

How now, my wench! How is't? What, not a word?—
Alas, poor soul, the tooth-ache plagues her sore.—   611
Well, my wench, here is an angel for to buy thee pins.
And I pray thee use mine house;
The oftener, the more welcome.   Farewell.

Exit Grime.

BETTRIS.   O blessed love, and blessed fortune both!
But, Bettris, stand not here to talk of love,
But hie thee straight unto thy George a Greene.
Never went roe-buck swifter on the downs
Then I will trip it till I see my George.

Exit Bettris.

Scene 8.

Before the cave of the old magician, near Wakefield.

*Enter the Earl of Kendal, Lord Bonfield, Sir Gilbert,
and Jenkin the clown.*

KEND.   Come away, Jenkin.   620
JENKIN.   Come; here is his house. *Calling.* Where
be you, ho?
GEORGE *within*.   Who knocks there?
KEND.   Here are two or three poor men, father,
Would speak with you.
GEORGE.   Pray, give your man leave to lead me forth.
KEND.   Go, Jenkin, fetch him forth.
JENKIN.   Come, old man.

Enter George a Greene disguised.

KEND.   Father, here is three poor men come to ques-
tion Thee a word in secret that concerns their lives.
GEORGE.   Say on, my sons.   630
KEND.   Father, I am sure you hear the news
How that the Earl of Kendal wars against the king.
Now, father, we three are gentlemen by birth,
But younger brethren that want revenues,
And for the hope we have to be preferred,
If that we knew that we shall win,
We will march with him;
If not, we will not march a foot to London more.
Therefore, good father, tell us what shall happen,
Whether the king or the Earl of Kendal shall win.   640
GEORGE.   The King, my son.
KEND.   Art thou sure of that?
GEORGE.   I, as sure as thou art Henry Momford,
The one Lord Bonfield, the other Sir Gilbert.

KEND. Why this is wondrous, being blind of sight,
His deep perception should be such to know us!

GIBB. Magic is mighty, and fortelleth great matters.
Indeed, father, here is the earl come to see thee;
And therefore, good father, fable not with him.

GEORGE. Welcome is the earl to my poor cell, 650
And so are you, my lords. But let me counsel you
To leave these wars against your king,
And live in quiet.

KEND. Father, we come not for advice in war,
But to know whether we shall win or lose.

GEORGE. Lose, gentle lords, but not by good King
Edward;
A baser man shall give you all the foil.

KEND. I, marry, father, what man is that?

GEORGE. Poor George a Greene, the pinner.

KEND. What shall he? 660

GEORGE. Pull all your plumes, and sore dishonor you.

KEND. He! As how?

GEORGE. Nay, the end tries all. But so it will fall
out.

KEND. But so it shall not, by my honor! Christ!
I'll raise my camp, and fire Wakefield town,
And take that servile pinner, George a Greene,
And butcher him before King Edward's face.

GEORGE. Good my lord, be not offended;
For I speak no more than art reveals to me:
And for greater proof, 670
Give your man leave to fetch me out my staff.

KEND. Jenkin, fetch him his walking staff.

Jenkin goes in and brings out George's staff.

JENKIN. Here is your walking staff.

GEORGE. I'll prove it good upon your carcasses
A wiser wizard never met you yet,
Nor one that better could foredoom your fall.

Now I have singled you here alone,
I care not though you be three to one.

Throws off his disguise.

KEND. Villain, hast thou betrayed us?

GEORGE. Momford, thou liest! never was I traitor
  yet;   680
Only devised this guile to draw you on
For to be combatants.
Now conquer me, and then march on to London!
It shall go hard, but I will hold you task.

GIBB. Come, my lord, cheerily. I'll kill him hand to
  hand.

KEND. A thousand pounds to him that strikes that
  stroke!

GEORGE. Then give it me, for I will have the first.

*Here they fight. George kills Sir Gilbert, and takes
the other two prisoners.*

BON. Stay, George! we do appeal.

GEORGE. To whom?

BON. Why, to the king;   690
For rather had we bide what he appoints,
Than here be murdered by a servile groom.

KEND. What wilt thou do with us?

GEORGE. Even as Lord Bonfield wished,
You shall unto the king;
And, for that purpose, see where the Justice is placed.

Enter Justice.

JUST. Now, my Lord of Kendal, where be all your
  threats?
Even as the cause, so is the combat fallen,
Else one could never have conquered three.

KEND. I pray thee, Woodroffe, do not twit me. 700

If I have faulted, I must make amends.

GEORGE.   Master Woodroffe, here is not a place for
   many words.

I beseech ye, sir, discharge all his soldiers,

That every man may go home unto his own house.

JUST.   It shall be so.   What wilt thou do, George?

GEORGE.   Master Woodroffe, look to your charge;

Leave me to myself.

JUST.   Come, my Lords.

Exeunt all but George.

GEORGE.   Here sit thou, George, wearing a willow
   wreath,

As one despairing of thy beauteous love.   710

Fie, George! No more!

Pine not away for that which cannot be.

I cannot joy in any earthly bliss

So long as I do want my Bettris.

Enter Jenkin.

JENKIN.   Who see a master of mine?

GEORGE.   How now, sirra! whither away?

JENKIN.   Whither away? why, who do you take me
   to be?

GEORGE.   Why Jenkin, my man.

JENKIN.   I was so once, indeed, but now the case is
   altered.

GEORGE.   I pray thee, as how?   720

JENKIN.   Were not you a fortune-teller today?

GEORGE.   Well, what of that?

JENKIN.   So sure am I become a juggler.

What will you say if I juggle your sweetheart?

GEORGE.   Peace, prating losel! Her jealous father

Doth wait over her with such suspicious eyes,

That, if a man but dally by her feet,

He thinks it straight a witch to charm his daughter.

> JENKIN.   Well, what will you give me if I bring her
> hither?
>
> GEORGE.   A suit of green, and twenty crowns be-
> sides.   730
>
> JENKIN.   Well, by your leave, give me room.

You must give me something that you have lately worn.

> GEORGE.   Here is a gown; will that serve you?

Throws him the gown.

> JENKIN.   Ay, this will serve me.   Keep out of my
> circle,

Least you be torn in pieces by she devils.

Mistress Bettris, once! twice! thrice!

He throws the gown in, and she comes out.

Oh, is this no cunning?

> GEORGE.   Is this my love, or is it but her shadow?
>
> JENKIN.   Ay, this is the shadow, but here is the sub-
> stance.
>
> GEORGE.   Tell me, sweet love, what good fortune   740

Brought thee hither?

For one it was that favored George a Greene.

> BETTRIS.   Both love and fortune brought me to my
> George,

In whose sweet sight is all my heart's content.

> GEORGE.   Tell me, sweet love, how camest thou from
> thy father's?
>
> BETTRIS.   A willing mind hath many slips in love:

It was not I, but Wily, thy sweet boy.

> GEORGE.   And where is Wily now?
>
> BETTRIS.   In my apparel, in my chamber still.
>
> GEORGE.   Jenkin, come hither.   Go to Bradford,   750

And listen out [1] your fellow Wily.—

---

[1] seek news of

Come, Bettris, let us in,
And in my cottage we will sit and talk.

Exeunt omnes

Scene 9

The Court of King Edward.

Enter King Edward, the King of Scots, Lord Warwick,
young Cuddie, and their train.

EDWARD.   Brother of Scotland, I do hold it hard,
Seeing a league of truce was late confirmed
'Twixt you and me, without displeasure offered
You should make such invasion in my land.
The vows of kings should be as oracles,
Not blemished with the stain of any breach,
Chiefly where fealty and homage willeth it.   760
   JAMES.   Brother of England, rub not the sore afresh;
My conscience grieves me for my deep misdeed.
I have the worst; of thirty thousand men,
There 'scaped not full five thousand from the field.
   EDWARD.   Gramercy, Musgrove, else it had gone hard.
Cuddie, I'll quit thee well ere we two part.
   JAMES.   But had not his old father, William Musgrove,
Played twice the man, I had not now been here.
A stronger man I seldom felt before.
But one of more resolute valiance   770
Treads not, I think, upon the English ground.
   EDWARD.   I wot well Musgrove shall not lose his hire.[1]
   CUDDIE.   And it please your Grace, my father was
Five score and three at midsummer last past;
Yet, had King Jamie been as good as George a Greene,
Yet Billy Musgrove would have fought with him.

---

[1] reward

EDWARD. As George a Greene! I pray thee, Cuddie,
Let me question thee.
Much have I heard, since I came to my crown,
Many in manner of a proverb say,   780
"Were he as good as George a Greene, I would strike
    him sure."
I pray thee tell me, Cuddie, canst thou inform me
What is that George a Greene?

    CUDDIE. Know, my lord, I never saw the man,
But mickle talk is of him in the country.
They say he is the pinner of Wakefield town;
But for his other qualities, I let alone.

    WAR. May it please your Grace, I know the man too
      well.

    EDWARD. Too well! why so, Warwick?

    WAR. For once he swinged me till my bones did
      ache.   790

    EDWARD. Why, dares he strike an earl?

    WAR. An earl, my lord! nay, he will strike a king,
Be it not King Edward.
For stature he is framed
Like to the picture of stout Hercules,
And for his carriage passeth Robin Hood.
The boldest earl or baron of your land
That offereth scath unto the town of Wakefield,
George will arrest his pledge unto the pound;
And whoso resisteth bears away the blows,   800
For he himself is good enough for three.

    EDWARD. Why, this is wondrous! My Lord of War-
      wick,
Sore do I long to see this George a Greene.
But leaving him, what shall we do, my lord,
For to subdue the rebels in the north?
They are now marching up to Doncaster.

    Enter one with the Earl of Kendal prisoner.

Soft! who have we there?

    CUDDIE.   Here is a traitor, the Earl of Kendal.

    EDWARD.   Aspiring traitor! how darest thou once
Cast thine eyes upon thy sovereign   810
That honored thee with kindness and with favor?
But I will make thee buy this treason dear.

    KEND.   Good my lord—

    EDWARD.   Reply not, traitor.—
Tell me, Cuddie, whose deed of honor
Won the victory against this rebel?

    CUDDIE.   George a Greene, the pinner of Wakefield.

    EDWARD.   George a Greene! Now shall I hear news
Certain what this pinner is.
Discourse it briefly, Cuddie, how it befell.   820

    CUDDIE.   Kendal and Bonfield, with Sir Gilbert Arm-
        strong,
Came to Wakefield town disguised,
And there spoke ill of your grace;
Which George, but hearing, felled them at his feet;
And, had not rescue come into the place,
George had slain them in his close of wheat.

    EDWARD.   But, Cuddie, canst thou not tell
Where I might give and grant some thing
That might please, and highly gratify the pinner's
        thoughts?

    CUDDIE.   This at their parting George did say to
        me: 830
"If the king vouchsafe of this my service,
Then, gentle Cuddie, kneel upon thy knee,
And humbly crave a boon of him for me."

    EDWARD.   Cuddie, what is it?

    CUDDIE.   It is his will your Grace would pardon them,
And let them live, although they have offended.

    EDWARD.   I think the man striveth to be glorious.
Well, George hath craved it, and it shall be granted,

Which none but he in England should have gotten.
Live, Kendal—but as prisoner;   840
So shalt thou end thy days within the tower.

KEND. Gracious is Edward to offending subjects.

K. JAMES. My Lord of Kend, you are welcome to the
court.

EDWARD. Nay, but ill come, as it falls out now;
Ay, ill come, indeed, were it not for George a Greene.
But, gentle king—for so you would aver—
And Edward's betters, I salute you both,

      He mockingly vails bonnet to them.

And here I vow, by good Saint George,
You will gain but little when your sums are counted!
I sore do long to see this George a Greene.   850
And for because I never saw the north,
I will forthwith go see it;
And for that to none I will be known,
We will disguise ourselves and steal down secretly,
Thou and I, King James, Cuddie, and two or three,
And make a merry journey for a month.
Away, then, conduct him to the tower.
Come on, King James, my heart must needs be merry,
If fortune make such havoc of our foes.

      Exeunt omnes.

      Scene 10

      Robin Hood's Forest

*Enter Robin Hood, Maid Marian, Scarlet, and Much,
the Miller's son.*

ROBIN. Why is not lovely Marian blithe of
cheer?   860
What ails my leman, that she 'gins to lour?
Say, good Marian, why art thou so sad?

MARIAN. Nothing, my Robin, grieves me to the heart
But whensoever I do walk abroad
I hear no songs but all of George a Greene;
Bettris, his fair leman, passeth me.
And this, my Robin, galls my very soul.

 ROBIN. Content thee. What recks it us though
    George a Greene be stout,
So long as he doth proffer us no scath?
Envy doth seldom hurt but to itself.   870
And therefore, Marian, smile upon thy Robin.

 MARIAN. Never will Marian smile upon her Robin,
Nor lie with him under the green wood shade,
Till that thou go to Wakefield on a green,
And beat the pinner for the love of me.

 ROBIN. Content thee, Marian; I will ease thy grief;
My merry men and I will thither stray.
And here I vow that, for the love of thee,
I will beat George a Greene, or he shall beat me.

 SCARLET. As I am Scarlet, next to Little John, 880
One of the boldest yeomen of the crew,
So will I wend with Robin all along,
And try this pinner what he dares to do.

 MUCH. As I am Much, the miller's son,
That left my mill to go with thee—
And nill repent that I have done;
This pleasant life contenteth me—
In aught I may, to do thee good,
I'll live and die with Robin Hood.

 MARIAN. And, Robin, Marian she will go with
    thee,   890
To see fair Bettris how bright she is of blee.[1]

 ROBIN. Marian, thou shalt go with thy Robin.

He turns to his followers.

Bend up your bows, and see your strings be tight,

[1] countenance

The arrows keen, and everything be ready;
And each of you a good bat on his neck,
Able to lay a good man on the ground.

SCARLET. I will have Friar Tuck's.

MUCH. I will have Little John's.

ROBIN. I will have one made of an ashen plank,
Able to bear a bout or two.—   900
Then come on, Marian, let us go!
For before the sun doth show the morning day,
I will be at Wakefield to see this pinner, George a
    Greene.

Exeunt omnes.

Scene 11.

The town of Bradford.

*Enter a Shoemaker, sits upon the stage at work. Jenkin
    to him.*

JENKIN. My masters, he that hath neither meat nor
    money,
And hath lost his credit with the alewife,
For anything I know may go supperless to bed.
But, soft! who is here? Here is a shoemaker.
He knows where is the best ale.—
Shoemaker, I pray thee tell me,
Where is the best ale in the town?   910

SHOE. Afore, afore; follow thy nose;
At the sign of the eggshell.

JENKIN. Come, shoemaker, if thou wilt,
And take thy part of a pot.

SHOE. Sirra, down with your staff!
Down with your staff!

JENKIN. Why, how now! is the fellow mad?
I pray thee tell me, why should I hold down my staff?

SHOE. You will down with him, will you not, sir?

JENKIN.   Why, tell me wherefore?   920

SHOE.   My friend, this is the town of merry Bradford,
And here is a custom held
That none shall pass with his staff on his shoulders
But he must have a bout with me;
And so shall you, sir.

JENKIN.   And so will I not, sir!

SHOE.   That will I try.   Barking dogs bite not the
sorest.

JENKIN *aside*.   I would to God I were once well rid
of him.

SHOE.   Now, what! will you down with your staff?

JENKIN.   Why, you are not in earnest, are you?   930

SHOE.   If I am not, take that.

Strikes him with his staff.

JENKIN.   You whoreson cowardly scab,
It is but the part of a clapperdudgeon
To strike a man in the street.
But darest thou walk to the town's end with me?

SHOE.   Ay, that I dare do!   But stay till I lay in my
tools, and I will go with thee to the town's end presently.

JENKIN *aside*.   I would I knew how to be rid of this
fellow.

SHOE.   Come, sir; will you go to the town's end now,
sir?

JENKIN.   Ay, sir; come.   940

They cross over the stage.

Now we are at the town's end.   What say you now?

SHOE.   Marry, come let us even have a bout.

JENKIN.   Ha! stay a little!   Hold thy hands, I pray
thee!

SHOE.   Why what's the matter?

JENKIN.   Faith, I am under-pinner of a town,
And there is an order, which if I do not keep,

I shall be turned out of mine office.

SHOE. What is that, sir?

JENKIN. Whensoever I go to fight with anybody,
I use to flourish my staff thrice about my head   950
Before I strike—and then show no favor.

SHOE. Well, sir, and till then I will not strike thee.

JENKIN. Well, sir, here is once, twice:—here is my
     hand;
I will never do it the third time.

SHOE. Why, then I see we shall not fight.

JENKIN. Faith, no. Come, I will give thee two pots
Of the best ale, and be friends.

SHOE. Faith, I see it is as hard to get water out of a
     flint,
As to get him to have a bout with me;
Therefore I will enter into him for some good
     cheer.—   960
My friend, I see thou art a faint-hearted fellow,
Thou hast no stomach to fight;
Therefore let us go to the alehouse and drink.

JENKIN. Well, content. Go thy ways, and say thy
     prayers
Thou 'scapest my hands today.

Exeunt omnes.

Scene 12.

Near George a Greene's house, Wakefield.

Enter George a Greene and Bettris.

GEORGE. Tell me, sweet love: how, is thy mind con-
     tent?
What, canst thou brook to live with George a Greene?

BETTRIS. Oh, George, how little pleasing are these
     words!

Came I from Bradford for the love of thee
And left my father for so sweet a friend. 970
Here will I live until my life do end.

Enter Robin Hood and Marian, and his train.

GEORGE. Happy am I to have so sweet a love.—
But what are these come tracing here along?
    BETTRIS. Three men come striking through the corn,
        my love.
    GEORGE. Back again, you foolish travelers!
For you are wrong, and may not wend this way.
    ROBIN HOOD. That were great shame!
Now, by my soul, proud sir,
We be three tall yeomen, and thou art but one.—
Come, we will forward in despite of him. 980
    GEORGE. Leap the ditch, or I will make you skip!
What, cannot the highway serve your turn,
But you must make a path over the corn?
    ROBIN. Why, art thou mad? Darest thou encounter
        three?
We are no babes, man; look upon our limbs.
    GEORGE. Sirra, the biggest limbs have not the stoutest
        hearts.
Were ye as good as Robin Hood and his three merry
        men,
I'll drive you back the same way that ye came.
Be ye men, ye scorn to encounter me all at once;
But be ye cowards, set upon me all three, 990
And try the pinner what he dares perform!
    SCARLET. Were thou as high in deeds
As thou art haughty in words,
Thou well mightest be a champion for the king;
But empty vessels have the loudest sounds,
And cowards prattle more than men of worth.

GEORGE. Sirra, darest thou try me?

SCARLET. I, sirra, that I dare.

They fight, and George a Greene beats him.

MUCH. How now! what! art thou down?
Come, sir, I am next.   1000

They fight, and George a Greene beats him.

ROBIN HOOD. Come, sirra, now to me. Spare me not,
For I'll not spare thee!

GEORGE. Make no doubt I will be as liberal to thee.

They fight; Robin Hood stays.

ROBIN HOOD. Stay, George! for here I do protest,
Thou art the stoutest champion that ever I laid
Hands upon.

GEORGE. Soft you, sir! by your leave, you lie;
You never yet laid hands on me.

ROBIN HOOD. George, wilt thou forsake Wakefield,
And go with me?   1010
Two liveries will I give thee every year,
And forty crowns shall be thy fee.

GEORGE. Why, who art thou?

ROBIN HOOD. Why, Robin Hood.
I am come hither with my Marian
And these my yeomen for to visit thee.

GEORGE. Robin Hood! Next to King Edward
Art thou lief to me.
Welcome, sweet Robin! Welcome, maid Marian!
And welcome, you my friends!   1020
Will you to my poor house?
You shall have wafer cakes your fill,
A piece of beef hung up since Martinmas,
Mutton, and veal. If this like you not,
Take that you find, or that you bring, for me.

ROBIN HOOD. God-a-mercies, good George;
I'll be thy guest today.

GEORGE. Robin, therein thou honorest me.
I'll lead the way.

Exeunt omnes.

Scene 13.

At Bradford.

Enter King Edward and King James disguised, with two staves.

EDWARD. Come on, King James. Now we are   1030
    thus disguised,
There is none, I know, will take us to be kings.
I think we are now in Bradford,
Where all the merry shoemakers dwell.

Enter a Shoemaker.

SHOEMAKER. Down with your staves, my friends!
Down with them!

EDWARD. Down with our staves? I pray thee, why
    so?

SHOE. My friend, I see thou art a stranger here,
Else wouldst thou not have questioned of the thing.
This is the town of merry Bradford,   1040
And here hath been a custom, kept of old,
That none may bear his staff upon his neck,
But trail it all along throughout the town,
Unless they mean to have a bout with me.

EDWARD. But hear you, sir, hath the king
Granted you this custom?

SHOE. King or kaiser, none shall pass this way,
Except King Edward;
No, nor the stoutest groom that haunts his court.
Therefore down with your staves!   1050

EDWARD. What were we best to do?

JAMES. Faith, my lord, they are stout fellows;
And because we will see some sport,
We will trail our staves.

EDWARD. Hear'st thou, my friend?
Because we are men of peace, and travellers,
We are content to trail our staves.

SHOE. The way lies before you; go along.

Enter Robin Hood and George a Greene, disguised.

ROBIN HOOD. See, George, two men are passing
Through the town,   1060
Two lusty men, and yet they trail their staves.

GEORGE. Robin, they are some peasants
Tricked in yeoman's weeds.—Hollo, you two travellers!

EDWARD. Call you us, sir?

GEORGE. Ay, you! Are ye not big enough to bear
Your bats upon your necks,
But you must trail them along the streets?

EDWARD. Yes, sir, we are big enough; but here is a
    custom
Kept, that none may pass, his staff upon his neck,
Unless he trail it at the weapon's point.   1070
Sir, we are men of peace, and love to sleep
In our whole skins, and therefore quietness is best.

GEORGE. Base minded peasants, worthless to be men!
What! have you bones and limbs to strike a blow,
And be your hearts so faint you cannot fight?
Wer't not for shame I would shrub your shoulders well,
And teach you manhood against another time.

SHOE. Well preached, sir Jack! Down with your
    staff!

EDWARD. Do you hear, my friends? and you be wise,
Keep down your staves,   1080

For all the town will rise upon you.

GEORGE.   Thou speakest like an honest quiet fellow!
But hear you me: In spite of all the swains
Of Bradford town, bear me your staves upon your
      necks—
Or, to begin withal, I'll baste you both so well,
You were never better basted in your lives.

EDWARD.   We will hold up our staves.

*George a Greene fights with the Shoemakers, and beats
      them all down.*

GEORGE.   What, have you any more?
Call all your town forth, cut and longtail.

The Shoemakers spy George a Greene.

SHOE.   What, George a Greene! is it you?   1090
A plague found [1] you!
I think you longed to swing me well.
Come, George, we will crush a pot before we part.

GEORGE.   A pot, you slave? we will have an hundred!
Here, Will Perkins; take my purse,
Fetch me a stand of ale, and set it in the market-place,
That all may drink that are athirst this day;
For this is for a fee to welcome Robin Hood
To Bradford town.

They bring out the stand of ale, and fall a drinking.

Here, Robin, sit thou here; for thou art the best
      man   1100
At the board this day.
You that are strangers, place your selves where you will.
Robin, here's a carouse to good King Edward's self.

[1] confound

And they that love him not, I would we had
The basting of them a little!

Enter the Earl of Warwick with other noble men, bring-
ing out the King's garments; then George a Greene
and the rest kneel down to the King.

EDWARD.   Come, masters, all fellows!
Nay, Robin, you are the best man at the board to-
    day;
Rise up, George.
  GEORGE.   Nay, good my liege, ill-nurtured we were,
    then.
Though we Yorkshire men be blunt of speech,   1110
And little skilled in court or such quaint fashions,
Yet nature teacheth us duty to our king;
Therefore, I humbly beseech you, pardon George a
    Greene.
  ROBIN.   And, good my lord, a pardon for poor Robin;
And for us all a pardon, good King Edward.
  SHOE.   I pray you, a pardon for the shoemakers.
  EDWARD.   I frankly grant a pardon to you all.
And, George a Greene, give me thy hand!
There is none in England that shall do thee wrong.
Even from my court I came to see thy self;   1120
And now I see that fame speaks nought but truth.
  GEORGE.   I humbly thank your royal Majesty.
That which I did against the Earl of Kendal,
It was but a subject's duty to his sovereign,
And therefore little merits such good words.
  EDWARD.   But ere I go, I'll grace thee with good deeds.
Say what King Edward may perform,
And thou shalt have it, being in England's bounds.
  GEORGE.   I have a lovely leman,
As bright of blee as in the silver moon;   1130
And old Grime, her father, will not let her match

With me, because I am a pinner,
Although I love her, and she me, dearly.

   EDWARD. Where is she?

   GEORGE. At home at my poor house,
And vows never to marry unless her father
Give consent; which is my great grief, my Lord.

   EDWARD. If this be all, I will dispatch it straight;
I'll send for Grime and force him give his grant.
He will not deny King Edward such a suit.   1140

Enter Jenkin, and speaks.

   JENKIN. Ho! who saw a master of mine?
Oh, he is gotten into company—and a body should rake
Hell for company.

   GEORGE. Peace, ye slave! see where King Edward is?

   EDWARD. George, what is he?

   GEORGE. I beseech your Grace pardon him; he is my
     man.

   SHOE. Sirra, the king hath been drinking with us,
And did pledge us too.

   JENKIN. Hath he so? Kneel; I dub you "gentle-
     men."

   SHOE. Beg it of the king, Jenkin.   1150

   JENKIN. I will—I beseech your worship grant me
     one thing.

   EDWARD. What is that?

   JENKIN. Hark in your ear.

He whispers the King in the ear.

   EDWARD. Go your ways, and do it.

   JENKIN. Come! down on your knees! I have got it.

   SHOE. Let us hear what it is first.

   JENKIN. Marry, because you have drunk with the
king, and the king hath so graciously pledged you, you
shall be no more called shoemakers, but you and yours,

to the world's end, shall be called "the trade of [1160
the gentle craft."

SHOE. I beseech your Majesty reform this which
he hath spoken.

JENKIN. I beseech your worship consume this which
he hath spoken.

EDWARD. Confirm it, you would say.—Well, he hath
done it for you; it is sufficient.—Come, George, we will
go to Grime, and have thy love.

JENKIN. I am sure your worship will abide; for
yonder is coming old Musgrove and mad Cuddie [1170
his son.—Master, my fellow Wily comes dressed like a
woman, and master Grime will marry Wily. Here they
come.

*Enter Musgrove and Cuddie, and master Grime, Wily,
Maid Marian, and Bettris.*

EDWARD. Which is thy old father, Cuddie?

CUDDIE. This, if it please your Majesty.

EDWARD. Ah, old Musgrove, rise up!
It fits not such gray hairs to kneel.

MUSGROVE. Long live my sovereign!
Long and happy be his days!
Vouchsafe, my gracious lord, a simple gift   1180
At Billy Musgrove's hand.
King James at Meddellom Castle gave me this;
This won the honor, and this give I thee.

He hands him a sword.

EDWARD. God-a-mercy, Musgrove, for this friendly
   gift.
And, for thou feldst a king with this same weapon,
This blade shall here dub valiant Musgrove knight.

MUSG. Alas, what hath your highness done? I am
   poor.

EDW. To mend thy living take thou Meddellom Castle,

And hold of me. And if thou want living, complain;
Thou shalt have more to maintain thine estate.   1190
George, which is thy love?

GEORGE. This, if please your Majesty.

EDWARD. Art thou her aged father?

GRIME. I am, and it like your Majesty.

EDWARD. And wilt not give thy daughter unto
    George?

GRIME. Yes, my lord, if he will let me marry
With this lovely lass.

EDWARD. What sayest thou, George?

GEORGE. With all my heart, my lord, I give consent.

GRIME. Then do I give my daughter unto
    George.   1200

WILY. Then shall the marriage soon be at an end.

Throws off his disguise.

Witness, my lord, if that I be a woman!
For I am Wily, boy to George a Greene,
Who for my master wrought this subtle shift.

EDWARD. What! is it a boy? What sayest thou to
    this, Grime?

GRIME. Marry, my lord, I think this boy hath
More knavery than all the world besides.
Yet am I content that George shall both have
My daughter and my lands.

EDWARD. Now, George, it rests I gratify thy
    worth.   1210
And therefore here I do bequeath to thee,
In full possession, half that Kendal hath;
And what as Bradford holds of men in chief,
I give it frankly unto thee for ever.
Kneel down, George.

GEORGE. What will your Majesty do?

EDWARD. Dub thee a knight, George.

GEORGE. I beseech your Grace, grant me one thing

EDWARD. What is that?

GEORGE. Then let me live and die a yeoman still. 1220
So was my father, so must live his son.
For 'tis more credit to men of base degree
To do great deeds, than men of dignity.

EDWARD. Well, be it so, George.

JAMES. I beseech your Grace dispatch with me,
And set down my ransom.

EDWARD. George a Greene, set down the King of
            Scots
His ransom.

GEORGE. I beseech your Grace pardon me;
It passeth my skill.   1230

EDWARD. Do it; the honor's thine.

GEORGE. Then let King James make good
Those towns which he hath burnt upon the borders;
Give a small pension to the fatherless,
Whose fathers he caused murdered in those wars;
Put in pledge for these things to your Grace;
And so return.

EDWARD. King James, are you content?

JAMES. I am content, and like your Majesty,
And will leave good castles in security.   1240

EDWARD. I crave no more.—Now, George a Greene,
I'll to thy house. And when I have supped I'll go to
            Aske,
And see if Jane a Barley be so fair
As good King James reports her for to be.
And for the ancient custom of "Vail Staff," keep it still;
Claim privilege from me:
If any ask a reason why, or how,
Say, English Edward vailed his staff to you.

Exeunt omnes.

(written about 1590, printed 1599)

LYRICS

SWEET ARE THE THOUGHTS THAT SAVOR OF CONTENT

(From *The Farewell to Folly*)

SWEET are the thoughts that savor of content;
  The quiet mind is richer than a crown;
Sweet are the nights in careless slumber spent;
  The poor estate scorns fortune's angry frown:
Such sweet content, such minds, such sleep, such bliss,
Beggars enjoy, when princes oft do miss.

The homely house that harbors quiet rest;
  The cottage that affords no pride nor care;
The mean that 'grees with country music best;
  The sweet consort of mirth and music's fare;   1C
Obscurèd life sets down a type of bliss:
A mind content both crown and kingdom is.

(1587)

WEEP NOT, MY WANTON

(From *Menaphon*)

WEEP not, my wanton, smile upon my knee,
When thou art old there's grief enough for thee.
       Mother's wag, pretty boy,
       Father's sorrow, father's joy;
       When thy father first did see
       Such a boy by him and me,
       He was glad, I was woe,
       Fortune changèd made him so,

When he left his pretty boy
Last his sorrow, first his joy.   **10**

Weep not, my wanton, smile upon my knee,
When thou art old there's grief enough for thee.
      Streaming tears that never stint,
      Like pearl-drops from a flint,
      Fell by course from his eyes,
      That one another's place supplies;
      Thus he grieved in every part,
      Tears of blood fell from his heart,
      When he left his pretty boy,
      Father's sorrow, father's joy.   **20**

Weep not, my wanton, smile upon my knee,
When thou art old there's grief enough for thee.
      The wanton smiled, father wept,
      Mother cried, baby leapt;
      More he crowed, more we cried,
      Nature could not sorrow hide:
      He must go, he must kiss
      Child and mother, baby bless,
      For he left his pretty boy,
      Father's sorrow, father's joy.   **30**

Weep not, my wanton, smile upon my knee,
When thou art old there's grief enough for thee.
                    (1589)

THE SHEPHERD'S WIFE'S SONG

(From *The Mourning Garment*)

Ah, what is love? It is a pretty thing,
As sweet unto a shepherd as a king;
      And sweeter too:

For kings have cares that wait upon a crown,
And cares can make the sweetest love to frown.
  Ah then, ah then,
If country loves such sweet desires do gain,
What lady would not love a shepherd swain?

His flocks are folded, he comes home at night,
As merry as a king in his delight;   10
  And merrier too:
For kings bethink them what the state require,
Where shepherds careless carol by the fire.
  Ah then, ah then,
If country loves such sweet desires do gain,
What lady would not love a shepherd swain?

He kisseth first, then sits as blithe to eat
His cream and curds as doth the king his meat;
  And blither too:
For kings have often fears when they do sup, 20
Where shepherds dread no poison in their cup.
  Ah then, ah then,
If country loves such sweet desires do gain,
What lady would not love a shepherd swain?

To bed he goes, as wanton then, I ween,
As is a king in dalliance with a queen;
  More wanton too:
For kings have many griefs affects to move,
Where shepherds have no greater grief than love.
  Ah then, ah then,   30
If country loves such sweet desires do gain,
What lady would not love a shepherd swain?

Upon his couch of straw he sleeps as sound,
As doth the king upon his bed of down;
    More sounder too:
For cares cause kings full oft their sleep to spill,
Where weary shepherds lie and snort their fill.
    Ah then, ah then,
If country loves such sweet desires do gain,
What lady would not love a shepherd swain?   40

Thus with his wife he spends the year, as blithe
As doth the king at every tide or sithe;
    And blither too:
For kings have wars and broils to take in hand
When shepherds laugh and love upon the land.
    Ah then, ah then,
If country loves such sweet desires do gain,
What lady would not love a shepherd swain?

                         (1590)

FIE, FIE ON BLIND FANCY!

(From *Groatsworth of Wit*)

    Fie, fie on blind fancy!
    It hinders youth's joy:
    Fair virgins, learn by me
    To count Love a toy.

When Love learned first the A B C of delight,
And knew no figures nor conceited phrase,
He simply gave to due desert her right,
He led not lovers in dark winding ways:
He plainly willed to love, or flatly answered no.
But now who lists to prove, shall find it nothing so.   10

> *Fie, fie, then, on fancy!*
> *It hinders youth's joy:*
> *Fair virgins, learn by me*
> *To count Love a toy.*

For since he learned to use the poet's pen,
He learned likewise with smoothing words to feign,
Witching chaste ears with trothless tongues of men,
And wronged faith with falsehood and disdain.
He gives a promise now, anon he sweareth no:
Who listeth for to prove, shall find his changings so.

> *Fie, fie, then, on fancy!*
> *It hinders youth's joy:*
> *Fair virgins, learn by me*
> *To count Love a toy.*

(1592)

THOMAS NASHE (1567-1601)

THE UNFORTUNATE TRAVELLER, OR THE LIFE OF JACK WILTON

ABOUT that time that the terror of the world, and fever quartan of the French, Henry the eighth (the only true subject of chronicles), advanced his standard against the two hundred and fifty towers of Turney and Turwin, and had the Emperor and all the nobility of Flanders, Holland, and Brabant as mercenary attendants on his full-sailed fortune, I, Jack Wilton (a gentleman at least) was a certain kind of an appendix or page, belonging or appertaining in or unto the confines of the English court, where what my credit was, a number of my creditors that I cosened can testify, *Caelum petimus stultitia*, which of us all is not a sinner.

Be it known to as many as will pay money enough to peruse my story, that I followed the court or the camp, or the camp and the court, when Turwin lost her maidenhead, and opened her gates to more than Jane Trosse did. There did I, (soft let me drink before I go any further) reign sole king of the cans and black-jacks, prince of the pigmies, county palatine of clean straw and provant, and, to conclude, lord high regent of rashers of the coals and redherring cobs. *Paulo maiora canamus.* Well, to the purpose. What strata-gemical acts and monuments do you think an ingenious infant of my years might enact? you will say it were suf-ficient if he slur a die, pawn his master to the utmost penny, and minister the oath of the pantofle artificially. These are signs of good education I must confess, and arguments of In grace and virtue to proceed. Oh but *Aliquid latet quod non patet,* there's a further path I must trace; examples confirm, list lordings to my pro-ceedings. Whosoever is acquainted with the state of a camp, understands that in it be many quarters, and yet not so many as on London Bridge. In those quar-ters are many companies: much company, much knavery, as true as that old adage, much courtesy, much subtility. Those companies, like a great deal of corn, do yield some chaff, the corn are cormorants, the chaff are good fellows, which are quickly blown to nothing, with bear-ing a light heart in a light purse. Amongst this chaff was I winnowing my wits to live merrily, and by my troth so I did: the prince could but command men spend their blood in his service, I could make them spend all the money they had for my pleasure. But poverty in the end parts friends, though I was prince of their purses, and exacted of my unthrifty subjects as much liquid allegiance as any kaiser in the world could do, yet where it is not to be had the king must lose his right, want cannot be withstood, men can do no more than they can do, what remained then, but the foxes case must help, when the lion's skin is out at the elbows.

There was a lord in the camp, let him be a lord of misrule if you will, for he kept a plain alehouse without welt or gard of any ivybush, and sold cider and cheese by pint and by pound to all that came (at the very name of cider I can but sigh, there is so much of it in Rhenish wine now-a-days.) Well, *Tendit ad sydera virtus,* there's great virtue belongs (I can tell you) to a cup of cider, and very good men have sold it, and at sea it is *Aqua cœlestis,* but that's neither here nor there, if it had no other patron but this peer of quart pots to authorize it, it were sufficient. This great lord, this worthy lord, this noble lord, thought no scorn (Lord have mercy upon us) to have his great velvet breeches larded with the droppings of this dainty liquor, and yet he was an old servitor, a cavalier of an ancient house, as might appear by the arms of his ancestors, drawn very amiably in chalk on the inside of his tent door.

He and no other was the man I chose out to damn with a lewd moneyless device, for coming to him on a day as he was counting his barrels and setting the price in chalk on the head of them, I did my duty very devoutly, and told his ale-y honor I had matters of some secrecy to impart unto him, if it pleased him to grant me private audience. With me young Wilton, quoth he, marry and shalt: bring us a pint of cider of a fresh tap into the three cups here, wash the pot, so into a back room he led me, where after he had spit on his finger, and picked off two or three moats of his old moth-eaten velvet cap, and sponged and wrung all the rheumatic drivel from his ill-favored goat's beard, he bade me declare my mind, and thereupon he drank to me on the same. I up with a long circumstance, alias, a cunning shift of the seventeens, discoursed unto him what entire affection I had borne him time out of mind, partly for the high descent and lineage from whence he sprung, and partly for the tender care and provident respect he had of poor soldiers, that whereas the vastity of that place, (which afforded them no indifferent supply of drink or of victuals) might humble them to some extremity, and so weaken their hands, he vouchsafed in his own person to be a victualler to the camp (a rare example of magnificence and honorable courtesy) and diligently provided that without far travel, every man might for his money have cider and cheese his belly full, nor did he sell his cheese by the way only, or his cider by the great, but abast himself with his own hands to take a shoemaker's knife, (a homely instrument for such a high personage to touch) and cut it out equally like a true justiciary, in little pennyworths, that it would do a man good for to look upon. So likewise of his cider, the poorman might have his moderate draught of it, (as there is a moderation in all things) as well for his doit or his dandiprat, as the rich man for his half-sous or his denier. Not so much quoth I, but this tapster's linen apron which you wear to protect your apparel from the imperfections of the spigot, most amply bewrays your lowly mind, I speak it with tears, too few such noble men have we that will draw drink in linen aprons. Why you are every child's fellow, any man that comes under the name of soldier and a good fellow, you will sit and bear company to the last pot, yea, and you take in as good part the homely phrase of "mine host, here's to you," as if one saluted you by all the titles of your barony. These considerations I say, which the world suffers to slip by in the channel of forgetfulness, have moved me in ardent zeal of your welfare, to forewarn you of some dangers that have beset you and your barrels. At the name of dangers he start up and bounced with his fist on the board so hard, that his tapster over-hearing him, cried, "anon, anon sir, by and by," and came and made a low leg [1] and asked him what he lacked. He was ready to have stricken his tapster, for interrupting him in attention of this his so much desired relation, but for fear of displeasing me he moderated his fury, and only sending for the other fresh pint, willed him look to the bar, and come when he is called, with a devil's name. Well, at his earnest importunity, after I had moistened my lips, to make my lie run glib to his journey's end, forward I went as followeth. It chanced me the other night, amongst other pages, to attend where the King with his lords and many chief leaders sat in counsel, there amongst sundry serious matters that were debated, and intelligences from the enemy given up, it was privily informed (no villains to these privy informers) that you, even you that I now speak to, had (O would I had no tongue to tell the rest; by this drink it grieves me so I am not able to repeat it). Now was my drunken lord ready to hang himself for the end of the full point, and over my neck he throws himself very lubberly, and entreated me as I was a proper young gentleman, and ever looked for pleasure at his hands, soon to rid him out of this hell of suspense, and resolve him of the rest, then fell he on his knees, wrung his hands, and I think, on my conscience, wept out all the cider that he had drunk in a week before, to move me to have pity on him, he rose and put his rusty ring on my finger, gave me his greasy purse with that single money that was in it, promised to make me his heir, and a thousand more favors, if I would expire the misery of his unspeakable

[1] deep bow

tormenting uncertainty. I being by nature inclined to mercy (for indeed I knew two or three good wenches of that name), bade him harden his ears, and not make his eyes abortive before their time, and he should have the inside of my breast turned outward, hear such a tale as would tempt the utmost strength of life to attend it, and not die in the midst of it. Why (quoth I) myself that am but a poor childish well-willer of yours, with the very thought, that a man of your desert and state, by a number of peasants and varlets should be so injuriously abused in hugger mugger,[1] have wept all my urine upward. The wheel under our city bridge, carries not so much water over the city, as my brain hath welled forth gushing streams of sorrow, I have wept so immoderately and lavishly, that I thought verily my palate had been turned to [a] conduit in London. My eyes have been drunk, outrageously drunk, with giving but ordinary intercourse through their sea-circled islands to my distilling dreariment. What shall I say? that which malice hath said is the mere overthrow and murder of these days. Change not your color, none can slander a clear conscience to itself, receive all your fraught of misfortune in at once.

It is buzzed in the King's head that you are a secret friend to the enemy, and under pretense of getting a license to furnish the camp with cider and such like provant, you have furnished the enemy, and in empty barrels sent letters of discovery, and corn innumerable.

I might well have left here, for by this time his white liver had mixed itself with the white of his eye, and both were turned upwards, as if they had offered themselves a fair white for death to shoot at. The truth was, I was very loth mine host and I should part with dry lips: wherefore the best means that I could imagine

[1] secret

to wake him out of his trance, was to cry loud in his ear, "Ho host, what's to pay? will no man look to the reckoning here?" And in plain verity it took expected effect, for with the noise he started and bustled, like a man that had been scared with fire out of his sleep, and ran hastily to his tapster, and all to belabored him about the ears, for letting gentlemen call so long, and not look in to them. Presently he remembered himself, and had like to fall into his memento again, but that I met him half ways, and asked his lordship what he meant, to slip his neck out of the collar so suddenly, and being revived strike his tapster so hastily?

Oh (quoth he) I am bought and sold for doing my country such good service as I have done. They are afraid of me, because my good deeds have brought me into such estimation with the commonalty. I see, I see, it is not for the lamb to live with the wolf.

The world is well amended (thought I) with your cidership; such another forty years' nap together as Epimenides had, would make you a perfect wise man. Answer me (quoth he) my wise young Wilton, is it true that I am thus underhand dead and buried by these bad tongues?

Nay (quoth I) you shall pardon me, for I have spoken too much already, no definitive sentence of death shall march out of my well meaning lips: they have but lately sucked milk, and shall they so suddenly change their food and seek after blood?

Oh, but (quoth he) a man's friend is his friend, fill the other pint, tapster: what said the King, did he believe it when he heard it? I pray thee say, I swear by my nobility; none in the world shall ever be made privy, that I received any light of this matter by thee.

That firm affiance (quoth I) had I in you before, or else I would never have gone so far over the shoes, to pluck you out of the mire. Not to make many words (since you will needs know) the King says flatly; you are a miser and a snudge,[1] and he never hoped better of you. Nay, then (quoth he) questionless some planet that loves not cider hath conspired against me. Moreover, which is worse, the King hath vowed to give Turwin one hot breakfast, only with the bungs that he will pluck out of your barrels. I cannot stay at this time to report each circumstance that passed, but the only counsel that my long cherished kind inclination can possibly contrive, is now in your old days to be liberal, such victuals or provision as you have, presently distribute it frankly amongst poor soldiers, I would let them burst their bellies with cider, and bathe in it, before I would run into my prince's ill opinion for a whole sea of it. The hunter pursuing the beaver for his stones, he bites them off, and leaves them behind for him to gather up, whereby he lives quiet. If greedy hunters and hungry tale-tellers pursue you, it is for a little pelf that you have, cast it behind you, neglect it, let them have it, lest it breed a farther inconvenience. Credit my advice, you shall find it prophetical: and thus have I discharged the part of a poor friend. With some few like phrases of ceremony, your honor's poor suppliant, and so forth, and farewell my good youth, I thank thee, and will remember thee, we parted. But the next day I think we had a dole of cider, cider in bowls, in scuppets, in helmets: and to conclude, if a man would have filled his boots full, there he might have it: provant thrust itself into poor soldiers' pockets whether they would or no. We made five peals of shot into the town together, of nothing but spigots and faucets of discarded empty barrels: every under-foot soldier had a distenanted tun, as Diogenes had his tub to sleep in. I myself got as many

[1] stingy fellow

confiscated tapsters' aprons as made me a tent, as big as any ordinary commander's in the field. But in conclusion my well-beloved baron of double beer got him humbly on his mary-bones to the King, and complained he was old and stricken in years, and had never an heir to cast at a dog, wherefore if it might please his Majesty to take his lands into his hands, and allow him some reasonable pension to live, he should be marvelously well pleased: as for wars he was weary of them, yet as long as his highness ventured his own person, he would not flinch a foot, but make his withered body a buckler to bear off any blow advanced against him.

The King, marveling at this alteration of his cider-merchant (for so he often pleasantly termed him), with a little farther talk bolted out the whole complotment. Then was I pitifully whipt for my holiday lie, though they made themselves merry with it many a winter's evening after. For all this, his good ass-headed-honor, mine host, persevered in his former request to the King to accept his lands, and allow him a beadsmanry or out-brothership of brachet: which through his vehement in-stancy took effect, and the King jestingly said, since he would needs have it so, he would distrain one part of his land for impost of cider, which he was behind with.

This was one of my famous achievements, insomuch as I never light upon the like famous fool; but I have done a thousand better jests, if they had been booked in order as they were begotten. It is pity posterity should be deprived of such precious records: and yet there is no remedy, and yet there is too, for when all fails, welfare a good memory. Gentle readers (look you be gentle now, since I have called you so), as freely as my knavery was mine own, it shall be yours to use in the way of honesty.

Even in this expedition of Turwin (for the King

stood not long a thrumming of buttons there) it happened me [to] fall in (I would it had fallen out otherwise for his sake) with an ugly mechanical [1] captain. You must think in an army, where truncheons are in their state-house, it is a flat stab once to name a captain without cap in hand. Well, suppose he was a captain, and had never a good cap of his own, but I was fain to lend him one of my lord's cast [-off] velvet caps, and a weather-beaten feather, wherewith he threatened his soldiers afar off, as Jupiter said, with the shaking of his hair to make heaven and earth to quake. Suppose out of the parings of a pair of false dice, I apparelled both him and myself many a time and oft: and surely, not to slander the devil, if any man ever deserved the golden dice the King of the Parthians sent to Demetrius it was I. I had the right vein of sucking up a die twixt the dints of my fingers, not a crevice in my hand but could swallow a quarter trey for a need: in the line of life many a dead lift did there lurk, but it was nothing towards the maintenance of a family. This Monsieur Capitano ate up the cream of my earnings, and *Crede mihi, res est ingeniosa dare,* any man is a fine fellow as long as he hath any money in his purse. That money is like the marigold, which opens and shuts with the sun: if fortune smileth or one be in favor, it floweth; if the evening of age comes on, or he falls into disgrace, it fadeth and is not to be found. I was my craftsmaster though I were but young, and could as soon decline *Nominativo hic Asinus,* as a greater clerk, wherefore I thought it not convenient my soldado should have my purse any longer for his drum to play upon, but I would give him Jacke Drum's entertainment,[2] and send him packing.

This was my plot: I knew a piece of service of intelli-

[1] common, vulgar   [2] a beating

gence, which was presently to be done, that required a man with all his five senses to effect it, and would overthrow any fool that should undertake it: to this service did I animate and egg my foresaid costs and charges, alias, Senior Velvet-cap, whose head was not encumbered with too much forecast; and coming to him in his cabin about dinner time, where I found him very devoutly paring of his nails for want of other repast, I entertained him with this solemn oration.

Captain, you perceive how near both of us are driven, the dice of late are grown as melancholy as a dog, high men and low men both prosper alike, langrets,[1] fullams,[1] and all the whole fellowship of them, will not afford a man his dinner, some other means must be invented to prevent imminent extremity. My state, you are not ignorant, depends on trencher service, your advancement must be derived from the valor of your arm. In the delays of siege, desert hardly gets a day of hearing: 'tis gowns must direct and guns enact all the wars that is to be made against walls. Resteth no way for you to climb suddenly, but by doing some rare stratagem, the like not before heard of: and fitly at this time occasion is offered.

There is a feat the King is desirous to have wrought on some great man of the enemy's side: marry it requireth not so much resolution as discretion to bring it to pass; and yet resolution enough should be shown in it too, being so full of hazardous jeopardy as it is, hark in your ear, thus it is: without more drumbling or pausing, if you will undertake it, and work it through stitch (as you may, ere the King hath determined which way to go about it) I warrant you are made while you live, you need not care which way your staff falls, if it prove not so, then cut off my head.

[1] false dice

Oh my auditors, had you seen him how he stretched out his limbs, scratched his scabbed elbows at this speech, how he set his cap over his eyebrows like a politician, and then folded his arms one in another, and nodded with the head, as who would say, let the French beware for they shall find me a devil: if (I say) you had seen but half the action that he used, of shrucking up his shoulders, smiling scornfully, playing with his fingers on his buttons, and biting the lip; you would have laughed your face and your knees together. The iron being hot, I thought to lay on load, for in any case I would not have his humor cool. As before I laid open unto him the brief sum of the service, so now I began to urge the honorableness of it, and what a rare thing it was to be a right politician, how much esteemed of kings and princes, and how diverse of mean parentage have come to be monarchs by it. Then I discoursed of the qualities and properties of him in every respect, how like the wolf he must draw the breath from a man long before he be seen, how like a hare he must sleep with his eyes open, how as the eagle in his flying casts dust in the eyes of crows and other fowls, for to blind them, so he must cast dust in the eyes of his enemies, delude their sight by one means or other that they dive not into his subtleties: how he must be familiar with all and trust none, drink, carouse, and lecher with him out of whom he hopes to wring any matter, swear and forswear, rather than be suspected, and in a word, have the art of dissembling at his fingers ends as perfect as any courtier.

Perhaps (quoth I) you may have some few greasy cavaliers that will seek to dissuade you from it, and they will not stick to stand on their three half-penny honor, swearing and staring that a man were better to be a hangman than an intelligencer,[1] and call him a sneaking eavesdropper, a scraping hedgecreeper, and a piperly pickthank, but you must not be discouraged by their talk, for the most part of these beggarly contemners of wit, are huge burly-bond butchers like Ajax, good for nothing but to strike right down blows on a wedge with a cleaving beetle, or stand hammering all day upon bars of iron.   The whelps of a bear never grow but sleeping, and these bear-wards having big limbs shall be preferred though they do nothing.   You have read stories (I'll be sworn he never looked in book in his life), how many of the Roman worthies were there that have gone as spialls into their enemy's camp? Ulysses, Nestor, Diomed, went as spies together in the night into the tents of Rhæsus, and intercepted Dolon the spy of the Trojans: never discredited the trade of intelligencers but Judas, and he hanged himself. Danger will put wit into any man.   Architas made a wooden dove to fly; by which proportion I see no reason that the veriest block in the world should despair of anything.   Though nature be contrary inclined, it may be altered, yet usually those whom she denies her ordinary gifts in one thing, she doubles them in another.   That which the ass wants in wit, he hath in honesty, who ever saw him kick or winch, or use any jade's tricks? though he live an hundred years you shall never hear that he breaks pasture.   Amongst men, he that hath not good wit, lightly hath a good iron memory, and he that hath neither of both, hath some bones to carry burthens. Blind men have better noses than other men: the bull's horns serve him as well as hands to fight withall, the lion's paws are as good to him as a pole-axe to knock down any that resist him, the boar's tusks serve him in better stead than a sword and buckler: what need the

[1] spy

snail care for eyes, when he feels the way with his two horns, as well as if he were as quick sighted as a decipherer. There is a fish, that having no wings supports herself in the air with her fins. Admit that you had neither wit nor capacity, as sure in my judgment there is none equal unto you in idiotism, yet if you have simplicity and secrecy, serpents themselves will think you a serpent, for what serpent is there but hides his sting: and yet whatsoever be wanting, a good plausible tongue in such a man of employment, can hardly be spared, which as the fore-named serpent, with his winding tail fetcheth in those that come near him, so with a ravishing tale it gathers all men's hearts unto him: which if he have not let him never look to engender by the mouth as ravens and doves do; that is, mount or be great by undermining. Sir, I am ascertained that all these imperfections I speak of in you have their natural residence. I see in your face, that you were born with the swallow to feed flying, to get much treasure and honor by travel. None so fit as you for so important an enterprise: our vulgar politicians are but flies swimming on the stream of subtilty superficially in comparison of your singularity, their blind narrow eyes cannot pierce into the profundity of hypocrisy, you alone with Palamed, can pry into Ulysses' mad counterfeiting, you can discern Achilles from a chamber maid, though he be decked with spindle and distaff: as Jove dining with Licaon could not be beguiled with human flesh dressed like meat, so no human brain may go beyond you, none beguile you, you gull all, all fear you, love you, stoop to you. Therefore good sir be ruled by me, stoop your fortune so low, as to bequeath yourself wholly to this business.

This silver-sounding tale made such sugared harmony in his ears, that with the sweet meditation, what a more than miraculous politician he should be, and what kingly promotion should come tumbling on him thereby, he could have found in his heart to have packed up his pipes, and to have gone to heaven without a bait: yea, he was more inflamed and ravished with it, than a young man called Taurimontanus was with the Phrygian melody, who was so incensed and fired therewith, that he would needs run presently upon it, and set a courtesan's house on fire that had angered him.

No remedy there was, but I must help to furnish him with money. I did so, as who will not make his enemy a bridge of gold to fly by. Very earnestly he conjured me to make no man living privy to his departure, in regard of his place and charge, and on his honor assured me, his return should be very short and successful. Ay, Ay, shorter by the neck (thought I) in the mean time let this be thy posy, *I live in hope to scape the rope.*

Gone he is, God send him good shipping to Wapping, and by this time if you will, let him be a pitiful poor fellow, and undone forever, for mine own part, if he had been mine own brother, I could have done no more for him than I did, for straight after his back was turned I went in all love and kindness to the marshal-general of the field, and certified him that such a man was lately fled to the enemy, and got his place begged for another immediately: what became of him after you shall hear. To the enemy he went and offered his service, railing egregiously against the King of England, he swore, as he was a gentleman and a soldier, he would be revenged on him: and let but the King of France follow his counsel, he would drive him from Turwin walls yet ere three days to an end. All these were good humors, but the tragedy followeth. The French King hearing of such a prating fellow that was come, desired to see him, but yet he feared treason, willing one of his minions to take upon him his person, and he would stand by as a private person while he was examined. Why should I use any delays? In was Captain Gog's-wounds brought, after he was thoroughly searched, not a louse in his doublet was let pass, but was asked *Quevela,* and charged to stand in the King's name, the molds of his buttons they turned out, to see if they were not bullets covered over with thread, the cod-piece in his devil's breeches (for they were then in fashion) they said plainly was a case for a pisol: if he had had ever a hob-nail in his shoes it had hanged him, and he should never have known who had harmed him, but as luck was, he had no mite of any metal about him, he took part with none of the four ages, neither the golden age, the silver age, the brazen, nor the iron age, only his purse was aged in emptiness, and I think verily a Puritan, for it kept itself from any pollution of crosses. Standing before the supposed King, he was asked what he was, and wherefore he came? To which, in a glorious bragging humor he answered, that he was a gentleman, a captain commander, a chief leader, that came from the King of England upon discontentment. Questioned of the particular cause, he had not a word to bless himself with, yet fain he would have patched out a polt-foot [1] tale, but (God knows) it had not one true leg to stand on.

Then began he to smell of the villain so rammishly, that none there but was ready to rend him in pieces, yet the minion King kept in his choler, and propounded unto him further, what of the King of England's secrets (so advantageable) he was privy to, as might remove him from the siege of Turwin in three days. He said divers, divers matters, which asked longer conference, but in good honesty they were lies, which he had not yet

[1] club-foot, lame

stamped. Hereat the true King stepped forth, and commanded to lay hand on the losel, and that he should be tortured to confess the truth, for he was a spy and nothing else.

He no sooner saw the wheel and the torments set before him, but he cried out like a rascal, and said he was a poor captain in the English camp, suborned by one Jack Wilton (a nobleman's page) and no other, to come and kill the French King in a bravery and return, and that he had no other intention in the world.

This confession could not choose but move them all to laughter, in that he made it as light a matter to kill their King and come back, as to go to Islington and eat a mess of cream, and come home again, nay, and besides he protested that he had no other intention, as if that were not enough to hang him.

Adam never fell till God made fools, all this could not keep his joints from ransacking on the wheel, for they vowed either to make him a confessor or a martyr with a trice: when still he sung all one song, they told the King he was a fool, and that some shrewd head had knavishly wrought on him, wherefore it should stand with his honor to whip him out of the camp and send him home. That persuasion took place, and soundly was he lashed out of their liberties, and sent home by a herald with this message, that so the King his master hoped to whip home all the English fools very shortly: answer was returned, that that shortly, was a long-lie, and they were shrewd fools that should drive the Frenchman out of his kingdom, and make him glad with Corinthian Dionisius to play the schoolmaster.

The herald being dismissed, our afflicted intelligencer was called *coram nobis,* how he sped judge you, but something he was adjudged, too. The sparrow for his

lechery liveth but a year, he for his treachery was
turned on the toe, *Plura dolor prohibet.*

Here let me triumph a while, and ruminate a line or
two on the excellence of my wit, but I will not breathe
neither till I have disfraughted all my knavery.

(1594)

* * *

THOMAS DEKKER (1570?-1641)

THE GULL'S HORN-BOOK.

Chapter 6.

HOW A GALLANT SHOULD BEHAVE HIMSELF IN A PLAY-HOUSE

The theater is your poets' royal exchange, upon which
their muses (that are now turned to merchants) meeting, barter away that light commodity of words for a
lighter ware than words, *Plaudites,* and the breath of
the great beast; which (like the threatenings of two
cowards) vanish all into air. Players and their factors,
who put away the stuff, and make the best of it they
possibly can (as indeed 'tis their parts so to do), your
gallant, your courtier, and your captain, had wont to be
the soundest paymasters; and I think are still the surest
chapmen; and these, by means that their heads are well
stocked, deal upon this comical freight by the gross:
when your groundling and gallery-commoner buys his
sport by the penny, and, like a haggler, is glad to utter
it again by retailing.

Since then the place is so free in entertainment, allowing a stool as well to the farmer's son as to your templer: that your stinkard has the selfsame liberty to be

there in his tobacco fumes, which your sweet courtier hath: and that your carman and tinker claim as strong a voice in their suffrage, and sit to give judgment on the play's life and death, as well as the proudest Momus among the tribes of critic: it is fit that he, whom the most tailors' bills do make room for, when he comes, should not be basely (like a viol) cased up in a corner.

Whether therefore the gatherers [1] of the public or private playhouse stand to receive the afternoon's rent, let our gallant (having paid it) presently advance himself up to the throne of the stage. I mean not into the lord's room (which is now but the stage's suburbs): no, those boxes, by the iniquity of custom, conspiracy of waiting women and gentlemen ushers, that there sweat together, and the covetousness of sharers, are contemptibly thrust into the rear, and much new satin is there damned, by being smothered to death in darkness. But on the very rushes where the comedy is to dance, yea, and under the state of Cambises himself must our feathered estridge,[2] like a piece of ordnance, be planted, valiantly (because impudently) beating down the mewes and hisses of the opposed rascality.

For do but cast up a reckoning, what large comings-in are pursed up by sitting on the stage. First, a conspicuous eminence is gotten; by which means, the best and most essential parts of a gallant (good clothes, a proportionable leg, white hand, the Persian lock, and a tolerable beard) are perfectly revealed.

By sitting on the stage, you have a signed patent to engross the whole commodity of censure; may lawfully presume to be a girder,[3] and stand at the helm to steer the passage of scenes; yet no man shall once offer to hinder you from obtaining the title of an insolent, overweening coxcomb.

[1] door-keepers   [2] ostrich   [3] mocker

By sitting on the stage, you may (without travelling for it) at the very next door ask whose play it is: and, by that 'quest of inquiry,' the law warrants you to avoid much mistaking: if you know not the author, you may rail against him: and peradventure so behave yourself, that you may enforce the author to know you.

By sitting on the stage, if you be a knight, you may happily get you a mistress; if a mere Fleet street gentleman, a wife: but assure yourself, by continual residence, you are the first and principal man in election to begin the number of 'we three.'

By spreading your body on the stage and by being a justice in examining of plays, you shall put yourself into such true scenical authority, that some poet shall not dare to present his muse rudely upon your eyes without having first unmasked her, rifled her, and discovered all her bare and most mystical parts before you at a tavern; when you most knightly shall, for his pains, pay for both their suppers.

By sitting on the stage, you may (with small cost) purchase the dear acquaintance of the boys, have a good stool for sixpence, at any time know what particular part any of the infants present, get your match lighted, examine the playsuits' lace, and perhaps win wagers upon laying 'tis copper, etc. And to conclude, whether you be a fool or a justice of peace, a cuckold or a captain, a Lord Mayor's son or a dawcock, a knave or an under-sheriff, of what stamp soever you be, current or counterfeit, the stage, like time, will bring you to most perfect light and lay you open. Neither are you to be hunted from thence though the scarecrows in the yard hoot at you, hiss at you, spit at you, yea, throw dirt even in your teeth; 'tis most gentlemanlike patience to endure all this and to laugh at the silly animals. But if the rabble, with a full throat, cry 'Away with the fool!' you were worse than a madman to tarry by it, for the gentleman and the fool should never sit on the stage together.

Marry, let this observation go hand in hand with the rest, or rather, like a country serving-man, some five yards before them. Present not yourself on the stage (especially at a new play) until the quaking Prologue hath (by rubbing) got color into his cheeks and is ready to give the trumpets their cue that he's upon point to enter; for then it is time, as though you were one of the properties, or that you dropped out of the hangings, to creep from behind the arras, with your tripos or three-footed stool in one hand and a teston[1] mounted between a forefinger and a thumb in the other; for, if you should bestow your person upon the vulgar when the belly of the house is but half full, your apparel is quite eaten up, the fashion lost, and the proportion of your body in more danger to be devoured than if it were served up in the Counter amongst the poultry: avoid that as you would the bastome.[2] It shall crown you with rich commendation to laugh aloud in the midst of the most serious and saddest scene of the terriblest tragedy, and to let that clapper (your tongue) be tossed so high that all the house may ring of it: your lords use it; your knights are apes to the lords, and do so too; your inn-o'-court man is zany[3] to the knights, and (marry, very scurvily) comes likewise limping after it. Be thou a beagle to them all and never lin[4] snuffing till you have scented them; for by talking and laughing (like a ploughman in a morris) you heap Pelion upon Ossa, glory upon glory: as first, all the eyes in the galleries will leave walking after the players and only follow you, the simplest dolt in the house snatches up your name, and, when he meets you in the streets, or

[1] shilling [2] cudgel [3] mimicking fool [4] cease

that you fall into his hands in the middle of a watch, his word shall be taken for you; he'll cry, 'He's such a gallant,' and you pass.   Secondly, you publish your temperance to the world, in that you seem not to resort thither to taste vain pleasures with a hungry appetite, but only as a gentleman to spend a foolish hour or two because you can do nothing else.   Thirdly, you mightily disrelish the audience, and disgrace the author; marry, you take up (though it be at the worst hand) a strong opinion of your own judgment and enforce the poet to take pity of your weakness, and, by some dedicated sonnet, to bring you into a better paradise, only to stop your mouth.

If you can (either for love or money) provide yourself a lodging by the waterside, for, above the convenience it brings to shun shoulder-clapping and to ship away your cockatrice betimes in the morning, it adds a kind of state unto you to be carried from thence to the stairs of your playhouse.   Hate a sculler—remember that— worse than to be acquainted with one o' th' scullery. No, your oars are your only sea-crabs.   Board them, and take heed you never go twice together with one pair; often shifting is a great credit to gentlemen, and that dividing of your fare will make the poor water-snakes be ready to pull you in pieces to enjoy your custom. No matter whether, upon landing, you have money or no; you may swim in twenty of their boats over the river upon ticket.[1]   Marry, when silver comes in, re- member to pay treble their fare, and it will make your flounder-catchers to send more thanks after you when you do not draw than when you do, for they know it will be their own another day.

Before the play begins, fall to cards.   You may win or lose (as fencers do in a prize) and beat one another

[1] credit

by confederacy, yet share the money when you meet at
supper. Notwithstanding, to gull the ragamuffins that
stand aloof gaping at you, throw the cards (having first
torn four or five of them) round about the stage, just,
upon the third sound, as though you had lost. It skills
not if the four knaves lie on their backs and outface
the audience; there's none such fools as dare take exceptions at them, because, ere the play go off, better knaves
than they will fall into the company.

Now, sir, if the writer be a fellow that hath either
epigrammed you, or hath had a flirt at your mistress, or
hath brought either your feather or your red beard, or
your little legs, etc. on the stage, you shall disgrace him
worse than by tossing him in a blanket or giving him
the bastinado in a tavern if, in the middle of his play
(be it pastoral or comedy, moral or tragedy) you rise
with a screwed and discontented face from your stool
to be gone. No matter whether the scenes be good or
no; the better they are, the worse do you distaste them.
And, being on your feet, sneak not away like a coward,
but salute all your gentle acquaintance that are spread
either on the rushes or on stools about you; and draw
what troop you can from the stage after you. The
mimics are beholden to you for allowing them elbow-
room; their poet cries, perhaps, 'A pox go with you,'
but care not you for that,—there's no music without
frets.

Marry, if either the company or indisposition of the
weather bind you to sit it out, my counsel is then that
you turn plain ape: take up a rush and tickle the earnest
ears of your fellow gallants to make other fools fall a
laughing; mew at passionate speeches; blare at merry;
find fault with the music; whew at the children's action;
whistle at the songs; and, above all, curse the sharers,
that whereas the same day you had bestowed forty shil-

lings on an embroidered felt and feather (Scotch fashion) for your mistress in the court, or your punk in the city, within two hours after you encounter the very same block on the stage, when the haberdasher swore to you the impression was extant but that morning.

To conclude: hoard up the finest playscraps you can get, upon which your lean wit may most savorly feed for want of other stuff, when the Arcadian and Euphuized gentlewomen have their tongues sharpened to set upon you. That quality (next to your shuttlecock) is the only furniture to a courtier that's but a new beginner, and is but in his A B C of compliment. The next places that are filled, after the playhouses be emptied, are (or ought to be) taverns; into a tavern then let us next march, where the brains of one hogshead must be beaten out to make up another.

Chapter 7.

HOW A GALLANT SHOULD BEHAVE HIMSELF IN A TAVERN

WHOSOEVER desires to be a man of good reckoning in the city, and (like your French lord) to have as many tables furnished as lackeys (who, when they keep least, keep none), whether he be a young quat [1] of the first year's revenue, or some austere and sullen-faced steward, who (in despite of a great beard, a satin suit, and a chain of gold wrapped in cypress) proclaims himself to any (but to those to whom his lord owes money) for a rank coxcomb, or whether he be a country gentleman, that brings his wife up to learn the fashion, see the tombs at Westminster, the lions in the Tower, or to take physic; or else is some young farmer, who many

[1] pimple, here upstart

times makes his wife (in the country) believe he hath suits in law, because he will come up to his lechery: be he of what stamp he will that hath money in his purse, and a good conscience to spend it, my counsel is that he take his continual diet at a tavern, which (out of question) is the only rendezvous of boon company; and the drawers [1] the most nimble, the most bold, and most sudden proclaimers of your largest bounty.

Having therefore thrust yourself into a case [2] most in fashion (how coarse soever the stuff be, 'tis no matter so it hold fashion), your office is (if you mean to do your judgment right) to inquire out those taverns which are best customed, whose masters are oftenest drunk (for that confirms their taste, and that they choose wholesome wines), and such as stand furthest from the counters; where, landing yourself and your followers, your first compliment shall be to grow most inwardly acquainted with the drawers, to learn their names, as Jack, and Will, and Tom, to dive into their inclinations, as whether this fellow useth to the fencing school, this to the dancing school; whether that young conjurer (in hogsheads) at midnight keeps a gelding now and then to visit his cockatrice, or whether he loves dogs, or be addicted to any other eminent and citizen-like quality: and protest yourself to be extremely in love, and that you spend much money in a year, upon any one of those exercises which you perceive is followed by them. The use which you shall make of this familiarity is this: if you want money five or six days together, you may still pay the reckoning with this most gentlemanlike language, 'Boy, fetch me money from the bar,' and keep yourself most providently from a hungry melancholy in your chamber. Besides, you shall be sure (if there be but one faucet that can betray neat wine to the bar) to

[1] bar-tenders   [2] suit of clothes

have that arraigned before you, sooner than a better
and worthier person.

The first question you are to make (after the discharg-
ing of your pocket of tobacco and pipes, and the household stuff thereto belonging) shall be for an inventory
of the kitchen: for it were more than most tailor-like,
and to be suspected you were in league with some
kitchen-wench, to descend yourself, to offend your
stomach with the sight of the larder, and haply to
grease your accoutrements. Having therefore received
this bill, you shall (like a captain putting up dear pays)
have many salads stand on your table, as it were for
blanks to the other more serviceable dishes: and according to the time of the year, vary your fare, as capon is a
stirring meat sometimes, oysters are a swelling meat
sometimes, trout a tickling meat sometimes, green goose
and woodcock a delicate meat sometimes, especially in
a tavern, where you shall sit in as great state as a
church-warden amongst his poor parishioners, at Pente-
cost or Christmas.

For your drink, let not your physician confine you
to any one particular liquor: for as it is requisite that
a gentleman should not always be plodding in one art,
but rather be a general scholar (that is, to have a lick
at all sorts of learning, and away) so 'tis not fitting a
man should trouble his head with sucking at one grape,
but that he may be able (now there is a general peace)
to drink any stranger drunk in his own element of
drink, or more properly in his own mist language.

Your discourse at the table must be such as that
which you utter at your ordinary: your behavior the
same, but somewhat more careless: for where your expense is great, let your modesty be less: and, though
you should be mad in a tavern, the largeness of the items
will bear with your incivility: you may, without prick

to your conscience, set the want of your wit against
the superfluity and sauciness of their reckonings.

If you desire not to be haunted with fiddlers (who by
the statute have as much liberty as rogues to travel
into any place, having the passport of the house about
them) bring then no women along with you: but if
you love the company of all the drawers, never sup
without your cockatrice: for, having her there, you
shall be sure of most officious attendance. Inquire what
gallants sup in the next room, and if they be any of
your acquaintance, do not you (after the city fashion)
send them in a bottle of wine, and your name, sweetened
in two pitiful papers of sugar, with some filthy apology
crammed into the mouth of a drawer; but rather keep
a boy in fee, who underhand shall proclaim you in every
room, what a gallant fellow you are, how much you
spend yearly in taverns, what a great gamester, what
custom you bring to the house, in what witty discourse
you maintain a table, what gentlewomen of citizens'
wives you can with a wet finger have at any time to sup
with you, and such like. By which encomiastics of his,
they that know you shall admire you, and think themselves to be brought into a paradise but to be meanly in
your acquaintance; and if any of your endeared friends
be in the house, and beat the same ivy bush that yourself does, you may join companies and be drunk together most publicly.

But in such a deluge of drink, take heed that no man
counterfeit himself drunk to free his purse from the
danger of the shot:[1] 'tis a usual thing now among gentlemen; it had wont be the quality of cockneys: I would
advise you to leave so much brains in your head as to
prevent this. When the terrible reckoning (like an indictment) bids you hold up your hand, and that you

[1] bill, reckoning

must answer it at the bar, you must not abate one penny in any particular, no, though they reckon cheese to you, when you have neither eaten any, nor could ever abide it, raw or toasted: but cast your eye only upon the totalis,[1] and no further; for to traverse the bill would betray you to be acquainted with the rates of the market, nay more, it would make the vintners believe you were *pater familias,* and kept a house; which, I assure you, is not now in fashion.

If you fall to dice after supper, let the drawers be as familiar with you as your barber, and venture their silver amongst you; no matter where they had it: you are to cherish the unthriftiness of such young tame pigeons, if you be a right gentleman: for when two are yoked together by the purse strings, and draw the chariot of Madam Prodigality, when one faints in the way and slips his horns, let the other rejoice and laugh at him.

At your departure forth the house, to kiss mine hostess over the bar, or to accept of the courtesy of the cellar when 'tis offered you by the drawers, and you must know that kindness never creeps upon them, but when they see you almost cleft to the shoulders, or to bid any of the vintners good night, is as commendable, as for a barber after trimming to lave your face with sweet water.

To conclude, count it an honor, either to invite or be invited to any rifling:[2] for commonly, though you find much satin there, yet you shall likewise find many citizens' sons, and heirs, and younger brothers there, who smell out such feasts more greedily than tailors hunt upon Sundays after weddings. And let any hook draw you either to a fencer's supper, or to a player's that acts such a part for a wager; for by this means you

[1] total   [2] raffle

shall get experience, by being guilty to their abominable
shaving.

Chapter 8.

HOW A GALLANT IS TO BEHAVE HIMSELF PASSING THROUGH
THE CITY, AT ALL HOURS OF THE NIGHT,
AND HOW TO PASS BY ANY WATCH

After the sound of pottle-pots is out of your ears,
and that the spirit of wine and tobacco walks in your
brain, the tavern door being shut upon your back, cast
about to pass through the widest and goodliest streets
in the city. And if your means cannot reach to the
keeping of a boy, hire one of the drawers, to be as a
lanthorne unto your feet, and to light you home: and,
still as you approach near any night-walker that is up
as late as yourself, curse and swear (like one that speaks
High Dutch) in a lofty voice, because your men have
used you so like a rascal in not waiting upon you, and
vow the next morning to pull their blue cases over their
ears, though, if your chamber were well searched, you
give only sixpence a week to some old woman to make
your bed, and that she is all the serving-creatures you
give wages to. If you smell a watch (and that you may
easily do, for commonly they eat onions to keep them
in sleeping, which they account a medicine against cold)
or, if you come within danger of their brown bills, let
him that is your candlestick, and holds up your torch
from dropping (for to march after a link is shoe-maker-
like), let *Ignis Fatuus,* I say, being within the reach of
the constable's staff, ask aloud, 'Sir Giles,' or 'Sir
Abram, will you turn this way, or down that street?'
It skills not, though there be none dubbed in your bunch;
the watch will wink at you, only for the love they bear

to arms and knighthood: marry, if the sentinel and his court of guard stand strictly upon his martial law and cry 'Stand,' commanding you to give the word, and to show reason why your ghost walks so late, do it in some jest (for that will show you have a desperate wit, and perhaps make him and his halberdiers afraid to lay foul hands upon you) or, if you read a *mittimus* [1] in the constable's book, counterfeit to be a Frenchman, a Dutchman, or any other nation whose country is in peace with your own; and you may pass the pikes: for being not able to understand you, they cannot by the customs of the city take your examination, and so by consequence they have nothing to say to you.

All the way as you pass (especially being approached near some of the gates) talk of none but lords, and such ladies with whom you have played at primero, or danced in the presence the very same day. It is a chance to lock up the lips of an inquisitive bell-man: and being arrived at your lodging door, which I would counsel you to choose in some rich citizen's house, salute at parting no man but by the name of Sir (as though you had supped with knights) albeit you had none in your company but your Perinado, or your ingle.[2]

Happily it will be blown abroad, that you and your shoal of gallants swum through such an ocean of wine, that you danced so much money out at heels, and that in wild fowl there flew away thus much: and I assure you, to have the bill of your reckoning lost of purpose, so that it may be published, will make you to be held in dear estimation: only the danger is, if you owe money, and that your revealing gets your creditors by the ears; for then look to have a peal of ordnance thundering at your chamber door the next morning. But if either your tailor, mercer, haberdasher, silkman, cutter, linen

[1] warrant for arrest   [2] crony

draper, or sempster, stand like a guard of Switzers about your lodging, watching your uprising, or, if they miss of that, your lying in one of the Counters, you have no means to avoid the galling of their small shot, than by sending out a light-horseman to call your apothecary to your aid, who, encountering this desperate band of your creditors, only with two or three glasses in his hand, as though that day you purged, is able to drive them all to their holes like so many foxes: for the name of taking physic is a sufficient *quietus est* to any endangered gentleman, and gives an acquittance (for the time) to them all, though the twelve companies stand with their hoods to attend your coming forth and their officers with them.

I could now fetch you about noon (the hour which I prescribed you before to rise at) out of your chamber, and carry you with me into Paul's Churchyard; where planting yourself in a stationer's shop, many instructions are to be given you, what books to call for, how to censure of new books, how to mew at the old, how to look in your tables and inquire for such and such Greek, French, Italian, or Spanish authors, whose names you have there, but whom your mother for pity would not give you so much wit as to understand. From thence you should blow yourself into the tobacco-ordinary, where you are likewise to spend your judgment (like a quack-salver) upon that mystical wonder, to be able to discourse whether your cane [1] or your pudding [2] be sweetest, and which pipe has the best bore, and which burns black, which breaks in the burning, etc. Or, if you itch to step into the barber's, a whole dictionary cannot afford more words to set down notes what dialogues you are to maintain whilst you are doctor of the

[1] tobacco in rolls, like cigars   [2] tobacco in bags

chair there. After your shaving, I could breathe you in a fence-school, and out of that cudgel you into a dancing school, in both which I could weary you, by showing you more tricks than are in five galleries, or fifteen prizes. And, to close up the stomach of this feast, I could make cockneys, whose fathers have left them well, acknowledge themselves infinitely beholden to me, for teaching them by familiar demonstration how to spend their patrimony and to get themselves names, when their fathers are dead and rotten. But lest too many dishes should cast into a surfeit, I will now take away; yet so that, if I perceive you relish this well, the rest shall be (in time) prepared for you. Farewell.

(1609)

FRANCIS BACON (1561-1626)

ESSAYS

1. OF TRUTH

What is truth? said jesting Pilate; and would not stay for an answer. Certainly there be that delight in giddiness; and count it a bondage to fix a belief; affecting free-will in thinking, as well as in acting. And though the sects of philosophers of that kind be gone, yet there remain certain discoursing wits, which are of the same veins, though there be not so much blood in them as was in those of the ancients. But it is not only the difficulty and labor which men take in finding out of truth; nor again, that when it is found, it imposeth upon men's thoughts; that doth bring lies in favor: but a natural though corrupt love of the lie itself. One of the later school of the Grecians examineth the matter, and is at a stand to think what should be in it, that men should love lies; where neither they make for pleasure, as with poets; nor for advantage, as with the merchant; but for the lie's sake. But I cannot tell: this same truth is a naked and open day-light, that doth not show the masques, and mummeries, and triumphs of the world, half so stately and daintily as candle-lights. Truth may perhaps come to the price of a pearl, that showeth best by day: but it will not rise to the price of a diamond or carbuncle, that showeth best in varied lights. A mixture of a lie doth ever add pleasure. Doth any man doubt, that if there were taken out of men's minds, vain opinions, flattering hopes, false valuations, imaginations as one would, and the like; but it would leave the minds of a number of men, poor shrunken things; full of melancholy and indisposition, and unpleasing to themselves? One of the fathers, in great severity, called poesy *vinum dæmonum,* because it filleth the imagination, and yet it is but with the shadow of a lie. But it is not the lie that passeth through the mind, but the lie that sinketh in, and settleth in it, that doth the hurt, such as we spake of before. But howsoever these things are thus in men's depraved judgments and affections, yet truth, which only doth judge itself, teacheth, that the inquiry of truth, which is the love-making, or wooing of it; the knowledge of truth, which is the presence of it; and the belief of truth, which is the enjoying of it; is the sovereign good of human nature. The first creature of God, in the works of the days, was the light of the sense; the last was the light of reason; and his Sabbath work ever since is the illumination of his Spirit. First he breathed light upon the face of the matter, or chaos; then he breathed light into the face of man; and still he breatheth and inspireth light into the face of his chosen. The poet that beautified the sect, that was otherwise inferior to the rest, saith yet excellently well: 'It is a pleasure to stand upon the shore, and to see ships tost upon the sea: a pleasure to stand in the window of a castle, and to see a battle, and the adventures thereof below; but no pleasure is comparable to the standing upon the vantage ground of truth, a hill not to be commanded, and where the air is always clear and serene: and to see the errors, and wanderings, and mists, and tempests, in the vale below': so always, that this prospect be with pity, and not with swelling or pride. Certainly it is heaven upon earth, to have a man's mind move in charity, rest in Providence, and turn upon the poles of truth.

To pass from theological and philosophical truth, to the truth of civil business; it will be acknowledged, even by those that practice it not, that clear and round dealing is the honor of man's nature; and that mixture of falsehood is like alloy in coin of gold and silver; which may make the metal work the better, but it embaseth it. For these winding and crooked courses are the goings of the serpent; which goeth basely upon the belly, and not upon the feet. There is no vice that doth so cover a man with shame, as to be found false and perfidious. And therefore Montaigne saith prettily, when he inquired the reason why the word of the lie should be such a disgrace, and such an odious charge? Saith he, 'If it be well weighed, to say that a man lieth, is as much as to say that he is brave towards God, and a coward towards man. For a lie faces God, and shrinks from man.' Surely the wickedness of falsehood, and breach of faith, cannot possibly be so highly expressed, as in that it shall be the last peal to call the judgments of God upon the generations of men: it being foretold,

that when Christ cometh *he shall not find faith upon
the earth.*

5. OF ADVERSITY

It was a high speech of Seneca, after the manner of
the Stoics, that the good things which belong to prosperity are to be wished, but the good things that belong
to adversity are to be admired: *Bona rerum secundarum
optabilia, adversarum mirabilia.* Certainly, if miracles
be the command over nature, they appear most in adversity. It is yet a higher speech of his than the other,
much too high for a heathen: It is true greatness to
have in one the frailty of a man, and the security of
a God: *Vere magnum, habere fragilitatem hominis, se-
curitatem Dei.* This would have done better in poesy,
where transcendencies are more allowed. And the poets
indeed have been busy with it; for it is in effect the
thing which is figured in that strange fiction of the
ancient poets, which seemeth not to be without mystery;
nay, and to have some approach to the state of a
Christian: that Hercules, when he went to unbind Prometheus, by whom human nature is represented, sailed the
length of the great ocean in an earthen pot or pitcher;
lively describing Christian resolution, that saileth in the
frail bark of the flesh through the waves of the world.
But to speak in a mean:[1] the virtue of prosperity is
temperance; the virtue of adversity is fortitude; which
in morals is the more heroical virtue. Prosperity is the
blessing of the Old Testament; adversity is the blessing
of the New, which carrieth the greater benediction, and
the clearer revelation of God's favor. Yet, even in the
Old Testament, if you listen to David's harp, you shall

[1] prosaic, restrained style

hear as many hearse-like airs as carols: and the pencil of the Holy Ghost hath labored more in describing the afflictions of Job than the felicities of Solomon. Prosperity is not without many fears and distastes; and adversity is not without comforts and hopes. We see in needle-works and embroideries, it is more pleasing to have a lively work upon a sad and solemn ground, than to have a dark and melancholy work upon a lightsome ground: judge therefore of the pleasure of the heart by the pleasure of the eye. Certainly virtue is like precious odors, most fragrant when they are incensed, or crushed; for prosperity doth best discover vice, but adversity doth best discover virtue.

7. OF PARENTS AND CHILDREN

The joys of parents are secret, and so are their griefs and fears; they cannot utter the one, nor they will not utter the other. Children sweeten labors, but they make misfortunes more bitter; they increase the cares of life, but they mitigate the remembrance of death. The perpetuity by generation is common to beasts; but memory, and merit, and noble works are proper to men; and surely a man shall see the noblest works and foundations have proceeded from childless men, which have sought to express the images of their minds where those of their bodies have failed; so the care of posterity is most in them that have no posterity. They that are the first raisers of their houses are most indulgent towards their children, beholding them as the continuance, not only of their kind, but of their work, and so both children and creatures.

The difference in affection of parents towards their several children is many times unequal, and sometimes unworthy, especially in the mother; as Solomon saith, 'A wise son rejoiceth the father, but an ungracious son shames the mother.' A man shall see, where there is a house full of children, one or two of the eldest respected, and the youngest made wantons; but in the midst, some that are as it were forgotten, who, many times, nevertheless, prove the best. The illiberality of parents in allowance towards their children, is a harmful error, and makes them base, acquaints them with shifts, makes them sort with mean company, and makes them surfeit more when they come to plenty; and therefore the proof is best when men keep their authority towards their children, but not their purse. Men have a foolish manner (both parents, and schoolmasters, and servants), in creating and breeding an emulation between brothers during childhood, which many times sorteth to discord when they are men, and disturbeth families. The Italians make little difference between children and nephews, or near kinsfolk; but so they be of the lump they care not, though they pass not through their own body. And, to say truth, in nature it is much a like matter; insomuch that we see a nephew sometimes resembleth an uncle, or a kinsman, more than his own parent, as the blood happens. Let parents choose betimes the vocations and courses they mean their children should take, for then they are most flexible; and let them not too much apply themselves to the disposition of their children, as thinking they will take best to that which they have most mind to. It is true, that if the affection, or aptness, of the children be extraordinary, then it is good not to cross it; but generally the precept is good. *Optimum elige, suave et facile illud faciet consuetudo.* Younger brothers are commonly fortunate, but seldom or never where the elder are disinherited.

8. OF MARRIAGE AND SINGLE LIFE

He that hath wife and children, hath given hostages to fortune; for they are impediments to great enterprises, either of virtue or mischief. Certainly the best works and of greatest merit for the public, have proceeded from the unmarried or childless men: which both in affection and means have married and endowed the public. Yet it were great reason, that those that have children should have greatest care of future times; unto which they know they must transmit their dearest pledges. Some there are, who though they lead a single life, yet their thoughts do end with themselves, and account future times impertinences. Nay, there are some other, that account wife and children but as bills of charges. Nay more, there are some foolish, rich, covetous men, that take a pride in having no children, because they may be thought so much the richer. For perhaps they have heard some talk, Such a one is a great rich man; and another except to it, Yea, but he hath a great charge of children: as if it were an abatement to his riches. But the most ordinary cause of a single life is liberty; especially in certain self-pleasing and humorous [1] minds, which are so sensible of every restraint, as they will go near to think their girdles and garters to be bonds and shackles. Unmarried men are best friends, best masters, best servants, but not always best subjects; for they are light to run away; and almost all fugitives are of that condition. A single life doth well with churchmen: for charity will hardly water the ground, where it must first fill a pool. It is indifferent for judges and magistrates: for if they be facile and corrupt, you shall have a servant five

[1] capricious, eccentric

times worse than a wife. For soldiers, I find the generals commonly, in their hortatives, put men in mind of their wives and children. And I think the despising of marriage amongst the Turks, maketh the vulgar soldiers more base. Certainly, wife and children are a kind of discipline of humanity: and single men, though they be many times more charitable, because their means are less exhaust; yet, on the other side, they are more cruel and hard-hearted, good to make severe inquisitors, because their tenderness is not so oft called upon. Grave natures, led by custom, and therefore constant, are commonly loving husbands; as was said of Ulysses, *Vetulam suam prætulit immortalitati.* Chaste women are often proud and froward, as presuming upon the merit of their chastity. It is one of the best bonds, both of chastity and obedience, in the wife, if she thinks her husband wise; which she will never do if she find him jealous. Wives are young men's mistresses; companions for middle age; and old men's nurses. So as a man may have a quarrel [1] to marry when he will. But yet he was reputed one of the wise men, that made answer to the question, when a man should marry? 'A young man not yet, an elder man not at all.' It is often seen, that bad husbands have very good wives; whether it be, that it raiseth the price of their husband's kindness when it comes; or that the wives take a pride in their patience. But this never fails if the bad husbands were of their own choosing, against their friends' consent; for then they will be sure to make good their own folly.

10. OF LOVE

The stage is more beholden to love, than the life of man. For as to the stage, love is ever a matter of

[1] debate

comedies, and now and then of tragedies; but in life it doth much mischief, sometimes like a siren, sometimes like a fury. You may observe, that amongst all the great and worthy persons, whereof the memory remaineth, either ancient or recent, there is not one that hath been transported to the mad degree of love; which shows, that great spirits and great business do keep out this weak passion. You must except nevertheless, Marcus Antonius, the half-partner of the empire of Rome, and Appius Claudius, the decemvir and lawgiver; whereof the former was indeed a voluptuous man and inordinate; but the latter was an austere and wise man: and therefore it seems, though rarely, that love can find entrance, not only into an open heart, but also into a heart well fortified, if watch be not well kept. It is a poor saying of Epicurus; *Satis magnum alter alteri theatrum sumus:* as if man, made for the contemplation of heaven, and all noble objects, should do nothing but kneel before a little idol, and make himself subject, though not of the mouth, as beasts are, yet of the eye, which was given him for higher purposes. It is a strange thing to note the excess of this passion; and how it braves the nature and value of things by this, that the speaking in a perpetual hyperbole is comely in nothing but in love. Neither is it merely in the phrase; for whereas it hath been well said, that the arch-flatterer, with whom all the petty flatterers have intelligence, is a man's self; certainly the lover is more. For there was never proud man thought so absurdly well of himself, as the lover doth of the person loved; and therefore it was well said, that it is impossible to love, and to be wise. Neither doth this weakness appear to others only, and not to the party loved, but to the loved most of all; except the love be reciproque.[1] For it is

[1] mutual

a true rule, that love is ever rewarded either with the reciproque, or with an inward and secret contempt: by how much the more men ought to beware of this passion, which loseth not only other things, but itself. As for the other losses, the poet's relation doth well figure them; that he that preferred Helena, quitted the gifts of Juno and Pallas: for whosoever esteemeth too much of amorous affection quitteth both riches and wisdom. This passion hath its floods in the very times of weakness, which are great prosperity, and great adversity; though this latter hath been less observed; both which times kindle love, and make it more fervent, and therefore show it to be the child of folly. They do best, who, if they cannot but admit love, yet make it keep quarter; and sever it wholly from their serious affairs and actions of life: for if it check once with business, it troubleth men's fortunes, and maketh men that they can no ways be true to their own ends. I know not how, but martial men are given to love: I think it is, but as they are given to wine; for perils commonly ask to be paid in pleasures. There is in man's nature a secret inclination and motion towards love of others, which, if it be not spent upon some one or a few, doth naturally spread itself towards many, and maketh men become humane and charitable; as it is seen sometimes in friars. Nuptial love maketh mankind; friendly love perfecteth it; but wanton love corrupteth and embaseth it.

11. OF GREAT PLACE

Men in great place are thrice servants: servants of the sovereign or state; servants of fame; and servants of business: so as they have no freedom, neither in their persons, nor in their actions, nor in their times. It is a strange desire, to seek power, and to lose liberty; or to seek power over others, and to lose power over a man's self. The rising into place is laborious; and by pains men come to greater pains; and it is sometimes base; and by indignities men come to dignities. The standing is slippery, and the regress is either a downfall, or at least an eclipse, which is a melancholy thing. *Cum non sis qui fueris, non esse cur velis vivere.* Nay, retire men cannot when they would; neither will they when it were reason: but are impatient of privateness, even in age and sickness, which require the shadow: like old townsmen, that will be still sitting at their street door, though thereby they offer age to scorn. Certainly great persons had need to borrow other men's opinions to think themselves happy; for if they judge by their own feeling, they cannot find it; but if they think with themselves what other men think of them, and that other men would fain be as they are, then they are happy as it were by report, when perhaps they find the contrary within. For they are the first that find their own griefs; though they be the last that find their own faults. Certainly men in great fortunes are strangers to themselves, and while they are in the puzzle of business, they have no time to tend their health either of body or mind. *Illi mors gravis incubat, qui notus nimis omnibus, ignotus moritur sibi.* In place there is license to do good and evil; whereof the latter is a curse; for in evil the best condition is not to will; the second not to can.[1] But power to do good is the true and lawful end of aspiring. For good thoughts, though God accept them, yet towards men are little better than good dreams, except they be put in act; and that cannot be without power and place; as the vantage and commanding ground. Merit and good works is the end of man's motion; and conscience of the same is the accomplish-

[1] know how

ment of man's rest. For if a man can be partaker of God's theater, he shall likewise be partaker of God's rest. *Et conversus Deus, ut aspiceret opera, quæ fecerunt manus suæ, vidit quod omnia essent bona nimis;* and then the Sabbath. In the discharge of thy place, set before thee the best examples; for imitation is a globe of precepts. And after a time set before thee thine own example; and examine thyself strictly, whether thou didst not best at first. Neglect not also the examples of those, that have carried themselves ill in the same place: not to set off thyself by taxing their memory; but to direct thyself what to avoid. Reform therefore, without bravery or scandal of former times and persons; but yet set it down to thyself, as well to create good precedents, as to follow them. Reduce things to the first institution, and observe wherein and how they have degenerated; but yet ask counsel of both times: of the ancient time what is best; and of the latter time what is fittest. Seek to make thy course regular; that men may know beforehand what they may expect: but be not too positive and peremptory; and express thyself well when thou digressest from thy rule. Preserve the right of thy place, but stir not questions of jurisdiction: and rather assume thy right in silence, and *de facto,* than voice it with claims and challenges. Preserve likewise the rights of inferior places; and think it more honor to direct in chief, than to be busy in all. Embrace and invite helps and advices touching the execution of thy place; and do not drive away such as bring thee information, as meddlers, but accept of them in good part. The vices of authority are chiefly four; delays, corruption, roughness, and facility. For delays; give easy access; keep times appointed; go through with that which is in hand; and interlace not business but of necessity. For corruption; do not only bind thine own

hands, or thy servants' hands, from taking, but bind the
hands of suitors also from offering. For integrity used
doth the one; but integrity professed, and with a manifest detestation of bribery, doth the other: and avoid
not only the fault, but the suspicion. Whosoever is
found variable, and changeth manifestly without manifest cause, giveth suspicion of corruption. Therefore
always when thou changest thine opinion or course,
profess it plainly, and declare it, together with the reasons that move thee to change; and do not think to steal
it. A servant or a favorite, if he be inward, and no
other apparent cause of esteem, is commonly thought
but a by-way to close corruption. For roughness, it is
a needless cause of discontent; severity breedeth fear,
but roughness breedeth hate. Even reproofs from authority ought to be grave, and not taunting. As for
facility, it is worse than bribery. For bribes come but
now and then; but if importunity or idle respects lead
a man, he shall never be without. As Solomon saith;
*to respect persons is not good; for such a man will
transgress for a piece of bread.* It is most true that
was anciently spoken, A place showeth the man: and it
showeth some to the better, and some to the worse;
omnium consensu, capax imperii, nisi imperasset, saith
Tacitus of Galba: but of Vespasian he saith; *solus im-
perantium Vespasianus mutatus in melius.* Though the
one was meant of sufficiency, the other of manners and
affection. It is an assured sign of a worthy and gener-
ous spirit, whom honor amends. For honor is, or should
be, the place of virtue: and as in nature things move
violently to their place, and calmly in their place; so
virtue in ambition is violent, in authority settled and
calm. All rising to great place is by a winding-stair;
and if there be factions, it is good to side a man's self
whilst he is in the rising; and to balance himself when

he is placed. Use the memory of thy predecessor fairly and tenderly; for if thou dost not, it is a debt will sure be paid when thou art gone. If thou have colleagues, respect them, and rather call them when they look not for it, than exclude them when they have reason to look to be called. Be not too sensible, or too remembering of thy place in conversation, and private answers to suitors; but let it rather be said, When he sits in place he is another man.

17. OF SUPERSTITION

It were better to have no opinion of God at all, than such an opinion as is unworthy of him; for the one is unbelief, the other is contumely: and certainly superstition is the reproach of the Deity. Plutarch saith well to that purpose: 'Surely,' saith he, 'I had rather a great deal, men should say there was no such a man at all as Plutarch than that they should say that there was one Plutarch, that would eat his children as soon as they were born'; as the poets speak of Saturn. And as the contumely is greater towards God, so the danger is greater towards men. Atheism leaves a man to sense, to philosophy, to natural piety, to laws, to reputation— all which may be guides to an outward moral virtue, though religion were not; but superstition dismounts all these, and erecteth an absolute monarchy in the minds of men. Therefore atheism did never perturb states; for it makes men wary of themselves, as looking no further; and we see the times inclined to atheism, as the time of Augustus Cæsar, were civil times; but superstition hath been the confusion of many states, and bringeth in a new *primum mobile* that ravisheth all the spheres of government. The master of superstition is the people; and in all superstition wise men follow fools;

and arguments are fitted to practice in a reversed order. It was gravely said, by some of the prelates in the Council of Trent, where the doctrine of the schoolmen bare great sway, that the schoolmen were like astronomers, which did feign eccentrics and epicycles, and such engines of orbs, to save the phenomena, though they knew there were no such things; and, in like manner, that the schoolmen had framed a number of subtle and intricate axioms and theorems to save the practice of the church. The causes of superstition are pleasing and sensual rites and ceremonies, excess of outward and pharisaical holiness, over-great reverence of traditions, which cannot but load the church; the stratagems of prelates for their own ambition and lucre; the favoring too much of good intentions, which openeth the gate to conceits and novelties; the taking an aim at divine matters by human, which cannot but breed mixture of imaginations; and, lastly, barbarous times, especially joined with calamities and disasters. Superstition without a veil is a deformed thing, for as it addeth deformity to an ape to be so like a man, so the similitude of superstition to religion makes it the more deformed. And as wholesome meat corrupteth to little worms, so good forms and orders corrupt into a number of petty observances. There is a superstition in avoiding superstition, when men think to do best if they go farthest from the superstition formerly received. Therefore care would be had that, as it fareth in ill purgings, the good be not taken away with the bad, which commonly is done when the people is the reformer.

42. OF YOUTH AND AGE

A man that is young in years, may be old in hours, if he have lost no time. But that happeneth rarely.

Generally youth is like the first cogitations, not so wise as the second. For there is a youth in thoughts, as well as in ages. And yet the invention of young men is more lively than that of old: and imaginations stream into their minds better, and as it were more divinely. Natures that have much heat, and great and violent desires and perturbations, are not ripe for action, till they have passed the meridian of their years: as it was with Julius Cæsar, and Septimius Severus. Of the latter of whom it is said, *Juventutem egit erroribus, imo furoribus, plenam.* And yet he was the ablest emperor almost of all the list. But reposed natures may do well in youth: as it is seen in Augustus Cæsar, Cosmos, duke of Florence, Gaston de Fois, and others. On the other side, heat and vivacity in age is an excellent composition for business. Young men are fitter to invent than to judge; fitter for execution than for counsel; and fitter for new projects than for settled business. For the experience of age, in things that fall within the compass of it, directeth them; but in new things abuseth them. The errors of young men are the ruin of business; but the errors of aged men amount but to this; that more might have been done, or sooner. Young men, in the conduct and manage of actions, embrace more than they can hold; stir more than they can quiet; fly to the end, without consideration of the means and degrees; pursue some few principles, which they have chanced upon, absurdly; care not to innovate, which draws unknown inconveniences; use extreme remedies at first; and, that which doubleth all errors, will not acknowledge or retract them; like an unready horse, that will neither stop nor turn. Men of age object too much, consult too long, adventure too little, repent too soon, and seldom drive business home to the full period; but content themselves with a mediocrity of success. Certainly it is good to compound employments of both; for that will be good for the present, because the virtues of either age may correct the defects of both: and good for succession, that young men may be learners, while men in age are actors: and, lastly, good for extern accidents, because authority followeth old men, and favor and popularity youth. But for the moral part, perhaps youth will have the pre-eminence, as age hath for the politic. A certain rabbin upon the text, *Your young men shall see visions, and your old men shall dream dreams;* inferreth, that young men are admitted nearer to God than old; because vision is a clearer revelation than a dream. And certainly the more a man drinketh of the world, the more it intoxicateth; and age doth profit rather in the powers of understanding, than in the virtues of the will and affections. There be some have an over-early ripeness in their years, which fadeth betimes: these are, first, such as have brittle wits, the edge whereof is soon turned; such as was Hermogenes the rhetorician, whose books are exceeding subtile; who afterwards waxed stupid. A second sort, is of those that have some natural dispositions, which have better grace in youth than in age: such as is a fluent and luxuriant speech; which becomes youth well, but not age. So Tully saith of Hortensius; *idem manebat, neque idem decebat.* The third is, of such as take too high a strain at the first; and are magnanimous, more than tract of years can uphold. As was Scipio Africanus, of whom Livy saith in effect; *ultima primis cedebant.*

50. OF STUDIES

Studies serve for delight, for ornament, and for ability. Their chief use for delight, is in privateness and retiring; for ornament, is in discourse; and for ability, is in the judgment and disposition of business. For expert men can execute, and perhaps judge of particulars, one by one; but the general counsels, and the plots and marshalling of affairs, come best from those that are learned. To spend too much time in studies, is sloth; to use them too much for ornament, is affectation; to make judgment wholly by their rules, is the humor of a scholar. They perfect nature, and are perfected by experience: for natural abilities are like natural plants, that need pruning by study; and studies themselves do give forth directions too much at large, except they be bounded in by experience. Crafty men contemn studies; simple men admire them; and wise men use them: for they teach not their own use; but that is a wisdom without them, and above them, won by observation. Read not to contradict and confute; nor to believe and take for granted; nor to find talk and discourse; but to weigh and consider. Some books are to be tasted, others to be swallowed, and some few to be chewed and digested: that is, some books are to be read only in parts; others to be read, but not curiously; and some few to be read wholly, and with diligence and attention. Some books also may be read by deputy, and extracts made of them by others; but that would be only in the less important arguments, and the meaner sort of books: else distilled books are like common distilled waters, flashy things. Reading maketh a full man; conference a ready man; and writing an exact man. And therefore if a man write little, he had need have a great memory; if he confer little, he had need have a present wit; and if he read little, he had need have much cunning, to seem to know that he doth not. Histories make men wise; poets, witty; the mathematics, subtile; natural philosophy, deep; moral, grave; logic and rhetoric, able to contend: *Abeunt studia in mores.* Nay, there is no stond or impediment in the wit, but may be wrought out by fit studies; like as diseases of the body may have appropriate exercises: bowling is good for the stone and reins; [1] shooting for the lungs and breast; gentle walking for the stomach; riding for the head; and the like. So if a man's wit be wandering, let him study the mathematics; for in demonstrations, if his wit be called away never so little, he must begin again: if his wit be not apt to distinguish or find differences, let him study the schoolmen; for they are *cymini sectores:* if he be not apt to beat over matters, and to call up one thing to prove and illustrate another, let him study the lawyer's cases: so every defect of the mind may have a special receipt.

(1597, 1612, 1625)

OF THE ADVANCEMENT OF LEARNING

(From Book II, *Natural Philosophy*)

IF THEN it be true that Democritus said, *That the truth of nature lieth hid in certain deep mines and caves,* and if it be true likewise that the alchemists do so much inculcate, that Vulcan is a second nature, and imitateth that dexterously and compendiously, which nature worketh by ambages [2] and length of time, it were good to divide natural philosophy into the mine and the furnace: and to make two professions or occupations of natural philosophers, some to be pioneers and some smiths; some to dig, and some to refine and hammer: and surely I do best allow of a division of that kind, though in more familiar and scholastical terms; namely, that these be the two parts of natural philosophy,—the *inquisition of causes,* and the *production of effects;*

[1] bladder and kidneys   [2] roundabout proceedings

speculative, and *operative; natural science* and *natural prudence.* For as in civil matters there is a wisdom of discourse and a wisdom of direction; so is it in natural. And here I will make a request, that for the latter, or at least for a part thereof, I may revive and reintegrate the misapplied and abused name of *natural magic;* which, in the true sense, is but *natural wisdom,* or *natural prudence;* taken according to the ancient acception, purged from vanity and superstition. Now although it be true, and I know it well, that there is an intercourse between causes and effects, so as both these knowledges, speculative and operative, have a great connection between themselves; yet because all true and fruitful natural philosophy hath a double scale or ladder, ascendent and descendent; ascending from experiments to the invention of causes, and descending from causes to the invention of new experiments; therefore I judge it most requisite that these two parts be severally considered and handled.

Natural science or *theory* is divided into *physic* and *metaphysic:* wherein I desire it may be conceived that I use the word metaphysic in a differing sense from that that is received: and in like manner, I doubt not but it will easily appear to men of judgment, that in this and other particulars, wheresoever my conception and notion may differ from the ancient, yet I am studious to keep the ancient terms. For hoping well to deliver myself from mistaking, by the order and perspicuous expressing of that I do propound, I am otherwise zealous and affectionate to recede as little from antiquity, either in terms or opinions, as many stand with truth and the proficience of knowledge. And herein I cannot a little marvel at the philosopher Aristotle, that did proceed in such a spirit of difference and contradiction towards all antiquity: undertaking not only to frame new words of science at pleasure, but to confound and extinguish all ancient wisdom: insomuch as he never nameth or mentioneth an ancient author or opinion, but to confute and reprove; wherein for glory, and drawing followers and disciples, he took the right course. For certainly there cometh to pass and hath place in human truth, that which was noted and pronounced in the highest truth: *Veni in nomine Patris, nec recipitis me; si quis venerit in nomine suo eum recipietis.* But in this divine aphorism, (considering to whom it was applied, namely to Antichrist, the highest deceiver,) we may discern well that the coming in a man's own name, without regard of antiquity or paternity, is no good sign of truth, although it be joined with the fortune and success of an *Eum recipietis.* But for this excellent person Aristotle, I will think of him that he learned that humor of his scholar, with whom, it seemeth, he did emulate, the one to conquer all opinions, as the other to conquer all nations; wherein nevertheless, it may be, he may at some men's hands that are of a bitter disposition get a like title as his scholar did:

> *Felix terrarum prædo, non utile mundo*
> *Editus exemplum, etc.*

So

> *Felix doctrinæ prædo.*

But to me, on the other side, that do desire as much as lieth in my pen to ground a sociable intercourse between antiquity and proficience, it seemeth best to keep way with antiquity *usque ad aras;* and therefore to retain the ancient terms, though I sometimes alter the uses and definitions, according to the moderate proceeding in civil government: where although there be some alteration, yet that holdeth which Tacitus wisely noteth, *Eadem Magistratuum vocabula.*

To return therefore to the use and acceptation of the term Metaphysic, as I do now understand the word; it appeareth, by that which hath been already said, that I intend *philosophia prima,* Summary Philosophy, and Metaphysic, which heretofore have been confounded as one, to be two distinct things. For the one I have made as a parent or common ancestor to all knowledge; and the other I have now brought in as a branch or descendent of natural science. It appeareth likewise that I have assigned to Summary Philosophy the common principles and axioms which are promiscuous and indifferent to several sciences: I have assigned unto it likewise the inquiry touching the operation of the relative and adventive characters of essences, as *quantity, similitude, diversity, possibility,* and the rest: with this distinction and provision; that they be handled as they have efficacy in nature, and not logically. It appeareth likewise that Natural Theology, which heretofore hath been handled confusedly with Metaphysic, I have inclosed and bounded by itself. It is therefore now a question which is left remaining for Metaphysic; wherein I may without prejudice preserve thus much of the conceit of antiquity, that Physic should contemplate that which is inherent in matter, and therefore transitory; and Metaphysic that which is abstracted and fixed. And again, that Physic should handle that which supposeth in nature only a being and moving; and Metaphysic should handle that which supposeth further in nature a reason, understanding, and platform. But the difference, perspicuously expressed, is most familiar and sensible. For as we divided natural philosophy in general into the *inquiry* of *causes,* and *productions* of *effects:* so that part which concerneth the inquiry of causes we do subdivide according to the received and found division of causes; the one part, which is Physic, inquireth and handleth the *material* and *efficient causes;* and the other, which is Metaphysic, handleth the *formal* and *final causes.*

Physic, taking it according to the derivation, and not according to our idiom for *medicine,* is situate in a middle term or distance between Natural History and Metaphysic. For natural history describeth the variety of things; physic, the causes, but variable or respective causes; and metaphysic, the fixed and constant causes.

> *Limus ut hic durescit, et hæc ut cera liquescit,*
> *Uno eodemque igni:*

Fire is the cause of induration, but respective to clay; fire is the cause of colliquation, but respective to wax; but fire is no constant cause either of induration or colliquation: so then the physical causes are but the efficient and the matter. Physic hath three parts; whereof two respect nature united or collected, the third contemplateth nature diffused or distributed. Nature is collected either into one entire total, or else into the same principles or seeds. So as the first doctrine is touching the contexture or configuration of things, as *de mundo, de universitate rerum.* The second is the doctrine concerning the principles or originals of things. The third is the doctrine concerning all variety and particularity of things; whether it be of the differing substances, or their differing qualities and natures; whereof there needeth no enumeration, this part being but as a gloss, or paraphrase, that attendeth upon the text of natural history. Of these three I cannot report any as deficient. In what truth or perfection they are handled, I make not now any judgment; but they are parts of knowledge not deserted by the labor of man.

For Metaphysic, we have assigned unto it the inquiry of formal and final causes; which assignation, as to the former of them, may seem to be nugatory and void; because of the received and inveterate opinion that the inquisition of man is not competent to find out essential Forms or true differences: of which opinion we will take this hold, that the invention of Forms is of all other parts of knowledge the worthiest to be sought, if it be possible to be found. As for the possibility, they are ill discoverers that think there is no land, when they can see nothing but sea. But it is manifest that Plato, in his opinion of Ideas, as one that had a wit of elevation situate as upon a cliff, did descry, *that Forms were the true object of knowledge,* but lost the real fruit of his opinion, by considering of Forms as absolutely abstracted from matter, and not confined and determined by matter; and so turning his opinion upon theology, wherewith all his natural philosophy is infected. But if any man shall keep a continual watchful and severe eye upon action, operation, and the use of knowledge, he may advise and take notice what are the Forms, the disclosures whereof are fruitful and important to the state of man. For as to the Forms of substances, man only except, of whom it is said, *Formavit hominem de limo terræ, et spiravit in faciem ejus spiraculum vitæ,* and not as of all other creatures, *Producant aquæ, producat terra;* the Forms of substances, I say, as they are now by compounding and transplanting multiplied, are so perplexed, as they are not to be inquired; no more than it were either possible or to purpose to seek in gross the Forms of those sounds which make words, which by composition and transposition of letters are infinite. But, on the other side, to inquire the Form of those sounds or voices which make simple letters is easily comprehensible; and being known, induceth and manifesteth the Forms of all words, which consist and are compounded of them. In the same manner to inquire the Form of a lion, of an oak, of gold; nay, of water, of air, is a vain pursuit: but to inquire the Forms of sense, of voluntary motion, of vegetation, of colors, of gravity and levity, of density, of tenuity, of heat, of cold, and all other natures and qualities, which, like an alphabet, are not many, and of which the essences, upheld by matter, of all creatures do consist; to inquire, I say, the true Forms of these, is that part of metaphysic which we now define of. Not but that Physic doth make inquiry, and take consideration of the same natures: but how? Only as to the *material and efficient causes* of them, and not as to the Forms. For example; if the cause of whiteness in snow or froth be inquired, and it be rendered thus, that the subtile intermixture of air and water is the cause, it is well rendered; but, nevertheless, is this the form of whiteness? No; but it is the efficient, which is ever but *vehiculum formæ.* This part of Metaphysic I do not find labored and performed: whereat I marvel not; because I hold it not possible to be invented by that course of invention which hath been used; in regard that men, which is the root of all error, have made too untimely a departure and too remote a recess from particulars.

But the use of this part of Metaphysic, which I report as deficient, is of the rest the most excellent in two respects: the one, because it is the duty and virtue of all knowledge to abridge the infinity of individual experience, as much as the conception of truth will permit, and to remedy the complaint of *vita brevis, ars longa;* which is performed by uniting the notions and conceptions of sciences: for knowledges are as pyramids, whereof history is the basis. So of natural philosophy, the basis is natural history; the stage next the basis is physic; the stage next the vertical point is metaphysic. As for the vertical point, *opus quod operatur Deus à principio usque ad finem,* the summary law of nature, we know not whether man's inquiry can attain unto it. But these three be the true stages of knowledge, and are to them that are depraved no better than the giant's hills:

> *Ter sunt conati imponere Pelio Ossam,*
> *Scilicet atque Ossæ frondosum involvere Olympum.*

But to those who refer all things to the glory of God, they are as the three acclamations, *Sancte, sancte, sancte!* holy in the description or dilatation of His works; holy in the connection or concatenation of them: and holy in the union of them in a perpetual and uniform law. And therefore the speculation was excellent in Parmenides and Plato, although but a speculation in them, that all things by scale did ascend to unity. So then always that knowledge is worthiest which is charged with least multiplicity; which appeareth to be metaphysic; as that which considereth the simple Forms or differences of things, which are few in number, and the degrees and co-ordinations whereof make all this variety.

The second respect, which valueth and commendeth this part of metaphysic, is that it doth enfranchise the power of man unto the greatest liberty and possibility of works and effects. For physic carrieth men in narrow and restrained ways, subject to many accidents of impediments, imitating the ordinary flexuous courses of nature; but *latæ undique sunt sapientibus viæ:* to sapience, which was anciently defined to be *rerum divinarum et humanarum scientia,* there is ever choice of means.

For physical causes give light to new invention in *simili materia;* but whosoever knoweth any Form, knoweth the utmost possibility of super-inducing that nature upon any variety of matter; and so is less restrained in operation, either to the basis of the matter, or the condition of the efficient; which kind of knowledge Salomon likewise, though in a more divine sort, elegantly describeth: *non arctabuntur gressus tui, et currens non habebis offendiculum.* The ways of sapience are not much liable either to particularity or chance.

The second part of metaphysic is the *inquiry of final causes,* which I am moved to report not as omitted, but as misplaced; and yet if it were but a fault in order, I would not speak of it: for order is matter of illustration, but pertaineth not to the substance of sciences. But this misplacing hath caused a deficience, or at least a great improficience in the sciences themselves. For the handling of final causes mixed with the rest in physical inquiries, hath intercepted the severe and diligent inquiry of all real and physical causes, and given men the occasion to stay upon these satisfactory and specious causes, to the great arrest and prejudice of further discovery. For this I find done not only by Plato, who ever anchoreth upon that shore, but by Aristotle, Galen, and others which do usually likewise fall upon these flats of discoursing causes. For to say *that the hairs of the eyelids are for a quickset and fence about the sight;* or that *the firmness of the skins and hides of living creatures is to defend them from the extremities of heat or cold;* or that *the bones are for the columns or beams, whereupon the frames of the bodies of living creatures are built:* or that *the leaves of trees are for protecting of the fruit;* or that *the clouds are for watering of the earth;* or that *the solidness of the earth is for the station and mansion of living creatures* and the like, is well inquired and collected in metaphysic, but in physic they are impertinent. Nay, they are indeed but *remoræ,* and hindrances to stay and slug the ship from further sailing; and have brought this to pass, that the search of the physical causes hath been neglected, and passed in silence. And therefore the natural philosophy of Democritus and some others (who did not suppose a mind or reason in the frame of things, but attributed the form thereof able to maintain itself to infinite essays or proofs of nature, which they term *fortune*) seemeth to me, as far as I can judge by the recital and fragments which remain unto us, in particularities of physical causes, more real and better inquired than that of Aristotle and Plato; whereof both intermingled final causes, the one as a part of theology, and the other as a part of logic, which were the favorite studies respectively of both those persons. Not because those final causes are not true, and worthy to be inquired, being kept within their own province; but because their excursions into the limits of physical causes hath bred a vastness and solitude in that track. For otherwise, keeping their precincts and borders, men are extremely deceived if they think there is an enmity or repugnancy at all between them. For the cause rendered, that *the hairs about the eye-lids are for the safeguard of the sight,* doth not impugn the cause rendered, that *pilosity is incident to orifices of moisture; muscosi fontes,* etc. Nor the cause rendered, *that the firmness of hides is for the armor of the body against extremities of heat* or *cold,* doth not impugn the cause rendered, *that contraction of pores is incident to the outwardest parts, in regard of their adjacence to foreign or unlike bodies:* and so of the rest: both causes being true and compatible, the one declaring an *intention,* the other a *consequence* only. Neither doth this call in question, or derogate from

Divine Providence, but highly confirm and exalt it. For as in civil actions he is the greater and deeper politic, that can make other men the instruments of his will and ends, and yet never acquaint them with his purpose, so as they shall do it and yet not know what they do, than he that imparteth his meaning to those he employeth; so is the wisdom of God more admirable, when nature intendeth one thing, and Providence draweth forth another, than if He communicated to particular creatures and motions the characters and impressions of His Providence. And thus much for metaphysic: the latter part whereof I allow as extant, but with it confined to his proper place.

Nevertheless there remaineth yet another part of Natural Philosophy, which is commonly made a principal part and holdeth rank with Physic special and Metaphysic, which is Mathematic; but I think it more agreeable to the nature of things and to the light of order to place it as a branch of Metaphysic: for the subject of it being *quantity* (not *quantity indefinite,* which is but a *relative,* and belongeth to *philosophia prima,* as hath been said, but *quantity determined or proportionable*) it appeareth to be one of the essential Forms of things; as that that is causative in nature of a number of effects; insomuch as we see, in the schools both of Democritus and of Pythagoras, that the one did ascribe figure to the first seeds of things, and the other did suppose numbers to be the principles and originals of things: and it is true also that of all other Forms, as we understand Forms, it is the most abstracted and separable from matter, and therefore most proper to Metaphysic; which hath likewise been the cause why it hath been better labored and inquired than any of the other Forms, which are more immersed in matter.

For it being the nature of the mind of man, to the

extreme prejudice of knowledge, to delight in the spacious liberty of generalities, as in a champain [1] region, and not in the inclosures of particularity; the Mathematics of all other knowledge were the goodliest fields to satisfy that appetite. But for the placing of this science, it is not much material: only we have endeavored in these our partitions to observe a kind of perspective, that one part may cast light upon another.

The Mathematics are either *pure* or *mixed*. To the Pure Mathematics are those sciences belonging which handle *quantity determinate,* merely severed from any axioms of natural philosophy; and these are two, Geometry and Arithmetic; the one handling quantity continued, and the other dissevered.

Mixed hath for subject some axioms or parts of natural philosophy, and considereth *quantity determined,* as it is auxiliary and incident unto them. For many parts of nature can neither be invented with sufficient subtilty, nor demonstrated with sufficient perspicuity, nor accommodated unto use with sufficient dexterity, without the aid and intervening of the mathematics; of which sort are *perspective, music, astronomy, cosmography, architecture, enginery,* and divers others.

In the Mathematics I can report no deficience, except it be that men do not sufficiently understand the excellent use of the Pure Mathematics, in that they do remedy and cure many defects in the wit and faculties intellectual. For if the wit be too dull, they sharpen it; if too wandering, they fix it; if too inherent in the sense, they abstract it. So that as tennis is a game of no use in itself, but of great use in respect it maketh a quick eye and a body ready to put itself into all postures; so in the Mathematics, that use which is collateral and intervenient is no less worthy than that which is principal

[1] open country

and intended. And as for the Mixed Mathematics, I may only make this prediction, that there cannot fail to be more kinds of them, as nature grows further disclosed. Thus much of Natural Science, or the part of nature speculative.

For Natural Prudence, or the part operative of Natural Philosophy, we will divide it into three parts, experimental, philosophical, and magical; which three parts active have a correspondence and analogy with the three parts speculative, natural history, physic, and metaphysic: for many operations have been invented, sometimes by a casual incidence and occurrence, sometimes by a purposed experiment: and of those which have been found by an intentional experiment, some have been found out by varying or extending the same experiments, some by transferring and compounding divers experiments the one into the other, which kind of invention an empiric may manage.

Again, by the knowledge of physical causes there cannot fail to follow many indications and designations of new particulars, if men in their speculation will keep one eye upon use and practice. But these are but coastings along the shore, *Premendo litus iniquum:* for it seemeth to me there can hardly be discovered any radical or fundamental alterations and innovations in nature, either by the fortune and essays of experiments, or by the light and direction of physical causes. If therefore we have reported Metaphysic deficient, it must follow that we do the like of natural Magic, which hath relation thereunto. For as for the Natural Magic whereof now there is mention in books, containing certain credulous and superstitious conceits and observations of sympathies and antipathies, and hidden properties, and some frivolous experiments, strange rather by disguisement than in themselves; it is as far differing in truth of nature from such a knowledge as we require, as the story of King Arthur of Britain, or Hugh of Bordeaux, differs from Cæsar's Commentaries in truth of story. For it is manifest that Cæsar did greater things *de vero* than those imaginary heroes were feigned to do; but he did them not in that fabulous manner. Of this kind of learning the fable of Ixion was a figure, who designed to enjoy Juno, the goddess of power; and instead of her had copulation with a cloud, of which mixture were begotten centaurs and chimeras. So whosoever shall entertain high and vaporous imaginations, instead of a laborious and sober inquiry of truth, shall beget hopes and beliefs of strange and impossible shapes.

And therefore we may note in these sciences which hold so much of imagination and belief, as this degenerate Natural Magic, Alchemy, Astrology, and the like, that in their propositions the description of the mean is ever more monstrous than the pretence or end. For it is a thing more probable, that he that knoweth well the natures of *weight,* of *color,* of *pliant,* and *fragile,* in respect of the hammer, of *volatile* and *fixed* in respect of the fire and the rest, may superinduce upon some metal the nature and Form of gold by such mechanic as belongeth to the production of the natures afore rehearsed, than that some grains of the medicine projected should in a few moments of time turn a sea of quicksilver or other material into gold: so it is more probable that he that knoweth the nature of arefaction, the nature of assimilation of nourishment to the thing nourished, the manner of increase and clearing of spirits, the manner of the depredations which spirits make upon the humors and solid parts, shall by ambages of diets, bathings, anointings, medicines, motions, and the like, prolong life or restore some degree of youth or vivacity, than that it can be done with the use of a few drops or scruples of a liquor or receipt. To conclude, therefore, the true Natural Magic, which is that great liberty and latitude of operation which dependeth upon the knowledge of Forms, I may report deficient, as the relative thereof is.

To which part, if we be serious, and incline not to vanities and plausible discourse, besides the deriving and deducing the operations themselves from Metaphysic, there are pertinent two points of much purpose, the one by way of preparation, the other by way of caution: the first is, that there be made a calendar, resembling an inventory of the estate of man, containing all the inventions, being the works or fruits of nature or art, which are now extant, and whereof man is already possessed; out of which doth naturally result a note, what things are yet held impossible, or not invented: which calendar will be the more artificial and serviceable, if to every reputed impossibility you add what thing is extant which cometh the nearest in degree to that impossibility; to the end that by these optatives and potentials man's inquiry may be more awake in deducing direction of works from the speculation of causes: and secondly, that those experiments be not only esteemed which have an immediate and present use, but those principally which are of most universal consequence for invention of other experiments, and those which give most light to the invention of causes; for the invention of the mariner's needle, which giveth the direction, is of no less benefit for navigation than the invention of the sails which give the motion.

Thus have I passed through Natural Philosophy, and the deficiencies thereof; wherein if I have differed from the ancient and received doctrines, and thereby shall move contradiction; for my part, as I affect not to dissent, so I purpose not to contend. If it be truth,

Non canimus surdis, respondent omnia sylvæ.

The voice of nature will consent, whether the voice of man do or no. And as Alexander Borgia was wont to say of the expedition of the French for Naples, that they came with chalk in their hands to mark up their lodgings, and not with weapons to fight; so I like better that entry of truth which cometh peaceably, with chalk to mark up those minds which are capable to lodge and harbor it, than that which cometh with pugnacity and contention.

(1605)

BEN JONSON (1573?-1637)

TIMBER, OR DISCOVERIES MADE UPON MEN AND MATTER

Censura de poetis.

NOTHING in our age, I have observed, is more preposterous than the running judgments upon poetry and poets; when we shall hear those things commended and cried up for the best writings which a man would scarce vouchsafe to wrap any wholesome drug in; he would never light his tobacco with them. And those men almost named for miracles, who yet are so vile that if a man should go about to examine and correct them, he must make all they have done but one blot. Their good is so entangled with their bad as forcibly one must draw on the other's death with it. A sponge dipped in ink will do all:—

> . . . *Comitetur Punica librum Spongia.* . . .
> *Et paulo post,*
> *Non possunt . . . multœ . . . una litura potest.*

Yet their vices have not hurt them; nay, a great many they have profited, for they have been loved for nothing else. And this false opinion grows strong against the best men, if once it take root with the ignorant. Cestius, in his time, was preferred to Cicero, so far as the ignorant durst. They learned him without book, and had him often in their mouths; but a man cannot imagine that thing so foolish or rude but will find and enjoy an admirer; at least a reader, or spectator. The puppets are seen now in despite of the players; Heath's epigrams and the Sculler's poems have their applause. There are never wanting those that dare prefer the worst preachers, the worst pleaders, the worst poets; not that the better have left to write or speak better, but that they that hear them judge worse; *Non illi pejus dicunt, sed hi corruptius judicant.* Nay, if it were put to the question of the water-rhymer's works, against Spenser's, I doubt not but they would find more suffrages; because the most favor common vices, out of a prerogative the vulgar have to lose their judgments and like that which is naught.

Poetry, in this latter age, hath proved but a mean mistress to such as have wholly addicted themselves to her, or given their names up to her family. They who have but saluted her on the by, and now and then tendered their visits, she hath done much for, and advanced in the way of their own professions (both the law and the gospel) beyond all they could have hoped, or done for themselves without her favor. Wherein she doth emulate the judicious but preposterous bounty of the time's grandees, who accumulate all they can upon the parasite or fresh-man in their friendship; but think an old client or honest servant bound by his place to write and starve.

Indeed, the multitude commend writers as they do fencers or wrestlers, who if they come in robustiously and put for it with a deal of violence, are received for the braver fellows; when many times their own rudeness is a cause of their disgrace, and a slight touch of their adversary gives all that boisterous force the foil. But in these things the unskilful are naturally deceived, and judging wholly by the bulk, think rude things greater than polished, and scattered more numerous than composed; nor think this only to be true in the sordid multitude, but the neater sort of our gallants; for all are the multitude, only they differ in clothes, not in judgment or understanding.

De Shakespeare nostrati.

I remember the players have often mentioned it as an honor to Shakespeare, that in his writing (whatsoever he penned) he never blotted out a line. My answer hath been, Would he had blotted a thousand. Which they thought a malevolent speech. I had not told posterity this, but for their ignorance, who chose that circumstance to commend their friend by, wherein he most faulted; and to justify mine own candor: for I loved the man, and do honor his memory, on this side idolatry, as much as any. He was (indeed) honest, and of an open and free nature; had an excellent phantasy, brave notions, and gentle expressions; wherein he flowed with that facility, that sometimes it was necessary he should be stopped. *Sufflaminandus erat,* as Augustus said of Haterius. His wit was in his own power, would the rule of it had been so too. Many times he fell into those things, could not escape laughter: as when he said in the person of Cæsar, one speaking to him, 'Cæsar, thou dost me wrong.' He replied, 'Cæsar did never wrong but with just cause,' and such like; which were ridiculous. But he redeemed his vices with his virtues. There was ever more in him to be praised than to be pardoned.

Dominus Verulamius.

One, though he be excellent, and the chief, is not to be imitated alone: for no imitator every grew up to his author; likeness is always on this side truth. Yet there happened in my time one noble speaker, who was full of gravity in his speaking. His language (where he could spare or pass by a jest) was nobly censorious. No man ever spake more neatly, more pressly,[1] more weightily, or suffered less emptiness, less idleness, in what he uttered. No member of his speech, but consisted of his own graces. His hearers could not cough, or look aside from him, without loss. He commanded where he spoke; and had his judges angry and pleased at his devotion. No man had their affections more in his power. The fear of every man that heard him was, lest he should make an end.

. . .

I have ever observed it to have been the office of a wise patriot, among the greatest affairs of the state, to take care of the commonwealth of learning. For schools, they are the seminaries of state; and nothing is worthier the study of a statesman than that part of the republic

[1] concisely

which we call the advancement of letters. Witness the care of Julius Cæsar, who, in the heat of the civil war, writ his books of Analogy and dedicated them to Tully. This made the late Lord St. Alban entitle his work *Novum Organum;* which, though by the most of superficial men, who cannot get beyond the title of nominals, it is not penetrated nor understood, it really openeth all defects of learning whatsoever, and is a book

Qui longum noto scriptori proroget ævum.

My conceit of his person was never increased toward him by his place or honors; but I have and do reverence him for the greatness that was only proper to himself, in that he seemed to me ever, by his work, one of the greatest men and most worthy of admiration, that had been in many ages. In his adversity I ever prayed that God would give him strength; for greatness he could not want. Neither could I condole in a word or syllable for him, as knowing no accident could do harm to virtue, but rather help to make it manifest.

Consuetudo, etc.

Custom is the most certain mistress of language, as the public stamp makes the current money. But we must not be too frequent with the mint, every day coming, nor fetch words from the extreme and utmost ages; since the chief virtue of a style is perspicuity, and nothing so vicious in it as to need an interpreter. Words borrowed of antiquity do lend a kind of majesty to style, and are not without their delight sometimes. For they have the authority of years, and out of their intermission do win themselves a kind of grace-like newness. But the eldest of the present, and newness of the past language, is the best. For what was the ancient language, which some men so dote upon, but the ancient custom? Yet when I name custom, I understand not the vulgar custom; for that were a precept no less dangerous to language than life, if we should speak or live after the manners of the vulgar: but that I call custom of speech, which is the consent of the learned; as custom of life, which is the consent of the good. Virgil was most loving of antiquity; yet how rarely doth he insert *aquai,* and *pictai!* Lucretius is scabrous and rough in these; he seeks them: as some do Chaucerisms with us, which were better expunged and banished. Some words are to be culled out for ornament and color, as we gather flowers to strow houses, or make garlands; but they are better when they grow to our style; as in a meadow, where though the mere grass and greenness delight, yet the variety of flowers doth heighten and beautify. Marry we must not play or riot with them too much, as in Paronomasies; nor use too swelling or ill-sounding words; *Quæ per salebras, altaque saxa cadunt.* It is true there is no sound but shall find some lovers, as the bitterest confections are grateful to some palates. Our composition must be more accurate in the beginning and end than in the midst, and in the end more than in the beginning; for through the midst the stream bears us. And this is attained by custom more than care or diligence. We must express readily and fully, not profusely. There is difference between a liberal and prodigal hand. As it is a great point of art, when our matter requires it, to enlarge and veer out all sail; so to take it in and contract it, is of no less praise, when the argument doth ask it. Either of them hath their fitness in the place. A good man always profits by his endeavor, by his help, yea, when he is absent, nay, when he is dead, by his example and memory. So good authors in their style: a strict and succinct style is that, where you can take away nothing without loss, and that loss to be manifest.

(printed 1641)

LYRICS.

HYMN TO DIANA

(From *Cynthia's Revels*)

QUEEN and huntress, chaste and fair,
Now the sun is laid to sleep,
Seated in thy silver chair,
State in wonted manner keep:
  Hesperus entreats thy light,
  Goddess excellently bright.

Earth, let not thy envious shade
Dare itself to interpose;
Cynthia's shining orb was made
Heaven to clear when day did close: 10
  Bless us then with wishèd sight,
  Goddess excellently bright.

Lay thy bow of pearl apart
And thy crystal-shining quiver;
Give unto the flying hart
Space to breathe, how short soever:
  Thou that makest a day of night,
  Goddess excellently bright.

(1600)

EPITAPH ON S[ALATHIEL] P[AVY]

(From *Epigrams*)

WEEP with me all you that read
      This little story;
And know, for whom a tear you shed,
      Death's self is sorry.
'T was a child, that so did thrive
      In grace and feature,
As heaven and nature seemed to strive
      Which owned the creature.
Years he numbered scarce thirteen
      When fates turned cruel;   10
Yet three filled zodiacs [1] had he been
      The stage's jewel;
And did act, what now we moan,
      Old men so duly;
As, sooth, the Parcæ thought him one,
      He played so truly.
So, by error, to his fate
      They all consented;
But viewing him since, alas, too late!
      They have repented;   20
And have sought, to give new birth,
      In baths to steep him;
But, being so much too good for earth,
      Heaven vows to keep him.

                                        (1616)

[1] three whole years

SONG

(From *The Poetaster*)

IF I freely may discover
What would please me in my lover,
I would have her fair and witty,
Savoring more of court than city;
A little proud, but full of pity;
Light and humorous in her toying;
Oft building hopes, and soon destroying;
Long, but sweet in the enjoying;
Neither too easy nor too hard:
All extremes I would have barred.   10

She should be allowed her passions,
So they were but used as fashions;
Sometimes froward, and then frowning,
Sometimes sickish, and then swowning;
Every fit with change still crowning.
Purely jealous I would have her;
Then only constant when I crave her;
'Tis a virtue should not save her.
Thus, nor her delicates would cloy me,
Neither her peevishness annoy me.   20

(1602)

TO CELIA

(From *The Forest*)

DRINK to me only with thine eyes,
     And I will pledge with mine;

Or leave a kiss but in the cup,
   And I'll not look for wine.
The thirst that from the soul doth rise,
   Doth ask a drink divine:
But might I of Jove's nectar sup,
   I would not change for thine.

I sent thee late a rosy wreath,
   Not so much honoring thee   10
As giving it a hope that there
   It could not withered be.
But thou thereon didst only breathe,
   And sent'st it back to me:
Since when it grows, and smells, I swear,
   Not of itself, but thee.

                       (1616)

SONG: TO CELIA

(From *Volpone*)

COME, my Celia, let us prove,
While we may, the sports of love;
Time will not be ours for ever:
He at length our good will sever.
Spend not then his gifts in vain:
Suns that set, may rise again;
But if once we lose this light,
'T is with us perpetual night.
Why should we defer our joys?
Fame and rumor are but toys.   10
Cannot we delude the eyes
Of a few poor household spies?
Or his easier ears beguile,
Thus removèd by our wile?

'T is no sin love's fruits to steal,
But the sweet theft to reveal:
To be taken, to be seen,
These have crimes accounted been.

(1605?)

SIMPLEX MUNDITIIS

(From *Epicœne*)

STILL to be neat, still to be drest,
As you were going to a feast;
Still to be powdered, still perfumed:
Lady, it is to be presumed,
Though art's hid causes are not found,
All is not sweet, all is not sound.

Give me a look, give me a face,
That makes simplicity a grace;
Robes loosely flowing, hair as free:
Such sweet neglect more taketh me   10
Than all the adulteries of art;
They strike mine eyes, but not my heart.

(1609?)

THAT WOMEN ARE BUT MEN'S SHADOWS

(From *The Forest*)

FOLLOW a shadow, it still flies you;
  Seem to fly it, it will pursue:
So court a mistress, she denies you;
  Let her alone, she will court you.
Say, are not women truly, then,
Styled but the shadows of us men?

At morn and even, shades are longest,
   At noon they are or short, or none:
So, men at weakest, they are strongest;
   But grant us perfect, they're not known.   10
Say, are not women truly, then,
Styled but the shadows of us men?

                       (1616)

ON MY FIRST SON

(From *Epigrams*)

FAREWELL, thou child of my right hand, and joy!
My sin was too much hope of thee, loved boy;
Seven years thou wert lent to me, and I thee pay,
Exacted by thy fate, on the just day.
Oh, could I lose all father now! For why
Will man lament the state he should envy—
To have so soon 'scaped world's and flesh's rage,
And, if no other misery, yet age?
Rest in soft peace, and, asked, say here doth lie
Ben Jonson his best piece of poetry: 10
For whose sake, henceforth, all his vows be such
As what he loves may never like too much.

                       (1616)

TO THE MEMORY OF MY BELOVED MASTER WILLIAM SHAKESPEARE

To DRAW no envy, Shakespeare, on thy name,
Am I thus ample to thy book and fame;
While I confess thy writings to be such
As neither man, nor muse, can praise too much.
'T is true, and all men's suffrage. But these ways
Were not the paths I meant unto thy praise;

For silliest ignorance on these may light,
Which, when it sounds at best, but echoes right;
Or blind affection, which doth ne'er advance
The truth, but gropes, and urgeth all by chance;   10
Or crafty malice might pretend this praise,
And think to ruin, where it seemed to raise.
These are, as some infamous bawd or whore
Should praise a matron. What could hurt her more?
But thou art proof against them, and, indeed,
Above the ill fortune of them, or the need.
I therefore will begin. Soul of the age!
The applause, delight, the wonder of our stage!
My Shakespeare, rise! I will not lodge thee by
Chaucer, or Spenser, or bid Beaumont lie   20
A little further off to make thee room:
Thou art a monument without a tomb,
And art alive still, while thy book doth live
And we have wits to read, and praise to give.
That I not mix thee so, my brain excuses,
I mean with great, but disproportioned Muses;
For if I thought my judgment were of years,
I should commit thee surely with thy peers,
And tell how far thou didst our Lyly outshine,
Or sporting Kyd, or Marlowe's mighty line.   30
And though thou hadst small Latin and less Greek,
From thence to honor thee, I will not seek
For names: but call forth thundering Æschylus,
Euripides, and Sophocles to us,
Pacuvius, Accius, him of Cordova dead,
To life again, to hear thy buskin tread,
And shake a stage; or, when thy socks were on,
Leave thee alone for the comparison
Of all that insolent Greece, or haughty Rome
Sent forth, or since did from their ashes come.   40
Triumph, my Britain, thou hast one to show,

To whom all scenes of Europe homage owe.
He was not of an age, but for all time!
And all the Muses still were in their prime,
When, like Apollo, he came forth to warm
Our ears, or like a Mercury to charm!
Nature herself was proud of his designs,
And joyed to wear the dressing of his lines,
Which were so richly spun, and woven so fit,
As, since, she will vouchsafe no other wit.   50
The merry Greek, tart Aristophanes,
Neat Terence, witty Plautus, now not please;
But antiquated and deserted lie,
As they were not of nature's family.
Yet must I not give nature all; thy art,
My gentle Shakespeare, must enjoy a part:
For though the poet's matter nature be,
His art doth give the fashion: and, that he
Who casts to write a living line, must sweat,
(Such as thine are) and strike the second heat   60
Upon the Muse's anvil; turn the same,
And himself with it, that he thinks to frame;
Or for the laurel, he may gain a scorn;
For a good poet's made, as well as born.
And such wert thou! Look how the father's face
Lives in his issue, even so the race
Of Shakespeare's mind and manners brightly shines
In his well turnèd, and true filèd lines;
In each of which he seems to shake a lance,
As brandished at the eyes of ignorance.   70
Sweet Swan of Avon! what a sight it were
To see thee in our water yet appear,
And make those flights upon the banks of Thames,
That so did take Eliza, and our James!
But stay, I see thee in the hemisphere

Advanced, and made a constellation there!
Shine forth, thou star of poets, and with rage,
Or influence, chide, or cheer the drooping stage,
Which, since thy flight from hence, hath mourned like
      night,
And despairs day, but for thy volume's light.   80
                      (1623)

TO HEAVEN

(From *The Forest*)

Good and great God! can I not think of thee,
But it must straight my melancholy be?
Is it interpreted in me disease,
That, laden with my sins, I seek for ease?
O be thou witness, that the reins dost know
And hearts of all, if I be sad for show;
And judge me after, if I dare pretend
To aught but grace, or aim at other end.
As thou art all, so be thou all to me,
First, midst, and last, converted One and Three!   10
My faith, my hope, my love; and, in this state,
My judge, my witness, and my advocate!
Where have I been this while exiled from thee,
And whither rapt, now thou but stoop'st to me?
Dwell, dwell here still! O, being everywhere,
How can I doubt to find thee ever here?
I know my state, both full of shame and scorn,
Conceived in sin, and unto labor born,
Standing with fear, and must with horror fall,
And destined unto judgment, after all.   20
I feel my griefs too, and there scarce is ground
Upon my flesh t' inflict another wound;

Yet dare I not complain or wish for death
With holy Paul, lest it be thought the breath
Of discontent; or that these prayers be
For weariness of life, not love of thee.

(1616)

NOTES

EARLY TUDOR LYRICS

Sir Thomas Wyatt, (1503?–1542) educated at Cambridge, a courtier and royal ambassador, wrote his lyrics under the influence of French and Italian fashions, imitating Petrarch in his sonnets and employing many new lyric forms. His verse is not smooth or fluent, but he did much to establish the vogue of the lyric in England. Most of his poems appeared long after his death in *Tottel's Miscellany*, 1557 (see *Introduction*, p. xxv).

Page   5, l. 1. This sonnet is a translation of Petrarch's sonnet 140; the next is from Petrarch's sonnet 156.

         6, l. 6. **Seneca.** Seneca, Roman Stoic philosopher and writer of tragedies (first century A.D.).

         7, l. 19. **John Poins.** A personal friend of Wyatt's, to whom he wrote other verse.

         9, l. 4. **Rood.** The Cross; an old English oath.

Henry Howard, the Earl of Surrey (1517?–1547), was a courtier-poet like Wyatt, but of higher rank and greater political power. Impetuous and proud, he aroused the envy and hatred of the cliques which formed about Henry VIII, and was finally beheaded for treason. His poetic gifts were greater than Wyatt's; his command of language and verse form, his lightness of touch, his easy assimilation of the poetic manners of the continental Renaissance, his happy alteration of the Italian sonnet into an English form—all combine to give him first place among the early Tudor writers. In his translation of Virgil's *Æneid* he used blank verse for the first time in English poetry, although Nicholas Grimald was then experimenting in this form. Most of Surrey's poems were published first in *Tottel's Miscellany*, 1557.

         12, l. 10. **Cyprus.** This island in the Mediterranean was one of Venus' favorite haunts.

         13, l. 9. This poem is similar to that by Heywood on the same theme (see p. 21).

         14, l. 14. **Martial.** The Roman poet (43–104 A.D.), who wrote the epigram here rendered into English.

         15, l. 5. **encreased by disdain,** *i.e.*, made better by his modesty toward them.

         l. 24. **none affect,** *i.e.*, no amount of affection or self-interest.

JOHN HEYWOOD (1497–1578?), a courtier, poet, musician, and writer of early comedies, shows in his work little of the influences of Petrarch or the humanists. He wrote many ballads and lyrics to accompany his music, and in most of his work shows a homely English quality quite different from the Italianate graces of Wyatt and Surrey (see *Introduction*, pp. xxii, xxviii).

18, l. 2. This is the earliest of many "Willow" ballads. Note *Othello*, act iv, scene 3; also the "Titwillow" song in *The Mikado*.

l. 23. **all amiss.** A pun is attempted in *almès* (alms) and *all amiss*. This playing upon words (as in the next poem, on the word *mean*) was a reputable poetic device in the sixteenth century.

l. 28. **sow,** *i.e.,* a large mass. (In pouring pig-iron, the central mass is still called the sow.)

21, l. 9. This poem was written in 1534 as a compliment to Princess Mary Tudor, on her eighteenth birthday. When it was later printed in *Tottel's Miscellany* it was changed so that the lady could not be identified as the Queen of England.

l. 19. **naked boy.** A cupid.

l. 27. **Phœnix.** A legendary bird which burned itself on the altar and rose from its ashes, renewed in youth.

THOMAS, LORD VAUX (1510–1556), a courtier-poet like Wyatt and Surrey, is more serious and reflective in tone than the others. He also wrote religious poems.

25, l. 17. **a pickaxe and a spade.** The grave-digger in *Hamlet*, act v, scene 1, sings a corrupted version of this song. Note also William Blake's song, *My silks and fine array*, stanza 3.

l. 21. **clark,** clerk. This pronunciation is still used in England.

THOMAS NORTON (1532–1584), a minor poet whose chief fame is derived from his collaboration with Thomas Sackville in writing *Gorboduc*, the first English tragedy, written in blank verse and employing the methods of Seneca (see *Introduction*, p. xxviii). In addition to some courtly lyrics, Norton wrote, with others, a lyrical version of the Psalms.

27, l. 2. **knot, etc.,** *i.e.,* a group of people of noble birth. Refers to the slaying of the suitors of Penelope by her returned husband, as told in Homer's *Odyssey*.

ANONYMOUS

l. 29. **feater cast.** A neater trick, or throw, as in dice.

28, l. 22. **lime.** Birdlime, a sticky substance used to catch small birds.

THOMAS SACKVILLE

THOMAS SACKVILLE (1536–1608), studied law at the Inner Temple, but gave much of his time to literary work. A cultivated gentleman, he was raised to the peerage, as Lord Buckhurst, in 1567. He became chancellor of Oxford University, and enjoyed many honors and high appointments. His *Induction* was written as a poetic introduction to the *Mirror for Magistrates*, and to this collection he also contributed one tale, the *Complaint of Henry, Duke of Buckingham* (see *Introduction*, p. xxiii). His work is the best in the *Mirror;* in fact, it is generally said that he is the best poet between Chaucer and Spenser. With Thomas Norton he wrote the first English tragedy, *Gorboduc.* The *Induction* is an interesting combination of medieval and renaissance elements. The use of the seven-line Chaucerian stanza, the lengthy astrological reference, and the extended treatment of allegorical figures are all derived from his Middle English predecessors. But as a renaissance student he draws on Virgil, especially the sixth book of the *Æneid*, and crowds his lines with allusions to classical myth and story. The scenes through which Sorrow leads him anticipate several episodes in Spenser's *Faerie Queene.*

THE INDUCTION

33, l. 11. **tapets.** Figurative reference to foliage. *Tapet* means tapestry.

l. 15. **Boreas.** The north wind.

34, l. 3. **Hermes.** Mercury, messenger of the gods.

l. 4. **Mars.** God of war.

l. 6. **Virgo.** The Virgin, a sign of the zodiac, a constellation.

l. 7. **Thetis.** A goddess of the sea.

l. 8. **Scorpio, Sagittarius.** Scorpion and Archer, signs of the zodiac.

l. 11. **Bear.** A constellation.

l. 15. **Phaeton.** Son of Phœbus Apollo; here, the god of the sun.

l. 18. **Erythius.** Erithius, one of the many titles of Apollo; "God of reapers."

l. 21. **Titan.** The sun. It seems that Sackville is confused in these various allusions to sun myths.

l. 22. **Cynthea.** Cynthia, the moon.

35, l. 9. **Phœbus.** The sun god. See Phaeton, above.

36, l. 29. **Furies.** The Eumenides, daughters of Night, who punished guilty souls.

37, l. 1. **Lethe.** The river Oblivion, in Hades.

38, l. 5. **Æolus.** God of the winds.

l. 26. **glass.** Mirror, as in the title, *Mirror for Magistrates.*

40, l. 14. **cleped is Avern,** *i.e.*, is called Avernus; a lake near Naples, believed to be the entrance to Hades.

42, l. 24. **toil.** Rimes with *while* in sixteenth century pronunciation.

43, l. 9. **Crœsus.** Wealthy king of Lydia, about 550 B.C. **Irus,** a beggar in Homer's *Odyssey*, whom Ulysses overcomes.

l. 14. **Sisters.** The three Fates.

44, l. 16. **went on three feet.** Recalls the ancient riddle; what animal walks in the morning on four feet, at noon on two, and in the evening on three? The answer is man, who as a child crawls on all fours, in his maturity walks on his two feet, and in his old age hobbles with a staff or crutch.

46, l. 7. **parde.** French *par Dieu*, here means indeed.

l. 29. **Darius.** King of Persia. Darius III was defeated by **Macedo** (p. 47, l. 1), or Alexander the Great, King of Macedon.

47, l. 4. **Hannibal.** Led Carthaginian army against Romans, victorious at River Trebia (218 B.C.), at Lake Trasimene (217), and at Cannæ (216) where the consul Paulus was killed. He was finally defeated by Scipio Africanus at Zama, in Africa.

l. 13. **Pompey and Cæsar.** Opponents in civil war, ending in Pompey's defeat and murder at Pharsalia, 48 B.C.

l. 17. **Sulla and Marius.** Antagonists in another Roman civil war, 88 B.C.

l. 19. **Cyrus.** Rebelled against his brother Artaxerxes of Persia, was defeated and slain at Cunaxa, 401 B.C. His mother, the Queen Parysatis, was said to have tortured and butchered his enemies which she captured.

l. 22. **Xerxes** (519?–464 B.C.). Was defeated at Salamis, in his invasion of Greece.

l. 26. **Thebes.** A city in Bœotia, Greece, destroyed by Alexander the Great.

l. 27. **Tyrus.** Tyre, in Phœnicia, which fell before Alexander.

48, l. 12. **Hector.** Son of Priam, king of Troy.

l. 26. **Cassandra.** A prophetess, daughter of Priam, taken as captive by Agamemnon from the temple of Pallas Athene.

49, l. 13. **Acheron.** One of the rivers in Hades over which old Charon ferried the souls of the dead.

l. 30. **three-sound bark.** From the three heads which the watch-dog Cerberus possessed.

JOHN FOXE

JOHN FOXE (1516–1587) studied at Oxford, where he took his A.B. and M.A. degrees, but because of his extreme Protestant views re-signal a fellowship and left the university in 1545. During Queen Mary's rule he avoided persecution by leaving the country, returning, under Elizabeth, to write his *Acts and Monuments*. This is a decidedly partisan account of the Protestant martyrs, and was later augmented by other material relating to general Christian martyrdom. It is valuable for the vivid picture it gives of the social and religious background of the English Renaissance.

Hugh Latimer (1491–1555) was a brilliant and forceful preacher who advocated the Protestant cause. He, like Cranmer, sanctioned Henry VIII's divorce from Katherine, and won thereby the enmity of their daughter Mary Tudor. He became Bishop of Worcester and adviser to Cranmer, Archbishop of Canterbury. He was convicted of heresy under Queen Mary, and was sentenced to die on Oct. 16, 1555.

Nicholas Ridley, like Latimer, attacked the Roman Catholic doctrine of transubstantiation, which eventually caused his death for heresy. He was chaplain to Archbishop Cranmer, and became Bishop of Rochester.

Acts and Monuments

52, l. 6. **Bocardo.** A prison in the building at the old North Gate at Oxford.

l. 7. **Cranmer.** Thomas, Archbishop of Canterbury, was here being tried for heresy. He was burned at the stake in 1556. Foxe gives a stirring account of his death.

53, l. 15. **Œcolampadians,** followers of John Œcolampadius (Hussgen) (1482–1531), a Swiss reformer, friend of Huldreich Zwingli, and a supporter of Luther. Although differing from Zwingli on minor points of doctrine, he agreed in general with all Protestant attitudes toward the Roman Catholic doctrines.

54, l. 34. **groat.** A silver coin of trifling value.

56, l. 34. **In manus tuas, etc.** "Into thy hands, O Lord, I commit my spirit."

ROGER ASCHAM

Roger Ascham (1515–1568) became prominent among English humanists through his studies at St. John's College, Cambridge. His *Toxophilus* (1545) combines a discussion of archery and learning, full of enthusiasm for the old English sport and patriotism, and won for him a royal pension. He was appointed tutor to Princess (later Queen) Elizabeth. He served as secretary under Queen Mary, and later led the Protestants in their opposition to Catholic influences from abroad. His theories on the education of youth were humane and enlightened.

The Schoolmaster

59, l. 8. This book, as Ascham states in his preface, was written at the instigation of Sir Richard Sackville, treasurer of the Exchequer, who sought Ascham's advice concerning the education of his grandson, Robert Sackville.

61, l. 15. Thomas Watson, (1513–1584) was a student, later fellow, at St. John's College, Cambridge. He was active in the humanist group there; a neo-classical play, *Absolom*, is chief among his literary exercises. He was pro-Catholic in his attitude, and through Bishop Gairdner became master of St. John's College, and was later made Bishop of Lincoln under Queen Mary. He was imprisoned and deprived of his bishopric early in Elizabeth's reign.

l. 18. barbarous riming. See *Introduction*, pp. xxxviii, xxxix.

62, l. 6. Pallas. Athene, goddess of wisdom.

l. 10. Alcinous. King of the Phæacians (Corfu), who with his daughter Nausicaa entertained Ulysses. This and the following allusions come from Homer's *Odyssey*. **Cyclops.** A race of one-eyed giants dwelling in Sicily. **Calypso.** A nymph of Ogygia, the island on which Ulysses was shipwrecked. **Scylla and Charybdis.** Sea monsters who commanded the Gulf of Messina, and who snatched at ships and sailors passing between them. **Circe.** An enchantress whose drink transformed her guests into swine. **Tiresias.** A seer, blinded by Athene, but given the knowledge of the language of the birds and the power to prophesy.

63, l. 1. moly, a fabled plant of magic properties. A wild garlic is known by the same name today.

64, l. 4. λήθην, etc. These words may be translated, respectively, forgetfulness, dulness, folly, insolence.

65, l. 1. Jeremiah. iv, 22. Ascham makes his own translation of this verse.

l. 9. Hesiod. Greek poet, eighth century B.C., who wrote the *Theogony*, the *Works and Days*, *The Shield of Heracles*.

l. 25. Dionysius. King of Syracuse, in Sicily, who invited Plato to set up his ideal republic in his land. They eventually quarreled, Plato was held captive and ransomed by a friend.

l. 28. Nolite, etc. "Be ye not as the horse, or as the mule." Ps. xxxii, 9.

66, l. 2. Diverte, etc. "Depart from evil, and do good." Ps. xxxiv, 14.

l. 24. Inglese, etc. An Italianate Englishman is a devil incarnate.

67, l. 25. Paul's Cross. A cross in the yard of St. Paul's, London, from which public sermons were preached.

l. 31. **Louvain.** From this Belgian city Catholic books and pamphlets were issued for use in the English religious controversy.

70, l. 16. **abominabiles, etc.** "Made detestable in their studies."

l. 17. **Dixit, etc.** "The fool hath said in his heart there is no God." Ps. xiv, 1.

l. 24. **Triumphs of Petrarch.** An allegorical poem, celebrating historic events and persons.

l. 25. **Tully's Offices.** Marcus Tullius Cicero's (106–43 B.C.) essay *De Officiis* (On Duties).

l. 26. **Boccaccio.** Reference is to his *Decamerone*, a collection of one hundred *novelle* (see *Introduction*, p. xxxiv).

71, l. 11. ἄθεοι, godless.

l. 26. **mysteries of Moses.** Ancient Jewish rites in Leviticus and Deuteronomy.

l. 32. **Credat, etc.** Let the Jew Appella believe it. Horace, *Satires*, i, 5, 100.

72, l. 12. **Pygius.** Albert Pighius (1490–1542), a Catholic controversialist and scholar whom Calvin opposed. **Machiavelli** (1469–1527), Italian courtier and writer, famous for his *The Prince*, a book which urges shrewd cunning rather than fairness and honesty in affairs of state.

73, l. 21. **Bridewell.** An old London prison.

l. 25. **present Pope.** Pius V (1566–1572).

74, l. 4. **Guelph.** The papal or Church party, opposed by the Ghibelines, the Roman Empire party, in a long struggle during the Middle Ages.

RALPH HOLINSHED

RALPH (or Raphael) HOLINSHED (died about 1580) was for many years the general editor of a project which was to have been a universal history, later confined to the chronicles of England, Scotland, and Ireland. This became the great, popular history of the Elizabethans (see *Introduction*, p. xxxvii). Most of the English chronicle he penned himself. The description of Elizabeth's procession through London is the work of George Ferrers (1500–1579), a gentleman who attended the Queen on this occasion. Ferrers was a courtier-poet, and one of the group which began the *Mirror for Magistrates*.

CHRONICLES OF ENGLAND, ETC.

76, l. 16. **Fores.** A castle and town on Moray Firth, northeast Scotland.

77, l. 18. **weird sisters.** In Old English *wyrd* was fate; these are comparable to the three Fates of classical myth.

78, l. 17. **pretend to the crown,** *i.e.,* lay claim to it, because Macbeth was Duncan's first cousin.

80, l. 31. **men of Cyprus.** Richard took affront at the inhospitality of the Cyprians when one of the ships of his fleet (bearing his betrothed bride) was stranded on their shore. He conquered the island and garrisoned it with his men.

l. 32. **Acres.** Acre, a sea-port in Syria which had been under siege for several years previous.

81, l. 30. **Saladin.** The Turkish Sultan.

82, l. 28. **Fleetbridge.** A bridge on Fleet Street, over Fleet Brook, just beyond Ludgate, outside the wall of the old city.

l. 29. **Westminster.** Then west of the old city, a separate town.

84, l. 13. **pikes.** Men armed with long poles tipped with iron points. **shot.** Men armed with firearms. **halberdiers.** Foot soldiers armed with pikes which had long blades.

l. 15. **Almaine rivets.** A light flexible armor of overlapping plates sliding on rivets; invented in Germany.

l. 16. **crafts and companies.** The crafts-guilds and liveried trades-guilds or corporations, surviving from the Middle Ages.

l. 21. **Bridges,** probably **Bruges.** In Belgium, famous for its cloth.

l. 22. **sarsenet.** A fine, soft silk used in linings.

85, l. 6. **Miles End.** An open green in the suburbs, about a mile east of the city limits, near Stepney Church. **St. George's field,** an open field, used for archery contests and games, near St. George's Church, on the south side of the Thames, southwest of the town of Southwark.

JOHN LYLY

JOHN LYLY (1554?–1606), was the grandson of William Lilly, the grammarian and humanist. He studied at Magdalen College, Oxford, where he took his M.A. in 1575. Lyly attempted to win his way as a courtier, and tried unsuccessfully several times to obtain the Mastership of the Queen's Revels. He was a minor official in the royal household. His *Euphues, The Anatomy of Wit* (1578) made him famous, and its immediate success moved him to write a sequel, *Euphues and his England* (1580), which made still more popular his ornate prose style. It even came to be the fashion to "speak Euphues" at the court of Elizabeth, (see *Introduction,* p. xxxiii, also p. xxxiv). Under the patronage of the Earl of Oxford, he succeeded in becoming the first of the court dramatists. Beginning in 1581, he produced a series of fanciful and witty comedies, eight of which have been preserved, (see *Introduction*, p. xxx). Lyly also engaged in the religious controversy between the Anglican party and the Puritans. This probably hurt his chances for preferment at court. Although his prose style is today a curiosity, and his dramatic work fell out of fashion after 1590, he represents to us the artifice and grace of the courtly literature during the height of Elizabeth's reign.

EUPHUES, THE ANATOMY OF WIT

86, l. 3. **A Cooling Card.** This witty essay is supposed to be a pamphlet written by the hero of the book, Euphues, to his friend Philautus. These two young men loved Lucilla, who after leaving Philautus for Euphues, deserted Euphues for another lover, Curio. Euphues here fortifies himself and all lovers against women by this pleasant diatribe. Incidentally, the passage is a free paraphrase of Ovid's *Remedies for Love.*

l. 24. **turn my tippet,** *i.e.,* to change sides; a folk saying.

l. 31. **old huddle, and twang, etc.,** *i.e.,* though Curio be cuddled, and sing "I'm the boy!"

87, l. 28. **Achilles's spear.** Lyly is here paraphrasing Ovid, *Rem. Am.* lines 41 ff.

l. 30. **Nerius.** Dogbane, a medicinal plant. It does not, however, poison sheep or other animals.

l. 34. **run with the hare, etc.** A folk saying, as is to carry fire, etc.

88, l. 7. **Phyllis.** A legendary Thracian princess, betrothed to Demophoon, son of Theseus, who hanged herself when deserted.

l. 9. **Pasiphae.** Legendary wife of Minos; mother of Ariadne, also of the Minotaur, a monster.

l. 10. **Phedra.** Phædra, who married Theseus, fell in love with his son Hippolytus, her step-son. This story is the subject of a tragedy by Euripides.

90, l. 10. **a town in Spain, etc.** This passage (like many others of Lyly's amazing natural history) comes from Pliny; viii.

l. 35. **wife of Darius, etc.** Reference taken from Plutarch's *Life of Alexander.*

91, l. 4. **Panthea.** Wife of Abradatus, king of Susa. The incident is taken from Xenophon's *Cyropædia,* and is also used by Plutarch.

l. 11. **Agesilaus.** Spartan king and conqueror (444?–360 B.C.).

l. 12. **Diogenes.** (Laertius) a Greek writer of second century. Reference probably taken from Erasmus' *Apophthegms.*

l. 30. **abbey-lubbers.** Monks; a Protestant epithet common in the sixteenth century.

93, l. 3. **Galen . . . Justinian, etc.,** *i.e.,* the practice of medicine is full of profit, of law, full of honors. Galen was a Greek philosopher and writer on medicine (131–201 A.D.). The Emperor Justinian I (483–565) codified the Roman law.

94, l. 6. **Silvacenda.** A confusion of Pliny's *silva ædua* (coppice-wood). Pharos is an island near Alexandria. The next sentence is also from Pliny, xvi.

98, l. 11. **stand thou on thy pantofles,** *i.e.,* be proud. Pantofles frequently had thick soles and heels of cork, and so increased the wearer's height.

l. 27. **Asiarchus.** Thought to be an imaginary character; Biarus also.

Songs from Plays

101, l. 7. **prick-song.** Music. The notes of music were called pricks or prickings.

l. 18. **Oyes.** From French *oyez,* "hear ye!"—a court summons.

SIR PHILIP SIDNEY

Sir Philip Sidney (1554–1586) seems to have embodied all the ideals of the renaissance gentleman. He was educated at Shrewsbury School and at Oxford. In 1571 he toured the continent, as was the fashion of young gentlemen of his rank. He became a trusted courtier and diplomat, as popular in the courts of Europe as at that of his Queen. He was a precocious and studious young man, an expert horseman and gallant soldier; he was esteemed as a scholar and philosopher by eminent humanists in Germany and Italy, with whom he corresponded, and was urged as a candidate for the throne of Poland; he was a patron of poets and artists, and himself a poet, romancer, literary critic, prominent among the great figures of his age. Because of his activities in opposition to the proposed marriage of the Queen to the Duke of Anjou, he was forced to retire from the court to Wilton, the home of his sister, the Countess of Pembroke, in 1580. While there he wrote his long romance, *Arcadia,* which circulated widely in manuscripts before its publication in 1595, (see *Introduction,* p. xxxv). Sidney's critical work, the *Defense of Poesie,* is the most important essay of its kind in the period. This is a reply to Stephen Gosson's *School of Abuse* (1579), an attack on poetry for its immorality. With grace and humor he establishes the moral elevation of poetry, and then proceeds to suggest improvements in the literary practice of his contemporaries, (see *Introduction,* p. xxxix.) In 1585 he was appointed Governor of Flushing, in the Low Countries. During the siege of Zutphen he was mortally wounded in an engagement with a Spanish convoy, and died in October, 1586.

THE DEFENSE OF POESIE

103, l. 20. **imputations.** Sidney here makes direct answer to Gosson's attack.

104, l. 2. **ere.** Chaucer (whom Sidney does not quote exactly) uses this expression, *Knight's Tale*, l. 28.

l. 8. **commonwealth.** Plato would exclude poets from his ideal republic. This attitude is not consistent with other statements which he makes about poetry.

l. 12. **petere principium.** To seek the beginning.

105, l. 13. **Nathan.** II Samuel, xii. Nathan tells the parable of the ewe lamb, and thus makes David judge his own conduct thereby.

l. 20. **Thebes.** Signs or placards were sometimes used in the theaters to tell the name and general locality of the action of plays. This is far from a general rule, however.

l. 35. **John a stile, John a noakes.** John at the stile. John at the oak; fictitious names used in legal action, like John Doe and Richard Roe.

106, l. 15. **lyric, elegiac, heroical.** Kinds of poetry which classical criticism had designated. Later neo-classical critics attempted to restrict each to a distinct style and subject matter.

107, l. 2. **Elkastike.** Truthful portrayal. **Phantastike.** Imaginative.

l. 11. **better hidden matters,** *i.e.,* of matters which would be better hidden.

108, l. 32. **Jubeo, etc.** I order him to be the fool gladly.

l. 34. **companion of the camps.** This bears on a popular renaissance discussion, concerning the relation of the gentleman to war and to literature. Sidney, in his life and writings, maintained that he should combine martial exercise and learning.

109, l. 1. **Orlando Furioso.** A renaissance epic poem, by the Italian Ariosto, 1516, about the romance hero Roland. This poem influenced Spenser in his *Faerie Queene*.

l. 3. **Ens.** Being. **Prima materia.** First substance. Sidney is here making fun of hair-splitting metaphysics.

l. 22. **Cato.** "The elder" (234–140 B.C.), a Roman patriot who fought against Hannibal and who persistently urged the destruction of Carthage. **Fulvius.** Friend and political ally of Caius Gracchus, slain in a riot, 121 B.C. **Ennius.** Quintus, a Roman epic poet (third century B.C.) of whose works only fragments remain. **Cato Uticensis.** "The younger" (95–46 B.C.), Stoic philosopher who killed himself when Cæsar overthrew the republic.

110, l. 2. **Scipio Nasica.** A senatorial leader against Tiberius Gracchus, second century B.C.

l. 34. **Simonides.** Of Ceos (556–468 B.C.), a Greek lyric poet. **Pindar.** (522–443 B.C.) a Greek lyric poet whose odes have a complexity of rhythm and stanza form.

111, l. 2. **Dionysius.** See note to p. 65, l. 25.

l. 6. **Phædrus.** A dialogue on metaphysics. **Symposium.** A dialogue on love.

l. 7. **discourse of love.** Plutarch's *Dialogue on Love*, concerning its nature, followed by a collection of sensational erotic stories.

l. 19. **twice two poets.** The poets are Epimenides of Crete, *On Oracles* (Titus, i, 12); Aratus of Cilicia, the *Phænomena* (Acts, xvii, 28); Cleanthes, *Hymn to Zeus* (Acts, xvii, 28); Menander, *Thais* (I Cor. xv, 33).

112, l. 8. **Julius Scaliger** (1484–1558). A much-quoted Italian literary critic, who influenced many renaissance writers. In his *Poetics* he builds upon the theories of Aristotle and Horace. The Latin passage means: by what authority do certain barbarians and crude men wish to utter abuse, to drive poets out of the country?

l. 16. **Ion.** This dialogue, between Socrates and Ion, a professional reciter of epic poems, discusses the nature of Homeric verse and poetic inspiration.

l. 32. **Lelius.** Caius Lælius, "the wise" (ca. 140 B.C.), orator and philosopher; the chief character of Cicero's *De Amicitia*.

l. 34. **Heautontimorumenos.** "The Self-Tormentor," a comedy by Terence.

114, l. 3. **Musa, etc.** Muse, bring to my mind the reasons; for the injury of what divinity? Virgil, *Æneid*, I, 12.

l. 6. **David, etc.** Note II Samuel, xxii. **Adrian.** Roman Emperor (A.D. 117–138), also wrote poetry and prose. **Sophocles.** Greek dramatic poet (495?–406 B.C.). **Germanicus.** Nephew of Emperor Tiberius; served in wars in Germany; wrote verse and prose (15 B.C.–A.D. 19).

l. 8. **Robert, King of Sicily, etc.** King of Naples (1309–1343). **Francis.** The first (1515–1547), outstanding among renaissance patrons of literature and art. **James.** Probably James I (1405–1436) who wrote

The King's Quair, imitative of Chaucer. It ⟨s possible, however, that Sidney refers to James VI⟨ early work. James VI became James I of Englan⟨ after Elizabeth's death.

l. 10. **Bembus and Bibiena.** Pietro Bembo (1470–1547⟨ and Bernardo da Bibbiena (1470–1520), both renaissance men of letters in Italy.

l. 11. **Beza and Melanchthon.** Theodore Beza (1519–1605), a French Calvinist and writer of Latin verse; Philip Melanchthon (1497–1560), a German theologian supporting Luther, who also wrote Latin poems.

l. 12. **Fracastorius and Scaliger.** Hieronymus Fracastorius (1483–1533), an Italian humanist and scientist, author of many Latin didactic poems. **Scaliger.** See note, p. 112, l. 8.

l. 13. **Pontanus and Muretus.** John Jovius Pontanus (1420–1503), an Italian writer of Latin verse and prose. Marc Antoine Muret (1526–1585), a French lawyer and poet.

l. 14. **George Buchanan** (1506–1582). A Scotch humanist, tutor to Mary, Queen of Scots, and her son James IV; wrote Latin tragedies in the fashion of Seneca.

l. 15. **Hospital of France.** Michel de l'Hôpital (1505–1573), Chancellor of France; also wrote Latin verse.

l. 27. **strew the house,** *i.e.*, to lay fresh rushes on the floor in preparation for distinguished company.

l. 29. **mountebanks at Venice.** During the sixteenth century Venice was notorious for its sharpers and quacks.

l. 32. **Vulcan.** Made a net to keep his wife from leaving him for her lover.

115, l. 4. **Epaminondas.** A Theban statesman (third century B.C.), who twice defeated the Spartans. He also regulated the sewers of Thebes.

l. 11. **Helicon.** A mountain in Boetia where the Muses lived.

l. 14. **Queis meliore, etc.** Whose heart-strings the Titan fastened with a better clay. Juvenal, *Satires*, xiv, 36.

116, l. 3. **Orator, etc.** The orator is made, the poet born.

l. 6. **Dædalus.** A legendary sculptor of Crete who invented wings for flying. He and his son Icarus were drowned during a flight.

l. 18. **Quodlibet.** What you will.

l. 20. **Quicquid conabor, etc.** Whatever I shall try to say will be verse. Ovid, *Tristia*, iv. 10.26.

117, l. 1. **I dare not allow.** See *Introduction*, p. xxvii. Theocritus, Virgil, Sannazaro all wrote pastoral poetry, and served as Spenser's models.

l. 13. **Gorboduc.** See *Introduction*, p. xxviii. This early tragedy, by Sackville and Norton, was prized by humanists for its adherence to classical technique. As Sidney further states, it does not observe the unity of place, which required that all action be localized at one place, or the unity of time, which limited the action to a single day. The "unities" were formulated as rules in the Renaissance, not by the classical dramatists themselves.

118, l. 17. **Eunuch in Terence.** A play by the Roman comedist (185–159 B.C.). This work violates the unity of time.

l. 20. **Plautus** (d. 184 B.C.). A Roman dramatist, whose comedies do not have the finish of style and form that Terence's have.

l. 33. **Pacolet's horse.** A magical flying horse, in the French romance *Valentine et Orson.*

119, l. 1. **Nuntius.** A messenger, employed in classical drama to relate action which takes place off stage.

l. 4. **Horace.** In his *Ars Poetica*, 147: *ab ovo*, from the very beginning; literally, from the egg.

l. 18. **Euripides.** The story here outlined forms the play *Hecuba* by Euripides.

l. 29. **mongrel tragi-comedy.** This very popular Elizabethan form of drama aroused the ire of most critics because it "mixed the kinds" of drama, which they considered inartistic.

l. 29. **Apuleius.** A Roman writer (second century A.D.) whose chief work is *The Golden Ass.*

l. 33. **Amphitruo.** A farce by Plautus, dramatizing an amour of Jove's with Alcmene, wife of Amphitrion.

121, l. 1. **Omphale's commandment.** This Queen of Lydia dressed her admirer Hercules as a woman, and made him spin yarn.

l. 17. **Nil habet, etc.** Wretched poverty has no worse ill than that it makes men ridiculous. Juvenal, *Satires*, iii, 152.

l. 20. **Thraso.** The braggart soldier, a character in Terence's play *The Eunuch.*

122, l. 17. **energia.** A rhetorical quality of style by which a thought is vividly impressed upon the reader; frequently figurative or metaphorical phrases.

l. 26. **coursing of a letter.** Sidney here hits at the writing of anagrams by lyric poets; also at arranging verses into patterns, such as diamonds, squares, flowers,

ship of the English gentry who were establishing themselves in his neighborhood. Sir Walter Raleigh's estate lay next to Spenser's, and to him, in 1589, Spenser showed the first three books of the *Faerie Queene*. (See *Introduction*, p. xxiii.) Raleigh, delighted with the work, took it and the poet to the court, where he was well received. No great rewards were forthcoming; a small pension was granted him by the Queen, sufficient to encourage him to continue his poem. He returned to Ireland in 1590, after seeing the first three books in print.

The writing of the *Faerie Queene* was pleasantly interrupted by the love, courtship, and marriage with Elizabeth Boyle (1593–94), so exquisitely celebrated in the *Amoretti* and *Epithalamion*. In 1595 the next three books of his *Faerie Queene* were ready. He took them to London, hoping that now he was to receive his reward in honors and pensions which would place him permanently at court. His political affiliations, however, were not with those who were in power. He again returned, disappointed, to his Irish estate, only to meet with greater trouble. In an uprising of the peasantry in 1598 his home was burned, and he, with the English landholders, was driven out of the district. Spenser, with his wife and four children, went to London, where he had an audience with the Queen, in December, 1598. A month later he died. The circumstances of his death are not known, but the legend that he died penniless and starving is highly improbable. The court and the literary world of his day paid homage to his memory. He was buried in Westminster Abbey; poets threw into his grave elegies written for the occasion. Spenser's life, like his greatest poem, was interrupted; a fragment of great promise, and yet of substantial and splendid achievement.

In the selections from Spenser, the sixteenth century spellings have not been modernized, in order that the student may appreciate the archaic quality for which Spenser deliberately wrote. Also, several rimes would be lost if reduced to modern spelling.

THE FAERIE QUEENE

136, l. 24. **Ariosto.** See note to page 109, l. 1.

l. 25. **Tasso.** Torquato Tasso (1544–1595), an Italian poet; wrote a religious epic, *Jerusalem Delivered*, in the renaissance style, using much of the chivalric romance.

l. 33. **twelve books.** Of which Spenser completed only six, and part of the seventh.

137, l. 10. **Xenophon** (ca. 431–ca. 341 B.C.). Greek soldier and historian. The work referred to is the *Cyropædia*, a historical romance on the education and life of Cyrus the Great, not the Cyrus of Xenophon's *Anabasis*.

l. 34. **Cynthia.** The name of a long poem by Raleigh,

celebrating Elizabeth. Only one book of the twenty-one is preserved.

138, l. 9. **these three books.** The first three books were published with this letter in 1590.

141, l. 7. **lowly Shepheards weeds.** Referring to his *Shepherd's Calendar.*

l. 17. **holy Virgin.** Either Calliope, muse of heroic poetry, or Clio, muse of history.

l. 21. **Tanaquill.** A legendary British princess, daughter of King Oberon; here Queen Elizabeth.

l. 22. **Briton Prince.** Arthur, the chief hero of his poem.

142, l. 9. **Goddesse.** Queen Elizabeth.

143, l. 17. **Gloriana.** Queen Elizabeth.

l. 24. **Dragon.** Sin. (Revelation, xii, 9.)

l. 26. **Ladie.** Una, truth.

144, l. 17. **Dwarfe.** Prudence, common sense.

l. 23. **Lemans lap.** Refers to old myth of Jove's love for the earth goddess.

145, l. 14. **sayling Pine.** Pine used in ships.

l. 16. **builder Oake.** Oak used for building.

l. 20. **weepeth, still,** *i.e.,* always exuding resin.

l. 24. **Mirrhe.** The Arabian myrtle which yields a fragrant gum. Myrrha, mother of Adonis, when wounded by her father was changed into this tree.

l. 25. **warlike Beech.** Lances were made of beech wood.

l. 27. **carver Holme.** Oak used for carving.

148, l. 19. **Elfe.** The knight belonged to fairy land.

149, l. 27. **bookes and papers,** *i.e.,* pamphlets written by Catholics against Protestantism.

152, l. 14. **that Armorie.** That armor of the Christian man.

153, l. 3. **aged Sire.** An enchanter, Archimago, exemplifying hypocrisy.

155, l. 14. **Ave-Mary.** Hail, Mary; a prayer to the Virgin.

l. 29. **Plutoes griesly Dame.** Proserpine, queen of the underworld.

156, l. 4. **Gorgon.** Demogorgon, an underworld magician whose dreadful name was not to be mentioned. **Cocytus** and **Styx.** Rivers in Hades.

l. 22. **Thetys.** The ocean. **Cynthia.** The moon.

157, l. 24. **dryer braine.** According to medieval science, a dry brain produced dreams; dampness was normal and healthy.

158, l. 1. **Hecate.** Queen of demons and witches.

159, l. 19. **boy.** Cupid.

160, l. 2. **Hymen Io Hymen.** Refrain of a Roman nuptial song, to Hymen, god of marriage.

162, l. 23. **Northerne wagoner.** The constellation Boötes, situated behind the Dipper, or Charles's Wain (wagon), "his seven fold teme."

l. 24. **stedfast starre.** The North star.

164, l. 20. **Hesperus.** The evening star; in other places in the poem, the morning star.

l. 26. **Tithones.** Tithonus, loved by Aurora (morning), and was at her request made immortal, but was not given eternal youth. (Note Tennyson's poem *Tithonus*.)

l. 28. **Titan.** The sun.

166, l. 2. **Proteus.** A sea god who could assume whatever form he wished.

l. 18. **St. George.** The patron saint of England. The Red Cross Knight is St. George in Spenser's typification of him as the Church of England.

l. 27. **Sans foy.** Faithless. This character, like others on the evil side of the story, is called a Saracen in the general sense of pagan.

167, l. 3. **Lady.** Duessa, falsehood, who also assumes the name Fidessa. She represents the Roman Catholic Church, and in a political interpretation, Mary, Queen of Scots.

l. 5. **mitre.** Here the papal crown.

168, l. 12. **reliques,** *i.e.,* their splintered lances.

169, l. 5. **from blame, etc.** *i.e.,* protected him from harm.

170, l. 15. **Emperor.** The Pope, at Rome, on the river Tiber.

l. 22. **Prince.** This may be the dauphin of France, first husband of Mary, Queen of Scots.

171, l. 19. **Sans joy.** Without happiness. **Sans loy.** Lawlessness.

172, l. 12. **dainty maketh derth,** *i.e.,* coyness makes one desirable.

174, l. 2. **Limbo.** Hades.

l. 10. **Fradubio.** The doubter.

175, l. 26. **Fraelissa.** Personifying such faith as is possible to a doubter.

179, l. 21. **touch,** *i.e.,* touchstone, by which gold is tested.

180, l. 19. **Lyon.** Probably represents reason or strength of mind.

182, l. 16. **A damzell.** Abessa, representing superstition.

183, l. 1. **her mother blind.** Corceca, representing blind devotion.

184, l. 9. **Aldeboran.** A bright star of the constellation Taurus.

l. 10. **Cassiopeia's chair.** Another constellation.

l. 12. **One.** Kirkrapine, or church robber.

186, l. 8. **Greeke.** Ulysses, in Homer's *Odyssey*.

189, l. 25. **Orions hound.** Sirius, the dog star. Orion was a hunter, accidentally slain by the goddess Artemis, and immortalized as a constellation.

l. 28. **Nereus crownes with cups,** *i.e.*, drinks to the sea god.

192, l. 14. **round lists,** *i.e.*, in tournaments or set combats, usually fought in circular arenas.

195, l. 11. **building.** The House of Pride. Pride is chief of the seven deadly sins.

196, l. 19. **Malvenu.** Ill-come, as contrasted with welcome.

197, l. 18. **fairest child.** Phaeton, son of Phœbus Apollo, who attempted to drive his father's chariot across the heavens.

198, l. 25. **six wizards.** The rest of the seven deadly sins.

200, l. 20. **Argus.** A giant who had a hundred eyes, killed by Hermes. Juno had his eyes placed on the tail of the peacock, her favorite bird.

l. 25. **With like . . . applyde,** *i.e.*, the beasts are of the same nature as their riders.

204, l. 20. **Whose greedy lust, etc.** *i.e.*, whose greedy desires were ungratified amidst greatest wealth.

205, l. 5. **chaw.** Jaw. In Elizabethan poetry it was good usage to rime two words whose sound was identical, provided the sense was different.

207, l. 4. **Saint Fraunces fire.** Probably should be St. Anthony's fire, or erysipelas.

211, l. 25. **Stygian shores.** The bank of the Styx, where spirits await Charon's ferry to Hades.

AMORETTI

213, l. 11. **brooke.** The fountain Hippocrene on Mt. Helicon, where the muses dwelt.

214, l. 8. **Lodowick.** Lodowick Bryskett, one of Spenser's friends, in the Irish civil service. This sonnet is a pleasant answer to Bryskett's urging that the *Faerie Queene* be completed.

l. 28. **Helice.** The constellation of the Great Bear. Spenser probably means the Lesser Bear, which contains the pole star.

217, l. 4. **this day.** Easter Sunday.

l. 20. **cote-armour.** A herald's tabard, or sleeveless coat, embroidered with the arms of the monarch.

EPITHALAMION

219, l. 20. **learned sisters.** The muses.

220, l. 27. **the sea that neighbors.** She lived at Kilcoran, on the bay of Youghal.

221, l. 12. **Mulla.** A stream near Kilcolman (now called the

Awbeg), emptying into Broadwater, the "rushy lake" below.

222, l. 22. **Hours.** The three Horæ, daughters of Jove, goddesses of the seasons, who give law and order to the world of nature.

l. 27. **three handmayds.** The three Graces who were attendants of Venus.

224, l. 7. **Phœbe.** One of the names of the moon goddess.

225, l. 15. **Medusa.** A monster, whose hair was serpents, and whose hideousness transformed to stone all who saw her.

227, l. 28. **Barnaby.** St. Barnabas' day, June 11th, which was in the old calendar the first day of summer.

l. 31. **Crab.** A sign of the zodiac (Cancer), the first of the summer period.

228, l. 33. **Arras.** A colored tapestry, made in the French town of this name.

229, l. 3. **Maia.** One of the Pleiades, who became the mother of Hermes.

l. 24. **Alcmena.** The mother of Hercules, by Jove; Hercules was supposed to have lived in the Greek town of Tiryns.

l. 27. **Majesty.** Night was regarded as the mother of all things; by her Jove begot Majesty.

230, l. 5. **Pouke.** Puck, a mischievous elf in English folk-lore.

231, l. 11. **Latmian shepherd.** Endimion, whose love for the moon goddess Cynthia many poets have sung, notably Lyly and Keats.

l. 29. **Genius.** A guardian deity which protected and assisted at the birth of each person.

232, l. 4. **Hebe.** Goddess of youth, cup-bearer to the gods.

l. 28. **hasty accidents,** *i.e.,* accidents caused by haste. It is thought that the wedding day was put earlier upon short notice.

SIR WALTER RALEIGH

SIR WALTER RALEIGH (1552?–1618), famous as a favorite of Queen Elizabeth's, as leader of an expedition to colonize Virginia, as soldier, politician, explorer, historian, and poet, well exemplifies in his career the varied and energetic activities of the renaissance Englishman. His political life was decidedly checkered. He was frequently in disfavor with Elizabeth. He made enemies as rapidly as he made friends, and his impetuosity and insolence brought him to many dangerous crises. In 1603 he was under sentence of death, but was reprieved to a long imprisonment in the Tower, during which he wrote his *History of the World.* Failing in an expedition against the Spaniards in South America, he was beheaded for treason in October, 1618.

The full title of this pamphlet reads, *A Report of the Truth of the Fight about the Isles of the Azores, this last Summer, Betwixt the Revenge, one of her Majesty's ships, and an Armada of the King of Spain.* It was reprinted by Richard Hakluyt in his *The Principal Navigations,* etc. (1598–1600). The patriotic exaggeration and boastfulness, as well as the religious animosity, which prompted Raleigh's pen illustrate the high feelings of his age. This spirited account provides a background for Tennyson's poem *The Revenge, A Ballad of the Fleet.*

THE FIGHT OF THE REVENGE

233, l. 16. **Sir Richard Grenville.** The real hero of this account was a cousin to Raleigh. He commanded a fleet to Virginia in 1585, and was vice-admiral of the fleet which attacked the Spanish treasure-ships in 1591.

l. 25. **invasion of this land.** Reference to the Great Armada of Spain, which failed in its attack on England, 1588.

234, l. 2. **Caracks.** Large merchant ships equipped with guns.

l. 7. **Lizard in Cornwall.** The southernmost point of England.

l. 8. **Portland.** A peninsula in Dorset, southern England.

235, l. 2. **Sant-Iago,** etc. These exploits of Drake were performed in 1585-6.

237, l. 2. **very hardly . . . wind,** *i.e.,* with difficulty caught sufficient wind to get under way.

241, l. 27. **galley,** *i.e.,* service as prisoners on galleys.

248, l. 16. **Agnus Dei.** "Lamb of God," a prayer beginning with these words.

l. 22. **Hispaniola.** Haiti.

LYRICS

250, l. 2. **Marlowe's Passionate Shepherd.** See p. 264. Marlowe's lyric should be read first.

251, l. 1. **This Conceit of the Faery Queen.** This sonnet was printed among congratulatory verses in the first edition of Spenser's poem.

l. 3. **Laura.** The Lady of Petrarch's sonnets.

254, l. 5. **His Pilgrimage.** Probably written in 1603 when he was under sentence of death.

l. 6. **scallop-shell.** Worn by pilgrims as a sign of a journey to the shrine of St. James at Compostella, Spain.

l. 14. **palmer.** Pilgrims to Jerusalem in the Middle Ages wore palms as a token of this religious work.

255, l. 18. **angels.** A pun; an angel is an English gold coin.

256, l. 8. **The Conclusion.** This lyric was found in his Bible,

and is said to have been written on the night before
his execution.

CHRISTOPHER MARLOWE

CHRISTOPHER MARLOWE (1564–1593), one of the most gifted poets
of his age, came to London from Cambridge, where he had received
his M.A. degree in 1587. Like many other poor men's sons who had
received a university education, he lived by his wits and his pen—a
turbulent and precarious existence. He seems to have been a government agent in several investigations of Catholic activities. His
plays made him famous in his own short day, exerting a powerful
influence toward the treatment of serious and exalted themes, (see
Introduction, p. xxx). He was killed by an associate in a tavern at
Deptford, in 1593.

Hero and Leander presents a sharp contrast to Spenser's work in
the field of poetic narrative. Here the attitude is pagan, completely
lacking in ethical or didactic purpose. In fact, at times there is a
lightness of tone which suggests that the poet is playing with his
material. Marlowe completed only the first two sestiads (or cantos),
and after his death George Chapman added four more to finish the
story, which was published in 1598.

HERO AND LEANDER

257, l. 8. **Adonis.** A youthful hunter whom Venus courted
because of his beauty. Note Shakespeare's poem,
Venus and Adonis.

l. 10. **blood of wretched lovers.** This is, of course, a
fanciful reference to what were probably red figures
in her kirtle or gown.

258, l. 12. **Musæus.** A Greek poet of the sixth century B.C.,
to whom is attributed a poem on this subject which
is the source of Marlowe's work.

l. 16. **Colchos.** Colchis, in Asia, where the Golden Fleece
was sought by Jason and the Argonauts.

l. 25. **Pelops.** Son of Tantalus, a legendary Phrygian
prince, one of whose shoulders was made of ivory.

259, l. 2. **Hippolytus.** Son of Theseus and Hippolyta, who
while driving recklessly on the seashore was drowned
by Poseidon.

l. 32. **star.** The moon, Cynthia, who loved Endimion,
the shepherd of Mt. Latmus.

260, l. 5. **Ixion's . . . race.** The centaurs. Ixion fell in love
with the goddess Hera; the gods gave him a phantom
resembling her, by whom these half-men, half-horses
were born.

l. 30. **Bacchus.** The god of cultivation and of wine.
Women were his chief devotees, and brought him
into association with the Venus cult.

261, l. 3. **Danae.** Beloved of Jove, and by him the mother of Perseus. She was shut up in a tower by her father, to keep her from her lover.

l. 4. **his sister.** Juno was Jove's sister as well as his wife.

l. 5. **Ganymede.** A beautiful boy, who because of Jove's affection was made cup-bearer to the gods, displacing Hebe.

l. 6. **Europa.** A sister of Cadmus, loved by Jove, and carried off to Crete by him in the form of a white bull.

l. 7. **Rainbow.** Iris, the messenger of Juno.

l. 9. **Vulcan.** Venus's lamed husband, who made a net to keep her from her lover, Mars.

l. 11. **Silvanus.** God of woods and rural life.

263, l. 2. **Alcides.** One of the names of Hercules.

264, l. 2. **sapphire-visaged god.** Neptune.

l. 3. **Triton.** A son of Neptune's, who with his horn ruled the waves.

ELIZABETHAN LYRICS

ANONYMOUS

271, l. 20. **fairings.** Gifts bought at fairs. Ballads were very popular fairings.

272, l. 15. **Rosemary, etc.** Ophelia quotes this passage, *Hamlet* IV, 5, 174, etc.

GEORGE GASCOIGNE (1535?–1577), studied at Cambridge, and lived a life of unrestraint in London. He is a pioneer of Elizabethan literary forms. His *Supposes* was the first prose comedy of the Elizabethan age; his *Certain Notes of Instruction* a precursor of literary critical writing; his *Steel Glass* an early verse satire. His lyrics are smooth and easy-going. He was surpassed, however, in all that he attempted by his successors, who came in a riper period of renaissance technique and power.

ANTHONY MUNDAY (1553–1633) was a prolific hack-writer whose work falls into all types of literature. He was an actor, and in collaboration with others wrote more than fifteen plays, and several civic pageants and shows. He wrote several romances which enjoyed a long popularity, and has a score of tracts and pamphlets to his credit. Perhaps his best work is in the lyric, although in this form he wrote many poems that are not above the average.

277, l. 2. **I serve a mistress.** This lyric is assigned to Munday, who had a hand in the writing of *Two Italian Gentlemen.*

SIR EDWARD DYER (1550?–1607), studied at Oxford, and after the customary foreign travel, became a courtier. He was a friend of

Sidney's and Spenser's, a member of their Areopagus, interested in critical problems and experimentation in quantitative verse. He was highly regarded in his own day for the dignity and seriousness of his poetry. Much that he has written has now been lost.

GEORGE PEELE (1558?–1598?) became interested in dramatic writing and acting while a student at Oxford. Most of his literary work was in the drama, in which he shows Greene's habit of following the fashion of the moment, writing whatever sort of thing would pay well. He had a gift for romantic and poetic themes, although there is good realism in some of his plays. His life was considered riotous and reprehensible by even his Bohemian fellow-writers, and his early death was caused directly by his excesses.

> 282, l. 21. **age his.** Age's. The Elizabethans frequently used the possessive pronoun thus to show a genitive case.

THOMAS LODGE (1558?–1625), one of the "university wits," studied at Oxford and then dabbled in law, which he gave up for literature. He wrote plays (chiefly in collaboration with others), took an adventurer's voyage to the new world, and upon his return wrote his famous romance *Rosalind* (see *Introduction*, p. xxxv) in which are found some of his loveliest lyrics. Several other romances followed this, and all enjoyed a modest success. He later took up the practice of medicine, and wrote several books and pamphlets on medicine and religion.

NICHOLAS BRETON (1545?–1626?), step-son of George Gascoigne, was a voluminous writer of trifles. His style is even and facile, equally ready to express pastoral gaiety or religious pathos. He, like Daniel and other greater poets, claimed Mary Sidney, the Countess of Pembroke, as a patroness. He wrote prose pamphlets, essays, and satires, but on his many volumes of lyric verse rests his modest fame. His best work is in the pastoral, with its background of the English countryside and its pleasant, homely customs.

> 288, l. 24. **Phyllida and Corydon.** Taken from the account of "The Honourable Entertainment given to the Queen's Majesty in Progress at Elvetham," 1591.

ROBERT SOUTHWELL (1561?–1595), received an education as a Catholic on the continent, and became a Jesuit priest. He joined the Jesuit mission in England, which attempted to reconvert the nation to Catholicism. This most hazardous undertaking is a measure of the sincerity and deep conviction of the man. He was eventually detected and hanged for what was then his treasonable offense. He has written many books, and well. His lyrics are all religious, but in them he employs the metaphorical devices found in secular themes. The Elizabethan fervor and passion, so characteristic in the poetry of the age, is in him sublimated into a lyrical mysticism.

SAMUEL DANIEL (1562–1619) was educated at Oxford, and after some foreign travel became tutor to William Herbert, later Earl of Pembroke. It was through this association that he became a protegé of Mary Sidney, the Countess of Pembroke, and a member of the literary group which centered in her home at Wilton. His early sonnets were printed with Sidney's *Astrophel and Stella*, without his permission. The next year, 1592, he published his sonnet sequence *Delia*, which established him as a poet. His *Civil Wars*, a long historical and patriotic poem, is the outstanding work from his pen. He also wrote some literary criticism, defending the use of rime in English verse.

> 295, l. 4. **Thames nor theaters,** *i.e.*, he is not writing about
> topics popular in London in order to receive reward.

WILLIAM SHAKESPEARE (1564–1616), has left us far more numerous traces of his genius than of his life. After his schooling and marriage in his native Stratford-on-Avon, he went to London and there became an actor. By 1592, when Greene refers to him in one of his pamphlets, he had made some reputation as a dramatist, largely, it is believed, in re-writing old plays. His *Venus and Adonis* (1593) and *The Rape of Lucrece* (1594), both narrative poems on classical themes, show that he had been working in other literary fields. Some of his sonnets also date from this decade. He evidently made a good living in his double connection with the theater, as actor and playwright. He became part-owner of the Globe theater, and bought an imposing home in Stratford. He was granted a coat-of-arms in 1599, thus establishing himself (through his father) as a gentleman. He seems to have given up acting in 1609, the year in which *The Sonnets* were printed. After 1611 he retired from London to live in Stratford, and with the exception of a few plays written in collaboration with John Fletcher, laid aside his immortal pen. (See *Introduction*, pp. xxx–xxxi.)

His plays are studded with lyrics which show him to be a master of this form. In them we can note a native English quality, a reference to village life and characters, showing abundant fancy and grace as well as human heartiness and pathos, free from the conventions of Petrarchism and its courtly artifices. His sonnets are more distinctive than those of any other Elizabethan. Problems of identification and of interpretation concerning the young friend and the dark lady should be postponed until after the reader has enjoyed the poetry which crowds his lines. Employing a conventional form and frequently conventional conceits and metaphors, he added a beauty of phrase and allusion which dominates his thought. Where his ideas are sometimes on the plane of common humanity and its experiences, his majestic expression transfigures them into a vast and universal commentary. At times his observation of the nature of human life is detached and profound. Perhaps the surest token of his genius is that he permits us to read into his poetry our own philosophies, and find in his verse a response to our desire for a synthesis of life and beauty.

296, l. 9. **the cuckoo.** Because of her habit of laying eggs in other birds' nests for hatching, the cuckoo was a popular symbol of domestic infidelity.

297, l. 11. **crabs.** Apples, cooked with spices and liquor to make a hot drink.

298, l. 13. **Philomel.** The nightingale. Philomela was changed into a nightingale to escape her ravisher, Tereus. From the bird's song, *philomela* also means a love-song.

308, l. 17. **suns.** A play on the word *son.*

314, l. 25. **seething bath.** Medicinal baths, hot springs. This and the next sonnet are literary exercises paraphrasing a fifth century Greek epigram which had been turned into Latin in the sixteenth century.

THOMAS CAMPION (?–1619) was educated at Cambridge and later studied law, which he did not practice. He was an accomplished musician, composing many airs for his lyrics. He also wrote a treatise on counterpoint. His lyrics show a classical background, an epigrammatic neatness combined with grace and melody. Campion practiced medicine in his later years, but continued to produce lyrics and songs of sustained excellence until his death.

318, l. 21. **"Cherry ripe."** A cry of the fruit venders.

MICHAEL DRAYTON (1563–1631) gave practically his entire career to poetry. He seems not to have gone to the universities, but was educated in the household of Sir Henry Goodere. He wrote *Idea, the Shepherd's Garland* (1593) in imitation of the pastorals of Spenser, and a series of *Sonnets to Idea* which he revised and added to in several editions. In 1598 appeared *England's Heroical Epistles*, a series of imaginary love letters of historical persons, and later he continued in this historical vein with *The Barons' Wars* (1603). His greatest work, the *Polyolbion* (1613) also shows his patriotic zeal in a poetic treatment of the history and topography of England. In his sonnets he makes a sharp break with the Petrarchian conventions which had long dominated lyric writers.

320, l. 3. **Bedlam.** Insane. The old London priory of St. Mary of Bethlehem was used for many years as an insane asylum.

323, l. 8. **Hakluyt.** The compiler of the *Voyages,* and *Principal Navigations,* (see *Introduction,* p. xxxvi).

l. 22. **King Harry.** Henry V, who invaded France in 1415 to maintain his claim to the French throne.

324, l. 25. **Poitiers and Cressy, 1356 and 1346.** Celebrated victories of the English over the French in the Hundred Years War.

JOHN FLETCHER (1579–1625) is famous for his plays, many of which were written in collaboration with Francis Beaumont, and several with Shakespeare, (see *Introduction*, p. xxxi). His blank verse was flexible and less bombastic than that of his predecessors, and his lyrics mark the beginning of a more restrained mood which heralds the decline of the Elizabethan poetic manner.

JOHN DONNE (1573–1631) is one of the most original minds of the late Elizabethan age. He was educated as a Catholic, attending Oxford at an early age, traveling on the continent, and studying law after his return to England. He eventually turned to the Church of England, and under the patronage of King James became the Dean of St. Paul's and one of the most brilliant divines of the period. Donne's literary work falls into two widely separated kinds: his prose, scholarly and philosophical, covering a wide range of learning, religious, historical, legal, and scientific; his poetry, chiefly lyric, running from early eroticism and satire to his later spiritual and religious verse. His poetry is most original in its attitudes and technique. He never strives for mere prettiness, he was careless of sound and meter, and indifferent to the conventions of Petrarchiaɪ lyrics and the classical allusions of renaissance poetry. His metaphors and allusions are novel, usually concrete, realistic, and forceful. A hard-hearted lady is one "who is dry cork and never cries"; those old Elizabethan lovers who vow eternal constancy are "some two or three poor heretics in love"; love is a circle and the lovers "as stiff twin compasses are two"; Christ is the "strong ram that batterest heaven for me."

Even in his love poetry there is an intellectual virility rather than a physical passion and its sublimated imagination. It is believed that those poems written about 1602 were addressed to Anne More, who became his wife. The gratification of his poetry comes only with an understanding of the force of his thinking. His lyrics were printed after his death, in 1633, but most of them belong to the times of Elizabeth and James.

330, l. 25. **mandrake.** A plant which contains a narcotic poison, long used in incantations and other folk superstitions.

332, l. 17. **She heard this not till now,** *i.e.*, Venus heard from the earlier love poets only vows of undying constancy, etc.

333, l. 17. **rebel and atheist.** Against the god of love and his worship.

l. 29. **Seven Sleepers.** A medieval legend of seven youths, hiding from persecution of Christians in a cave near Ephesus, who miraculously were put to sleep for nearly two hundred years.

339, l. 25. **done.** A pun on his own name.

ROBERT GREENE

ROBERT GREENE (1560?–1592), one of the most facile and diligent writers of the period, was educated at Cambridge. After traveling on the continent, he returned to his native Norwich, where he married. Later he deserted his wife and child to go to London, where he led a riotous and disorderly life, probably exaggerated by him in his pamphlets about his repentances. Greene wrote with remarkable ease in any form, upon any subject which would bring a good sale. His collected works fill fifteen good-sized volumes. Of his plays, *Friar Bacon and Friar Bungay* was the most popular, and in the list of his novels, *Pandosto* and *Menaphon* stand out for their romantic power. He wrote numerous pamphlets on the iniquities of London's underworld, and an interesting series of confessions about himself. Although it may be unfair to describe his tracts and pamphlets as journalism, written with an eye to good copy and large sales, he did, nevertheless, capitalize his own weaknesses and the life of his literary group in a brilliant way, (see *Introduction*, p. xxvi). He died prematurely, worn out by his self-indulgence, after composing a final tract of repentance and warning.

The play *George a Greene, the Pinner of Wakefield* is assigned to Greene with no degree of certainty. It resembles his work, and a contemporary actor said that Greene wrote it. It was popular for many years, and the form in which we have it is probably a shortened version, cut down in plot and in number of characters, for use on tour. No single play can serve to illustrate the breadth and variety of Elizabethan drama. There is nothing eminent about this play, either in plot organization or in conception of character. The blank verse has been corrupted so that only a suggestion of its rhythm remains. Yet there is an interesting combination of popular themes in it. The chronicle-history element, of King James against King Edward, and the rebellion of Kendal; the sturdy manhood of the English villages, represented by George a Greene and the Shoemaker of Bradford; the exaltation of the common man and his craft; the ever-appealing presence of Robin Hood and sportsmanlike contests of strength—all combine to hold and delight the average audiences of the 1590's. The modern editions by Collins, Dickinson, Adams, and Schelling show a continued interest in this play.

GEORGE A GREENE

343, l. 3. **George a Greene.** The name *a Greene* meant originally "of the green." A pinner is one who impounds stray cattle and other beasts.

345, l. 26. **Tamberlaine.** The warlike hero of two very popular plays by Christopher Marlowe.

354, l. 2. **Helena.** Daughter of Leda by Jove, who disguised himself as a swan to deceive Leda.

l. 30. **give . . . the horn.** An expression of the day, signifying marital infidelity.

357, l. 17. **sousewife.** A woman who sells soused or pickled pork.

376, l. 16. **my masters.** Addressed to the audience.

THOMAS NASHE

THOMAS NASHE (1567–1601), after seven years of study at Cambridge, went to London and became a hack-writer. He was soon famous in his literary group for the satiric power of his work. He wrote a few plays, and then turned his pen to pamphlets in the Martin Marprelate controversy, taking the side of the bishops against the Puritans. He also engaged in a personal controversy with Gabriel Harvey, a fellow of Cambridge, which produced several pamphlets of extreme acrimony. Other tracts and some lyrics of real merit were written by him, but his chief contribution to literature was *The Unfortunate Traveller* (see *Introduction*, p. xxxv).

THE UNFORTUNATE TRAVELLER

393, l. 20. **fever quartan.** A malarial fever in which the attack comes every fourth day.

l. 22. **Turney and Turwin.** Henry VIII captured Tournay and Térouanne in the summer of 1513.

l. 30. **Caelum, etc.** We stupidly seek heaven.

394, l. 9. **Paulo, etc.** Let us sing of somewhat greater matters.

l. 13. **slur a die.** To cheat at dice by preventing the piece from rolling fairly.

l. 14. **oath of the pantofle.** A student initiation ceremony, in which the newcomer swears his oath on an old slipper.

l. 17. **Aliquid, etc.** Something lies hidden which is not well known.

l. 21. **London Bridge.** The bodies of criminals and traitors were often quartered and exposed on London Bridge.

395, l. 6. **ivybush.** The customary sign of a drinking-house. Note the proverb, "Good wine needs no bush."

l. 9. **Tendit, etc.** Virtue reaches to the stars.

l. 12. **Aqua cælestis.** Water of heaven.

398, l. 32. **fair white.** The center of archery targets (the bull's eye) was usually white.

399, l. 20. **Epimenides.** A poet and prophet of Crete (seventh century B.C.), who is said to have slept in a cave for 57 years. (See note to p. 111, l. 19.)

401, l. 21. **brachet.** A hunting dog. The passage means that he be given a minor office or post by royal appointment.

402, l. 12. **parings . . . dice,** *i.e.,* shaving dice to make them roll to certain numbers, hence, by crooked dice-play.

l. 18. **swallow a quarter trey,** *i.e.,* throw a four and a three by cheating.

l. 21. **Crede, etc.** Believe me, it is a shrewd thing to give.

l. 29. **Nominativo, etc.** This ass, in the nominative case.

405, l. 14. **Ulysses, etc.** Refers to the episode of Book 10 of Homer's *Iliad.*

l. 18. **Architas.** Of Tarentum, a philosopher and mathematician of the fourth century B.C.

406, l. 24. **Palamed, etc.** Palamedes exposed Ulysses, who assumed madness to avoid going to Troy.

l. 27. **Licaon.** Lycaon, king of Arcadia, was host at dinner to Jove, who was disguised as a poor man. When human flesh was served him, he punished Lycaon by changing him into a wolf.

408, l. 5. **Quevela.** Qui va la, who goes there.

l. 17. **crosses.** A nickname for coins. The Tudor coins had crosses stamped on them.

409, l. 33. **coram nobis.** In our presence.

410, l. 2. **Plura, etc.** Sorrow forbids telling more.

THOMAS DEKKER

THOMAS DEKKER (1570?–1641) is one of the best examples of the Elizabethan professional writer. A Londoner by birth and career, he drew heavily upon the life of his city for copy. No writer of the age has given us more vivid pictures of Elizabethan London. In his numerous plays, some written in collaboration with other dramatists, he colors with a romantic and poetic imagination the realism of the city, and skilfully adapts his matter to the public taste. He suffered periodically from lack of funds, and found himself frequently in prison because of his debts. He also wrote civic pageants, lyrics, tracts, pamphlets—anything which would bring in some money.

His *Gull's Hornbook* is not only interesting and pleasant reading; it preserves for us details of the London theaters which otherwise would be lost. This pamphlet, full of mockery and satire, and yet of good-spirits, shows up the follies of his age as has no amount of contemporary puritanic denunciation.

THE GULL'S HORNBOOK

410, l. 8. **Hornbook.** A book bound in horn to prevent its tearing. Children's primers were thus protected, hence the title means a primer for gulls, or fools.

l. 24. **groundling.** The occupant of the ground or pit of the theater, the cheapest place.

l. 28. **templer.** A resident of the Temple, or an inn of court.

411, l. 4. **Monus.** The god of censure and mockery.

l. 19. **state of Cambises.** The canopy of the king in a popular bombastic tragedy.

412, l. 11. **'we three.'** A popular jest, a picture of two fools or asses, of which the beholder makes the third.

413, l. 19. **Counter.** The name of a London prison.

l. 30. **Pelion upon Ossa.** Two mountains of Greece, which the Titans placed together in order to attack the gods of heaven.

423, l. 10. **quietus est.** He must be quiet.

FRANCIS BACON

FRANCIS BACON (1561–1626) descended from an aristocratic family, and studied at Cambridge where he became interested in science and philosophy, eventually disagreeing with the scholarship which the past had accumulated in these branches of learning. He left the university to study law at Gray's Inn, and, after the death of his father, was admitted to legal practice. In 1584 he entered Parliament, and began his long political career. He was ambitious, and sought advancement through his friendships with powerful politicians and statesmen. He was knighted by King James in 1603, after which followed a series of honors and appointments which lifted him into high place: solicitor-general (1607), attorney-general (1613), privy councillor (1616), lord keeper of the great seal (1617), lord chancellor and Baron Verulam (1618), Viscount St. Alban (1621). Here his rise halted, and in this year, from this eminence, he fell. At the instigation of political rivals, he was impeached for corruption in office. His only defense against the charges of bribery was that he had never been affected in a judicial decision by the gifts he received, and that the acceptance of such gifts was a common practice and abuse in the age. He admitted the charges, and was fined, imprisoned, and deprived of office. The fine was converted by the king into a trust fund for his benefit, and he was promptly released from the Tower. He spent the remaining five years of his life in seclusion and study.

His literary work comes from his active and busy public life as well as from his retirement, (see *Introduction*, p. xxxvii, and p. xxxviii). Its importance and value was recognized in his own day, and ever since. The poet Cowley pays tribute to him as the first modern, scientific philosopher in his poem celebrating the founding of the Royal Society in 1662. The *Advancement of Learning* and the *Novum Organum* have been called the foundations of modern science.

THE ESSAYS

424, l. 18. **Pilate.** See John, xviii, 38. Bacon assumes that this question was asked cynically.

l. 22. **philosophers.** The Skeptics, who believed that absolute knowledge is impossible and that we can know things only in their relationship to other things.

425, l. 6. masques, mummeries, triumphs. Semi-dramatic shows and pageants presented at court for entertainment.

l. 17. fathers. This term was given to early Christian writers; Augustine and Jerome attacked poetry because of its imaginative and worldly nature.

l. 18. vinum dæmonum. Wine of devils.

426, l. 1. the poet. Lucretius, an Epicurean, in his poem, *On the Nature of Things*.

l. 25. Montaigne (1533–1592). Celebrated French essayist. The reference is to his *Essays*, II, 18.

l. 34. foretold. In Luke, xvii, 8.

427, l. 3. Of Adversity. Written after his fall and degradation from the position of Lord Chancellor; first printed in 1625.

l. 20. Prometheus. The legendary Titan, a friend to man, who stole fire from heaven. He was chained to a rock by angry Jove, and birds of prey attacked him daily. He was eventually freed by Hercules.

429, l. 1. Solomon. In Proverbs, x, 1.

l. 31. precept. Attributed to Pythagoras, quoted by Plutarch, *De Exilo*, 8; "choose the best, custom will make it pleasant and easy."

431, l. 13. Vetulam, etc. He preferred his aged wife to immortality.

l. 21. one of the wise men. Thales of Miletus (640–546 B.C.), one of the "seven wise men" of Greece.

432, l. 9. Marcus Antonius (83–30 B.C.). Famous as the lover of Cleopatra. **Appius Claudius** (fifth century B.C.) From whose lust the daughter of Virginius was protected by meeting death at the hands of her father.

l. 16. Satis, etc. We are for each other a spectacle great enough.

433, l. 6. Helena. Paris awarded the apple of discord to Venus, and received Helen as his reward, rejecting the offers of rule over all Asia, and fame in war, made by the other goddesses.

434, l. 6. Cum non, etc. Since you are not what you were, there is no reason why you should care to live. From Cicero's Epistles, *Ad Marium*, after the defeat of his cause at the battle of Pharsalia, 48 B.C.

l. 24. Illi mors, etc. Death presses heavily upon him who dies known too well by all, but unknown to himself. From Seneca, *Thyestes*, xi.

435, l. 3. Et conversus, etc. And God, turning, looked upon the works which his hands had made and saw that they were all very good. Bacon turns into his own Latin Genesis, I, 31.

l. 24. **de facto.** As a matter of fact.

436, l. 19. **Solomon saith, etc.** From Proverbs, xxviii, 21.

l. 24. **omnium, etc.** If he had not governed, all would have thought him capable of governing. Tacitus, *History*, I, 49. Vespasian alone as emperor changed for the better. *Vespasian, History*, I, 50.

437, l. 14. **Plutarch.** In his essay *Of Superstition*.

l. 19. **Saturn.** The Greek Kronos, who was forewarned that he would be overthrown by one of his children, and so ate them as soon as they were born. Zeus escaped this fate and revolted against his father.

l. 31. **primum mobile.** First cause the origin of all motion, according to classical astronomy.

438, l. 2. **Council of Trent.** Held 1545–1563, to discuss and combat the doctrines of Protestantism.

439, l. 10. **Juventutem, etc.** He spent a youth full of errors, even of madness.

l. 13. **Cosmos, etc.** Cosimo de Medici (1519–1574), the famous renaissance Grand Duke of Tuscany. **Gaston de Fois** (1489–1512). French general, killed by the Spaniards in the battle of Ravenna.

440, l. 9. **A certain rabbin.** The great Hebrew scholar and exponent of Old Testament writings, Isaac Abrabanel (1437–1508).

l. 19. **Hermogenes.** A Greek scholar, second century A.D., said to have lost his memory at the age of 25.

l. 25. **Tully.** Cicero, *Brutus*, 95. Hortensius was a Roman orator, and Cicero's rival. The passage means he remained the same when it was no longer becoming.

l. 29. **ultima, etc.** The last fell short of the beginning.

441, l. 35. **Abeunt, etc.** Studies develop into manners.

442, l. 10. **cymini sectores.** Literally "dividers of cumin seed," (hair-splitters). Cumin is an oriental plant with a small, aromatic seed.

THE ADVANCEMENT OF LEARNING

l. 18. **Democritus** (ca. 400–ca. 357). A Greek philosopher who held that the universe was formed by atoms in motion.

l. 21. **Vulcan,** *i.e.*, the crafts of forging, smelting, and refining.

443, l. 6. **magic.** Bacon in the *Novum Organum*, ii, 9, 51, gives this term its proper association with learning and philosophy, "purged of vanity and superstition," as he says.

l. 33. **Aristotle** (384–322 B.C.). Scientist and philosopher, the greatest man of learning of classical antiquity. Bacon particularly admires the practicality and untraditional nature of his thinking.

444, l. 7. **Veni in,** etc. "I am come in my Father's name, and ye receive me not; if another shall come in his own name, him ye will receive." John, v, 43.

l. 14. **Eum recipietis,** *i.e.,* one who is well received.

l. 17. **scholar.** Aristotle was the teacher of Alexander the Great.

l. 22. **Felix terrarum,** etc. The happy plunderer of lands, producing a useless example to the world.
Felix doctrinæ, etc. The happy plunderer of learning.

l. 29. **usque ad aras.** To the altars, *i.e.,* in all affection or friendliness.

445, l. 1. **Eadem,** etc. The same terminology as that of the magistrates. *Annals,* i, 3.

446, l. 12. **Limus,** etc. As this clay hardens, and this wax dissolves by one and the same fire. Virgil, *Eclogues,* viii, 80.

l. 24. **de mundo,** etc. Concerning the earth, of the universality of things.

447, l. 24. **Formavit,** etc. "He formed man of the dust of the ground, and breathed into his nostrils the breath of life." Genesis, ii, 7.

l. 26. **Producant,** etc. "Let the waters bring forth —, let the earth bring forth —." Gen., i, 20, 24.

448, l. 21. **vehiculum formæ.** A vehicle of form.

l. 32. **vita brevis,** etc. Life is short, art is long.

449, l. 4. **opus quod,** etc. "The work that God maketh from the beginning to the end." Eccle., iii, 11.
Bacon's scientific interest compels him to disregard the first half of this sentence.

l. 9. **Ter sunt,** etc. Thrice they tried to place Ossa upon Pelion, and to roll woody Olympus upon Ossa. Virgil, *Georgics,* i, 281. This refers to the Titans' war against the gods; see note to p. 413, l. 30.

l. 17. **Parmenides and Plato.** Parmenides was a Greek philosopher of the fifth century B.C., a forerunner of Plato in his idealism. The reference is to the treatise attributed to Plato, *On Parmenides,* 165.

l. 31. **latæ,** etc. The roads from all directions are broad to the wise.

l. 32. **rerum,** etc. The knowledge of divine and human things.

450, l. 2. **simili materia.** Similar things or matter.

l. 8. **non arctabuntur,** etc. "When thou goest thy steps

shall not be restrained, and when thou runnest thou shalt not stumble." Ps., iv, 12.

451, l. 2. **remoræ.** Obstacles.

l. 27. **moscosi fontes.** Mossy springs.

454, l. 23. **Premendo, etc.** By keeping close to the treacherous shore. Horace, *Odes*, II, x, 3.

455, l. 5. **de vero.** In reality.

l. 10. **centaurs and chimeras.** See note to p. 260, l. 5.

457, l. 4. **Non canimus, etc.** We do not sing to the deaf— the woods answer everything. Virgil, *Eclogues*, x, 8.

BEN JONSON

BEN JONSON (1573?–1637) is one of the most significant figures among the Elizabethans. He was the stepson of a bricklayer, but received a good education at Westminster School. He may have gone to Cambridge for a short time. He took up bricklaying as a young man, but grew discontented and enlisted for the wars in Flanders. After his return, about 1595, he became an actor and playwright. He was imprisoned for killing a man in a duel, and on his release wrote plays for the dramatic company of which Shakespeare was a member. His dramatic work covers several periods of his life, (see *Introduction*, p. xxxii). He is a realist, with sound ideas in adapting the method and technique of the classical dramatists. His "comedy of humors" presents its characters under the domination of a single outstanding trait, and thus gives to each a definite personality, which greatly simplified his plots. He began a comedy of manners which long affected the course of English comedy. Jonson next turned to satirical drama and tragedy, and exploited the life of the city about him. His critical virility was not confined to dramatic principles; he commented with shrewdness and force upon his contemporaries, his fellow-poets, and their work. He indulged in controversy and personal attack, and made trouble for himself. He was the central figure in the "war of the theatres," during which the audiences were delighted with plays which lampooned competing dramatists of the day.

In 1613 he travelled in France as the tutor of the son of Sir Walter Raleigh, and later received royal appointments and pensions. In addition to his plays, he wrote court masques, of great poetic novelty and beauty. His non-dramatic poetry includes numerous lyrics, satiric verse, and epigrams, all tinged by his admiration for classical poetry. There are also a large number of miscellaneous verses— elegies, epitaphs, dedications, epistles, etc. His *Timber, or Discoveries*, printed after his death, is a collection of notes or abbreviated essays, frequently translations from classical authors, with his comments thereon, sometimes judgments and criticisms of contemporary men and matters. These, with the notes made from his conversations with William Drummond, show us more directly than his dramas, the critical interests and insight of the man.

TIMBER, OR DISCOVERIES

457, l. 18. **Censura de poetis.** Opinion concerning poets.

458, l. 2. **Comitetur, etc.** Let a Punic sponge go with the book. And a little later; many erasures are not enough . . . a single sponging will suffice. Martial, IV, 10.

l. 9. **Cestius.** Pius, a Roman orator and rhetorician of Greek birth, living in the age of Cæsar Augustus.

l. 15. **Heath.** John, a Jacobean translator and author of collections of rather mediocre *Epigrams*, 1610, 1619. **Sculler.** John Taylor, nicknamed the "water poet," a facile rimester and a Thames boatman, whom Jonson knew. His *Sculler* (1612) was an attack on Coryate, and was a notorious book among literary men.

459, l. 20. **De Shakespeare nostrati.** Of our countryman Shakespeare.

460, l. 1. **Sufflaminandus erat.** He should have been clogged. Cæsar Augustus' comment on Haterius, a senator and rhetorician. Seneca, *Exerpta Controv.*, 4.

l. 11. **Dominus Verulamius.** Lord Verulam (Francis Bacon).

461, l. 9. **Qui longum, etc.** Which will secure a long age for the noted writer. Horace, *Ars Poetica*, 346.

l. 20. **Consuetudo, etc.** Custom, etc. (in literary style).

462, l. 11. **aquai, pictai.** Old Latin forms of *aquæ, pictæ.*

l. 12. **Chaucerisms.** Is Jonson hitting at the archaic diction of Spenser, in which he imitates Chaucer's language?

l. 20. **Paronomasies.** Puns and playing upon words.

l. 21. **Quæ per, etc.** Which fall by rough ways and lofty rocks.

LYRICS

464, l. 2. **Salathiel Pavy.** One of the choir-boys in the Queen's Chapel; an accomplished actor of female parts, who probably acted in some of Jonson's comedies.

l. 18. **Parcæ.** The three Fates, who cut at will the thread of human life.

466, l. 16. **Song: To Celia.** This is a free translation of a lyric by Catullus, a Latin poet (84–54 B.C.).

467, l. 6. **Simplex Munditiis** *i.e.*, of simple neatness; from a line in one of Horace's *Odes.*

468, l. 26. **thy book.** The first collected edition of Shakespeare's plays, 1623, in which this poem appeared as a preface.

469, l. 23. **sporting Kyd.** Thomas Kyd (1558–1594), a friend

of Marlowe's; wrote *The Spanish Tragedy* and other
early Elizabethan tragedies. The epithet "sporting"
is not suited to the tone of Kyd's work, and is
merely evoked by his name.

l. 28. **Pacuvius** (220?–130 B.C.). A Roman poet and
playwright.

Accius (170–90 B.C.). A Roman tragic poet.

him of Cordova. Reference to Seneca, who was
born in Spain.

470, l. 10. **Aristophanes** (454–388 B.C.). The greatest writer
of Greek comedy; extremely satiric and fanciful in
his work.

l. 32. **banks of Thames.** Most of the London theaters
were situated on the Bankside, along the south river-
front, in Southwark.

INDEX OF AUTHORS

INDEX OF TITLES

513

INDEX OF FIRST LINES OF POETRY

517

May 4 - Venus and Adonis
        Hero and Meander

Sonnet sequences
1892 "Delia" - Samuel Daniel
   5
1580 "Astrophel and Stella": Philip
                                Sidney

1609 Shakespeare's Sonnets

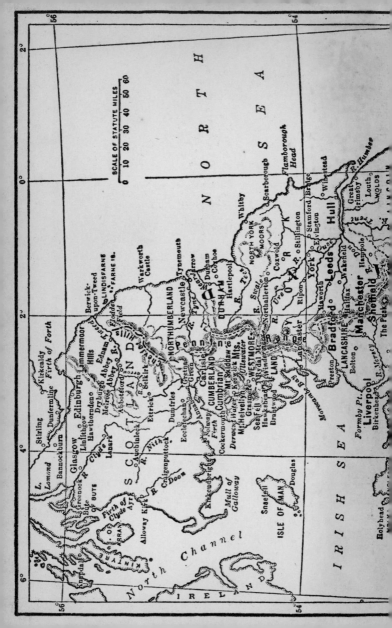